Sculpting the Blender Way

Explore Blender's 3D sculpting workflows and latest features, including Face Sets, Mesh Filters, and the Cloth brush

Xury Greer

BIRMINGHAM—MUMBAI

Sculpting the Blender Way

Copyright © 2022 Packt Publishing

Group Product Manager: Rohit Rajkumar

Publishing Product Manager: Kaustubh Manglurkar

Senior Editor: Hayden Edwards

Content Development Editor: Abhishek Jadhav

Technical Editor: Saurabh Kadave

Copy Editor: Safis Editing

Project Coordinator: Manthan Patel

Marketing Co-ordinator: Elizabeth Varghese

Proofreader: Safis Editing

Indexer: Tejal Daruwale Soni

Production Designer: Shyam Sundar Korumili

First published: January 2022

Production reference: 1231221

Published by Packt Publishing Ltd.
Livery Place
35 Livery Street
Birmingham
B3 2PB, UK.

ISBN 978-1-80107-387-5

www.packt.com

To my friends in SeaBUG: The Seattle Blender User Group. Thank you all for helping me grow as a 3D artist. Because of you, I've learned so much and had a chance to share my passion. I'm excited to finally send this book out into the world where I hope it will inspire others as much as this group has inspired me!

- Xury Greer

Contributors

About the author

Xury Greer is a digital media generalist and educator in the Greater Seattle area. He earned his bachelor's degree in game design from Lake Washington Institute of Technology. He specializes in 3D characters, and technical art, and loves to share his knowledge. Xury is an avid member and co-organizer of the Seattle Blender User Group, and aims to help others by teaching Blender, as well as other 3D content creation tools. He is always excited to get new users started on their digital media production journey.

About the reviewer

Mohamed Essam El Deen Farouk is a 3D character artist from Egypt. He has a passion for sculpting 3D character models using Blender 3D's Substance Painter and Unreal Engine pipeline.

Making 3D models for video games has been his primary objective since college, which is why he decided to learn how to make 3D models with such an amazing pipeline as Blender 3D sometime after graduation.

Table of Contents

2
Overview of Blender's Sculpting Workflows

3
Sculpting a Simple Character Head with Basic Brushes

4
How to Make a Base Mesh for a 3D Sculpture

5

Learning the Power of Subdivision and the Multiresolution Workflow

6

Using Advanced Features and Customizing the Sculpting Brushes

7

Making Eyeballs

8
Making Accessories and Clothing

10
Rendering Sculptures for Your Portfolio

Index

Other Books You May Enjoy

Preface

Blender 3D is a free and open source program that can be used for every part of the 3D production pipeline. It has several robust feature sets for creating 3D art that have contributed to its rising popularity in the last few years. Sculpting is perhaps the most enjoyable and artistic method for creating 3D art as it relies less on technical knowledge and focuses on artistic brushes. The latest release of Blender makes the sculpting feature set more powerful than ever, so now is an excellent time to learn it! This book covers the expansive list of features in the Blender 2.93 LTS release, as well as the exciting all-new Blender 3.0 release. This book will be an excellent resource for professionals who need a production-ready long-term support release of the software, as well as hobbyists looking for a cutting-edge experience.

Sculpting the Blender Way will demonstrate how to navigate Blender's user interface and take you through the core workflows. You'll gain a detailed understanding of how the sculpting features work, including basic sculpting, Dyntopo, the Voxel Remesher, QuadriFlow, and Multiresolution. This Blender book will cover a wide range of brushes, as well as all of the latest additions to the sculpting feature set, such as Face Sets, Mesh Filters, and the Cloth brush. You'll learn how to customize these brushes and features to create fantastic 3D sculptures that you can share with the ever-growing Blender community.

By the end of this book, you'll have gained a complete understanding of the core sculpting workflows and be able to use Blender to bring your digital characters to life.

Who this book is for

This book is for artists who want to get started with the exciting new sculpting features in Blender 3D. Whether you have experience using ZBrush or traditional sculpting, or are completely new to sculpting, this book will have something new for you to learn. Prior experience with Blender or other 3D software may be helpful but is not required.

However, a graphics tablet from Wacom, XP-Pen, or Huion is highly recommended to be able to follow along with the concepts and examples covered in the book.

What this book covers

Chapter 1, Exploring Blender's User Interface for Sculpting, gets us started with Blender's user interface as it pertains to sculpting. We'll learn how to install the latest version of Blender and learn about the important areas of the UI. We'll cover viewport shading options, basic navigation, and how to set up your graphics tablet for sculpting in Blender.

Chapter 2, Overview of Blender's Sculpting Workflows, covers which workflows should be used at any given stage of the sculpting process. We'll discover the components that make up a 3D sculpture and learn how brushes can be used to manipulate these components. We will learn the difference between Blender's basic sculpting tools, the Dyntopo feature, the Voxel Remesher workflow, and finally the Multiresolution modifier. Learning the difference between these features is key to making high-quality 3D sculptures in Blender.

Chapter 3, Sculpting a Simple Character Head with Basic Brushes, takes us through a simple character sculpture project. We will learn how to use several of the basic sculpting brushes to make the large features of a sculpture. We'll learn some beginner techniques for creating a head, neck, ears, nose, brow, cheeks, eyes, and mouth. We'll practice with a variety of brushes for each of these tasks and build familiarity with the Voxel Remesher workflow.

Chapter 4, How to Make a Base Mesh for a 3D Sculpture, explores several ways to create base meshes that we can use as the foundation for multiresolution sculpting. These methods range from the classic Box Modeling approach to some of Blender's fun features, including the Skin modifier, Metaballs, and the Lasso Trim tool.

Chapter 5, Learning the Power of Subdivision and the Multiresolution Workflow, explains how subdivision surfaces work and why they are so powerful. We will dive deeper into understanding how the components of a 3D sculpture work together to form a topology that can be used for the multiresolution workflow. We'll explore the difference between a mesh with dynamic topology, voxel remeshed topology, and all-quad topology that will retain its shape during subdivision. Once we have an understanding of how subdivision works, we will learn how to use the Multiresolution modifier to sculpt high-resolution details into a subdivided mesh.

Chapter 6, Using Advanced Features and Customizing the Sculpting Brushes, explains how Blender's brushes can be customized to suit our advanced sculpting needs. We'll learn how to adjust the brush falloff, use custom stroke settings, and add alpha textures to our brushes for sculpting intricate details. We'll practice using some advanced tools and brush settings and learn how to control our brushes with automatic masking options, Face Sets, and the Sculpt Expand operator.

Chapter 7, Making Eyeballs, shows off several ways of making eyeballs for our sculptures. Sculptures can be made in many art styles, so we will learn how to make eyes that fit a variety of styles, including standard clay eyeballs, hand-painted eyes, realistic eyeballs, insect eyes, elongated cartoon eyes, and stylized anime eyes. We'll also learn how to use constraints to aim the eyes at a target for an intuitive way to pose the eyes.

Chapter 8, Making Accessories and Clothing, showcases how sculpting can be supplemented with other 3D modeling techniques to create accessories for our 3D models. We'll start with some modeling tools for creating earrings. Next, we'll learn about several ways of creating cloth for our sculptures using the Mask Extract operator, Cloth brush, and the Cloth Filter. We'll cover basic cloth simulation tools, as well as some tips for manually sculpting cloth, including the Radial Symmetry feature.

Chapter 9, Creating Teeth, Eyebrows, and Hair, highlights the importance of creating secondary features for our characters. We'll learn how to create teeth as separate objects and place them in a character's mouth. We'll explore several ways of making hair, including mesh hair, particle hair, sculpted hair, and hair curves. We will see several practical examples of these techniques used for making eyebrows and hair.

Chapter 10, Rendering Sculptures for Your Portfolio, brings us to the end of the sculpting process. We'll learn how to render our sculptures so that they can be displayed in a portfolio. We'll start by setting up our render settings and learn about Blender's two render engines: Cycles and Eevee. We'll cover basic three-point lighting, environment lighting with an HDRI, and how to set up basic materials for the sculpture. We'll learn how to set up a camera and a 360-degree turntable for rendering. Our finished renders can then be uploaded to our portfolios and shared with the world!

To get the most out of this book

You will need an internet connection to download the latest version of Blender and the source files for the projects (an internet connection is not required after downloading the software and the files).

Blender requires about 670 MB of storage space to install. The project files in this book are approximately 1.1 GB all together (you do not need to download them all at once). It's a good idea to have at least 1 GB of additional free storage so that you can create your own 3D sculptures and renders. In total, about 3 GB of space should be enough for everything covered in this book.

This book has been tested for Blender 2.93 LTS. Blender 3.0 was released shortly before this book's publication and is also compatible, although there are some very subtle user interface differences from the reference images. Future Blender releases should remain compatible as well, however the Blender Foundation is always looking for ways to improve software.

A graphics tablet with pressure sensitivity is highly recommended for following along with this book.

A graphics card from Nvidia is recommended for the best experience in *Chapter 10, Rendering Sculptures for Your Portfolio*, although the Blender Foundation is actively working to support graphics cards from other brands.

Software/hardware covered in the book	Operating system requirements
Blender 2.93 LTS / Blender 3.0	Windows 8.1, 10, and 11 macOS 10.13 Intel / 11.0 Apple Silicon Linux
A graphics tablet from Wacom, XP-Pen, or Huion	Windows, and macOS drivers are supported by all major graphics tablet manufacturers. Linux drivers may require third-party drivers.

The Blender Foundation maintains several versions of Blender at the same time. Version 2.93 LTS is a Long-term Support release for users who want the most stable version of the software. You can download it here: `https://www.blender.org/download/lts/2-93/`.

Version 3.0 is the latest release with new features. This cutting-edge version has not been available as long as the LTS version, so some bugs may be present. You can download it here: `https://www.blender.org/download/`.

Either version of Blender will be perfect for following along in this book. However, version 3.0 or later is recommended for following along with *Chapter 10, Rendering Sculptures for Your Portfolio*, since there have been major performance improvements for the Cycles render engine.

Download the example files

You can download the example files for this book from GitHub at `https://github.com/PacktPublishing/Sculpting-the-Blender-Way`. If there's an update to the file, it will be updated in the GitHub repository.

We also have other code bundles from our rich catalog of books and videos available at `https://github.com/PacktPublishing/`. Check them out!

Sculpting in Action

The Sculpting in Action videos for this book can be viewed at `https://bit.ly/3IyA20X`.

Download the color images

We also provide a PDF file that has color images of the screenshots and diagrams used in this book. You can download it here: `https://static.packt-cdn.com/downloads/9781801073875_ColorImages.pdf`.

Conventions used

There are a number of text conventions used throughout this book.

`Code in text`: Indicates code words in the text, database table names, folder names, filenames, file extensions, pathnames, dummy URLs, user input, and Twitter handles. Here is an example: "We will continue where we left off in the previous section, using the `childHead.blend` file."

Bold: Indicates a new term, an important word, or words that you see on screen. For instance, words in menus or dialog boxes appear in **bold**. Here is an example: "Click on the **Type:** drop-down menu next to the **Cavity** checkbox."

> **Tips or Important Notes**
> Appear like this.

Get in touch

Feedback from our readers is always welcome.

General feedback: If you have questions about any aspect of this book, email us at `customercare@packtpub.com` and mention the book title in the subject of your message.

Errata: Although we have taken every care to ensure the accuracy of our content, mistakes do happen. If you have found a mistake in this book, we would be grateful if you would report this to us. Please visit `www.packtpub.com/support/errata` and fill in the form.

Piracy: If you come across any illegal copies of our works in any form on the internet, we would be grateful if you would provide us with the location address or website name. Please contact us at `copyright@packt.com` with a link to the material.

If you are interested in becoming an author: If there is a topic that you have expertise in and you are interested in either writing or contributing to a book, please visit `authors.packtpub.com`.

Share Your Thoughts

Once you've read *Sculpting the Blender Way*, we'd love to hear your thoughts! Scan the QR code below to go straight to the Amazon review page for this book and share your feedback.

https://www.amazon.in/review/create-review/error?asin=%3C1801073872%3E

Your review is important to us and the tech community and will help us make sure we're delivering excellent quality content.

1

Exploring Blender's User Interface for Sculpting

Welcome to *Sculpting the Blender Way*. **Blender** is a free and open-source 3D modeling suite, which means it has tools for creating 3D art with many different workflows. The **sculpting workflow** is widely considered to be the most fun and artistic approach. Blender includes all of the sculpting features you need to create amazing organic 3D artwork and characters. Blender has seen countless improvements to the sculpting process over the last year, so now is an excellent time to learn how to sculpt in Blender.

In this chapter, we will learn how to use Blender's user interface as it pertains to sculpting. No prior knowledge of 3D modeling or sculpting is required to follow along with this book, so don't worry if this is your first experience making 3D art of any kind. The Blender Foundation has created a list of features that you can read about here: `https://www.blender.org/features/`. This book will be focusing on the sculpting feature set, so we will not be going in depth on the other features. All concepts and workflows in this book will be introduced from the perspective of 3D sculpting.

We'll start with how to install the software. Next, we'll learn about the editors within Blender's user interface and how we can customize the interface for a streamlined sculpting workflow. We'll learn about Blender's powerful viewport customization features for shading and overlays. We'll have a look at the Toolbar and the Sidebar within the 3D Viewport. And we'll practice navigation in 3D since we will be doing that a lot during our sculpting workflow. We'll wrap up this chapter by learning the importance of using a graphics tablet and how to set up the drivers for the best sculpting experience.

By the end of this chapter, you'll have a foundational understanding of the Blender software and its user interface, and you'll be prepared to try out the sculpting features in the next chapter.

The topics in this chapter are as follows:

- Installing Blender
- Understanding Blender's user interface
- Expanding and collapsing the Toolbar and the Sidebar
- Exploring the viewport shading modes
- Customizing solid shading mode with the pop-over menu
- Using viewport overlays
- Navigating the 3D Viewport
- Setting up your graphics tablet's stylus buttons

Technical requirements

For sculpting in Blender, you will of course need a computer that can run the latest version of Blender. Blender works on all major operating systems, including Windows 8.1, 10, and 11, macOS 10.13+, and Linux. 3D sculpting primarily utilizes the CPU and RAM. A high-end graphics card (GPU) can help for rendering and viewport performance but isn't as important for sculpting performance as the CPU and RAM. You can read more about Blender's hardware requirements here: `https://www.blender.org/download/requirements/`.

We will need a recent version of Blender that has the latest sculpting features. The features we need are available in Blender version 2.93 and later. Blender 2.93 is a **Long-Term Support (LTS)** release, so it will get continued support and fixes until June 2023. Blender does not currently have an auto-updater, so if you've downloaded Blender before, you should check that you have at least version 2.93.6 before following along with this book.

> **Important Note**
> Blender receives several major features updates every year; version 3.0 will be released around the same time as this book's publication. Version 3.0 begins a new series of Blender releases; it comes with many new features and a slightly adjusted color scheme for the user interface. However, all of the sculpting information and examples in this book will be will still be 100% relevant and up to date for Blender 3.0.

It is possible to follow along with this book using a mouse, but it is highly recommended that you use a graphics tablet for all sculpting. Because this book is primarily about the sculpting features in Blender, you will not get the intended experience unless you have a graphics tablet.

This book includes several files that we've prepared for you to help demonstrate some of the sculpting features. You can download the files to follow along with this book at the GitHub link here: `https://github.com/PacktPublishing/Sculpting-the-Blender-Way`.

Installing Blender

First, we'll need to download the latest version of Blender. Blender is available through the Blender Foundation's official website. You do not need to register an account or pay license fees or anything like that; Blender is 100% free and open source!

Getting ready

Make sure your computer meets the requirements for Blender, as mentioned in the *Technical requirements* section, and then head over to the download page of the Blender website: `https://www.blender.org/download/`. The website will automatically detect your computer's operating system so you don't have to worry about choosing the correct version.

Now, let's install Blender.

How to do it...

To install Blender from the Blender Foundation website, follow these instructions:

1. Navigate to `https://www.blender.org/download/`.
2. Click on the **Download Blender...** button.
3. Once the installer file has been downloaded, click to open the installation wizard.
4. Follow the prompts in the installation wizard to finish installing Blender.

If you prefer to use a portable version of Blender that you can install to a thumb drive, follow these instructions:

1. Click on the **macOS, Linux, and other versions** drop-down list.

2. Choose the **Windows Portable (.zip)** option.

3. Once the `.zip` file finishes downloading, unzip it to your portable thumb drive so that you can take it with you.

4. Blender can be launched from your thumb drive by double-clicking on the `blender.exe` executable file.

And that's all there is to it! Congratulations – you're ready to use Blender!

How it works...

The installer version of Blender will automatically put the appropriate files into your computer's default program files directory. The portable version keeps all of the unzipped files in a portable directory so that you can take Blender with you on a thumb drive.

There's more...

Alternatively, Blender can be installed via the Microsoft Store or the Steam client. You will need an account to install Blender from these services, but the software is still 100% free. Using one of these services is completely optional.

If you prefer to manage your Blender installation with either the Microsoft Store or the Steam client, you can choose the appropriate store page from the drop-down list on the Blender website or use the following links:

*   **Microsoft Store**: `https://www.microsoft.com/en-us/p/blender/9pp3c07gtvrh`

*   **Steam**: `https://store.steampowered.com/app/365670/Blender/`

See also

As stated at the beginning of this chapter, this book will focus on Blender's sculpting features. If you would like to learn more about Blender's other features in a project-based workflow, check out *Blender 3D by Example (2nd Edition)* from Packt Publishing.

Understanding Blender's user interface

Blender's **User Interface** (**UI**) is highly customizable and offers several presets for different workflows. For this book, we will take a look at Blender's UI as it pertains to the sculpting workflow. Luckily for us, Blender includes a project template specifically for sculpting, so getting started will be easy and we'll be well on our way to exploring the UI.

Getting ready

Launch Blender so that we can take a look at the UI. You'll be greeted by Blender's **splash screen**. The splash screen is a little floating window that provides quick access to your recent Blender projects and a few helpful links. The first time you launch Blender, the splash screen will provide you with a **Quick Setup** option, as you can see in the following screenshot:

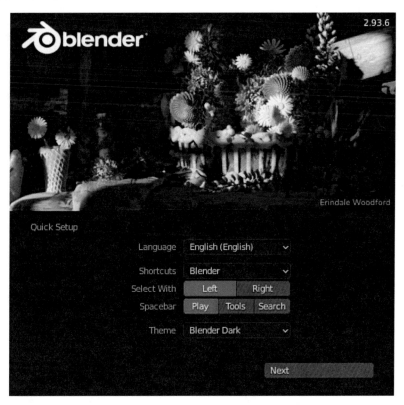

Figure 1.1 – The Blender splash screen

We recommend leaving all of these settings at their defaults so that your keyboard shortcuts and other settings will match the instructions in this book. You can close the splash screen by clicking anywhere in the UI outside of the splash screen area.

Once the quick setup is finished and the splash screen is closed, we can load the sculpting preset so that the UI won't be cluttered with features that we don't need. Then, we can explore the UI as it pertains to sculpting.

How to do it...

Before we explore the UI, let's load the sculpting preset so that the UI won't be cluttered with features that we don't need:

1. Click on the **File** menu in the top-left corner of the UI.

2. Choose **New | Sculpting** to start a new file with the sculpting preset.

    Blender's UI is broken into several sections called **editors**. Each editor provides a unique way for us to see the contents of the Blender file. In the sculpting preset, there are three editors available to us, as you can see in the following screenshot:

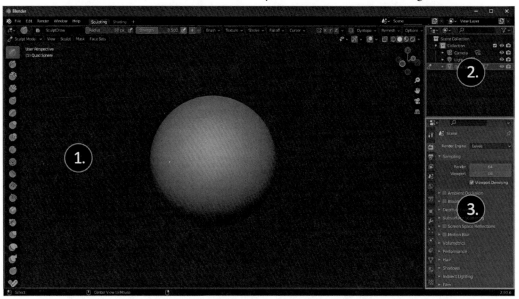

Figure 1.2 – The three editors in the sculpting preset

Let's take a look at each editor:

1. The **3D Viewport** is the largest part of the UI, and it's where we will be spending most of our time while sculpting. Here, we can see our 3D sculpture and work with our sculpting tools.

2. The **Outliner** provides us with a list of all objects in the scene. We won't be doing a lot of work in this editor early on, but it will become very useful for organizing the contents of our Blender files later.

3. The **Properties** editor gives us lots of extra control over our models; from here, we can apply **modifiers**, **materials**, and add other advanced features to our sculptures. We will use this editor from time to time, especially in the later chapters in this book.

At the very top of every editor is a **header**. The top-left corner of the header has an icon for the editor type. For example, the top-left corner of the 3D Viewport has an icon representing its editor type, as you can see in the following screenshot:

Figure 1.3 – The 3D Viewport icon as seen in the top-left corner of the 3D Viewport header

Clicking this icon will allow us to replace this editor with another type of editor and customize the UI for our needs. Luckily, the sculpting preset has already arranged the UI for the sculpting workflow, so we don't need to make any changes.

The 3D Viewport is the most important editor for our sculpting workflow. Not only does it contain a window for us to see our sculpture but it also contains brushes, settings, and other advanced ways for us to interact with our sculpture. The 3D Viewport can be further broken down into several **regions**. The regions are highlighted in the following screenshot:

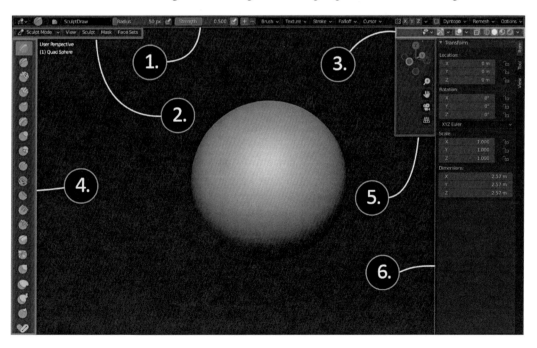

Figure 1.4 – The six regions in the 3D Viewport

The first three regions are part of the header:

1. Along the top of the header for the 3D Viewport is a list of **tool settings**. We will use these options for customizing our sculpting tools. Settings for our tools can be accessed in a number of places in Blender's UI, but the tool settings section in the header is the most convenient.

2. Slightly below the tool settings along the left side of the header, we can see the **mode and menus** for the 3D Viewport. The **Interaction Mode** determines the toolset and workflow we are currently using. Since we created this file with the sculpting preset, the Interaction Mode is set to **Sculpt Mode**. We will spend most of our time in this book using **Sculpt Mode**. However, there will be times where we switch to **Object Mode** or **Edit Mode** to make extra changes to our sculptures outside of the sculpting workflow. This region also has several menus: **View**, **Sculpt**, **Mask**, and **Face Sets**. These menus have lots of operations that we can perform while in Sculpt Mode; we will learn to use some of these operations later.

3. The final part of the header can be found in the top-right corner. This section has options for customizing the **display and shading** settings for the viewport; here, we can adjust the **viewport gizmos**, **overlays**, **shading**, and more.

   Below the header, there are several regions that can be found along the left and right sides of the 3D Viewport. Continuing the numbering shown in the previous image, these regions are as follows:

4. Along the left side of the 3D Viewport, we have the **Toolbar**. The Toolbar is full of icons for the brushes that we will use for sculpting.

5. Moving over to the right side of the viewport, we have the **navigation gizmo**. This can be used for viewport navigation and will allow us to look at our sculpture from different angles.

6. Lastly, we have the **Sidebar**. The Sidebar contains extra information about our objects, such as **Location**, **Rotation**, and **Scale**. It also provides an alternative area of the UI where we can adjust tool settings. We won't be using the Sidebar often during our sculpting workflow, so don't worry about it for now.

You may have noticed that the Sidebar is missing from the sculpting preset. This is because it is collapsed by default, but many regions can be expanded or collapsed to suit our needs. Check out the next topic of this chapter to see how to expand/collapse the Sidebar.

Expanding and collapsing the Toolbar and the Sidebar

Both the Toolbar on the left side and the Sidebar on the right side of the 3D Viewport can be expanded to show more of their contents or collapsed entirely while we aren't using them.

We will spend a lot of time with the Toolbar since all of our sculpting brushes can be found there. Tools can be chosen from the Toolbar by clicking on them. Only one tool can be active at a time; the active tool will be highlighted blue. By default, the Toolbar is in a minimized state, so all we can see are icons. It can be very helpful to expand the Toolbar and display the names of the tools next to the tool icons. Expanding the Sidebar will also give us more information while we work with our tools.

Let's learn how to expand and collapse the Toolbar and the Sidebar.

Getting ready

If you haven't already loaded the sculpting preset, do so now. The tools available on the Toolbar will be different for each Interaction Mode, so make sure you're still in **Sculpt Mode** before trying to follow along.

How to do it...

The Toolbar can be partially expanded to have two vertical columns, or it can be expanded fully to display the names of the tools. Let's expand it now:

1. Hover your mouse over the right-side edge of the Toolbar until your mouse pointer changes to the resizing cursor.

2. Click and drag to the right to expand the Toolbar, as shown in the following screenshot:

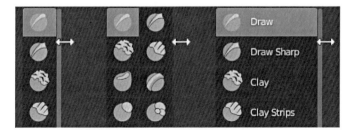

Figure 1.5 – Expanding the Toolbar

Being able to see the names of the tools will be helpful while we practice using the tools later in this book.

Just like the Toolbar on the left side, the Sidebar on the right side can be expanded or collapsed. In the sculpting preset, the Sidebar is collapsed by default. While a region is collapsed, you will see a little arrow indicating that the region can be expanded. In this case, the indicator can be seen along the right side of the 3D Viewport near the navigation gizmo, as shown in the following screenshot:

Figure 1.6 – The "<" indicator for expanding the Sidebar

This indicator can be clicked on to expand the Sidebar. Let's try expanding the Sidebar now:

3. Hover your mouse over the expand region indicator.

4. Either click once and release or click and drag the indicator to the left to expand the Sidebar.

The expanded Sidebar can be seen in the following screenshot:

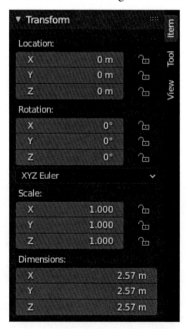

Figure 1.7 – The expanded Sidebar

The contents of the Sidebar are organized into several vertical tabs, including **View**, **Tool**, and **Item**. The **Item** tab contains transform data for our active object, the **Tool** tab contains lots of settings for our active tool, and the **View** tab contains settings for our viewport, camera, and 3D Cursor. We will learn to use some of these settings as they become relevant to our workflow. Many of these settings can also be accessed from the header of the 3D Viewport, which is why the Sidebar is collapsed by default in the sculpting preset.

Let's collapse the Sidebar again to get it out of our way:

1. Hover your mouse over the left-side edge of the expanded Sidebar.
2. Click and drag the edge of the Sidebar to the right until it collapses back into the side of the 3D Viewport.

We'll learn much more about the tools and the settings in the Sidebar throughout the rest of this book.

There's more...

You can gain quick access to these two regions with hotkeys. Hover your mouse inside the 3D Viewport before pressing a hotkey, then press the *T* hotkey to open or close the Toolbar, or press the *N* hotkey to open or close the Sidebar.

Exploring the viewport shading modes

As we saw earlier in this chapter, the 3D Viewport has a region for customizing the display and shading settings. In this topic, we will take a look at the different viewport shading modes available to us.

Getting ready

The viewport shading modes that we are about to see will work in any Blender project. However, it will be difficult to show off these modes without a proper model. We have provided the `childHead.blend` file for you so that you can follow along with this topic. You can download the file here: `https://github.com/PacktPublishing/Sculpting-the-Blender-Way/blob/main/Chapter01/childHead.blend`.

Once you've downloaded the example file, open it in Blender by either double-clicking the file or dragging the file into the Blender window and choosing **Open**. Inside this file, you'll find a nearly identical setup to the sculpting preset we saw earlier. However, this file contains a character sculpture instead of a basic sphere, as you can see in the following screenshot:

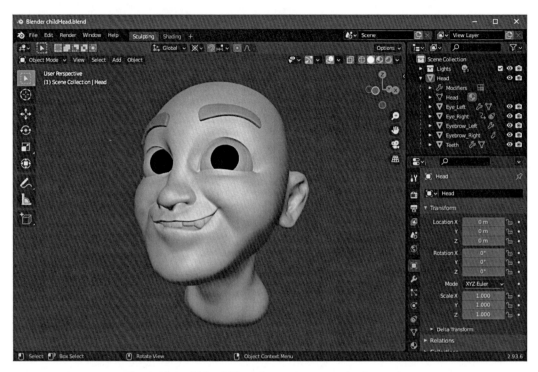

Figure 1.8 – The childHead.blend file with a sculpture on display in the 3D Viewport

Now that we have a proper file to demonstrate with, let's explore the shading modes.

How to do it...

Let's focus our attention on the shading modes in the top-right corner of the 3D Viewport. The right half of the display and shading region has several options for viewport shading, as you can see in the following screenshot:

Figure 1.9 – Viewport shading options

In this section, we have an icon for toggling the **X-ray** feature, followed by four small sphere icons for toggling between our shading modes: **Wireframe**, **Solid**, **Material Preview**, and **Rendered**. The second of the four sphere icons will be highlighted, indicating that we are currently using solid shading mode. Solid shading is the default when we create new projects in Blender.

Now, let's work our way through these shading options and see how they affect the viewport shading:

1. Click the **Toggle X-Ray** button to turn on the X-ray feature. Have a look at what the X-ray feature has done to the display of the sculpture:

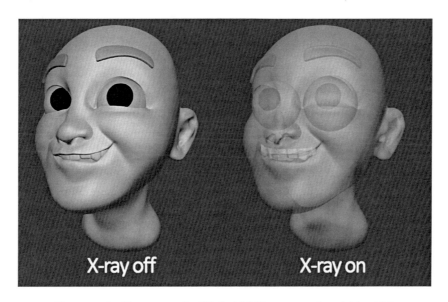

Figure 1.10 – X-ray turned off (left side)/X-ray turned on (right side)

It looks a little creepy, but it can be helpful for determining the intersection and depth of multiple objects. In this case, we can see that the character's eyeballs are much larger than they originally appeared to be. We can turn on this feature whenever we need it, but we're done with it for now, so let's turn it off and move on.

2. Click the **Toggle X-Ray** button to turn the X-ray feature off again.

> **Tip**
>
> Toggling X-ray mode on and off can also be done with the *Alt + Z* keyboard shortcut, as long as we have our mouse hovering over the 3D Viewport.

Up next are the four shading modes. These four spheres icons are organized from left to right in order of our typical workflow as well as how much processing power is required to display them. Let's work our way from left to right:

3. Click on the first of the four sphere icons to set the shading mode to **Wireframe**:

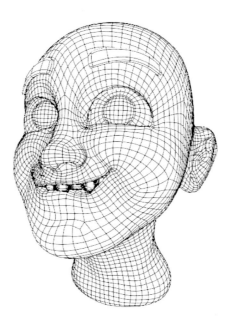

Figure 1.11 – Wireframe shading mode

Wireframe mode doesn't render the surface of the sculpture; it only draws the edges that make up the geometry of the model. There's not much to see here, so let's move on to the other shading modes. We already saw the second shading mode, **Solid**. This was the default setting when we first opened this file, so we'll skip it and move on to the third shading mode, **Material Preview**.

4. Click on the third of the four sphere icons to set the shading mode to **Material Preview**:

Figure 1.12 – Material Preview shading mode

Material Preview gives our sculpture a much more interesting look. Note how the skin has color and translucency, the eyes are shiny, and the character's nose, ears, and lips have slight red coloration. This is all because Material Preview mode gives us far more control over the materials that our sculptures are made of. For this file, the colors were painted, and the materials were set up ahead of time (you're welcome). For your own sculptures, you'll have to do this work yourself. The only thing that's missing from this mode is some lighting; that's where the fourth and final shading mode comes in, so let's look at it now.

5. Click on the fourth and final of the four sphere icons to set the shading mode to **Rendered**:

Figure 1.13 – Rendered shading mode

The difference here is subtle, but in this shading mode, we can set up custom lighting for our sculptures. We have to set up the lighting ourselves, but there's no better way to display a finished sculpture in all its glory than a final rendered image!

Now we have successfully explored the different viewport shading modes.

How it works...

For the majority of this book, we will only be using solid shading mode; it is the most practical shading mode because it offers the fastest sculpting performance while we work on our sculptures.

X-ray mode can be toggled on or off whenever you think it will help. In this example, being able to see the size and placement of the character's eyeballs can be very helpful while sculpting the eyelids and cheeks for the character.

Wireframe shading mode isn't very useful for sculpting, it is primarily used in other 3D modeling workflows, but it can be helpful for highlighting the geometry that the sculpture is made of. We'll learn more about the geometry of our sculptures in *Chapter 2, Overview of Blender's Sculpting Workflows*.

Material Preview gives us much better control over the materials that our object is made out of and looks a lot better than our previous modes. However, this comes at a price. Firstly, this display mode takes a lot of processing power, which means our sculpting tools won't work very well while we're in this mode. The other drawback is that we have to spend time setting up how these materials will look.

Rendered mode is used after we finish setting up our materials. We can set up our custom lighting in this final mode. Most digital art you will find in portfolios is created with this mode since it produces the highest-quality image. We'll learn how to show off our sculptures using this mode in *Chapter 10, Rendering Sculptures for Your Portfolio*.

Customizing solid shading mode with the pop-over menu

Now that we've seen the different shading modes available to us, let's take a look at how to adjust some of the settings for solid shading mode. Using the correct settings can help for optimizing sculpting performance as well as give us the best visual feedback during our sculpting workflow.

Getting ready

The viewport customization that we are about to explore will work in any Blender project. However, many of the settings will be difficult to demonstrate without a proper model, so we will be using the `childHead.blend` file again.

How to do it...

Have another look at the viewport shading options in the top-right corner of the 3D Viewport. We need to return to solid shading mode so that we can learn how to customize the solid shading:

1. Click on the second of the four sphere icons to set the shading mode to **Solid**.

    On the far-right side of the four shading mode icons, there is a little arrow for opening a **pop-over menu**. This menu will give us full control over the viewport shading options.

2. Click on the little down arrow to the right of the four sphere icons to open the **Viewport Shading** pop-over menu, as shown in the following screenshot:

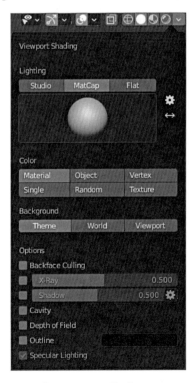

Figure 1.14 – The Viewport Shading pop-over menu

Excellent – now we can customize how our solid shading looks. First of all, we have our **Lighting** style. We have three options: **Studio**, **MatCap**, and **Flat**.

The sculpting preset for Blender sets our lighting mode to **MatCap** by default. **MatCap** stands for **Material Capture**. It is highly optimized for viewport performance since it does not actually require our computers to calculate lighting on the model while we sculpt. We highly recommend you stay in **MatCap** mode whenever sculpting, especially if you notice your computer slowing down while trying to sculpt. **MatCap** shading has an added benefit of overriding the materials in the viewport with a previously captured material.

Right now, we're using a gray clay material, but let's try swapping out our **MatCap** with a different material:

3. Click on the **MatCap** button if it isn't already active.

4. Click on the colored sphere below the **MatCap** button to open a list of materials, as seen in the following screenshot:

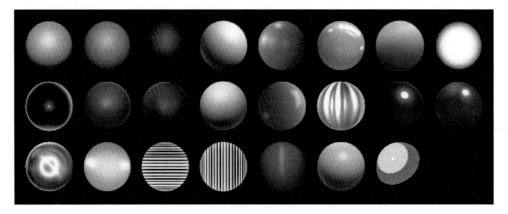

Figure 1.15 – The default selection of MatCaps

5. Click on the MatCap you would like to use.

We will continue the rest of this book with the standard gray clay MatCap, but feel free to use whichever MatCap works best for you.

If we can't get the level of customization that we need from MatCaps, we can use the next best thing, **studio lighting**. The eyes for this character look kind of lifeless; this is mostly because there is no reflectivity in the eyes when we use MatCaps. Let's fix that now.

6. Click on the **Studio** button to activate studio lighting mode:

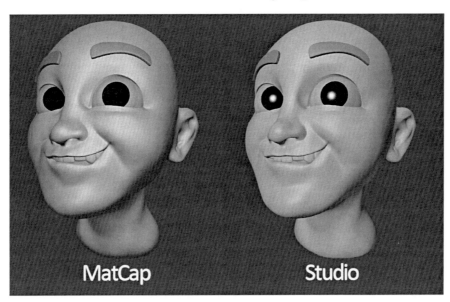

Figure 1.16 – MatCap lighting (left side)/Studio lighting (right side)

There, that's looking a lot better. In studio lighting, individual materials can be set to have different amounts of roughness. In this case, the eyes were set up ahead of time to have a very low roughness, so they look shiny.

The final of the three lighting options is **flat lighting**. Flat lighting can be useful for painting colors because it eliminates all shading from the surface of the sculpture. But right now, that's not a particularly helpful thing to do, so let's move on to our other settings.

We'll take a look at one more helpful shading option in the pop-over menu before we wrap up this section, **Cavity** (don't worry, our character doesn't have to go to the dentist; these are the good kind of cavities!). Let's take a look:

7. Check the box for **Cavity** in the pop-over menu.

    This option highlights the ridges and valleys of our sculpture. We have two types of cavity displays, **Screen Space** and **World Space**. We can even use both at the same time!

8. Click on the **Type:** drop-down menu next to the **Cavity** checkbox.

9. Choose **Both**.

Turning on both types of cavity displays can be very helpful for determining how sharp we need to make the edges of our sculptures. We can also more easily see how convex or concave a particular surface is. We recommend using this cavity feature while sculpting; you can turn it on for any of your sculpting projects.

There are other shading options for you to explore, but these are the most important shading options for sculpting.

How it works...

MatCaps are a standard feature in sculpting software because they look pretty good and they require very little processing power. This is a good thing because it means our computers can run fast while we sculpt. You may choose any MatCap you like. Obviously, some will be more practical than others. Most users stick to the gray or red clay, but some of the MatCaps are great for previewing other materials, such as 3D printed resin, car paint, or chrome.

Some of these MatCaps may look strange and impractical, but they can be very helpful. For instance, the vertically and horizontally striped MatCaps are excellent for helping to preview how lumpy or smooth the surface of a sculpture is.

Studio lighting gives us more accurate lighting and specular highlights. It's fine to use this mode while sculpting, but if you notice your computer slowing down, you may need to switch to MatCap lighting.

The cavity feature is very helpful while trying to visualize how smooth a surface is. We can also see shadows and highlights in the valleys and ridges of the sculpture, which is helpful for making sharp edges such as eyelids. You may even find that it helps for finding areas that have been over-sharpened.

Remember that you'll have to set these settings for each of your sculpting projects.

Using viewport overlays

Very similar to the shading options, we have another set of features called **overlays**. Overlays are extra parts of the viewport that are drawn on top of the regular shading features. This includes things like object outlines and grids.

Let's learn how to use viewport overlays to turn on features that will help us visualize some of the details of our scene, such as the position of the sculpture in 3D space.

Getting ready

We will continue where we left off in the previous topic using the childHead.blend file.

How to do it...

Overlays can be turned on and off either as a group, or individually. Turning overlays on can give us valuable information while we work on our sculptures, but sometimes all the visual clutter can be distracting while we work. Let's learn how to toggle our overlays.

Overlays can be accessed with the icon directly to the left of the shading icons in the top-right corner of the 3D Viewport. You can see the **Overlays** icon in the following screenshot:

Figure 1.17 – Viewport overlays

Clicking on the **Overlays** icon will toggle all overlays on and off:

1. Click the **Overlays** icon to turn off all overlays.

    Right now, we don't have very many overlays turned on, so this won't make much of a difference. But you will notice that the **Text Info** in the top-left corner of the 3D Viewport has disappeared. Let's turn the overlays back on and then learn how we can customize the overlays.

2. Click the **Overlays** icon again to turn the overlays back on.

    > **Tip**
    > Toggling overlays on and off can also be done with the *Shift + Alt + Z* keyboard shortcut.

Just like the viewport shading options, there is a pop-over menu that we can use to customize the overlays.

3.   Click on the little down arrow to the right of the **Overlays** icon to open the **Viewport Overlays** pop-over menu, as shown in the following screenshot:

Figure 1.18 – The Viewport Overlays pop-over menu

We can see that there are only a few options turned on. This is because the sculpting preset turns off many of the features that we don't need for the sculpting workflow. But we can turn some of these features back on as needed.

4.   Check the box for **Floor** in the pop-over menu to turn on the grid floor.

We can also turn on colored axis lines to go along with this floor.

5.   Click to turn on the toggles for **X** and **Y** next to the **Axes** label in the pop-over menu.

Isn't that neat? We've got a grid floor displayed below the character now. This can help us identify where our character is in relation to the center of the 3D scene, as you can see in the following screenshot:

Figure 1.19 – The grid floor and axes displayed below the character

Some of the most useful overlays are reserved for **Sculpt Mode**, but at the moment we are viewing this character in Object Mode. Let's change that now.

6. Click on the drop-down list labeled **Object Mode** in the top-left corner of the 3D Viewport.

7. Choose **Sculpt Mode** from the list to switch to **Sculpt Mode**.

8. Open the **Viewport Overlays** pop-over menu again.

    We have a few new options available now, including **Fade Inactive Geometry**, **Mask**, and **Face Sets**.

9. Check the box for **Fade Inactive Geometry** in the pop-over menu.

10. Click and drag the slider next to the checkbox to adjust the amount of fade.

Note how the eyes, eyebrows, and teeth all fade to gray as you adjust the slider. This overlay can be helpful for easily identifying which object we are currently sculpting on. We will learn about some of the other overlays later in this book, including the **Mask** overlay in *Chapter 3, Sculpting a Simple Character Head with Basic Brushes*, and the **Face Sets** overlay in *Chapter 6, Using Advanced Features and Customizing the Sculpting Brushes*.

How it works...

Most of the overlays are completely optional, especially for the sculpting workflow.

The **Mask** and **Face Sets** options will be very important later in this book, so don't be surprised if we visit this menu frequently to make adjustments to these overlays.

Toggling the overlays off entirely is helpful for looking at our sculptures without the extra visual noise. But some of the overlays provide useful information while we work, so we usually want the overlays on.

Navigating the 3D Viewport

Navigating in 3D space is fundamental to being able to create 3D art. We have to be able to look at our model from multiple angles while we work.

3D navigation can be broken down into three types of movement: **orbit**, **zoom**, and **pan**. We can see gizmos for these types of navigation in the top-right corner of the 3D Viewport:

Figure 1.20 – The navigation gizmo

Clicking on these gizmos will allow us to orbit, zoom, and pan respectively. However, navigation in 3D is very important, and it is best to use a dedicated button on your mouse or graphics tablet for these functions instead of relying on the gizmos. Orbit, pan, and zoom are all accessible from the middle mouse button, plus one of several modifier keys (*Alt*, *Ctrl*, and *Shift*).

In this topic, we will learn how to perform basic 3D Viewport navigation.

Getting ready

We will continue where we left off in the previous recipe using the `childHead.blend` file. It will be helpful to turn on the *X* and *Y* axis overlays, as well as the floor overlay.

Once you've opened the file and enabled these overlays, we'll be ready to try out 3D Viewport navigation.

How to do it...

Now, let's practice the three types of viewport navigation. We'll want to get comfortable navigating in the viewport so that we can look at our objects from multiple vantage points while we sculpt.

First up is orbiting, which will allow us to rotate our view around the sculpture:

1. Hover your mouse anywhere inside of the 3D Viewport.

2. Press and hold the middle mouse button and drag the mouse to orbit.

   And that's all there is to it!

   > Tip
   > Alternatively, we can click and drag on the colorful part of the navigation gizmo to orbit.

   We can also snap the view to align with any of the three-dimensional axes (*X*, *Y*, and *Z*):

3. Begin orbiting by pressing the middle mouse button and dragging.

4. While dragging with the middle mouse button, hold the *Alt* modifier key to snap the viewport to the closest angle.

   Similarly, we can flick the viewport into place for an even faster approach:

5. Hold the *Alt* modifier key before pressing the middle mouse button.

6. While holding the *Alt* modifier key, press the middle mouse button and flick the mouse slightly in the direction of the axis you would like to snap to.

   Being able to quickly snap our viewport like this is very helpful for checking the proportions of our sculptures.

   > Tip
   > Alternatively, we can click on any of the colored indicators of the navigation gizmo to snap to the corresponding axis (*X*, *Y*, *Z*, *-X*, *-Y*, and *-Z*).

Our next type of viewport navigation is zooming, which will allow us to get closer or further away from the sculpture:

7. Hold the *Ctrl* modifier key before pressing the middle mouse button.

8. While holding the *Ctrl* modifier key, press and hold the middle mouse button and drag up and down to zoom in and out.

> **Tip**
>
> If you have a mouse with a scroll wheel, you can scroll up and down to zoom in and out. However, we recommend sculpting with a graphics tablet, so you probably won't have access to a scroll wheel while sculpting. Another alternative is to click and drag on the magnifying glass icon in the navigation gizmo.

Lastly, we have panning, which will allow us to slide our view around, kind of like sliding a piece of paper around on a desk:

9. Hold the *Shift* modifier key before pressing the middle mouse button.

10. While holding the *Shift* modifier key, press and hold the middle mouse button and drag to pan.

    If you ever pan too far away from your sculpture, you can recenter the view from the **View** menu:

11. Open the **View** menu in the top-left corner of the 3D Viewport.

12. Choose **Frame Selected** to recenter the view on the active object.

And that wraps up our navigation controls. Practice these controls, as sculpting is a three-dimensional art form, so we need to be looking at our sculptures from all vantage points while we work. We'll be using these navigation controls very often while sculpting.

There's more...

Orbiting can be performed in one of two modes, **Turntable** and **Trackball**.

The default behavior is Turntable. In this mode, the viewport behaves as if the contents of the 3D scene are on a potter's wheel. It can be rotated around, and we can look up and down. This mode will always keep our view orientation aligned in a predictable way, which makes orbiting easy to get used to.

The alternative mode is Trackball. This mode allows us to take complete control over our viewport orientation, including tilted angles that would be impossible to achieve with the Turntable style of orbiting. This is more freeing but can be a little more difficult to get used to.

Choosing an orbit method is up to personal preference; most artists pick one style of orbiting and stick with it permanently. If you would like to try changing the orbit style, open the **Edit** menu from Blender's Topbar and choose **Preferences**. Once the **Blender Preferences** window appears, click on the **Navigation** tab. From here, you can choose the **Orbit Method** by clicking on the **Turntable** button or the **Trackball** button.

See also

To read more about Blender's viewport navigation, you can find the official documentation here: `https://docs.blender.org/manual/en/latest/editors/preferences/navigation.html`.

Setting up your graphics tablet's stylus buttons

Using a **graphics tablet** for sculpting makes a huge difference in ease of use and fine control over our brushstrokes. In particular, graphics tablets offer **pressure sensitivity**, which will allow us to control the strength of our brushstrokes on the fly.

Graphics tablets come in a variety of forms: pen tablets, pen displays, and touchscreen devices with integrated stylus support.

Pen tablets are often the most affordable option. They can be placed on your desk or held in your lap. Pen tablets do not have an integrated display, so you will have to look up at your computer's display while you move your pen across the tablet. This is not as difficult as it may sound; it's a lot like using a mouse.

Pen displays cost a lot more because they include a display underneath the drawing surface. They usually need lots of extra desk space and a stand to hold up the device. Many artists prefer these types of tablets because they allow them to use the pen directly on top of the art.

Some devices, such as Microsoft Surface with a Surface Pen, effectively have a graphics tablet built in, which is great for on-the-go 3D sculpting! Make sure your device is compatible with a pen stylus before use; if it is not compatible, you may damage your device.

Any graphics tablet brand should work for following along with this book, but we recommend **Wacom**, **Huion**, or **XP-PEN**. Wacom tablets are the most popular but also the most expensive; the other brands are just as capable and are much more affordable, with several entry-level tables available for under $50.

Getting ready

Most graphics tablets have a set of drivers that need to be installed for the tablet to work properly. Make sure you go to your graphics tablet manufacturer's website and install the latest drivers. Instructions will come with your device.

How to do it...

Let's set up our tablet's stylus buttons. It is easiest to use Blender if we have access to all three mouse buttons. Pressing with the tip of our stylus will mimic the left mouse button. Many styluses have one or two extra buttons along their side. If you have two buttons on your stylus, we recommend setting up one button for the middle mouse button and one button for the right mouse button.

We will use Wacom as an example for this topic; if you're using a different brand of tablet, follow the manual that came with the device to learn how to customize pen button bindings:

1. Open the tablet properties for your graphics tablet (if you have a Wacom tablet, this is called **Wacom Tablet Properties**):

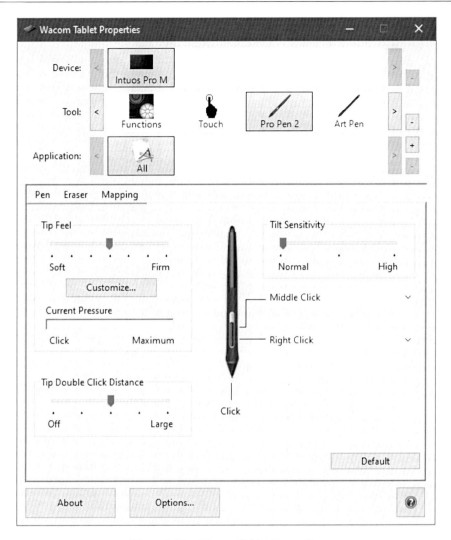

Figure 1.21 – Wacom Tablet Properties

Look at the bindings for the pen buttons on your tablet. If your tablet does not have a middle click button assigned, we will need to assign one now.

2. Find the section of the tablet properties for customizing pen buttons (If you have a Wacom tablet, these settings can be found in the **Pen** tab).

3. If your pen has two side buttons, bind the lower button to **Right Click**.

4. Again, if your pen has two side buttons, bind the upper button to **Middle Click**.

If your pen only has one side button, prioritize the middle-click binding. Blender uses a middle click for navigation, so this will be very helpful.

If your stylus does not include any side buttons like this, then you can use the navigation gizmo in the top-right corner of the 3D Viewport for navigation instead of pressing one of the side buttons on your pen.

See also

If you are using Windows, some users experience lag and other issues with graphics tablets. This is usually because Windows has some troublesome features turned on by default, such as Flicks and Press and hold right click These features interfere with graphics tablets, so they should be disabled. If you're still having graphics tablet issues, there are many community resources available online. Here's one from Boutique Retouching that is helpful for diagnosing issues with Wacom devices: `https://www.youtube.com/watch?v=fcrMJCgL8ss`.

2
Overview of Blender's Sculpting Workflows

This book is about art, so we're going to try not to get too technical about how sculpting works. However, digital sculpting is performed on a computer, and we will have the best experience with the software if we gain a basic understanding of what's going on under the hood. In this chapter, we will identify and explain how Blender's sculpting features work and demystify how each of the sculpting workflows should be used at each stage of the sculpting process.

The sculpting process can be broken up into four separate workflows: **Basic Sculpting**, **Dynamic Topology** (**Dyntopo** for short), **Voxel Remeshing**, and **Multiresolution**. Each of these workflows has upsides and downsides. We will learn how to use them at the correct stages of our sculpting projects so that we can maximize the upsides and minimize the downsides. If used appropriately, these workflows will give us artistic control, optimized performance, and final results of the highest quality.

By the end of this chapter, you'll have a good understanding of the components that 3D sculptures are made from and how the computer represents them to us in the 3D Viewport. Additionally, you'll understand how basic sculpting mode works and get a feel for several of the most common sculpting brushes. You'll understand how to use dynamic topology and voxel remeshing workflows to overcome the limitations of basic sculpting mode. Finally, you'll get a glimpse of the multiresolution workflow, which we will learn about, in more depth, in *Chapter 5, Learning the Power of Subdivision and the Multiresolution Workflow*.

The main topics in this chapter are as follows:

- Understanding the components of a 3D sculpture

- Pushing polys with the basic sculpting mode

- Discovering the limitations of the basic sculpting mode

- Creating dynamic topology with Dyntopo

- Practicing the basics of the Voxel Remesher

- Using the Voxel Remesher in a low-to-high detail workflow

- Exploring the most powerful sculpting mode – multiresolution

Technical requirements

For general requirements, please refer back to the *Technical requirements* section that was laid out in *Chapter 1, Exploring Blender's User Interface for Sculpting*.

In this chapter, we will be dealing with high-resolution models, so you will need at least 1GB of RAM available to open some of the example files. Example files for this book can be downloaded from the GitHub link at https://github.com/PacktPublishing/Sculpting-the-Blender-Way.

Understanding the components of a 3D sculpture

First, we're going to learn how 3D sculptures are represented by the computer. Traditional sculpting is often done with clay. Clay is an earthy blobby mess with no real structure; it's just out there waiting for us to play with it and make art! Digital sculpting in software such as Blender tries to capture the creativity and free-form nature of traditional sculpting. However, in digital sculpting, there is an underlying structure that we need to be aware of as artists. Although we like to think of our digital sculptures as clay, they are actually 3D models that are made up of small geometric shapes called **polygons**. The word polygon refers to a flat shape with multiple corners. Polygons are made up of three main components, as presented in the following diagram:

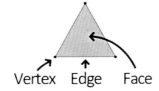

Figure 2.1 – The components of a polygon

The three main components of a polygon are as follows:

- **Vertex** (the plural form of the word is **Vertices**): These are the corners of a polygon; each vertex represents a single point in 3D space.

- **Edge**: This is a line that connects two vertices, edges make up the sides of a polygon.

- **Face**: This is the solid inner area of a polygon that forms the visible surface between three or more edges.

A vertex by itself is not a polygon; it has no dimension. An edge can be made between two vertices; however, an edge by itself is not a polygon either. We require at least three vertices and three edges in order to create a polygon. There are three types of polygons that we need to know about to make 3D art:

- The simplest polygons are **Triangles** (often abbreviated to **Tris**). Triangles have three vertices, three edges, and one face.

- The most common type of polygons are **Quadrilaterals** (often abbreviated to **Quads**). These have four vertices, four edges, and one face.

- Polygons with more than four vertices are known as **n-gons**. We do not usually use n-gons because they can cause issues with the surfaces of our 3D models.

Collectively, these simple geometric shapes are known as the **geometry** of the 3D model. When we interconnect all the little pieces of geometry together, they create a **mesh**. A mesh is the primary type of 3D model that we use when creating 3D models (that includes our sculptures).

We promised not to get too technical in this chapter, so that's plenty of information for now. Let's examine these components in the context of a 3D scene.

Getting ready

Launch Blender and start a new project with the sculpting preset by choosing **File | New | Sculpting**. We'll start this section by enabling a few viewport overlays that will show us the components of the model in the 3D Viewport.

How to do it...

First, let's enable our **Statistics** overlay so that Blender will display information about the model:

1. Locate the **Viewport Overlays** pop-over menu in the upper-right corner of the 3D Viewport.

2. Click on the little down arrow to open the pop-over menu..

3. Check the box labeled **Statistics**.

Perfect! Now we have some additional information in the upper-left corner of the 3D Viewport, as shown in the following image::

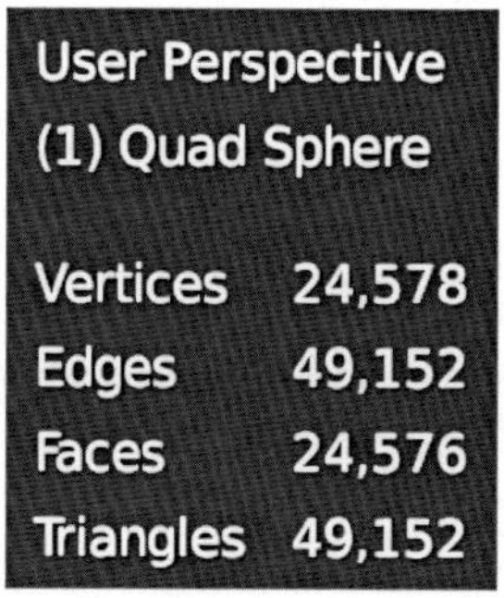

User Perspective
(1) Quad Sphere

Vertices	24,578
Edges	49,152
Faces	24,576
Triangles	49,152

Figure 2.2 – The statistics overlay as seen in the upper-left corner of the 3D Viewport

Here, the name of our active object is displayed. In this example, the object is called **Quad Sphere**. The statistics for the geometry are displayed beneath the name. These statistics serve as a summary of the model, but we can do better than that. Let's turn on another overlay so that we can view the polygons:

1. Open the **Viewport Overlays** pop-over menu again.

2. Check the box labeled **Wireframe**.

3. Use the slider next to the **Wireframe** checkbox to increase the value from 0.500 to 1.000 so that the full wireframe will be displayed.

Now we can view the little quadrilaterals that the Quad Sphere's mesh is made out of. It should appear similar to the following diagram:

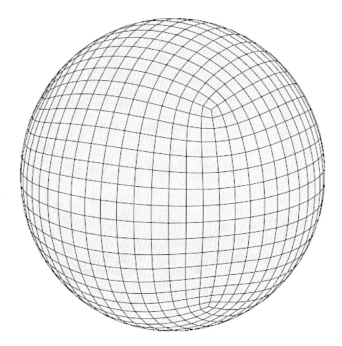

Figure 2.3 – The wireframe of the sphere (this diagram has been simplified for better visibility in this book)

This overlay is helpful when trying to understand how the geometry of the sculpture is arranged. Usually, we don't want to leave it turned on while we're sculpting because it can be a visual distraction. In this chapter, we'll be toggling this overlay on and off several times to help demonstrate what happens to the polygons as we sculpt. For now, we're done with this overlay. Toggle it back off so that we can move on and try out some sculpting tools!

How it works...

As you will have observed from the statistics, the Quad Sphere model has *24,578* vertices, *49,152* edges, and *24,576* faces. That's more information than we need. As a general rule, we only care about the number of polygons, which is referred to as the model's **poly count**. However, the poly count isn't always the most accurate representation of the complexity of our model. If we divide all of the quads and n-gons into their simplest forms, we will get the number of triangles in the model, which is known as the **tri count**. Blender includes the tri count for the model in the statistics overlay, so we can see that this model has *49,152* triangles.

That sounds like a lot, right? Wrong! This is actually a relatively low number of polygons when it comes to 3D sculptures. The `childHead.blend` example model that we explored in *Chapter 1*, *Exploring Blender's User Interface for Sculpting*, has 241,200 triangles, and even that is just scraping the surface of how many polygons Blender can handle.

So, why are there so many? Well, it's pretty simple. Triangles are always flat. We can't have a triangle with curved edges. So, we need to combine lots of triangles together to make the model look as though it's made out of clay with smooth round forms. When observed from afar, all of these tiny pieces of flat geometry should look smooth and round.

Some 3D modeling workflows are focused on arranging the geometry into specific patterns that give us good results without requiring many polygons. However, sculpting is designed around allowing us to create the shapes of the sculpture without having to focus on the geometry. To achieve this, the poly count is greatly increased – sometimes, into the millions. Once we have enough polygons, we can push them around with our sculpting tools to make any shape that we like.

Pushing polys with the basic sculpting mode

Your patience has paid off. It's finally time to try out some sculpting tools! In this section, we will discover how the basic **Draw** brush can be used to push the polygons of the model around to change the shape of the sculpture.

Getting ready

Let's pick up where we left off in the *Understanding the components of a 3D sculpture* section. We have a fresh file using the sculpting preset, and we have the Statistics overlay turned on.

Since we will be using tools, it would be helpful to expand the Toolbar on the left-hand side of the 3D Viewport so that we can view the names of the tools. Please refer back to the *Expanding and collapsing the Toolbar and the Sidebar* section of *Chapter 1, Exploring Blender's User Interface for Sculpting*.

Don't forget to use a graphics tablet as you follow along with the sculpting instructions. Please refer back to the *Setting up your graphics tablet's stylus buttons* section of *Chapter 1, Exploring Blender's User Interface for Sculpting*.

Important Note

If you do not have a graphics tablet, you can click with the left mouse button to use brushes instead of pressing down with the pen tip. Additionally, you can use the middle mouse button instead of the upper side button on the pen for navigation.

You might also experience inconsistencies with brush functionality because a mouse has no pressure sensitivity. If your brushes aren't working while using a mouse, check that the pen pressure for **Radius** and **Strength** are turned off in the **Tool Settings** menu.

How to do it...

As you can see in the upper-left corner of the 3D Viewport header, the sculpting preset has already set our Interaction Mode to **Sculpt Mode**, so we're ready to go! Now we can try out the **Draw** brush to begin sculpting:

1. Locate the **Draw** brush at the top of the Toolbar.

2. The active brush will be highlighted in blue. If the **Draw** brush is not already active, click on it to activate it.

3. Hover your pen over your graphics tablet and align the pointer over the top of the Quad Sphere model.

4. Press the tip of your pen onto your graphics tablet to begin drawing on the surface of the Quad Sphere.

Try drawing several brush strokes all over the surface of the model. It doesn't matter what you draw – we're just practicing. You can draw a smiley face, sign your name, or play a game of tic-tac-toe! Fill up the whole surface of the Quad Sphere, just as we've done in the following example:

Figure 2.4 – The Quad Sphere after using the Draw brush

Eventually, we will run out of surface area to draw on, so we need to rotate the 3D Viewport around the sculpture so that we can sculpt the other areas of the Quad Sphere. Let's use the upper side button on our tablet pen to orbit around the model:

1. Hover your pen over the 3D Viewport (do not press the tip of the pen down – keep it hovering slightly above the surface of the graphics tablet).

2. Press and hold the upper side button on your pen (this button should be bound to the middle mouse button).

3. While holding the upper side button, drag the pen to orbit around the model until you see an area of the Quad Sphere that you have not yet sculpted on.

4. Let go of the upper side button of the pen to stop orbiting.

We will be doing this a lot, so practice this style of navigating until you're comfortable enough to move on. Don't forget that sculpting is a 3D process; we must keep orbiting around our object to sculpt details on all sides.

Additionally, it is important to zoom in and out while working on our sculptures. By default, the size of the Draw brush is relative to the view, so the effective size changes as we zoom in and out. If we zoom far away from our model, we can make very large brush strokes, and if we zoom very close to the surface of the model, we can draw finer details. Let's try this now:

1. Hover your pen over the 3D Viewport (do not press the tip of the pen down – keep it hovering slightly above the surface of the graphics tablet).

2. Press and hold the *Ctrl* key on your keyboard and the upper side button on your pen.

3. While holding the *Ctrl* key and the upper side button, drag the pen downward to zoom out far away from the Quad Sphere.

4. Let go of the *Ctrl* key and the upper side button of the pen to stop zooming.

5. Use your pen to draw on the quad Quad Sphere.

   Notice that because we are far away from the Quad Sphere, our brush strokes have a much larger impact on the sculpture. Next, let's try the opposite.

6. While holding the *Ctrl* key and the upper side button, drag the pen upward to zoom in up close to the surface of the Quad Sphere.

7. Let go of the *Ctrl* key and the upper side button of the pen to stop zooming.

8. Use your pen to draw on the Quad Sphere again.

This time, we can make small details with each stroke of the brush.

It's very common to zoom out and increase the brush size while working on larger forms and, conversely, to zoom in and decrease the brush size while working on smaller details. However, zooming in and out isn't the most practical way to change the brush size. Quite often, we will want to change the brush size without changing our view.

Let's learn how to adjust the brush settings. Take a look at the **Tool Settings** section in the header of the 3D Viewport. Most of the settings we require are easily accessible from here:

Figure 2.5 – The Tool Settings section for the Draw brush

The size of the brush is determined by the **Radius** setting. By default, the radius of the Draw brush is set to 50 px. This radius unit is relative to the view, so 50 px means that the brush radius is 50 pixels on our screen. You can change the size of the brush by clicking and dragging the **Radius** slider.

This is simple enough, but we have a bit of a disadvantage to using this slider. We aren't able to easily view the size of the brush while we're adjusting it. Let's learn a hotkey for adjusting the brush radius instead:

1. Hover your pen over the 3D Viewport before pressing the following hotkey.

2. Press the *F* hotkey to begin changing the brush radius.

3. Drag your pen to the left to decrease the radius, or drag your pen to the right to increase the radius.

4. When you've got a brush radius you like, tap your pen down onto the graphics tablet.

Wasn't that easier than using the slider? Having this visual feedback while we adjust the brush size speeds up our workflow.

The next brush setting that we can adjust is the **Strength** setting. The strength determines how intense the brush effect will be. With a strength of 0.000, we will have no intensity at all, and the brush will do nothing. With a strength of 1.000, our brush will be at full intensity. Most brushes in Blender default to half strength, 0.500, which we can see in the **Tool Settings** at the top of the 3D Viewport.. So far, we've been using the Draw brush at half strength, so let's try turning it up to full:

1. Click and drag the **Strength** slider to increase the intensity of the brush to 1.000.

2. Use your pen to draw on the Quad Sphere again.

    Notice how we can raise the polygons twice as high now? Being able to adjust the strength is very useful, but we're not done yet. There is a pressure icon next to the **Strength** slider. By default, this button is turned on. But what does it do? While this feature is toggled on, we can control the intensity of our brush by varying the pressure on our pen tablet. Let's try it.

3. If the **pressure** button isn't already highlighted blue, click on it to activate the strength pressure.

4. Use your pen to draw on the Quad Sphere.

5. While drawing, press your pen harder against your graphics tablet to increase the intensity of the brush.

    Pen pressure can be modulated as much as you like during brush strokes. This gives us a lot of control over our brush strokes, and it is one of the main reasons we use graphics tablets for sculpting instead of a mouse. Just like adjusting the radius, we can also use a keyboard shortcut to adjust the brush strength.

6. Hover your pen over the 3D Viewport before pressing the following keyboard shortcut.

7. Press the *Shift + F* keyboard shortcut to begin changing the brush strength.

8. Drag your pen to the left to decrease the strength, or drag your pen to the right to increase the strength.

9. When you've got a brush strength that you like, tap your pen down onto the graphics tablet.

    The Draw brush behaves in a pretty straightforward manner. As we draw, it raises the surface of the model upward, but it can also be used to press the surface inward if we reverse the direction of the brush. The **Direction** of the brush is represented by the little + and - buttons in the **Tool Settings** at the top of the 3D Viewport.. Currently, the direction is set to **Add**, as indicated by the blue highlight on the + button. Let's try changing it to **Subtract**.

10. Locate the + and - buttons in the **Tool Settings** section of the 3D Viewport header.

11. Click on the - button to change the brush direction to **Subtract**.

12. Use your pen to draw on the surface of the Quad Sphere model.

    Excellent! Now we can subtract from the model to create grooves in the surface. Once again, we have a hotkey that we can use instead of having to reach up to the **Tool Settings**.

13. Hold the *Ctrl* key to temporarily invert the brush direction.

14. While holding *Ctrl*, use your pen to draw on the surface of the Quad Sphere model.

15. Let go of the *Ctrl* key to return to the original brush direction.

Very good. Since the *Ctrl* key makes switching direction very accessible, we should switch the Draw brush direction back to its default direction to avoid confusion. Switch the direction to **Add** by clicking on the + button in **Tool Settings**.

There are, of course, other brush settings, but we'll save those for later.

How it works...

Customizing our brush settings gives us a lot of control over how each brush feels. A large radius will allow us to make very large changes to the sculpture, while a small radius is helpful for smaller details. We tend to change brush radius very often while sculpting, so you should get used to using the *F* hotkey.

Strength is also important for getting our brush to behave exactly the way we want. When combined with pressure, the strength setting works as an upper bound to how intense the brush stroke will be. If strength is set to `1.000`, then we will get full intensity while pressing firmly on the tablet. If it is set to `0.500`, then we will max out at half intensity while pressing firmly on the tablet. Since we are using a graphics tablet with pressure sensitivity, we can usually keep the strength around `0.800` and press firmly or less firmly to get the intensity we like. Feel free to adjust the strength whenever you need to; just don't set it to `0.000` because no strength means that the brush will have no effect at all.

The direction of the brush gives us quick access to move the surface inward and outward with a single toggle. This gives each brush dual functionality and opens up a lot of possibilities. Some of the advanced brushes don't have a direction, but they can still be toggled to a secondary function while we hold the *Ctrl* key.

There's more...

Everything we did in this section utilized the basic sculpting mode. In this mode, the brushes push around the geometry to modify the shape of the model. If you read the information in the statistics overlay, you'll notice that the tri count of the Quad Sphere stayed exactly the same while we used the Draw brush. That's because basic Sculpt Mode can only modify the polygons that we already have; it does not create or remove polygons.

The basic Sculpt Mode is useful for all types of modeling. We can temporarily hop into basic sculpting mode and push the polygons around, then hop back out of the Sculpt Mode once we've made the changes we like. However, for the purposes of this book, the basic sculpting mode runs into limitations very quickly. So, what happens when we need more polygons? For that, we require a more advanced sculpting mode, which we will learn about in the next section.

Discovering the limitations of the basic sculpting mode

So far, we've only made changes to the **surface details** of the Quad Sphere using the Draw brush. These changes are pretty cool, but the whole thing still just looks like a sphere with some details on it because the **major forms** haven't changed. We can think of the major forms of a model as large building blocks. If you squint and look at any object, you can roughly block it out into its major forms: cubes, spheres, cylinders, the head, the neck, appendages, protrusions, horns, the nose, eyeballs, and more.

The Draw brush is not well suited to making new major forms, so we will require a new kind of brush – one that pushes the polygons around in a very different way. In this section, we will try out the **Snake Hook** brush to begin creating new major forms on our sculpture.

Getting ready

In this section, we can either start with a new sculpting project or pick up where we left off in the *Pushing polys with the basic sculpting mode* section. If you start a new file, make sure that you turn on the statistics overlay so that you can see the tri count.

How to do it...

Let's try using the Snake Hook brush to create new major forms on our Quad Sphere:

1.   Locate the **Snake Hook** brush from the Toolbar.
2.   Click to activate the **Snake Hook** brush.
3.   Increase the brush **Radius** setting to around 250 px.
4.   Hover your pen over your graphics tablet and align the pointer over part of the Quad Sphere model.
5.   Press the tip of your pen onto your graphics tablet to begin using the Snake Hook brush.
6.   Draw in an outward direction from the Quad Sphere to pull a piece of the sphere outward.

The Snake Hook brush is much better at moving around large areas of the sculpture than the Draw brush. Your results should appear similar to the following diagram:

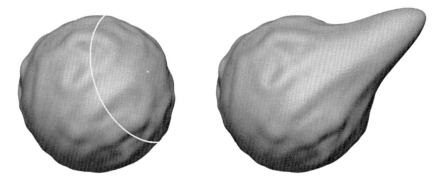

Figure 2.6 – The Snake Hook brush used to pull out a new segment of the Quad Sphere

Pretty cool! But we're starting to run into a problem. As we discovered in the *Pushing polys with the basic sculpting mode* section, the basic Sculpt Mode can only push around polygons that already exist in the model. The polygons of our Quad Sphere are getting a bit stretched out. To better visualize how stretched out these polygons have become, let's turn on the wireframe overlay:

1.   Open the **Viewport Overlays** pop-over menu.

2.   Check the box labeled **Wireframe**.

3.   Use the slider next to the wireframe checkbox to set the wireframe value to `1.000`.

The polygons of the Quad Sphere will now be visible. They should appear similar to the following diagram:

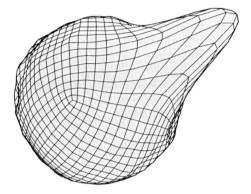

Figure 2.7 – The wireframe after using the Snake Hook brush (this diagram has been simplified for better visibility in this book)

Notice how the protrusion we created has led to large, stretched-out polygons? The further we pull these polygons away from the Quad Sphere, the more stretched out they will become.

So, let's examine what happens if we try taking this even further. Let's make a curvy shape using the Snake Hook brush:

1.   Use the Snake Hook brush to extend the protrusion further.

2.   As you draw, try making a curvy, swoopy S-shaped pattern.

You've probably noticed the problem by now. Our polygons have become so stretched out that they can't represent this shape properly, as you can see in the following diagram:

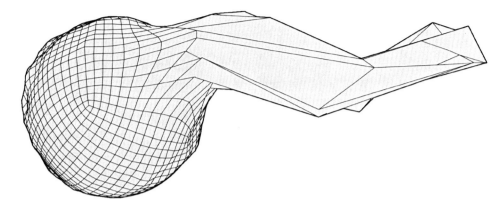

Figure 2.8 – The wireframe after making a curvy segment with the Snake Hook brush (this diagram has been simplified for better visibility in this book)

Oh, no! We ruined it. The Snake Hook brush did not play nicely with the polygons of our Quad Sphere. This is a major limitation of the basic sculpting mode. If we try to add new major forms to our models, we will end up with ruined, stretched-out geometry.

Stretched-out geometry such as this will always produce bad results in our finished sculptures. If you start to observe this happening to your sculptures, it means we are pushing the polygons too far. We need to do something else if we are going to overcome this limitation of the basic sculpting mode.

Creating dynamic topology with Dyntopo

As we discovered in the *Discovering the limitations of the basic sculpting mode* section, the basic sculpting mode doesn't work very well for introducing new major forms in our sculptures. But that's no good. How can we make beautiful art if we're stuck with a boring sphere? To solve this problem, we will have to learn a little bit about topology.

Topology is a term we use to describe how all the geometry of a mesh is interconnected. This Quad Sphere is made up of quadrilaterals that form a clean and simple set of grid patterns. The grid patterns in the Quad Sphere are arranged nicely to create a smooth sphere shape. One way to think about this is to say that the topology for this mesh *wants* to be a sphere. Of course, topology is not a living thing and can't truly *want* anything, but it can still be helpful for us to think of it in this way. The problem we ran into in our previous example is that the topology *doesn't want* to have a protrusion coming out of it – it's trying to stay a sphere.

So, if we want to introduce a new major form to this mesh, we need some way of adjusting the topology so that it will support the new major form we are trying to add.

One easy-to-use solution that we can try is called **Dynamic Topology (Dyntopo)**. Dyntopo is a feature that will dynamically update our sculpture's topology to fit the new shapes that we sculpt into the model. Dyntopo comes with its own set of limitations; however, before we concern ourselves with that, let's play around with it and have some fun.

Getting ready

We ruined our Quad Sphere in the *Discovering the limitations of the basic sculpting mode* section, so let's start over with a new sculpting project from the sculpting preset by choosing **File | New | Sculpting**. Turn on the statistics overlay again so that we can observe what happens to our topology as we work.

How to do it...

We're going to try out the Snake Hook brush again. However, this time, we will first enable the **Dyntopo** feature:

1. Locate the **Dyntopo** options in the upper-right corner of the 3D Viewport header.
2. Click the checkbox to activate dynamic topology.
3. Click on the **Dyntopo** option next to the checkbox to open the pop-over menu.
4. Change the **Detail Size** setting to 8.00 px.

You can view the Dyntopo settings in the following screenshot:

Figure 2.9 – The Dyntopo pop-over menu

Now, let's try the Snake Hook brush again with this new sculpting mode enabled:

1. Click on the **Snake Hook** brush in the Toolbar to activate it.
2. Set the **Radius** setting of the brush to 250 px.

3. Use the Snake Hook brush to pull a piece of the quad sphere outward.

4. As you draw, try making a curvy, swoopy S-shaped pattern.

That's looking much better than our previous attempt. Your result should appear similar to the following diagram:

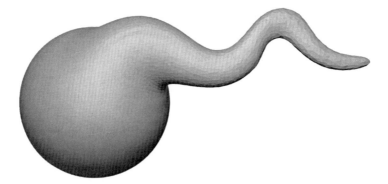

Figure 2.10 – The curvy segment we created with the Snake Hook brush and Dyntopo

Because we are using the Dyntopo feature, the topology of the Quad Sphere was altered when we used the Snake Hook brush. Let's turn on our statistics and wireframe overlays so that we can find out what happened:

1. Open the **Viewport Overlays** pop-over menu.

2. Check the box labeled **Statistics**.

3. Check the box labeled **Wireframe**.

4. Use the slider next to the **Wireframe** checkbox to set the wireframe value to `1.000`.

Your sculpture should appear similar to the following diagram:

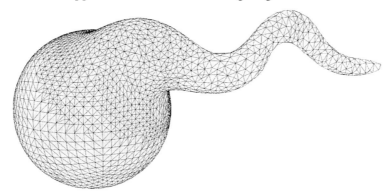

Figure 2.11 – The wireframe after making a curvy segment with the Snake Hook brush and Dyntopo
(this diagram has been simplified for better visibility in this book)

Isn't that interesting? Dyntopo has created new polygons to support the curvy protrusion that we just made. Go ahead and have some fun with this sculpting mode before moving on.

How it works...

Dyntopo is able to detect when our polygons are becoming too stretched out. When the edges of the polygons exceed the detail size we specified in the pop-over menu, new polygons are created to support the new shape. The technical term for this is **tessellation**.

Check the statistics: how many triangles did you end up with? In our example, we got 48,302. That's actually fewer than our original tri count of 49,152 because Dyntopo didn't just add polygons that we needed for our curvy shape, it also removed polygons that were no longer needed. This is because Dyntopo is using a **Refine Method** setting called **Subdivide Collapse**. These settings can be customized further to get exactly the effect you're looking for.

Take note of the fact that the arrangement of our topology is more important than the exact number of polygons. Greater or fewer polygons don't inherently mean we can create new major forms. We must support our new shapes with topology that *wants* to be the shape we are trying to make.

There's more...

This book would have been incomplete if we hadn't covered the Dyntopo feature, but admittedly, this feature has fallen out of favor in the Blender community because it has many downsides:

- Sometimes, the surfaces can fracture into scattered triangles that create holes and other issues with the surface of the mesh.

- It has the poorest performance of all the sculpting workflows and our computers will often slow down while performing highly detailed work.

- We cannot join separate pieces of geometry together.

- If we aren't careful, we can accidentally remove details from our sculptures that are too small for our current detail size.

- The tessellation creates lumpy surfaces that don't look very pleasing in a final model.

- The density of the polygons varies throughout the model. Areas of high detail have tiny polygons, while areas of low detail have very large polygons. This uneven polygon density can make it difficult to sculpt details into the model's surface.

For these reasons, we do not recommend that you utilize the Dyntopo feature for most of your sculpting workflows. It's fun while we're getting started, and it works well with the Snake Hook brush, but the flaws of this feature become very apparent when we get into high detail work.

Don't worry, though. Next, we will learn about an alternative feature that we can use to adjust the mesh of our sculptures while we work.

See also

Much of the information presented throughout this chapter is directly informed by the lead developer behind Blender's sculpting features: Pablo Dobarro. If you would like to view his original presentation on these sculpting workflows, please check out *The new sculpting workflow in Blender - Pablo Dobarro*, which is available on the official Blender YouTube channel at `https://www.youtube.com/watch?v=lxkyA4Xslzs`.

This presentation is a few years old and is presented from a highly technical standpoint. However, if you would like to view the techy inner workings of the software, there's no better resource than this.

Practicing the basics of the Voxel Remesher

We've learned about the importance of topology in relation to the shape of our sculptures. We understand that we can only push polygons around a short distance before they become too stretched out to properly represent the shape we are trying to make. In the *Creating dynamic topology with Dyntopo* section, we discovered one solution to this problem, but it was riddled with little issues that would make our workflow very difficult later down the line.

In this section, we will explore a better alternative for adjusting the topology while we sculpt. Blender has several methods for analyzing a mesh to determine which polygons are necessary to support any given shape. After analyzing the shape of a model, Blender can replace the original polygons with a completely new set of polygons to create a new mesh that better fits the shape we are trying to represent. This process is known as **Remeshing**.

There are several types of remeshing, but for sculpting, we require a really fast method. Luckily, we have an almost instantaneous type of remeshing called **Voxel Remeshing**. Voxels are three-dimensional volume elements, which is a nerdy way of saying: voxels are little cubes.

If we analyze a sphere, we can visualize its volume as being filled with little cubes. This tends to make our objects look extremely blocky, so we can follow it up by smoothing out all of the corners of the voxels, which will give us a nice new mesh. You can see a visualization of this process in the following diagram:

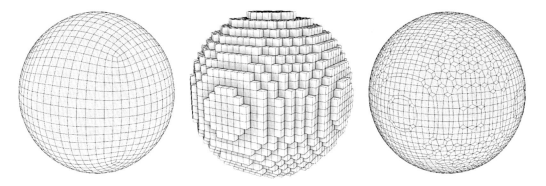

Figure 2.12 – The original Quad Sphere on the left-hand side, converted into voxels in the middle, and smoothed out into a new sphere-shaped mesh on the right-hand side

This process works for any shape. It's also extremely fast, so we can voxel remesh our sculpture as often as we need to. Let's try it out.

Getting ready

The Voxel Remesher utility will work with any object, but working with a sphere is boring, so let's try it with an example file. Download the devilishlyHandsomeGuy. blend example file from the GitHub repository at https://github.com/ PacktPublishing/Sculpting-the-Blender-Way/blob/main/Chapter02/ devilishlyHandsomeGuy.blend.

Once you've downloaded the example file, open it in Blender by either double-clicking on the file or dragging the file into the Blender window and choosing **Open**. Inside this file, you'll find a sculpture of a devilishly handsome guy, which you can see in the following diagram:

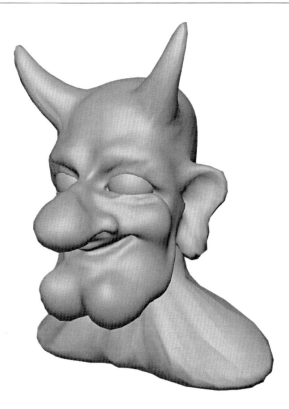

Figure 2.13 – The devilishly handsome guy

This character has been sculpted out of a basic Quad Sphere. The topology of this model is being stretched too far apart, which is causing issues. Notice how the shading around the neck, the base of the horns, and the ears have become blocky and distorted? This is a clear sign that the polygons have been stretched too far.

It's not just a shading issue; we don't have enough polygons in these areas to keep sculpting new details on this character. So, let's practice using the Voxel Remesher on this character to create new polygons and solve these issues.

How to do it...

Start by turning on the wireframe overlay so that we can see what the topology of the model looks like before and after we remesh it. As we can observe in the following diagram, the topology of this devilishly handsome guy has been stretched:

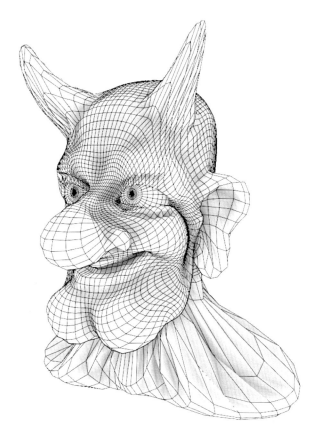

Figure 2.14 – The devilishly handsome guy before remeshing (this diagram has been simplified for better visibility in this book)

Take a look at the nose, horns, neck, shoulders, ears, and chin. These areas have all been stretched way too far. This character will greatly benefit from some extra polygons. Let's fix this now:

1. Locate the **Remesh** options in the upper-right corner of the 3D Viewport header.

2. Click on **Remesh** to open the pop-over menu.

Here, we can view the settings for the Voxel Remesher:

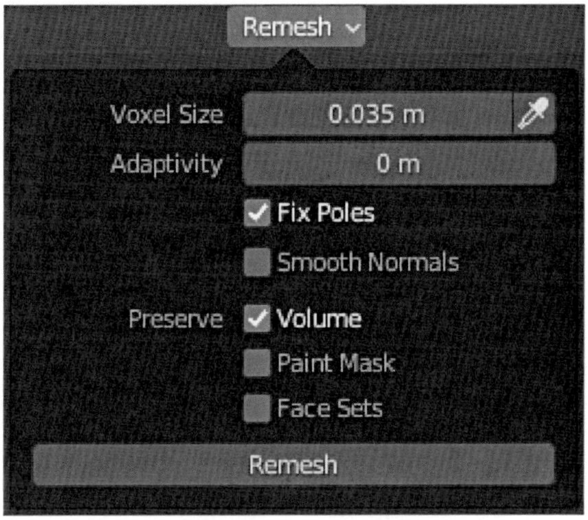

Figure 2.15 – The Remesh pop-over menu

To get a good result, we must choose a voxel size that can capture the details of the sculpture. If our voxel size is too high, we will lose details. If our voxel size is too low, we will have too many polygons and our sculpture will be difficult to work with. Luckily, we don't have to guess which size to use; we can use the eyedropper tool to pick a size from the model.

3. Click on the eyedropper icon next to the **Voxel Size** setting.

4. Use the eyedropper to click on an area of the model that isn't stretched too thin; the character's forehead is a good choice.

5. Open the **Remesh** pop-over menu again.

    You'll notice that the **Voxel Size** setting has been updated to match the size of the polygons on the character's forehead, which is 0.087872 m in our example. (Don't worry about getting this number exactly right; it just has to be close.) Now, we can run the Voxel Remesher to generate new polygons.

6. Click on the **Remesh** button at the bottom of the pop-over menu.

You can view how our example turned out in the following diagram:

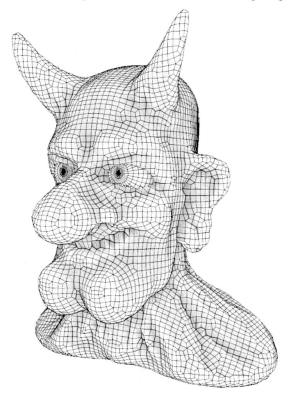

Figure 2.16 – The devilishly handsome guy after remeshing (this diagram has been simplified for better visibility in this book)

Excellent! The character has a fresh set of polygons for us to work with!

How it works...

The Voxel Remesher is the preferred method for many artists in the Blender community since it avoids many of the downsides from Dyntopo, but it still allows us to update the topology of the model to fit the shape while we work. The only real downside of the Voxel Remesher is that we have to manually run the remesher to update the geometry. This makes the Snake Hook brush slightly harder to use. Other than that, this method is better for an optimized workflow.

This character might look a little blocky now, but that's actually a good thing. When working with the Voxel Remesher, we are meant to start sculpting the major forms that have a low level of detail. As we make changes to the major forms, we can run the Voxel Remesher over and over again each time our polygons become stretched out.

Unfortunately, some of the details in this character didn't turn out very well. The mouth ended up pretty blocky because the voxel size we used wasn't small enough to represent that shape. Also, the neck has become somewhat distorted. This is because the original polygons in the neck were stretched so far that the Voxel Remesher couldn't really make sense of them. Problems such as this can easily be smoothed out, but this character really should have been remeshed earlier in the sculpting process to avoid these issues.

In the next section, we will gain additional practice with using the Voxel Remesher at the correct time and with the right detail size to avoid these issues.

Using the Voxel Remesher in a low-to-high detail workflow

Sculpting is an artistic process. In a lot of ways, it is similar to drawing. When we are trying to draw a character, we don't start with the finer details such as the nostrils, the anatomy of the ear, the individual hairs of the eyebrows, or anything like that. First, we block out the major forms, then work our way to finer and finer details. It's the same with sculpting.

The Voxel Remesher is meant to be used in this same way. Typically, we start with the voxel size set very large so that we are working with just a few polygons while we block out a shape. Then, when we don't have enough polygons to represent the forms we are trying to create, we reduce the voxel size and run the remesher again.

In this section, we will practice this workflow and learn a few hotkeys that can help us.

Getting ready

We're going to start this section from scratch. Launch Blender and create a new project with the sculpting preset. Once the new project has been created, we can practice with the Voxel Remesher workflow.

How to do it...

This time, we're not going to use the eyedropper to sample a voxel size from the model. Instead, we can set the voxel size by using a keyboard shortcut:

1. Hover your pen over the 3D Viewport before pressing the following keyboard shortcut.

2. Press the *Shift + R* keyboard shortcut to begin changing the voxel size.

    A visualization of the voxel size will appear over the model, as you can see in the following screenshot:

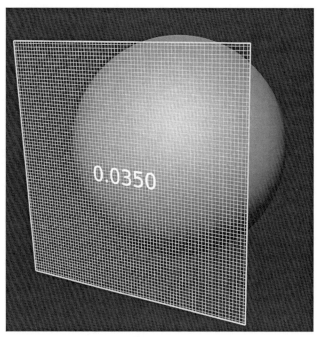

Figure 2.17 – The voxel size can be visualized using this grid pattern

3. Drag your pen to the left to increase the voxel size to around 0.2500.

4. Tap your pen down onto the graphics tablet to confirm the new voxel size.

Perfect! Increasing the voxel size also increases the size of the polygons that will be generated when we run the Voxel Remesher. This also means we will have fewer polygons, which, in this case, is a good thing. Having fewer polygons will make the sculpture easier to work with while we block out the largest of our major forms.

> **Important Note**
> Be careful with this setting – if you set the voxel size too low, it will take a very
> long time for your computer to calculate the new mesh. Usually, we don't need
> to go any lower than 0.01 m. If you try to use the Voxel Remesher with
> a setting that is much lower than this, you could crash Blender and lose
> your sculpture.

We also have a keyboard shortcut to run the Voxel Remesher. Let's use it now:

1. Hover your pen over the 3D Viewport before pressing the following keyboard
    shortcut.
2. Press the *Ctrl + R* keyboard shortcut to run the Voxel Remesher.

The sphere will be remeshed to have very few and very large polygons, as you can see in
the following screenshot:

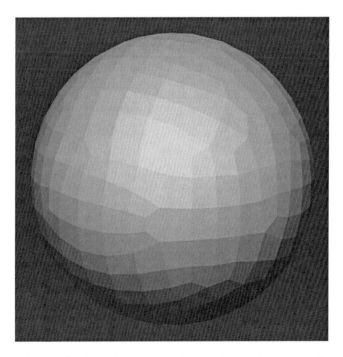

Figure 2.18 – The Quad Sphere after running the Voxel Remesher at a voxel size of 0.2500

Reducing the poly count is helpful at this stage because we can stay focused on the appropriate level of detail. Let's try pulling out a protrusion using the Snake Hook brush:

1. Click on the **Snake Hook** brush from the Toolbar to activate it.

2. Set the **Radius** setting of the brush to 250 px.

3. Use the Snake Hook brush to pull a piece of the sphere outward. Be careful not to create an overly curvy shape that the polygons can't properly support.

    When working with the Voxel Remesher, we have to make our changes in small increments; we make a change with our brushes, then we run the remesher again. Now that we have a protrusion coming out of the sphere, we need to remesh the polygons so that they support the new form.

4. Press *Ctrl + R* to run the Voxel Remesher again.

Notice that new polygons have been created to support the protrusion, but the rest of the sphere stayed the same. That's a good thing! If you can't see the difference, you can turn on the wireframe overlay to view the before and after, as we've done in the following diagram:

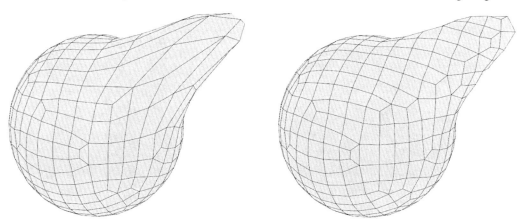

Figure 2.19 – The wireframe of the sphere before and after voxel remeshing a second time (this diagram has been simplified for better visibility in this book)

You might be wondering whether it's excessive to use the Voxel Remesher in this way. Not at all! This is how it's meant to be used. We can run the remesher as many times as we need to. Any time we begin to work on a new form and the polygons become stretched out, it's time to run the remesher again. You might run the Voxel Remesher 10, 50, 100, or even 1,000 times during a sculpting session; that's why we have the keyboard shortcuts.

Go ahead and practice this before moving on. Once we have all of the largest forms settled in, we need to use a smaller voxel size so that we can work on the smaller details:

1. Use the *Shift + R* keyboard shortcut to begin changing the voxel size.

2. Drag your pen to the right to decrease the voxel size to around 0.1000.

3. Tap your pen down onto the graphics tablet to confirm the new voxel size.

4. Press *Ctrl + R* to run the Voxel Remesher again.

Perfect! Now we can add more details at this new voxel size. We should avoid decreasing the voxel size too much too quickly. If we go too quickly, we will end up with jagged artifacts on the surface of our mesh. If you recall back to our example in the *Practicing the basics of the Voxel Remesher* section, this is what happened to the character's neck. If we end up with some of these jagged edges, we will have to find a way to smooth them out later. So, it's easier if we simply don't introduce these issues in the first place.

We will get plenty more practice with the Voxel Remesher throughout this book, as it will be the main method we use while creating all of the major forms of our sculptures.

How it works...

Working from low detail to high detail is the best way to achieve good results in our sculptures. Another way to think about voxel size is in terms of **resolution**. Resolution describes the amount of detail we can achieve based on the current size and density of the polygons.

This is the same concept in raster graphics and digital images. An image with few pixels has a **low resolution** and can only support a very low level of detail. An image with millions of pixels has a **high resolution** and can support a very high level of detail. An example of this can be seen in the following diagram:

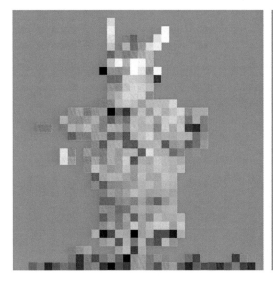

Figure 2.20 – A low-resolution image with 32 x 32 pixels on the left-hand side versus a high-resolution image with 1024 x 1024 pixels on the right-hand side

Resolution in an image and resolution in a 3D sculpture work very similarly. However, we have an advantage in 3D sculptures: we can increase the resolution by decreasing the voxel size, then running the Voxel Remesher.

This method will serve us well in the early stages of our sculpting workflow. However, we will eventually get to a point where the Voxel Remesher causes problems. Sometimes, we need to be able to work with extremely high-frequency details such as skin pores, fingernails, scars, scales, or other fine textures. Attempting to use the Voxel Remesher for these details becomes problematic for performance and workflow reasons.

To get around this, we need to learn about the final sculpting workflow – multiresolution.

Exploring the most powerful sculpting mode – multiresolution

The previous techniques in this chapter focused on the early stages of sculpting. Dyntopo and the Voxel Remesher are both focused on adding new polygons to support new major forms to our sculptures. But what do we do when we're done adding new major forms? Eventually, we'll want to start adding details to our sculptures, and for that, we require a very high resolution. If we want to get down to the highest frequency details such as skin pores, we're going to need hundreds of thousands, if not millions, of polygons.

However, increasing our resolution with something like the Voxel Remesher tends to make our work unwieldy. Often, our computers will slow down while working with anything over a few hundred thousand polygons. The Voxel Remesher is not designed for that.

Instead, what we need is a way to keep our model at a low resolution, but somehow also store a high-resolution version of the model that we can sculpt details onto. Luckily, we have a feature that does exactly that: it's called **multiresolution**.

For the sake of completeness in this chapter, we'll take a quick look at how multiresolution works. However, this is a very deep subject, so we won't go into much depth until *Chapter 5, Learning the Power of Subdivision and the Multiresolution Workflow.*

Getting ready

To demonstrate the power of the multiresolution workflow, we need a finished sculpture as an example.

Download the `multiResolutionHand.blend` example file from the GitHub repository at `https://github.com/PacktPublishing/Sculpting-the-Blender-Way/blob/main/Chapter02/multiResolutionHand.blend`.

Once you've downloaded the example file, open it in Blender by either double-clicking on the file or dragging the file into the Blender window and choosing **Open**. Inside this file, you'll find a sculpture of a hand, which you can view in the following diagram:

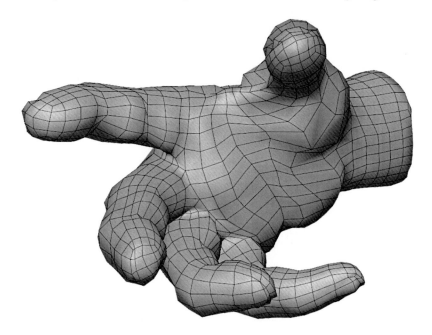

Figure 2.21 – The hand model as it appears in the .blend file

This hand is looking a little anticlimactic, isn't it? Where are all the high-resolution details? Good question. If you lower your expectations, all art can be beautiful! Just kidding! This is the low-resolution version of the hand sculpture. If you take a look at the information in the statistics overlay, you can see that this hand has **2,794** triangles. Most multiresolution sculptures start with a low tri count such as this before adding in the higher resolution.

Let's find out how we can activate the high-resolution details of this hand sculpture.

How to do it...

To activate the high-resolution details of this sculpture, we need to turn our attention to the **Properties** editor. Currently, the **Properties** editor is displaying the modifiers for the active object. In this case, the hand has a **Multires** modifier, as you can see in the following screenshot:

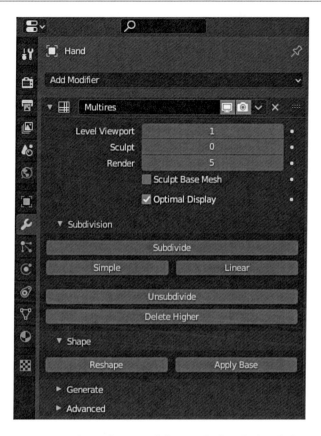

Figure 2.22 – The Multires modifier attached to the hand object

This modifier helps our computers to stay running fast by allowing us to preview the sculpture at different resolutions. Since we are in Sculpt Mode, the modifier is using the setting for the **Sculpt** resolution level, which can be found between the **Level Viewport** and **Render** resolution levels at the top of the modifier.

Right now, the **Sculpt** resolution is set to 0, which means that none of the extra details are being displayed. Let's increase it and see what happens:

1. Hover your mouse or pen over the right-hand side edge of the **Sculpt** level number field.

2. Two arrow indicators will appear along the left-hand and right-hand edges of the field. Clicking on these arrows acts as a quick shortcut to increase or decrease the number in the field.

3. Click or tap your pen on the right arrow indicator, >, to increase the **Sculpt** resolution to 1:

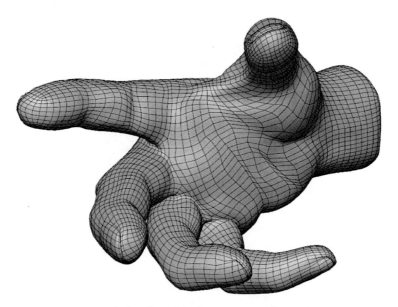

Figure 2.23 – The hand model after increasing the resolution to 1

Neat! If we check the statistics, we'll see that the hand now has **11,176** triangles. That's a pretty big jump from the previous resolution. In fact, it's exactly four times as many triangles as we had before. Each level or resolution quadruples the number of triangles in the sculpture, so the poly count is going to skyrocket by the time we're done.

From this point forward, the wireframe is just a visual distraction. Let's turn it off and increase the resolution again:

1. Use the **Viewport Overlays** popover menu to turn off the **Wireframe** setting.

2. Increase the **Sculpt** resolution level in the **Multires** modifier to 2.

    Notice that the details of the hand are starting to appear; the fingernails are starting to come in and a few of the creases in the palm are showing up as well.

3. Increase the **Sculpt** resolution level in the **Multires** modifier to 3.

Depending on how powerful your computer is, this might be as high as we can go. However, this sculpture has extra details that can only be viewed if we go all the way up to level **5**. If your computer can handle it, take it all the way up, and examine the details of the hand.

You can view the highest resolution in the following diagram:

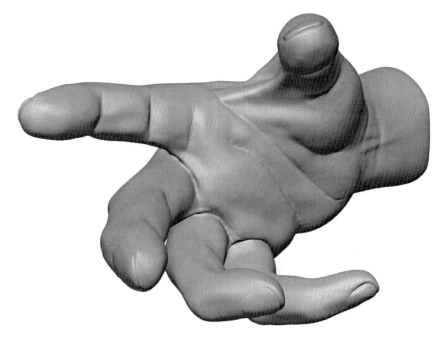

Figure 2.24 – The hand model after increasing the resolution to 5

Pretty cool! Feel free to orbit around the model and observe the details of the high-resolution hand.

How it works...

The Multiresolution modifier has allowed us to store all of this high-resolution detail in an optimized way. Additionally, we have access to a performance-saving feature called **Fast Navigate**. This feature is on by default; however, it can be toggled under the **Options** pop-over menu in the upper-right corner of the header of the 3D Viewport. The fast navigate feature will display the highest resolution of the sculpture while we are looking at the model and sculpting it, and it will toggle down to a lower resolution while we orbit around the sculpture so that our computers can stay running fast while we navigate around the scene.

Multiresolution is the gold standard of sculpting workflows. The other workflows, Dyntopo and voxel remeshing, are intended to be used before this stage in the sculpting process, with the ultimate goal of preparing a mesh for multiresolution.

Note that we do not go back to the Voxel Remesher or Dyntopo once we begin using multiresolution. We begin multiresolution once all of our major forms are in place. To prepare for multiresolution, we need to arrange our topology in a particular fashion that is well optimized for the multiresolution workflow. A mesh that has been prepared for multiresolution is called a **Base Mesh**. We will learn how to create a base mesh in *Chapter 4, How to Make a Base Mesh for a 3D Sculpture*.

There's more...

Here's a quick summary of the workflows that we discussed in this chapter:

- **Basic sculpting mode**: This is useful for pushing polygons around, but we run into limitations pretty quickly when we need to add major forms or add high-resolution details.

- **Dyntopo**: This is a way to quickly add polygons while sculpting. It is particularly helpful when paired with the Snake Hook brush. Dyntopo has fallen out of favor and is no longer considered the best way to sculpt by most sculptors.

- **Voxel Remesher**: This allows us to quickly block out major forms and remesh the sculpture to support any new shapes that we create. It is useful for the early stages of our model as we work our way from low detail to high detail.

- **Multiresolution**: This is the golden standard of sculpting. The goal is to get to this point so that we can add high-frequency details and work with millions of polygons in an optimized way.

If you're coming from the popular sculpting software of ZBrush, you might already be familiar with the features discussed in this chapter but under different names. For reference, here is a list of the equivalent features between ZBrush and Blender:

- ZBrush's **Sculptris Pro** feature is equivalent to Blender's Dyntopo.

- ZBrush's **Dynamesh** feature is equivalent to Blender's Voxel Remesher.

- ZBrush's **Subdivision Levels** feature is equivalent to Blender's multiresolution.

Now we have a solid foundation for our technical sculpting knowledge. Understanding these workflows is important for us to be able to make informed decisions for our artistic sculpting processes. Now that we understand how Blender does things under the hood, we'll have a much easier time creating sculptures!

3
Sculpting a Simple Character Head with Basic Brushes

By now, it should be no surprise to you that **brushes** are the main type of tool that we use while working on sculptures. Blender comes with an excellent selection of brushes that give us plenty of artistic control right out of the box.

Brushes can also be customized to behave exactly the way we want. We'll learn how to customize the brushes in *Chapter 6, Using Advanced Features and Customizing the Sculpting Brushes*, but for now, the basic brushes are more than enough to try sculpting a simple character head.

By the end of this chapter, you will understand how to use many of the default brushes in Blender. You will also gain experience using these brushes for several tasks related to sculpting a simple character. As this is your first time sculpting, we will focus on introducing the brushes and how they can be used, rather than trying to make the character anatomically correct or appealing. We can always refine the character design later.

The main topics in this chapter are as follows:

- Creating the large forms of the head with the Grab brush
- Using masks to add the neck and ears

- Building up the nose and brow with the Clay Strips brush
- Smoothing the lumpy and jagged surfaces of the sculpture
- Creating a bulbous nose and cheeks with the Inflate brush
- Adding basic eyes and eyelids to the character
- Adding detail to the ears with the Crease brush
- Creating the mouth with the Draw Sharp brush
- Sharpening details with the Pinch brush

Technical requirements

For general requirements, refer back to the *Technical requirements* laid out in *Chapter 1, Exploring Blender's User Interface for Sculpting.*

We will be building on the fundamental knowledge from *Chapter 2, Overview of Blender's Sculpting Workflows.* Throughout this chapter, we will be using the Voxel Remesher.

You can download the files to follow along with this book at the GitHub link here: `https://github.com/PacktPublishing/Sculpting-the-Blender-Way`.

> **Important Note**
>
> A major part of sculpting involves subtle adjustments and techniques that are nearly impossible to describe properly in these written step-by-step instructions. This chapter includes a *Sculpting in Action* video to help demonstrate the brushes in each section, which you can view online here: `https://bit.ly/3y93Dt5`. The video has demonstrations for each section of this chapter, as well as a bonus timelapse section showing how you can refine the shape of your character using all of the brushes we will learn about in this chapter.

Creating the large forms of the head with the Grab brush

Let's start by creating the main shape for a human head. This is an excellent time to introduce the **Grab** brush. In the *Discovering the limitations of the basic sculpting mode* section of *Chapter 2, Overview of Blender's Sculpting Workflows*, we tried out the Snake Hook brush, which let us pull around major forms of the model. The Grab brush is very similar, but it is less aggressive, and it does not taper in the same way.

When used with a large radius, the Grab brush is excellent for moving around the large shapes of our sculpture, which allows us to completely reshape the model. If we run the Voxel Remesher frequently in our sculpting workflow, we can turn the default sphere into nearly any shape we want. The Grab brush is the go-to method for most artists when beginning a sculpture, so we will start our character head using this brush.

Getting ready

Launch Blender, and then start a new project using the sculpting preset. If you like, you may turn on extra shading options and overlays, such as **Statistics** and **Cavity**, which we learned about in *Chapter 1, Exploring Blender's User Interface for Sculpting.* Many artists prefer the cavity feature turned on because it highlights sharp edges in the sculpture.

The default **Quad Sphere** model that comes with the sculpting preset has far more polygons than are necessary for this first stage of the sculpture. These unneeded polygons are going to make the Grab brush less responsive and difficult to use. Before we start blocking out the major forms of the head, we should reduce the poly count of the Quad Sphere by using the Voxel Remesher; a **Voxel Size** value of 0.2500 should be a good starting point. If you need a reminder of how to do this, refer back to the *Using the Voxel Remesher in a low-to-high detail workflow* section of *Chapter 2, Overview of Blender's Sculpting Workflows.*

Once we have a more manageable number of polygons, we can begin creating the major forms of the head with the Grab brush.

How to do it...

Before we make any changes to the model, let's turn on **X-Axis Symmetry** so that our sculpture stays symmetrical:

1. Find the symmetry settings in the top-right corner of the 3D Viewport header next to the little butterfly icon:

Figure 3.1 – The symmetry settings

2. Click the **X** toggle to activate **X-Axis Symmetry** (this option will be highlighted blue when it is active).

Perfect – now our model's left and right sides will stay symmetrical while we sculpt.

Let's think about our goal with this section before we continue. We're working from low to high detail. It's too early to add things like the ears, the nose, the eyes, or anything else like that. We're just focused on the largest shapes, such as the cranium and the jaw. Here is a simple visualization of the shapes we are trying to make in this section:

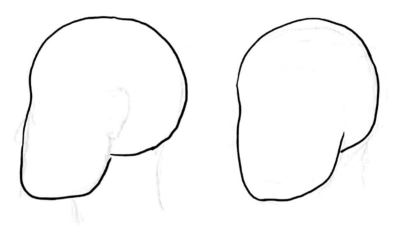

Figure 3.2 – The simplified shape of the head

Now that we know what we're trying to make, let's use the **Grab** brush to begin turning the sphere into a human head shape.

3. Find the **Grab** brush on the Toolbar and click to activate the brush.

4. Increase the brush **Radius** value to around 250 px.

We'll start by flattening out the sides of the sphere.

5. Hover your pen over your tablet and align the pointer over the right side of the sphere:

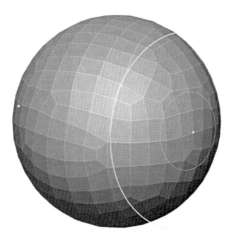

Figure 3.3 – The Grab brush indicator hovering over the right side of the sphere

6. Press the tip of your pen onto your graphics tablet to begin using the Grab brush.

7. Pull the sides of the Quad Sphere inward to flatten them out.

    You may need to do this with multiple brushstrokes; keep going until the sides of
    the sphere are flattened out. Our example looks like this so far:

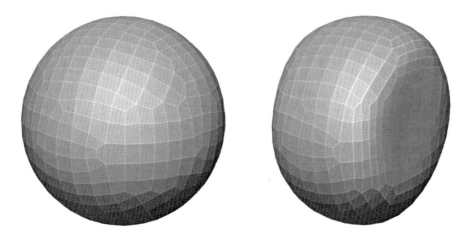

Figure 3.4 – The sides of the sphere flattened by the Grab brush

Believe it or not, this is a good start. For the next few steps, we'll have an easier time
if we work from the side view. So, let's lock the view to the side.

8. Find the **Navigation Gizmo** in the top-right corner of the 3D Viewport and click on
    the red **X Axis** indicator to snap the 3D Viewport to the side view.

9. Once the view is locked to the side, use the Grab brush to drag the bottom-left corner down and to the left to begin creating the jaw shape.

So far, our sculpture should look something like this:

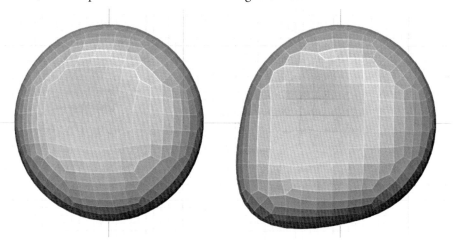

Figure 3.5 – The jaw shape pulled out from the bottom-left corner of the flattened sphere

Continue to shape the head with the Grab brush, using *Figure 3.2* as a reference point. Feel free to orbit the viewport around the sculpture and change the brush radius as needed. With just a few more brushstrokes, we can arrive at a shape like this:

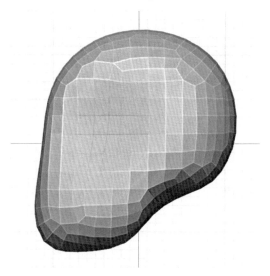

Figure 3.6 – The head after being shaped with the Grab brush

> **Important Note**
> As you shape the head, don't forget to use the *Ctrl + R* hotkey to run the Voxel Remesher any time the polygons get stretched too far. This may be necessary if you decide to make a character with a very large jaw.

At this point, we've taken the head shape about as far as possible from this vantage point. For the best results, we must remember to orbit the 3D Viewport frequently while using the Grab brush so that we can adjust the shape from all angles.

Chances are your head looks pretty good from the side but is probably not the correct shape when you look at it head-on. Use several 3D Viewport angles and brushstrokes to finish shaping the head.

Our example turned out like this:

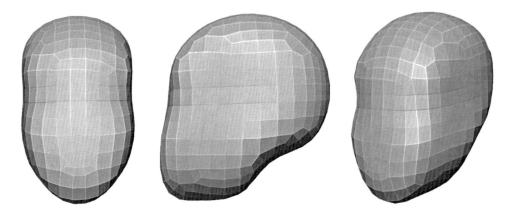

Figure 3.7 – The finished head shape as seen from the front, the side, and a three-quarters view

You don't have to make your head look exactly the same as our example. Try out different proportions and stylizations – that's part of the fun in sculpting!

This head will serve as a good base for trying other sculpting brushes throughout this chapter.

How it works...

By default, the Grab brush moves polygons around relative to our viewing angle. For instance, if we press and drag our pen upward, the polygons move upward relative to the screen. By orbiting our 3D Viewport around the sculpture, we can gain a new vantage point and push the polygons around in whichever direction we need.

The Grab brush is very similar to the Snake Hook brush that we tried in *Chapter 2, Overview of Blender's Sculpting Workflows*. The differences are difficult to describe, but the Snake Hook brush feels a bit gooey (like wet clay) and tapers off as we pull the polygons around. Some artists prefer the Snake Hook brush over the Grab brush; try them both for yourself.

There's more...

Many of the brushes can be accessed with hotkeys; for the Grab brush, we can use the *G* hotkey.

It is quite common to snap the 3D Viewport to a specific axis; we can do this by clicking on the appropriate axis in the navigation gizmo, but a faster way is to hold the *Alt* key while orbiting the viewport. This will snap the view to the closest viewing angle.

Using masks to add the neck and ears

There are a few utilities that we have at our disposal that can make sculpting easier; one of these utilities is a **mask**. A mask can be applied to parts of a sculpture to prevent our brushstrokes from affecting the masked area. This is just like using masking tape in traditional painting or using a mask layer in digital painting software.

The simplest way to apply a mask is by using the Mask brush. Instead of pushing polygons around like a regular brush, the Mask brush allows us to paint a mask onto the surface of the sculpture. This will be helpful for creating the ears and the neck of our character.

Getting ready

We will be adding ears and a neck to the head model that we started in the *Creating large forms of the head with the Grab brush* section of this chapter. If you would rather start this section using our example, download and open the `simpleCharacterHead_02_ Start.blend` file here: `https://github.com/PacktPublishing/Sculpting- the-Blender-Way/blob/main/Chapter03/simpleCharacterHead_02_ Start.blend`.

The ears are a higher-resolution detail than the rest of the head that we've sculpted so far, so let's start by decreasing our voxel size to about `0.1000` and running the Voxel Remesher. Once our head has been remeshed, we'll be ready to make masks for the ears and neck.

> **Important Note**
> Masks are only visible when our **Viewport Overlays** are active. Make sure you have the Viewport Overlays toggled on and check the pop-over menu to make sure that the **Mask** overlay is enabled under the **Sculpt** section.

How to do it...

We're going to paint a little ear shape on the side of the head using the Mask brush; then we can use the Grab brush to pull out an ear shape from the side of the head:

1. Find the **Mask** brush on the Toolbar and click to activate the brush.

2. Set the brush **Radius** value to something small, around 25 px.

3. Use your graphics tablet to draw a small ear shape on the side of the head:

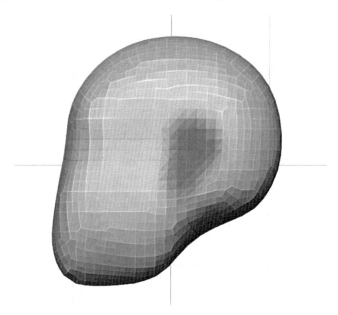

Figure 3.8 – The mask for the ear painted onto the side of the head

Don't worry about being precise; right now, we don't have enough polygons to be very detailed (we can refine the shape of the ear later).

Our mask is looking pretty good, but we have one small problem – it's inside out. The dark areas of the mask are the areas that won't be affected by our brushes, so we need to invert the mask.

4. Find the **Mask** menu in the top-left corner of the 3D Viewport.

5. Open the menu and choose the **Invert Mask** option. The light parts will become dark and the dark parts will become light, as you can see in the following screenshot:

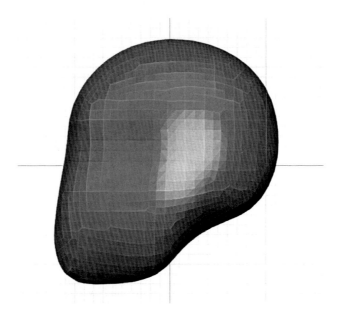

Figure 3.9 – The mask for the ear inverted

Perfect – now we can try using one of the other brushes to add the ears. We learned how to use the Draw brush in the *Pushing polys with the basic sculpting mode* section of *Chapter 2, Overview of Blender's Sculpting Workflows*. We'll use the Draw brush now to raise the ear shapes out of the masked area.

6. Find the **Draw** brush on the Toolbar and click to activate the brush.

The great thing about using masks is that Blender will not let us make edits to the dark parts of the model. We don't have to worry about being precise with our **Draw** brush because we've masked out the head, leaving only our ear shape in the non-masked area.

7. Use your graphics tablet to draw over the backside of the masked ear shape to raise up the polygons and begin forming the ears:

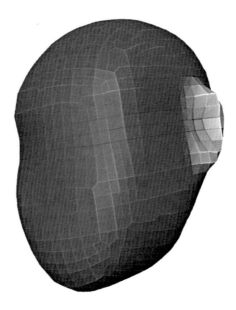

Figure 3.10 – The ear drawn on the side of the head

Once we've got the basic shape of the ears, we don't need the mask anymore, so we can remove it.

8. Find the **Mask** menu in the top-left corner of the 3D Viewport.

9. Open the menu and choose the **Clear Mask** option to remove the previous mask.

Let's learn one more technique for the Grab brush that we can use to create the character's neck. We'll start by making another mask for the neck.

10. Activate the **Mask** brush.

11. Set the brush **Radius** value to something small, around 50 px.

12. Orbit the 3D Viewport so that we can see the underside of the head.

13. Draw a neck-sized circle mask around the base of the cranium of the head.

14. Invert the mask by choosing **Mask | Invert Mask**. Our example can be seen in the following screenshot:

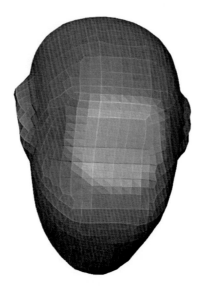

Figure 3.11 – The mask for the neck

Great! We could use the Draw brush again to raise the neck out of the masked area; however, we have a better option available. In the *Pushing polys with the basic sculpting mode* section of *Chapter 2, Overview of Blender's Sculpting Workflows*, we briefly mentioned that some of the sculpting brushes have a secondary function that can be accessed by holding the *Ctrl* key. The Grab brush is one of those brushes.

The secondary function of the Grab brush uses each polygon's own orientation as the direction for movement. So, we can push and pull the polygons inward and outward instead of moving them relative to the orientation of our viewport. Let's try this now:

1. Find the **Grab** brush on the Toolbar and click to activate the brush.

2. Set the brush **Radius** value to be larger than the masked area, around 250 px.

3. Hold down the *Ctrl* key to engage the Grab brush's secondary function.

4. While holding *Ctrl*, use your pen to draw over the masked area of the neck.

5. Drag toward the right to pull the polygons outward:

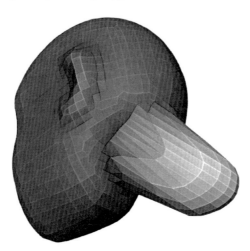

Figure 3.12 – The neck pulled out with the secondary function of the Grab brush

Perfect – this method can take some getting used to, but it's easier than trying to align the 3D Viewport to an exact angle. Once you're happy with the neck, we should clear the mask by choosing **Mask | Clear Mask**. Then, run the Voxel Remesher again to fix the stretched-out polygons.

Now we've got the major forms for the ears and the neck, but chances are these shapes will need to be adjusted. Take some time to look at the model from multiple angles, compare it to reference images, and keep adjusting these new features with the Grab brush until the proportions look correct. When you're finished, run the Voxel Remesher again. Our example turned out like this:

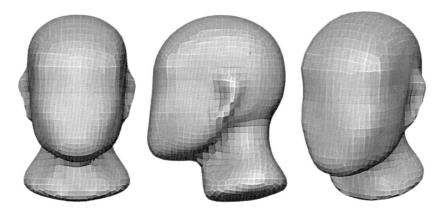

Figure 3.13 – The finished ear and neck shapes as seen from the front, the side, and a three-quarters view

So far, so good. The neck and ears will make it easier to get a sense of the proportions of the head. We can continue adjusting these forms as often as we need to as we add other facial features to the head.

How it works...

Masks are useful for limiting the areas that can be affected by our brushstrokes. We'll see other ways that masks can be used later in this book.

There are many ways to further customize the masks that we make; we can invert them, soften or sharpen them, grow or shrink them. Or we can use entirely different methods to create them, such as box selections and lassos. Explore the **Mask** menu for more options.

There's more...

Many of the brushes can be accessed with hotkeys; for the Mask brush, we can use the *M* hotkey. We can also bring up a pie menu full of **Mask Edit** options by pressing the *A* hotkey.

Building up the nose and brow with the Clay Strips brush

Our head sculpture is coming along nicely. So far in this chapter, we've made the basic shape of the head in the *Creating large forms of the head with the Grab brush* section, and then we followed up by adding ears and a neck in the *Using masks to add the ears and neck* section. At this point, we are ready to build up the nose and brow area.

In the *Understanding the components of a 3D sculpture* section of *Chapter 2, Overview of Blender's Sculpting Workflows*, we learned that 3D sculptures are made out of polygons. However, once we have enough resolution, the polygons start to visually blend together, and we can start thinking about them as a blob of clay. Several of the brushes in Blender attempt to emulate traditional techniques of clay sculpting, such as layering clay onto the sculpture to build up new forms.

For this section, we're going to try the **Clay Strips** brush, which will let us lay down thick tubes of clay to quickly build up the nose and brow.

Getting ready

We will continue working with our head model. If you would rather start this section using our example, download and open the `simpleCharacterHead_03_Start.blend` file here: `https://github.com/PacktPublishing/Sculpting-the-Blender-Way/blob/main/Chapter03/simpleCharacterHead_03_Start.blend`.

Once we've got our head model open in Blender, let's decrease our voxel size to about `0.0500` and run the Voxel Remesher. Now we're ready to try out the Clay Strips brush.

How to do it...

We're going to start by building up the bridge of the nose:

1. Find the **Clay Strips** brush on the Toolbar and click to activate the brush.

2. Set the brush **Radius** value to around `50 px`.

3. Set the brush **Strength** value to `1.000`.

4. Use your graphics tablet to draw the bridge of the nose.

5. Redraw over the same area multiple times to build up the bridge of the nose.

6. Run the Voxel Remesher as often as you need to while building up the bridge of the nose:

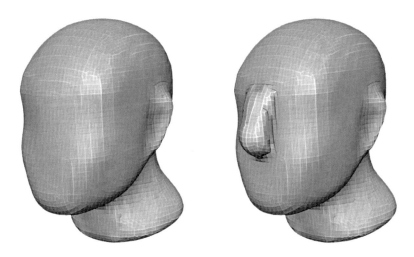

Figure 3.14 – The nose built up with the Clay Strips brush

Once you're happy with the shape of the nose, extend the bridge of the nose up and to the side to begin creating the brow. We will start to see the eye socket take shape underneath the brow; our example looks like this so far:

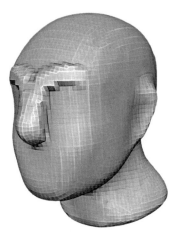

Figure 3.15 – The shape of the brow built up with the Clay Strips brush

Perfect – now, to complement the brow shape, we can start to carve away the eye socket. To do this, we will use the subtraction direction of the Clay Strips brush.

7. Make sure the **Clay Strips** brush is still active and hold the *Ctrl* key to invert the direction of the brush.

8. Use your graphics tablet to draw underneath the brow and begin carving out the eye socket:

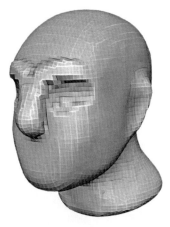

Figure 3.16 – The eye socket carved with the Clay Strips brush

It's starting to look like a proper face – how exciting! Don't forget to orbit the 3D Viewport around the model and check it from multiple viewing angles. Feel free to refine the sculpture using any of the brushes we've learned about so far.

We can build up the cheekbone and add the outside bumps for the nostrils with the Clay Strips brush. After a little touch-up, our example looks like this:

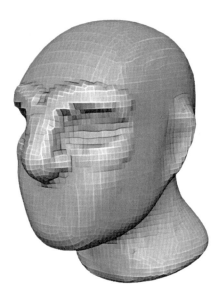

Figure 3.17 – Cheekbone and outer nostrils added to the head

> **Important Note**
>
> Resist the temptation of adding tiny details like the holes of the nostrils, as we don't have enough resolution at our current voxel size to support these small features yet. If we try to add details that are smaller than the current voxel size, they will be erased the next time we run the Voxel Remesher. We can come back and add these small features toward the end of our low-to-high resolution workflow.

Our head is looking a bit lumpy, but overall, it's starting to take shape.

How it works...

The Clay Strips brush is an excellent choice for quickly building up and carving away large areas. It is very similar to the Draw Brush that we tried in *Chapter 2, Overview of Blender's Sculpting Workflows*. The Clay Strips brush is a bit more aggressive and more square-shaped than the Draw brush. Play around with both of these brushes and get a feel for them; you'll quickly come to know which brush you like better for any given task.

Smoothing the lumpy and jagged surfaces of the sculpture

At this point in our sculpture, we're starting to get some pretty lumpy and jagged surfaces. The Clay Strips brush in particular tends to make rough edges. The Voxel Remesher can also introduce rough surfaces if we increase the resolution too quickly.

It's time to make a confession – one of the most important brushes in Blender has been kept secret from you until now. In this section, we'll learn how to fix up these problem areas with the **Smooth** brush, along with the smooth **Mesh Filter**.

Getting ready

To show off the Smooth brush, we'll need a lumpy model. The head model we've been working on throughout this chapter is a perfect candidate. You can either continue with the model you've been making, or if you would rather start this section using our example, download and open the simpleCharacterHead_04_Start.blend file here: https://github.com/PacktPublishing/Sculpting-the-Blender-Way/blob/main/Chapter03/simpleCharacterHead_04_Start.blend.

Once we've got the lumpy head model open in Blender, we'll be ready to try the Smooth brush.

How to do it...

We'll start by using the Smooth brush to touch up the brow area:

1. Find the **Smooth** brush on the Toolbar and click to activate the brush.

2. Use your graphics tablet to draw over the lumpy surface of the brow.

    A little smoothing goes a long way; use light pressure with your pen to make the smoothing effect more subtle. Here's how our character's brow looks after a little smoothing:

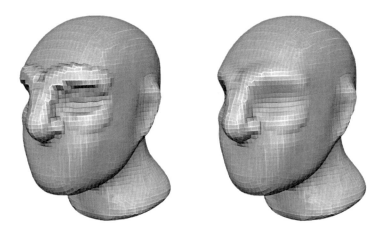

Figure 3.18 – Our character before and after smoothing the brow

Nice – the areas that we created with the Clay Strips brush were some of the most jagged parts of the model; however, the whole model is looking a bit rough. This is because we've been changing the resolution and running the Voxel Remesher. The more dramatic the shift in resolution, the more lumpy the surface will become. Speaking of which, let's set the voxel size to around 0.0250 and run the Voxel Remesher again before moving on.

If you've got the **Cavity** setting turned on in the **Viewport Shading** options, you'll notice that many little edges are being highlighted throughout the model. These highlighted edges are sharp peaks in the geometry that are causing the surface of the model to look rough, as you can see in the following screenshot:

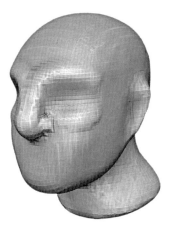

Figure 3.19 – Our character after voxel-remeshing at a voxel size of 0.0250

A quick fix for this would be to smooth out the whole model. To do this, we can try using a smooth Mesh Filter.

3.   Find the **Mesh Filter** tool on the Toolbar and click to activate the tool (you may need to scroll down to find it).

4.   Find **Tool Settings** at the top of the 3D Viewport.

5.   Use the drop-down list to change **Filter Type** to **Smooth**.

Now our Mesh Filter tool is ready to use; however, this tool doesn't work exactly the same way as our brushes. We don't draw on the surface of the model with brushstrokes; rather, we can think of it more like a virtual slider. We can press our pen down on the tablet, and then slide right or left to increase or decrease the effect of the filter.

6.   Hover your pen over your graphics tablet near the middle of the 3D Viewport.

7.   Press the tip of your pen onto your graphics tablet to begin using the Mesh Filter.

8.   Keep your pen pressed to the tablet and drag the pen to the right to begin smoothing the whole model.

9.   Lift up the pen when you're happy with the amount of smoothing.

Important Note

If you accidentally smooth too much, you can drag your pen to the left to reduce the intensity of the filter. But you must do this before lifting your pen off of the tablet. Otherwise, you need to press *Ctrl + Z* to undo the Mesh Filter and try again.

Excellent – our model is looking a lot less rough around the edges. Be careful not to over-smooth the model; we don't want to lose the details we've sculpted so far. Here's how our example turned out:

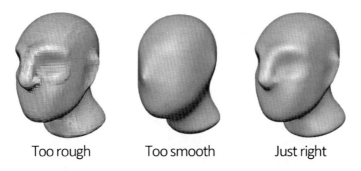

Too rough   Too smooth   Just right

Figure 3.20 – The head sculpture before and after smoothing

Smoothing doesn't have to be used exclusively for correcting issues; the Smooth brush is also valuable for creating smooth transitions between shapes in our sculptures. Get used to using this brush alongside the other brushes that we've learned so far.

How it works...

Smoothing is a really important part of the sculpting process. As we increase the resolution of the sculpture, the surfaces become prone to lumpiness. The best way to combat this is to smooth the sculpture while we work – sculpt a little, smooth a little, sculpt a little, smooth a little, and so on.

It is very common for artists to make brushstrokes with some of the regular brushes and then immediately follow up those brushstrokes with a little bit of smoothing. Because of this, the Smooth brush has its own special hotkey. While we are using any of the regular brushes, simply hold down the *Shift* key to temporarily switch to the Smooth brush. As soon as you let go of the *Shift* key, the previous brush will become active again.

> Important Note
>
> The *Shift* key will only switch to the Smooth brush if one of the regular brushes is active. For instance, **Draw**, **Grab**, and **Clay Strips** work with this hotkey, but **Mask** and **Mesh Filter** do not work with this hotkey.

Mesh Filters are an excellent way to make adjustments to the whole sculpture all at once. In this case, the Smooth filter was able to smooth out lumpiness across the entire model. Just be careful – the Smooth filter can come on really strong and smooth away all of the details of the sculpture.

Creating a bulbous nose and cheeks with the Inflate brush

In the *Smoothing the lumpy and jagged surfaces of the sculpture* section of this chapter, we removed a lot of rough surface artifacts in the character sculpture. This improved the model in a lot of ways, but it also deemphasized many of our character's facial features. Let's try to enhance some of those features by going over them with the **Inflate** brush.

Getting ready

You can either continue with the model you've been making so far, or if you would rather start this section using our example, download and open the `simpleCharacterHead_05_Start.blend` file here: `https://github.com/PacktPublishing/Sculpting-the-Blender-Way/blob/main/Chapter03/simpleCharacterHead_05_Start.blend`.

Once we've got our character model open in Blender, we'll be ready to try out the Inflate brush.

How to do it...

We'll start by activating the Inflate brush and enlarging the nose:

1. Find the **Inflate** brush on the Toolbar and click to activate the brush.

2. Set the brush **Radius** value to around 50 px.

3. Set the brush **Strength** value to 1.000.

4. Use your graphics tablet to draw over the tip of the nose.

   Depending on the type of character you would like to make, you can inflate just a little or a lot by varying the pressure and going over the same area multiple times. You can also wiggle your brush around in a small circular fashion to continuously inflate the same area. We've gone with a very bulbous nose, as you can see in the following screenshot:

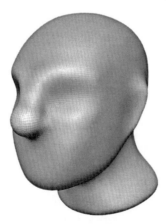

Figure 3.21 – The nose after using the Inflate brush

In our example, the bridge of the nose has become quite thick. We can use the subtraction direction of the Inflate brush to deflate this area to a more reasonable size:

5. Make sure the **Inflate** brush is still active and hold the *Ctrl* key to invert the direction of the brush.

6. While holding *Ctrl*, use your graphics tablet to draw along the sides of the bridge of the nose to deflate it:

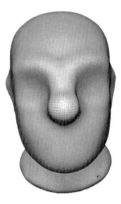 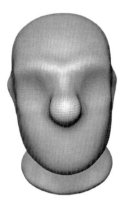

Figure 3.22 – The bridge of the nose after using the subtraction direction of the Inflate brush

Bulbous clown noses are fun, but you can make any type of nose you like.

Most noses need nostrils though, and the nostrils on this character have been almost completely smoothed away; let's fix this now.

7. Decrease the brush **Radius** value to around 25 px.

8. Release the *Ctrl* key to return the Inflate brush to its default direction.

9. Use your graphics tablet to draw over the nostrils:

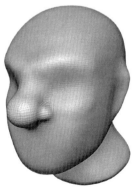

Figure 3.23 – The nostrils after using the Inflate brush

This character's cheeks would also benefit from a little inflation. Use the Inflate brush over the cheeks in a triangular pattern to make the character's cheeks look fuller, like our example here:

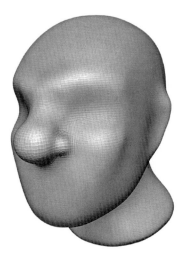

Figure 3.24 – The cheeks after using the Inflate brush

Perfect – the nose and the cheeks are looking a lot more defined thanks to the Inflate brush. If you have any areas that look lumpy, use the Smooth brush to fix up those areas before moving on.

How it works...

The Inflate brush pushes the polygons on the sculpture outward along their individual orientations. This can be used to enhance details that we've created with our other brushes.

There's more...

Many of the brushes can be accessed with hotkeys; for the Inflate brush, we can use the *I* hotkey.

Adding basic eyes and eyelids to the character

Our character is missing something important - eyes! Eyes are one of the most important parts of a character; they can take a lot of tweaking to get right. We'll explore how to make many different types of eyes in *Chapter 7, Making Eyeballs*, but for this chapter, we are going to keep it simple and provide you with a pair of eyes that you can add to your sculpture.

Eyes are typically created as a separate object instead of sculpting them directly into the character. We'll learn how to **append** a pair of pre-made eyes from an external `.blend` file. Then, we'll learn how to position the eyes with Blender's **transformation** tools. Once the eyes are added, we can make eyelids for the character. To make the eyelids, we can try using the **Crease** brush along with some of our other brushes.

Getting ready

You can either continue with the model you've been making so far, or if you would rather start this section using our example, you can download it here: `https://github.com/PacktPublishing/Sculpting-the-Blender-Way/blob/main/Chapter03/simpleCharacterHead_06_Start.blend`.

You will also need the pair of pre-made eyes, which you can download here: `https://github.com/PacktPublishing/Sculpting-the-Blender-Way/blob/main/Chapter03/simpleEyes.blend`.

Once you've downloaded the files, open your character head sculpture or open the `simpleCharacterHead_06_Start.blend` example file.

Once we've got our character model open in Blender, we can add the eyes to our sculpture.

How to do it...

For this project, we need to change which Interaction Mode we are using. Right now, we are in **Sculpt Mode**, as we can see in the top-left corner of the 3D Viewport header. Let's begin by switching to **Object Mode**:

1. Find the **Interaction Mode** drop-down list in the header of the 3D Viewport.

2. Click on the list and choose **Object Mode**.

    In this mode, you'll notice that the Toolbar has changed. We no longer have our sculpting brushes; instead, we have tools for moving objects around. Now, we can add the eyes from the example file.

3. Open the **File** menu.

4. Choose **Append**.

5. Use the file browser to locate the `simpleEyes.blend` file:

Figure 3.25 – The simpleEyes.blend file as seen from the file browser

6. Double-click on the file to explore its contents.

7. Double-click the `Collection` folder to browse the collections that belong to this `.blend` file.

8. Double click on the `Eyes` collection to import the eyes into our current `.blend` file.

Excellent – the eyes have been added to the scene. You might not be able to see the eyes yet because they are stuck inside of the head. We learned how to use the X-ray feature in the *Exploring the viewport shading modes* section of *Chapter 1, Exploring Blender's User Interface for Sculpting*. Let's turn on the X-ray feature now (found in the top-right corner on the 3D Viewport header) so that we can see the eyes inside of the head:

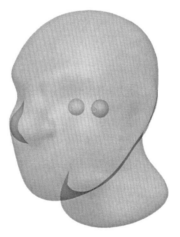

Figure 3.26 – The eyes can be seen inside of the head with X-ray toggled on

Now that we can see the eyes more clearly, let's learn how to position them. To make things easier, these eyes have been pre-made in such a way that we only need to position the left eye; the right eye will copy the position, size, and rotation to match it on the other side. Now, let's move the left eye into place:

9. Find the **Move** tool on the Toolbar and click to activate the tool.

    A gizmo with colored arrows will appear on top of the left eye:

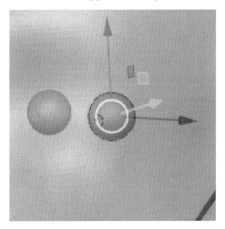

Figure 3.27 – The Move tool gizmo

It will be easiest to position the eye while our viewport is snapped to specific viewing angles.

10. Use the navigation gizmo in the top-right corner of the 3D Viewport to snap to the front view by clicking on the green -Y axis indicator.

11. Use the Move tool gizmo to move the eye into position by clicking and dragging on the blue and red arrows:

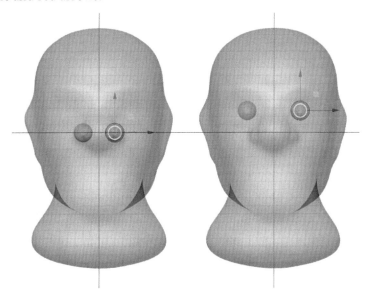

Figure 3.28 – The eyes before and after being positioned from the front view

12. Click on the red *X* axis indicator on the navigation gizmo to snap the 3D Viewport to the side view.

13. Click and drag on the green arrow on the Move tool gizmo to finish moving the eye into position:

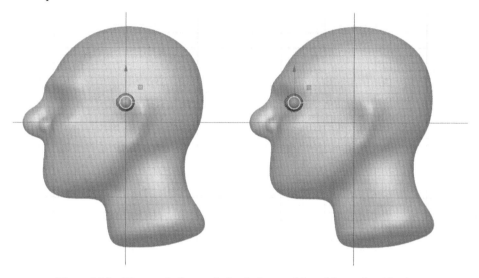

Figure 3.29 – The eyes before and after being positioned from the side view

If the eyes aren't the correct size, we can adjust the scale next.

14. Find the **Scale** tool on the Toolbar and click to activate the tool.

A gizmo with colored indicators will appear on top of the left eye. This gizmo also includes two white circles; these can be used to change the size while maintaining proportions:

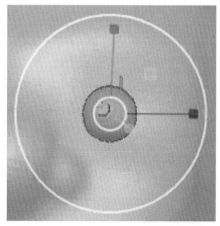

Figure 3.30 – The Scale tool gizmo

15. Hover your mouse inside of the large white circle (avoid the colored indicators).

16. Click and drag away from the eye to increase the size of the eyes:

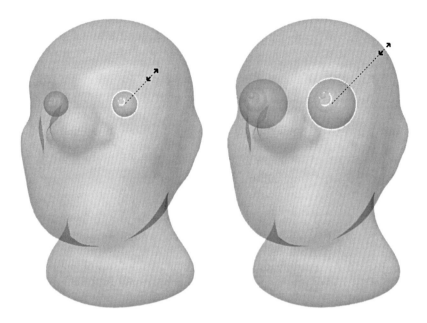

Figure 3.31 – The eyes before and after being scaled up

Once the eyes are in position and scaled to the correct size, we need to return to the head object and sculpt in the eyelids.

17. Toggle the X-ray feature back off.

18. Click on the head sculpture to select it.

19. Once the sculpture is the active object, change the Interaction Mode back to **Sculpt Mode**.

   Let's try using the Crease brush to create the eyelids. Our brushstrokes will only affect the active object, so the eyeballs will not be modified when we sculpt the eyelids:

20. Zoom into the eye so we can see it in detail.

21. Find the **Crease** brush on the Toolbar and click to activate the brush.

22. Set the brush **Radius** value to around 50 px.

23. Set the brush **Strength** value to around 0.750.

24. Draw over the corners of the eye to give them a sharp indent:

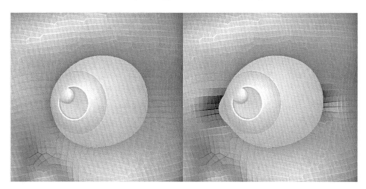

Figure 3.32 – The first crease drawn across the eye socket will form the corners of the eye

That's a good start; now, let's build up the eyelids by using the opposite direction of the Crease brush.

25. Hold the *Ctrl* key to invert the direction of the brush and draw around the upper part of the eye to build up the upper eyelid.

26. Keep the *Ctrl* key held down and draw around the lower part of the eye to build up the lower eyelid:

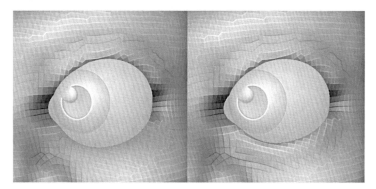

Figure 3.33 – The upper and lower eyelids are formed using the inverted Crease brush

Once we have the basic shapes for the eyelids, we can use our other brushes to adjust the shape. The Grab brush will be particularly useful. Use the Grab brush to reposition the eyelids as needed. If necessary, you can return to **Object Mode** to adjust the position and size of the eyeballs. When you're finished, run the Voxel Remesher. Our example turned out like this:

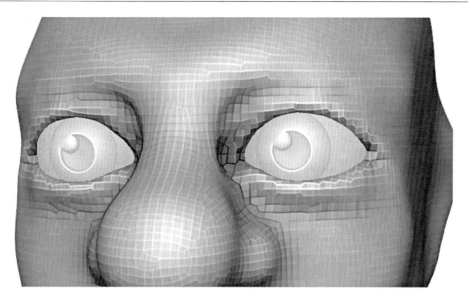

Figure 3.34 – The finished eyes after making many adjustments with the Grab brush

Eyes are hard, but don't get discouraged. Find some reference images that match the style you're trying to emulate. Also, remember that the character isn't finished yet; we can continue to refine the character in the subsequent sections as we add more details. Before the end of this chapter, we'll try out some brushes that will let us sharpen the details of the sculpture, including the eyelids.

How it works...

Appending objects and collections is an easy way for us to reach into an external .blend file and copy its contents into our current file. Many sculptors save time by using pre-made pieces as starting points for their sculptures. If you stick with sculpting for a long time, you can build up a large library of your own sculpting pieces that you can append into new projects.

The Crease brush indents the sculptures, similar to the subtractive mode of the Draw brush; however, it also pulls the vertices of the polygons together in order to make the indented area sharp.

The opposite direction of the Crease brush is good for making sharp ridges, such as eyelids.

There's more...

Many of the brushes can be accessed with hotkeys; for the Crease brush, we can use the *Shift + C* hotkey.

See also

Try not to get discouraged in this section - eyes are hard, and they take time and practice! Any time I'm getting discouraged about my sculptures, I remember a quote from one of the top sculptors in the Blender community, Julien Kaspar. He said, *"...For the longest time while sculpting on anything...your model is going to look [bad]. You'll get there eventually, it just takes a bit of time and effort."*

This quote comes from a presentation at the 2019 Blender Conference, *Speed Sculpting Live Session*, which you can watch here: `https://www.youtube.com/ watch?v=YaVEJTLDD3Y&t=732`.

Adding detail to the ears with the Crease brush

When we originally created the ears for the character, we were in the very early stages of the sculpting process. We have increased resolution with the Voxel Remesher several times since then as per our low-to-high detail workflow.

One of the goals with the Voxel Remesher is to create all of the major forms of the sculpture; surface details can always be added later. Most of the details of the ear can be saved for later, but at this stage, we have enough resolution that we ought to bring some definition back into the outer helix of the ear and separate it from the side of the head.

This is a relatively simple task, and we can get most of the way there with a combination of the Crease brush and the Smooth brush.

Getting ready

You can either continue with the model you've been making so far, or if you would rather start this section using our example, download and open the `simpleCharacterHead_07_Start.blend` file here: `https://github.com/ PacktPublishing/Sculpting-the-Blender-Way/blob/main/Chapter03/ simpleCharacterHead_07_Start.blend`.

Once we've got our character model open in Blender, we'll be ready to add detail to the ears.

How to do it...

We'll start by using the inverted direction of the Crease brush to build up the perimeter of the ear:

1. Orbit the 3D Viewport so we can clearly see the ear.

2. Activate the **Crease** brush on the Toolbar.

3. Set the brush **Radius** value to around 50 px.

4. Set the brush **Strength** value to around 0.750.

5. Hold the *Ctrl* key to invert the direction of the brush.

6. Draw around the perimeter of the ear to give it more definition:

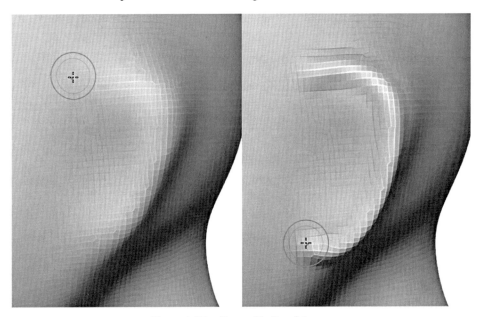

Figure 3.35 – Creased helix of the ear

7. Run the Voxel Remesher to create new polygons around the ear to help separate it from the side of the head.

    So far, so good. Now, we need to start carving away the backside of the ear so that it's not glued to the side of the head anymore. We will have to run the Voxel Remesher several times to properly detach the helix of the ear from the side of the head.

8. Orbit the 3D Viewport so that we can see the backside of the ear.

9. Let go of the *Ctrl* key so that we can use the default direction of the Crease brush.

10. Draw around the perimeter of the ear to give it more definition.

11. Run the Voxel Remesher.

12. Repeat these steps until the back of the ear is separated properly:

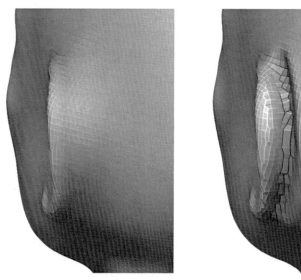

Figure 3.36 – The back of the ear separated from the side of the head

Use the Smooth brush to fix up the side of the head. Using a mask here may be helpful so that you can smooth the side of the head without smoothing the ear:

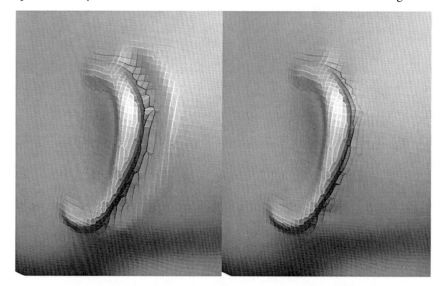

Figure 3.37 – The back of the ear before and after smoothing

Check the head from all angles; how do the ears look? If the ears look wonky, use the Grab brush to adjust them.

> **Important Note**
>
> Separating the back of the ear from the side of the head was the most important part of this process. This is because our current focus is to use the Voxel Remesher to create supporting geometry for the major forms of the sculpture. The details of the inner ear are optional at this stage because they can always be added and refined later in a high-resolution detail pass.

If you would like to sculpt the inner ear, the additive and subtractive directions of the Crease brush are both excellent ways to quickly add details. We've done a quick pass at ear details in the following example:

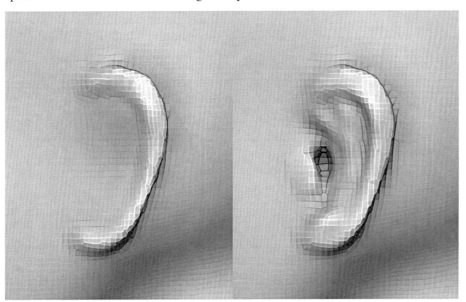

Figure 3.38 – Optional details of the ear

You may choose to style your ear in a more cartoony fashion that simplifies these details into basic shapes. Proper anatomy for the ear is something that will take a higher resolution, so our example is just a quick and dirty approximation.

How it works...

We're starting to get to the point where we've got all of our major shapes in the sculpture. Once we've finished adding major shapes, we won't need to rely on the Voxel Remesher anymore. It can be tricky to make decisions about which details we want to include at this stage; the ear details are a bit of a toss-up. A finished sculpture usually has to be touched up in the late stages anyway, so there's not much sense in trying to make the ears perfect right now. As long as we've captured the major forms, we'll be fine; that's why we focused on separating the back of the ear from the side of the head.

Creating the mouth with the Draw Sharp brush

We don't want our character to starve, so it's time to make a mouth! We're going to use a technique that creates the defining lines first, and then we can adjust the shape until it looks right. We're going to use the **Draw Sharp** brush to draw in a few key lines on and around the mouth. The Draw Sharp brush is closely related to the Crease brush, but it's even more aggressive and needs lots of polygons for the best results. Once we're done laying down our lines, we can use some of our other brushes to clean up the mouth shape.

Warning – this is going to look ugly at first; trust the process and we'll arrive at a proper-looking mouth by the end.

Getting ready

You can either continue with the model you've been making so far, or if you would rather start this section using our example, download and open the `simpleCharacterHead_08_Start.blend` file here: `https://github.com/PacktPublishing/Sculpting-the-Blender-Way/blob/main/Chapter03/simpleCharacterHead_08_Start.blend`.

Once we've got our character model open in Blender, we'll be ready to make a mouth.

How to do it...

Start by voxel-remeshing the character one last time so we have more polygons; a voxel size of around `0.0175` should work. If you need to, you can use the Smooth Mesh Filter to fix up any roughness that is introduced to the sculpture. Now, let's draw some lines for the mouth:

1. Click on the green *-Y* axis indicator on the navigation gizmo to snap the 3D Viewport to the front view.

2. Zoom in so that we can see the area where we're going to draw the mouth lines.

3. Find the **Draw Sharp** brush on the Toolbar and click to activate the brush.

4. Set the brush **Radius** value to around 20 px.

5. Set the brush **Strength** value to 1.000.

   We're going to make a set of guidelines for the mouth. Use this screenshot as a reference for the following instructions:

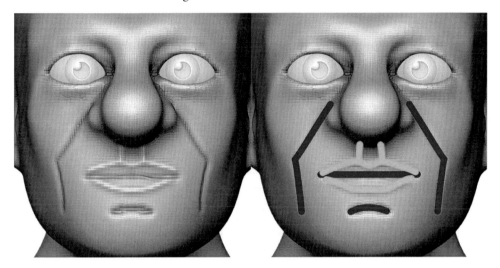

Figure 3.39 – The guidelines for the mouth (blue lines are grooves and orange lines are ridges)

Using the previous screenshot as a reference, let's use the **Draw Sharp** brush to draw the lines of the mouth.

6. Draw one horizontal deep groove for the middle of the mouth where the upper and lower lips meet.

7. Hold the *Ctrl* key to invert the direction of the brush and draw a horizontal ridge above the first line to form the ridge of the upper lip and Cupid's bow.

8. Hold the *Ctrl* key to invert the direction of the brush and draw a small vertical line above the upper lip toward the nose to outline the philtrum.

9. Hold the *Ctrl* key to invert the direction of the brush and draw a small, slightly rounded horizontal ridge below the middle of the mouth line to form the lower lip.

10. Let go of the *Ctrl* key and draw a short horizontal line below the lower lip to create the indentation between the mouth and the chin.

11. Finally, draw the lines that define the region between the mouth area and the cheeks. These lines cross over the top of the nostrils and angle inward near the corners of the mouth, as you can see in the preceding screenshot.

Remember how we warned you it was going to look ugly? This is that part; these lines will be our guide for sculpting the mouth. Now, we need to make it look good; we'll use several of the brushes we've learned throughout this chapter. This is going to take a lot of tweaking. Be patient and persist; we'll make it through.

We'll start by giving the lips some dimension. In a real mouth, the lips are pushed outward by the teeth underneath. Let's lift the lips away from the face by using the secondary function of the Grab brush.

12. Orbit the viewport to the side so we can see the silhouette of the mouth while we work (right now, the silhouette has no definition since the lips are flat against the face).

13. Activate the **Grab** brush from the Toolbar.

14. Set the **Radius** value large enough to cover the lips.

15. Switch to the **Grab** brush's secondary functionality by holding the *Ctrl* key.

16. Tap with your pen and drag outward to pull the lips away from the face.

Lift the lips far enough away from the face that they have some dimension; you can see our example in the following screenshot:

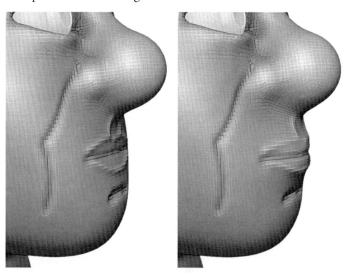

Figure 3.40 – The mouth before and after being raised up to give the lips some dimension

Next, we can smooth some of the lines so they don't look so jarring.

17. Orbit the viewport back near the front of the face.

18. Hold the *Shift* key to use the **Smooth** brush.

19. Smooth the indentation below the lips.

20. Use very light pressure to slightly smooth out the ridges of the lips and the philtrum.

    Be careful not to completely smooth away the lips. You can see how our example looks so far in the following screenshot:

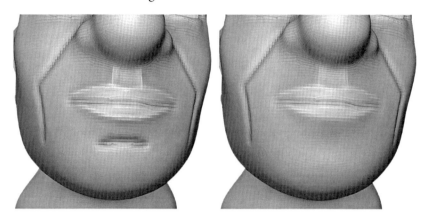

Figure 3.41 – The lines of the mouth before and after being smoothed

Next, we can do some inflating to bring out the lips and the cheeks.

21. Activate the **Inflate** brush.

22. Inflate the upper and lower lip to the desired thickness.

23. Inflate the cheek slightly in the area above the groove that outlines the mouth region.

24. Hold shift to use the **Smooth** brush and smooth the groove slightly.

    You can see the progress on our example in the following screenshot:

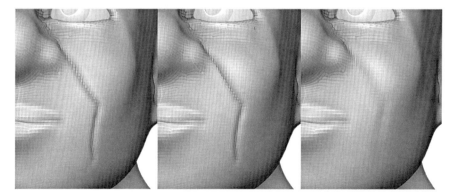

Figure 3.42 – The cheek after being inflated then smoothed

Now all of our key pieces are in place, we can use the **Grab** brush to reshape the philtrum, adjust the lips, bring in the cheeks a bit, and make any other necessary tweaks to the sculpture. Our example turned out like this:

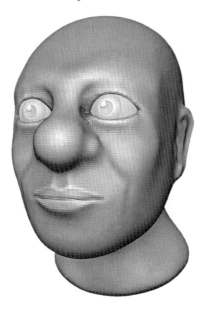

Figure 3.43 – The finished mouth

We've made a lot of progress. It may take you a while to tweak the mouth into a shape you're happy with, but don't get discouraged. Use reference images to help guide you to the mouth shape you're looking for. By the end of this chapter, we'll learn how to sharpen some of the details, such as the lines of the lips. A little sharpness will help the lips look a lot nicer.

Sharpening details with the Pinch brush

In this final section, we'll try out a brush that will help us refine the high-resolution details of the character. Some of the brushes in Blender work better when we have more polygons in our sculpture. In particular, the **Pinch** brush is a great way to get crisp edges, but it only works if we have lots of polygons in the sculpture.

> **Important Note**
>
> One issue with using the Pinch brush is that the Voxel Remesher tends to erase many of the sharpened details created by the Pinch brush. We're done with the Voxel Remesher now. Do not use it past this point; otherwise, many of our pinched details will be erased.

Before we get started with sharpening details, we'll take a moment to switch our model to using smooth shading, which will make the surface look like it's made out of clay instead of polygons.

Getting ready

You can either continue with the model you've been making so far, or if you would rather start this section using our example, download and open the `simpleCharacterHead_09_Start.blend` file here: `https://github.com/PacktPublishing/Sculpting-the-Blender-Way/blob/main/Chapter03/simpleCharacterHead_09_Start.blend`.

Once we've got our character model open in Blender, we'll be ready to sharpen the details of the sculpture.

How to do it...

Up until this point, we've been using **flat shading**, which makes all of the polygons look flat. We'll start this section by changing to **smooth shading**, which will help the surface of our sculpture look smooth:

1. Use the drop-down list in the header of the 3D Viewport to switch to **Object Mode**.

2. Open the **Object** menu from the header of the 3D Viewport.

3. Choose the **Shade Smooth** option.

4. Use the drop-down list in the header of the 3D Viewport to switch back to **Sculpt Mode**.

   That was easy. Many artists prefer to leave the shading set to flat during the early stages because it makes it easy to see the current resolution of the mesh. Now that we're done remeshing, we can use smooth shading to make our model look nicer.

   Speaking of looking nicer, let's try out the Pinch brush to make our character's eyelids look sharp.

5. Zoom in so that we can see the eyelid up close.

6. Activate the **Pinch** brush on the Toolbar.

7. Set the brush **Radius** value to around `100 px`.

8. Set the brush **Strength** value to around `1.000`.

9. Trace over the eyelids to pinch the polygons together to make the eyelids really sharp.

    This may take several passes. As the polygons get closer together, the eyelids will look sharper.

    Let's give the lips the same treatment.

10. Trace over the upper lip with the **Pinch** brush.

11. Trace over the lower lip with the **Pinch** brush.

12. Trace over the groove between the lips with the **Pinch** brush.

    Much better – as you can see in the following screenshot, our character looks a lot better after pinching the eyelids and the lips:

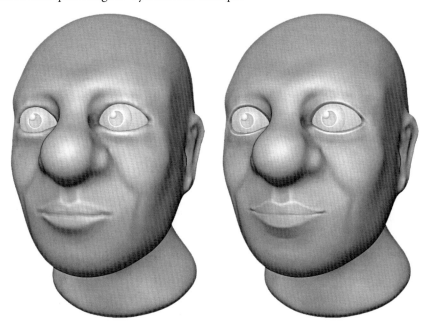

Figure 3.44 – Our finished character before and after pinching the eyelids and lips

If you like, you can use the Inflate brush over the lips. Inflating next to a pinched groove will intensify the groove. The Pinch brush can also be used with a large radius to sharpen the transitions between large forms; try using it to sharpen the jawline.

Pinching makes a big difference when refining details. Our sculpture is starting to look like a proper character with detailed facial features. If you like, you can keep adjusting the character with your favorite brushes.

There's more...

Many of the brushes can be accessed with hotkeys; for the Pinch brush, we can use the *P* hotkey.

Congratulations on getting through this chapter. We learned about lots of awesome brushes and got to try them out in a practical application for character creation. How did it go? Don't worry if you struggled with the eyes or the lips; these things take practice. Struggling your way through your first sculpture is part of the process. Stick with it and you'll get faster and better at sculpting!

If you're coming from the popular sculpting software ZBrush, you may already be familiar with some of the brushes discussed in this chapter but under different names. For reference, here is a list of the equivalent brushes between ZBrush and Blender:

- ZBrush's **Move** brush is equivalent to Blender's Grab brush.

- ZBrush's **MaskPen** brush is equivalent to Blender's Mask brush.

- ZBrush's **Standard** brush is equivalent to Blender's Draw brush.

- ZBrush's **ClayTubes** brush is equivalent to Blender's Clay Strips brush.

- ZBrush's **DamStandard** brush is equivalent to Blender's Draw Sharp brush.

- ZBrush doesn't have a direct equivalent to Blender's Crease brush; its functionality is somewhere between Standard and DamStandard.

- **SnakeHook**, **Smooth**, **Inflate**, and **Pinch** are all equivalent in both name and functionality between ZBrush and Blender.

- ZBrush's **Deformation** sub-palette is equivalent to Blender's Mesh Filters.

We've only scratched the surface of Blender's brushes. Feel free to explore the Toolbar and discover which brushes you like using. You may prefer the Clay brush over the Draw brush, or the Multi-Plane Scrape brush instead of the Pinch brush. There are so many to experiment with. Try playing around and taking your character to the next level of detail!

See also

Check out the *Sculpting in Action* video for this chapter for a visual demonstration of how these brushes can be used: `https://bit.ly/3y93Dt5`. The video for this chapter includes a bonus timelapse section at the end that demonstrates how the shape of this character can be refined using the brushes we've learned about throughout this chapter. You can see the refined version of the sculpture in the following image:

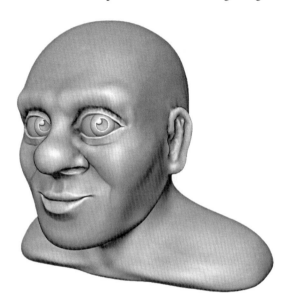

Figure 3.45 – The finished character after refining the details in the bonus timelapse video

You can read more about Blender's default brushes in the official Blender manual here: `https://docs.blender.org/manual/en/latest/sculpt_paint/sculpting/tools/index.html`.

4
How to Make a Base Mesh for a 3D Sculpture

The sculpting workflow has two distinct parts. In the first part, we create the major forms of the sculpture, such as the torso, legs, arms, fingers, head, nose, ears, and mouth. In the second part, we create the minor forms and details of the sculpture, such as the tight creases of the sculpture's lips, fingernails, wrinkles, skin pores, scars, and more.

The mesh that we create in the first phase is known as a **base mesh**. A base mesh is a model with simple geometry that supports all of the major forms that we want to have in our final sculpture. Once we have a base mesh, we can enter the second phase with the powerful multiresolution workflow and begin adding details to the model. We will learn all about this second phase in *Chapter 5, Learning the Power of Subdivision and the Multiresolution Workflow*.

Creating major forms of the model can be done in numerous ways. One way is to begin with a basic sphere and sculpt in the major forms with the Grab brush and other brushes. We used this approach throughout *Chapter 3, Sculpting a Simple Character Head with Basic Brushes*. This approach works well if you want a completely free-form sculpting experience, but sometimes, it can be helpful to create sculptures from a more structured base shape instead of starting from a sphere.

In this chapter, we'll learn about alternative ways to create a base mesh, starting with classic **box modeling** techniques. We will also explore various interactive ways of creating a base mesh with Blender's **modifiers**, including the **Skin** modifier and **Boolean** modifier. We'll use **Metaballs** to create implicit surfaces with interesting shapes. We'll also try using a special sculpting utility called **Lasso Trim** to add and cut away geometry in a free-form fashion.

Any of these techniques can be useful all by themselves. However, it is important to finish preparing our base mesh correctly by following a few steps, as laid out in the *Making sure our base mesh is ready for sculpting* section of this chapter. Be sure to follow these base mesh creation techniques with the process that's laid out in that section. Otherwise, our base meshes may not be compatible with the sculpting tools.

By the end of this chapter, you'll have plenty of techniques at your disposal for creating base meshes for anything you would like to sculpt.

The main topics in this chapter are as follows:

- Creating and transforming primitive objects
- Creating a base mesh with box modeling
- Using the Skin modifier to turn wireframe structures into thick skins
- Using Metaballs to build blob-like 3D forms
- Inserting meshes and cutting holes with Booleans
- Using the Lasso Trim tool to add and remove geometry
- Making sure our base mesh is ready for sculpting

Technical requirements

For the general requirements, please refer to the *Technical requirements* section of *Chapter 1, Exploring Blender's User Interface for Sculpting*.

You can download the files to follow along with this book at the GitHub link here: `https://github.com/PacktPublishing/Sculpting-the-Blender-Way`.

Creating and transforming primitive objects

Blender is a full 3D production suite; it includes many features that don't directly relate to Sculpt Mode. But that doesn't mean we can't use some of the extra features to supplement our sculpting workflows. In this section, we will learn how to create and transform objects that we can use to build up basic shapes for our sculptures.

We got our first taste of this process in the *Adding basic eyes and eyelids to the character* section of *Chapter 3, Sculpting a Simple Character Head with Basic Brushes*. In this section, we will dive a little deeper and get some practice constructing objects out of **primitive** objects. Primitive objects are simple geometric shapes, such as cubes, cylinders, spheres, and toruses that can be used as a starting point for our 3D models.

Getting ready

We will begin this project from a fresh Blender project. Choose **File | New | Sculpting** to create a new Blender project with the sculpting preset. Change the Interaction Mode from **Sculpt Mode** to **Object Mode** using the menu in the top-left corner of the 3D Viewport. Once we're in Object Mode, we can add and remove objects.

How to do it...

We don't need the default **Quad Sphere** object for this section, so we can delete it:

1. Find the **Object** menu in the top-left corner of the header of the 3D Viewport. Open the menu and choose **Delete**.

    Now that we've removed the sphere, we can try adding a different mesh. New objects in Blender are created at the location of the 3D Cursor. In the **Sculpting** preset, the **3D Cursor** isn't visible, so let's turn it on in the **Viewport Overlays** pop-over menu.

2. Open the **Viewport Overlays** pop-over menu and activate **3D Cursor**.

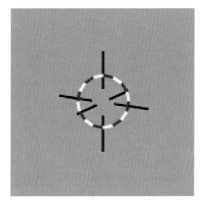

Figure 4.1 – The 3D Cursor as it appears in the 3D Viewport

You may find it helpful to turn on some of the other overlays, such as **Floor**, **X and Y Axes**, and **Statistics**. Once we can see the position of the 3D Cursor, we're ready to add a new primitive object.

3. Find the **Add** menu in the top-left corner of the header of the 3D Viewport.

4. Open the menu and choose **Mesh | Cube**.

Once the cube has been added, we can try transforming it with our **Move**, **Rotate**, and **Scale** tools. You will have an easier time exploring these tools if you expand the Toolbar so that the tool names are displayed.

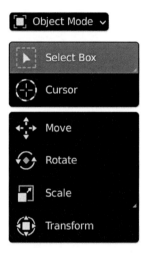

Figure 4.2 – The Toolbar in Object Mode contains transformation tools

First, let's try the **Move** tool to adjust the position of the object:

5. Find and activate the **Move** tool from the Toolbar.

    The colored gizmo for the **Move** tool will appear on top of the cube object.

Figure 4.3 – The Move tool gizmo as it appears in the 3D Viewport

6. Try clicking and dragging the colored arrows to move the cube to a new location.

    The colored arrows on the **Move** tool gizmo each correspond to the three axes – *X*, *Y*, and *Z*:

- Use the red arrow to move the cube along the global X axis (left and right).
- Use the green arrow to move the cube along the global Y axis (forward and backward).
- Use the blue arrow to move the cube along the global Z axis (up and down).
- We can also use the white area of the gizmo to move the cube along multiple axes at once.

Once the cube is in a position where you like it, we can try out the **Rotate** tool to change its orientation:

1. Find and activate the **Rotate** tool from the Toolbar.

    The colored gizmo for the **Rotate** tool will appear on top of the cube object.

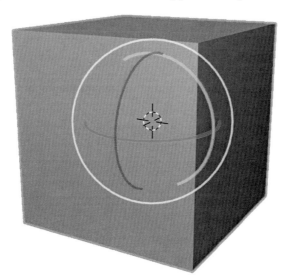

Figure 4.4 – The Rotate tool gizmo as it appears in the 3D Viewport

The **Rotate** tool behaves in the same way as the **Move** tool – each colored ring corresponds to the three axes.

2. Try clicking and dragging the colored rings to rotate the cube.

Lastly, let's try the **Scale** tool to change the size of the object:

1. Find and activate the **Scale** tool from the Toolbar.

    The colored gizmo for the **Scale** tool will appear on top of the cube object.

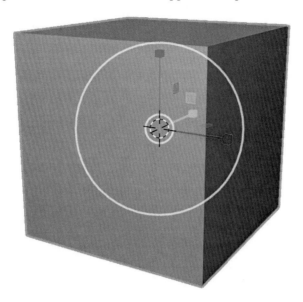

Figure 4.5 – The Scale tool gizmo as it appears in the 3D Viewport

Using these tools to transform our objects is often good enough for sculpting, but sometimes, precision is important. To be more precise, we can take a look at the Sidebar.

2. Open the Sidebar by clicking the < indicator in the top-right corner of the 3D Viewport near the **Navigation** gizmo, or by pressing the *N* hotkey.

    Once the Sidebar is open, we will see information about the selected object in the **Item** tab. Specifically, we can see the **Transform** information about the object, including the current **Location**, **Rotation**, and **Scale** of the object.

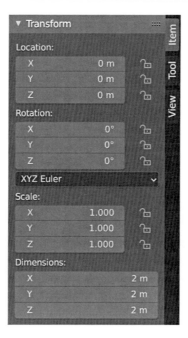

Figure 4.6 – The Item tab of the Sidebar displays Transform information for the active object

From here, we can type in exact values for the transforms of our object.

> **Tip**
>
> In Blender, all number fields like this can be used as sliders. To do this, simply click and drag left to right on the number field.

Another thing to know about the **Transform** tools is that we can change the orientation of the tools. By default, the **Transform** tools operate relative to the world using the **Global** orientation. We can see the orientation of the tool listed in the middle of the header of the 3D Viewport. By clicking on this option, we can change to an alternative orientation.

Figure 4.7 – The Transform Orientations settings in the header of the 3D Viewport

If we change the transform orientation to **Local** instead of **Global**, we will see the difference it makes to our transformation tool's gizmo.

Figure 4.8 – The Transform Orientations setting changed from Global (left) to Local (right)

Sometimes, this can be helpful when we're trying to move or scale an object, as the gizmo is now aligned with the object's local rotation instead of the world rotation.

Try adding several primitive mesh objects to the scene and using the **Transform** tools to build up a simple character shape.

Important Note

For this section, only use primitives from the **Mesh** section of the **Add** menu. We will learn about several other types of objects throughout this book, but only mesh objects will be compatible with each other if you use what we've learned in this section.

You can make anything you like this way, but here is an example:

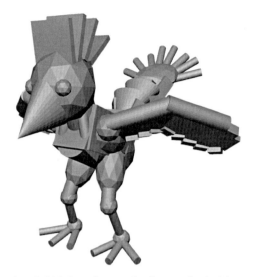

Figure 4.9 – A weird bird made completely out of primitive mesh objects

These transformation tools are critical for many workflows inside Blender, and we will make good use of them throughout the rest of this book.

How it works...

Primitive objects are an excellent starting point for our sculptures. Arranging the objects in this way would normally create problematic disjointed surfaces, but when we're done, we can use the Voxel Remesher to join them all together to create a base mesh. See the *Making sure our base mesh is ready for sculpting* section at the end of this chapter for more information on joining these shapes together.

We can be specific about how objects are placed using the Sidebar. This is especially handy for symmetrical sculptures. If we want to center an object along the X axis, we can simply type 0 in the **X Location** slot.

There's more...

Most of the operations we covered in this section have hotkeys for quick access:

- Instead of using the **Move** tool, we can quickly grab objects and move them around by pressing the G hotkey.

- Instead of using the **Rotate** tool, we can quickly rotate objects by pressing the R hotkey.

- Instead of using the **Scale** tool, we can quickly scale objects by pressing the S hotkey.

There are a couple of other useful tools on the Toolbar that can help us when adding primitive objects:

- The **Cursor** tool can be used to move the 3D Cursor to a new location. New primitive objects will always be added to the location of the 3D Cursor.

- The brand new **Add Cube** tool can be used to quickly draw out cubes by hand. Click and hold the **Add Cube** tool to find similar tools for adding cones, cylinders, and spheres.

Creating a base mesh with box modeling

This book focuses on sculpting workflows, but sculpting is just one of many techniques we can use for modeling in 3D software. We can augment our sculpting workflow with other techniques as we block out the shapes for a base mesh. A classic style of modeling that will be useful to us is **box modeling**. Box modeling is one of the oldest styles of 3D modeling. It's fairly straightforward; we start with a primitive shape (usually a cube), and then use a small set of tools to extrude, inset, and add edge loops to the model to begin modeling out the major forms of the object.

Getting ready

For this section, we'll use the **General** preset to create a new project, since we will be working with Blender's modeling tools instead of the sculpting tools. Choose **File | New | General** to create a new Blender project with the **General** preset. Once we have a fresh scene, we can try out a new type of Interaction Mode called **Edit Mode**, which we can use to edit the components of the default cube.

The general preset starts with a default cube model in the center of the scene. With the default cube selected, change the Interaction Mode from **Object Mode** to **Edit Mode** using the drop-down menu in the top-left corner of the header of the 3D Viewport.

There are several notable changes to Blender's UI when we enter **Edit Mode**. First of all, we can see three new icons next to the Interaction Mode in the header of the 3D Viewport. These three icons represent the three types of components of the mesh (vertices, edges, and faces).

Figure 4.10 – Edit Mode and the three component icons

In this mode, we can select and edit the individual components. We can specify the type of component we want to edit by clicking on these buttons, which will toggle between **Vertex Select**, **Edge Select**, and **Face Select**. We can also press the *1*, *2*, and *3* hotkeys to switch between these selection modes.

Some of our **Edit Mode** tools will behave differently, depending on which components we have selected. Speaking of **Edit Mode** tools, most of the tools on the Toolbar are the same between **Object Mode** and **Edit Mode**. However, **Edit Mode** provides us with several extra tools, as shown in the following diagram:

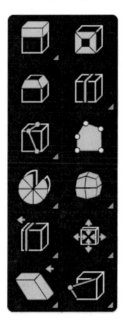

Figure 4.11 – Extra tools available on the Toolbar in Edit Mode

There are many tools to explore here, but we are mostly interested in **Extrude Region**, **Inset Faces**, and **Loop Cut**. With these tools, we can turn our cube into a much more interesting shape.

How to do it...

Let's start with the most famous box modeling tool – extrude:

1. Switch to **Face Select** mode by clicking the corresponding icon in the header of the 3D Viewport or by pressing the *3* hotkey.
2. Click on the top face of the cube to select it.
3. Find and activate the **Extrude Region** tool from the Toolbar.

A yellow gizmo for the **Extrude Region** tool will appear on top of the cube, as shown in the following diagram:

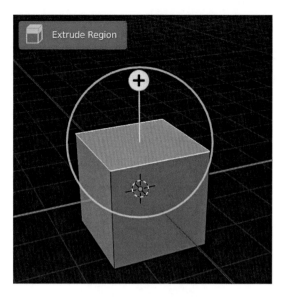

Figure 4.12 – The Extrude Region tool gizmo

We can use this gizmo to extrude the face, which will create new geometry around the perimeter of the selected face as we pull it upward:

1. Click and drag upward on the yellow + icon of the **Extrude Region** gizmo.

    The face will be extruded upward, as shown in the following screenshot:

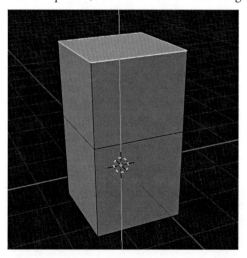

Figure 4.13 – The cube after the top face has been extruded upward

2.   Release the mouse button to finish extruding the face.

     This did not just make the cube taller; this has left behind an extra loop of edges in the original place of the extruded face. This effectively sections off the top and bottom of this cube. We can perform more extrusions on some of the faces on the top without affecting the faces on the bottom.

3.   Select one of the faces on the top half of the object.

4.   Use the **Extrude Region** tool to extrude the selected face.

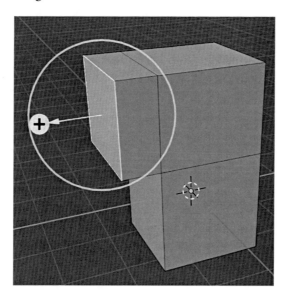

Figure 4.14 – The object after extruding one of the upper faces to the side

Extruding is a powerful way to quickly block out objects in a box-like manner, hence this type of modeling being called **box modeling**. We have a similar tool called **Inset Faces**, which will let us section off the inner regions of the faces. Let's try this tool now.

5.   Click on a face to select it (we've selected the large upper face nearest to us in our example).

6. Find and activate the **Inset Faces** tool from the Toolbar.

    A yellow gizmo for the **Inset Faces** tool will appear on top of the selected face.

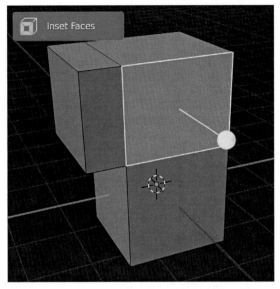

Figure 4.15 – The Inset Faces tool gizmo

We can use this gizmo to inset a loop of faces inward from the selected face.

7. Click and drag the yellow gizmo inward toward the center of the selected face.

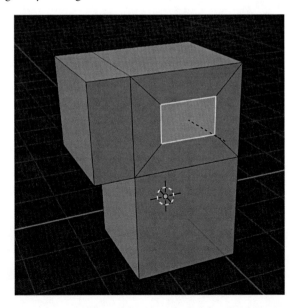

Figure 4.16 – The object after the selected face has been inset

This tool works well for defining new regions that we can extrude from. Try using the **Extrude Region** tool again to extrude the face that has been inset.

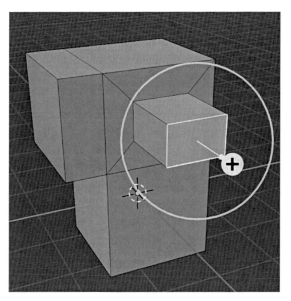

Figure 4.17 – Another extrusion, this time made from the inset face

Each of these extrusions has left behind a region that is bordered by a loop of edges. These edge loops offer an excellent place for us to insert new geometry. If we want to place a new edge loop in our model, we can do so with the **Loop Cut** tool.

8. Switch to **Edge Select** mode by clicking the corresponding icon in the header of the 3D Viewport or by pressing the *2* hotkey.

9. Find and activate the **Loop Cut** tool from the Toolbar.

    This time, we will not see a gizmo until we hover the mouse over a part of the mesh.

10. Hover your mouse over an area of the mesh that you would like to cut an edge loop through.

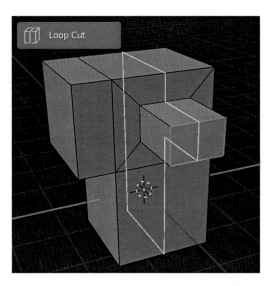

Figure 4.18 – The Loop Cut highlight running through the area we want to cut through

11. Click to cut a new edge loop through the mesh.

Keep cutting edge loops through the mesh until you've got enough divisions to make some interesting shapes. You can see the three edge loops we cut for our example in the following diagram:

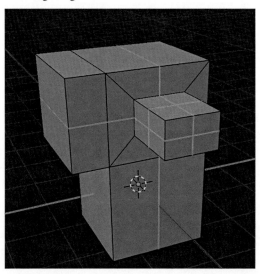

Figure 4.19 – Three new edge loops cut through the mesh using the Loop Cut tool

Once again, this tool works well for dividing faces into smaller regions that we can extrude from.

12. Switch back to **Face Select** mode by clicking the corresponding icon in the header of the 3D Viewport or by pressing the *3* hotkey.

13. Try using the **Extrude Region** tool again to extrude several new faces.

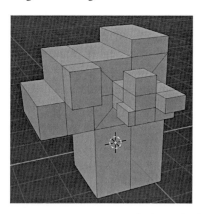

Figure 4.20 – Many new extrusions made from the divided faces

When combined with the transformation tools (**Move**, **Rotate**, and **Scale**), we can create all kinds of interesting shapes, which we can then use as base meshes for sculpting. It takes practice to create more organic forms since these tools aren't as artistic as our sculpting tools. Here's an example of a quadrupedal animal base mesh created entirely with these tools:

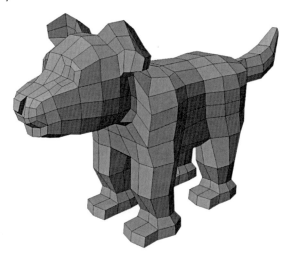

Figure 4.21 – An example animal base mesh created using the Extrude Region, Inset Faces, Loop Cut, and Transformation tools in Edit Mode

Don't worry about the character looking blocky as this is box modeling, after all; blockiness is inevitable. Just focus on getting all of the major forms of the model in place. In our example, we have a body, head, tail, four legs, a nose, ears, and an inset for the eyes.

How it works...

Back in the earliest days of 3D sculpting, there was no Voxel Remesher. If we wanted to create a sculpture, we started by box modeling all of the major forms of the object with these basic tools before entering Sculpt Mode. Today, box modeling techniques are still useful, especially if you intend to create mechanical parts that have blocky shapes.

Some parts of our characters lend themselves to this workflow more than others. For example, accessories such as earrings are often more easily created through box modeling techniques. Box modeling will come in handy in *Chapter 8, Making Accessories and Clothing*.

There's more...

Most of the operations we have covered in this section have hotkeys for quick access:

- Instead of using the **Extrude Region** tool, we can extrude the selection by pressing the *E* hotkey.

- Instead of using the **Inset Faces** tool, we can inset the selection by pressing the *I* hotkey.

- Instead of using the **Loop Cut** tool, we can insert edge loops by pressing the *Ctrl* + *R* hotkey.

Feel free to explore the rest of the **Edit Mode** Toolbar. There are lots of useful tools.

Edit Mode is also useful for making small tweaks and resolving issues in our models and sculptures. Just be careful when entering **Edit Mode** for objects that have hundreds of thousands of vertices because this will cause your computer to slow down to a crawl.

Box modeling has a lot of potential when combined with a **Subdivision Surface** modifier. We will learn all about this in *Chapter 5, Learning the Power of Subdivision and the Multiresolution Workflow*.

See also

There's so much more to learn about box modeling techniques, but this is a book about sculpting, so we won't focus any more time on this area. If you would like to learn more about other areas of Blender like this, we recommend picking up a copy of *Blender 3D By Example (2nd Edition)*, from Packt Publishing.

Using the Skin modifier to turn wireframe structures into thick skins

In the *Creating a base mesh with box modeling* section of this chapter, we tried out several tools in **Edit Mode**. These techniques will be useful for several other types of base mesh creation. One way to enhance our modeling workflow is to use modifiers.

Modifiers are a type of non-destructive editing in Blender. They work by taking input geometry (the unmodified model), then dynamically performing some kind of modification, and outputting that modified result. This is excellent because we can keep changing the input geometry and have the result update automatically while we work.

In this section, we'll take a look at a modifier that will create thickness around the edges of a model to create a base mesh for a character's body.

Getting ready

We'll start this section with the **General** preset. Choose **File | New | General** to create a new Blender project. Once we have a fresh scene, we can try adding a Skin modifier to the default cube and edit its components. We recommend turning on the **Cavity** option in the **Viewport Shading** options to help visualize the depth of the objects in the scene.

We'll be moving components around with our transformation tools, so make sure you understand the tools that were laid out in the *Creating and transforming primitive objects* and *Creating a base mesh with box modeling* sections of this chapter.

How to do it...

To add the Skin modifier to the cube, we'll use the Properties editor:

1. Navigate to the **Modifier** tab (represented by the blue wrench icon) in the Properties editor.

2. Click **Add Modifier**.

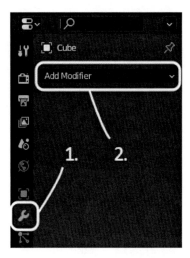

Figure 4.22 – The Modifier tab in the Properties editor

3. Choose **Skin** from the **Generate** column of the list of modifiers.

Perfect – the cube has been given thickness around its edges.

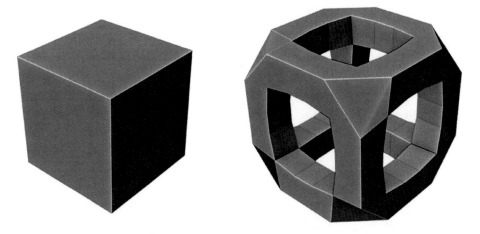

Figure 4.23 – The cube before and after adding the Skin modifier

The original six faces of the cube have been ignored; only the edges are contributing to the skin when this modifier is in use. The modifier then generates new faces to surround the edges of the input geometry.

To get the most out of this modifier, let's enter **Edit Mode** for the cube and extrude some vertices:

1. Change the Interaction Mode from **Object Mode** to **Edit Mode** using the drop-down menu in the top-left corner of the header of the 3D Viewport.

2. Make sure you're using **Vertex Select** mode by clicking the corresponding icon in the header of the 3D Viewport or by pressing the *1* hotkey.

3. This skin is blocking our view of the input geometry, so turn on **X-ray** from the shading options in the top-right corner of the 3D Viewport.

    Now, we can see the original input geometry of the cube, with the generated skin partially visible on top.

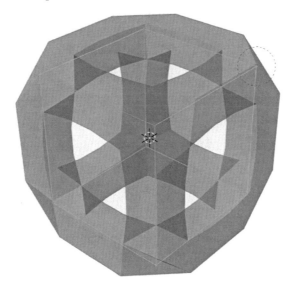

Figure 4.24 – The input geometry visible through the X-rayed skin

The faces for this input geometry aren't being used, so we can remove them to make the geometry simpler.

4. Find the **Mesh** menu in the top-left corner of the 3D Viewport. Open the menu and choose **Delete | Only Faces**.

    Perfect – now, we only have vertices and edges in our mesh.

5. Next, we can try extruding some vertices to edit the skin. For this, select a vertex.

6. Extrude the vertex either by using the **Extrude Region** tool or by pressing the *E* hotkey.

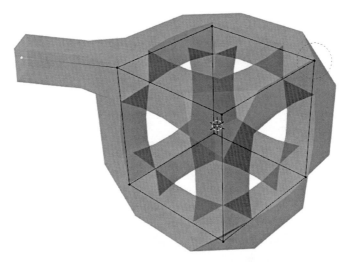

Figure 4.25 – The top-left vertex has been extruded to form a new edge

Excellent – by extruding this vertex, we've extended the geometry outward and created a new edge. The **Skin** modifier immediately takes this new edge into account and dynamically adds polygons to surround the edge with a thick skin.

Try extruding many times to create a body for a character (sort of like a stick figure). Use the **Move** tool to reposition the extruded segments as needed. Our example looks like this:

Figure 4.26 – A skinned stick figure made from vertices and edges

You can, of course, delete unwanted vertices. Our example looks like it's wearing a backpack made out of the vertices from the original cube mesh. If you don't like this, simply select the vertices of the *backpack* and choose **Mesh | Delete | Vertices**.

This might break the **Skin** modifier if you delete the **root** vertex. The **Skin** modifier uses the root vertex as a center point for the skin to stem outward from. Our example character looks like this after deleting the *backpack*, which contained the root vertex:

Figure 4.27 – The Skin modifier is broken after removing the root vertex

If the root vertex is removed, we'll see the following warning at the bottom of the **Skin** modifier:

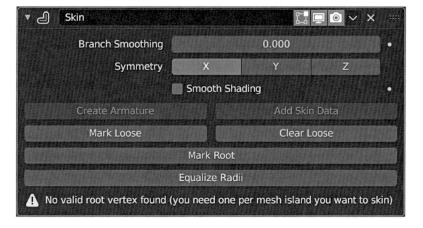

Figure 4.28 – The "No valid root" warning displayed at the bottom of the Skin modifier

We can fix this by choosing a new root vertex.

1. Select a vertex that should act as the new root for the skin (the pelvis is usually a good choice).

2. Click the **Mark Root** button from the **Skin** modifier settings in the Properties editor.

   And there we go, a beautiful skin. Well, to be honest, it could use a little work before we can call it beautiful. It would look a lot nicer with some varied thickness. We can apply different amounts of thickness to each vertex by adjusting the **Radius X** and **Radius Y** properties in the **Item** tab in the Sidebar, or simply by pressing the *Ctrl + A* hotkey.

3. To adjust the thickness, select a vertex that you would like to add thickness to.

4. Press the *Ctrl + A* hotkey to begin editing the vertex skin radius.

5. Drag your mouse outward or inward to increase or decrease the skin radius.

6. Left-click to confirm the adjustment to the radius.

   By adjusting the radius of individual parts, we can create a much more appealing character skin:

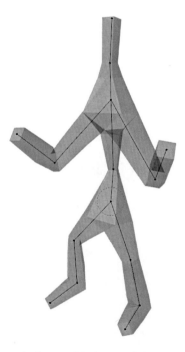

Figure 4.29 – Thickness added to several vertices in the skin

And that's it! The **Skin** modifier is an excellent way to quickly build up limbs for a character and create a base mesh that we can use for sculpting. Get creative – make lots of little extrusions, make hands, make horns, or make any large forms that you want to represent in the final base mesh.

How it works…

This **Skin** modifier uses the edges of the mesh as input and then generates new polygons surrounding the edges to form a thick skin that we can use for sculpting. Before we can use this result as a base mesh, we must convert the modifiers into geometry that is compatible with the sculpting tools. See the *Making sure our base mesh is ready for sculpting* section at the end of this chapter for more details.

There's more…

If you want the skinned mesh to look smoother, we can add an extra modifier to the object. Try adding a **Subdivision Surface** modifier from the **Generate** column of the **Add Modifier** menu.

This modifier is not necessary, but many artists use it in conjunction with the **Skin** modifier because it makes the results of the skinned mesh look much nicer. We will learn how to unlock the full potential of the **Subdivision Surface** modifier in *Chapter 5, Learning the Power of Subdivision and the Multiresolution Workflow*.

Another modifier we can try out is the **Mirror** modifier, which can also be found under the **Generate** column of the **Add Modifier** menu. Once added, we can activate the **Bisect X** option to throw away half of the model and mirror the other half on the other side, creating a perfectly symmetrical object.

Using Metaballs to build blob-like 3D forms

So far, the primary types of objects we've looked at in this book have been mesh objects. As we learned in the *Understanding the components of a 3D sculpture* section of *Chapter 2, Overview of Blender's Sculpting Workflows*, a mesh is made from vertices, edges, and faces. However, there are other types of objects that can be useful for creating basic shapes for our sculptures. In this section, we will use **Metaballs** to create blob-like forms out of mathematical 3D directing structures. Don't worry – it's not as technical as it sounds. It's easy and fun!

Getting ready

We'll start this section with a fresh Blender scene by using the **File | New | General** preset. Remove the default cube object by choosing **Object | Delete** from the menu in the top left of the 3D Viewport.

We'll be adding and moving objects around with our transformation tools, so make sure you understand the tools that were laid out in the *Creating and transforming primitive objects* section of this chapter.

How to do it...

We'll start by creating a single Metaball. Metaballs are not the same as primitive mesh objects. They can be found in their own section under the **Add** menu. We'll start by creating a basic object that we can modify:

1. Make sure you are in **Object Mode**.
2. Open the **Add** menu and choose **Metaball | Ball**.

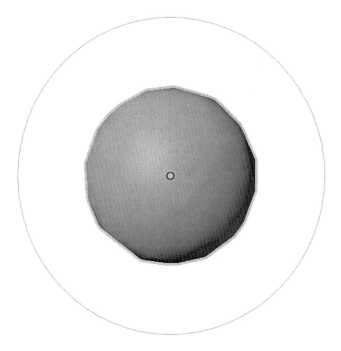

Figure 4.30 – Our new Metaball looks like a basic sphere

One Metaball by itself isn't particularly interesting, so let's switch to **Edit Mode** and add another Metaball.

3. Switch to **Edit Mode** using the drop-down menu in the top-left corner of the header of the 3D Viewport.

4. Use the **Add** menu to add another **Metaball | Ball**.

    Because we are in **Edit Mode**, this second Metaball has been added as part of the first Metaball object. It's also been added to the same spot as the first Metaball, so it doesn't look like much has changed. Let's move this second Metaball off to the side and watch the magic happen.

5. Use the **Move** tool to move the new Metaball around:

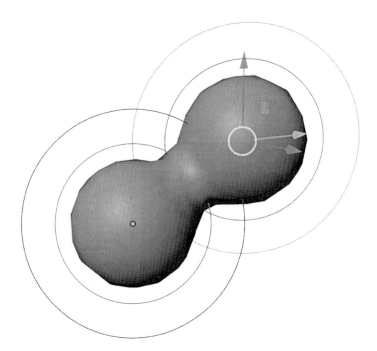

Figure 4.31 – Our second Metaball has been glued to the side of the first one,
creating an interesting shape

Notice how the two Metaballs stick together when they get close? Weird! Gross! Neat! Try building out an interesting shape by adding several Metaballs. You can press the *Shift + D* hotkey to quickly duplicate the selected objects instead of using the **Add** menu over and over. You can also use the **Scale** tool to adjust the size of the Metaballs.

If you get bored of the sphere-shaped Metaballs, you can add other types of Metaballs from the **Add** menu – there's **capsule, plane, ellipsoid**, and **cube** to choose from. You can make all sorts of interesting shapes when you combine several Metaballs, as shown in this example of a blob monster:

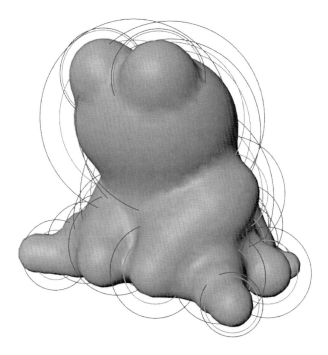

Figure 4.32 – An example blob monster made entirely out of Metaballs

This blob monster could use some eyes and a mouth. Metaballs can also be used to cut away from the defined area. To do this, let's turn our attention to the Properties editor:

1. Navigate to the **Object Data** tab (represented by the green icon) in the Properties editor.

2. Click the **Negative** checkbox to change the selected Metaball into a negative field.

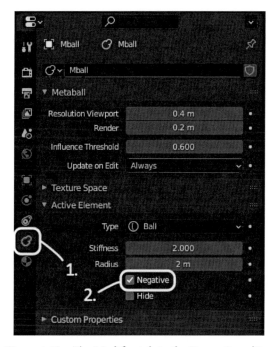

Figure 4.33 – The Modifier tab in the Properties editor

Perfect – we can place negative Metaballs anywhere we would like to cut a hole. In our example, we've added a hole for each eye and used three plane-shaped Metaballs to make a hole for the mouth:

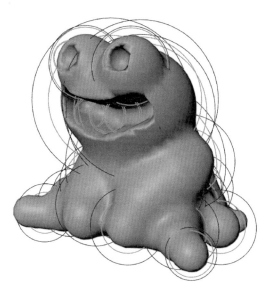

Figure 4.34 – The blob monster with negative Metaballs for the eyes and mouth

While we move the Metaballs around, our computers have to do a lot of processing. So, the resolution of the surface starts at a low default value of **0.4 m** (as seen in the Properties editor in *Figure 4.33*). When we're done moving the Metaballs around, we can increase the quality by setting the **Resolution Viewport** value to a lower value, such as **0.05 m**.

Figure 4.35 – The blob monster in high resolution

And there you have it – another interesting way to create a base mesh for sculpting. This approach is a fun way to create blobby creatures and organic shapes.

How it works...

Metaballs create shapes based on their proximity to one another. All sorts of organic shapes can be created in this way. However, this type of object is incompatible with sculpting, so it must be converted into a mesh before we can use our sculpting brushes on it. See the *Making sure our base mesh is ready for sculpting* section at the end of this chapter to learn how to convert Metaballs into a mesh.

See also

If you would like to learn more about Metaballs, you can read the official documentation here: https://docs.blender.org/manual/en/latest/modeling/metas/index.html.

Inserting meshes and cutting holes with Booleans

In the *Creating and transforming primitive objects* section of this chapter, we learned about adding new primitive shapes. This can help us create new shapes, but what about carving holes in geometry? We saw how useful carving a negative shape out of a model can be in the *Using Metaballs to build blob-like 3D forms* section of this chapter. However, the **Negative** option only works for Metaballs. If we want to do something similar to a mesh object, we have to use the Boolean modifier.

Getting ready

We'll start this section with a fresh Blender scene by using the **File | New | Sculpting** preset. Turn on the **Cavity** Viewport shading option so that we can visualize the depth of our geometry.

We'll be adding and moving objects around with our transformation tools, so make sure you understand the tools that were laid out in the *Creating and transforming primitive objects* section of this chapter.

How to do it...

Sculpt Mode does not have an **Add** menu, so to add an object, we must first switch to **Object Mode**:

1. Switch to **Object Mode** using the drop-down menu in the top-left corner of the header of the 3D Viewport.

2. Use the **Add** menu to add a **Mesh | Cube**.

3. Transform the cube with the **Move** and **Scale** tools so that it intersects the **Quad Sphere** object, as shown in the following diagram:

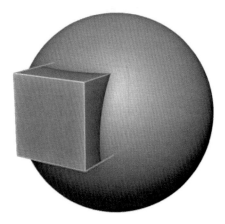

Figure 4.36 – A cube mesh intersecting the Quad Sphere object

Now, we're going to attach a Boolean modifier to the **Quad Sphere** object so that we can cut a hole in its surface using the shape of the cube:

1. Select the **Quad Sphere** object.

2. Navigate to the **Modifier** tab (represented by the blue wrench icon) in the Properties editor.

3. Click **Add Modifier** and choose the **Boolean** modifier from the **Generate** column.

4. In the settings for the **Boolean** modifier, click the **Object** slot and choose **Cube**.

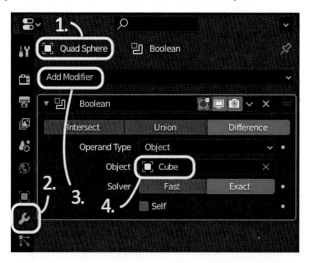

Figure 4.37 – The settings for the Boolean modifier in the Quad Sphere object

Excellent – we have a hole that's been cut in the **Quad Sphere** object. There's just one problem: the **Cube** object is blocking our view of the hole. We can fix this by adjusting the **Cube** object's Viewport display settings:

1. Select the **Cube** object.

2. Navigate to the **Object** tab (represented by the orange icon) in the Properties editor.

3. Scroll down the list of options and click to expand the **Viewport Display** section.

4. Click on the **Display As: Textured** drop-down list and choose **Bounds**.

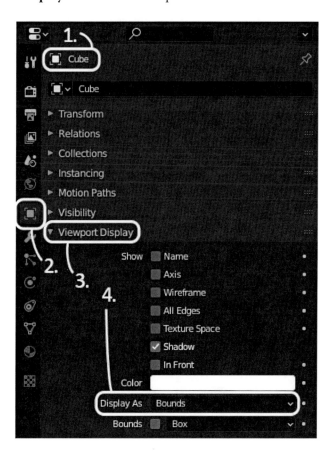

Figure 4.38 – The Viewport Display settings

That should do the trick. The **Cube** object will now only be visible as a bounding box, and we should be able to see through it into the hole in the **Quad Sphere** object.

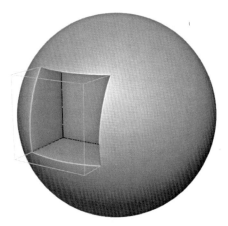

Figure 4.39 – The cube-shaped hole cut in the Quad Sphere using the Boolean modifier

What's super cool about this is that it's done dynamically through modifiers. If we want to change the placement of this hole, it's as easy as using the **Move** tool to reposition the **Cube** object. The **Boolean** modifier will keep cutting the hole wherever we move the cube to (this may run a little slow on your computer).

There are two other options for the **Boolean** modifier that we can use. Right now, we have it set to **Difference** (as seen in the Properties editor in *Figure 4.37*), which removes the **Cube** shape from the **Quad Sphere** object. We can use the **Union** mode as a way to merge the objects and connect the geometry. We can also try the **Intersect** mode, which keeps all of the geometry that both objects occupy but removes the rest. Try these three modes and see what interesting results you can come up with. Here are some examples:

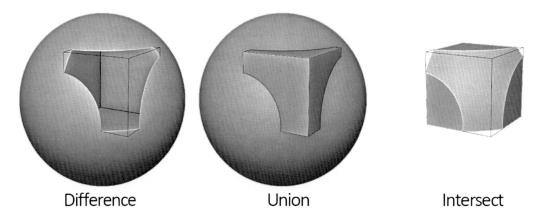

Figure 4.40 – The three Boolean operations performed on the Quad Sphere with the cube

Boolean modifiers are a lot of fun, and we can boolean together much more complex shapes as well. This is an excellent way to insert meshes into a sculpture (not just **Quad Sphere** objects).

How it works...

Booleans are a fairly expensive operation for our 3D software to perform. Be careful before applying a Boolean modifier. Always save your work in case the software can't handle the operation and crashes.

Boolean operations predate Blender's Voxel Remesher features and used to be the only way that we could properly merge two meshes. When we use the **Union** mode, the geometry isn't just intersecting; it removes all of the internal polygons and connects the components where the two objects touch, creating a perfectly sealed surface. Without this, we would just have two disconnected objects floating inside of each other, which wouldn't work well in sculpting.

See also

The Blender developers are always working hard on new features. Keep an eye out for the **Insert Mesh** brushes, which are currently in development by Blender's lead sculpt developer, Pablo Dobarro: `https://twitter.com/pablodp606/status/1321589952493326336`.

Using the Lasso Trim tool to add and remove geometry

We have one more technique to show off in this chapter. We'll be heading back to **Sculpt Mode** to try out the **Lasso Trim** tool. This tool offers an artistic approach to base mesh creation that 2D artists will appreciate. With this tool, we can draw shapes that become 3D geometry.

Getting ready

We'll start this section with a fresh Blender scene by using the **File** | **New** | **Sculpting** preset. Once we have our fresh scene, we can get started.

How to do it...

We're going to start by activating the **Lasso Trim** tool, which is hidden underneath the **Box Trim** tool:

1. Find the **Box Trim** tool on the Toolbar. This tool has a small arrow indicator in the bottom-right corner to let us know that there are similar tools stacked underneath it.

2. Click and hold the **Box Trim** tool to open a list of similar tools.

3. Choose the **Lasso Trim** tool from the list.

    Now, we need to adjust some settings for the tool. Take a look at the **Tool Settings** section of the header of the 3D Viewport:

Figure 4.41 – Tool Settings for the Lasso Trim tool

4. Change **Trim Mode** to **Join**.

5. Activate the checkbox labeled **Use Cursor for Depth**.

    Great – now, we can use our graphics pen to draw new shapes in the 3D Viewport.

6. Start with your pen on top of the **Quad Sphere** object so that the new shape will be created so that it matches the sphere's depth.

7. Press and hold your pen down on the tablet's surface. While held down, draw with your pen to create a lasso in the shape you would like to make.

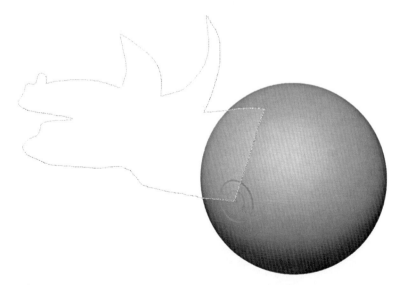

Figure 4.42 – A shape drawn with the Lasso Trim tool

8. Lift your pen to complete the shape.

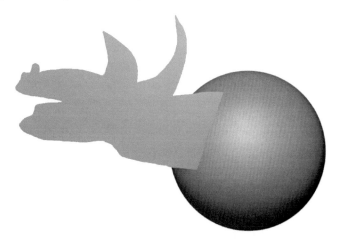

Figure 4.43 – The shape is turned into geometry

Have a look at the shape from other angles by orbiting the viewport around it. It has a thickness that reaches the depth of the 3D Cursor (right, now the 3D Cursor is invisible, but it is in the center of the **Quad Sphere** object).

> **Important Note**
> If your shape has no thickness, then that is because it didn't start with a depth far enough away from the 3D Cursor. You can undo this with the *Ctrl + Z* hotkey, and then try making a new shape. It can be helpful to zoom out so that the depth of the shape begins farther away from the 3D Cursor.

Try making several new shapes to create the shape of a creature.

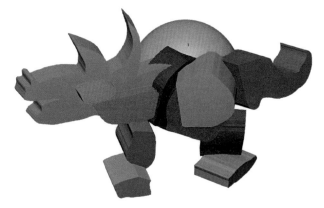

Figure 4.44 – Several lasso shapes can be used to design a creature

You'll notice that the new shapes have random colors. These colors are Blender's way of grouping the faces of these shapes. These colored groups of faces are called **Face Sets**.

> **Important Note**
> **Face Sets** are only visible when our **Viewport Overlays** are active. Make sure that you have **Viewport Overlays** toggled on and check the pop-over menu to make sure that the **Face Sets** overlay is enabled under the **Sculpt** section.

Face Sets are useful for defining specific areas of our sculptures. Once we have the areas defined with face sets, we can perform brush strokes and apply Mesh Filters to these areas; the effects of our tools will only apply within the specified face set. We can even hide or delete the faces that belong to a face set. To clean up this little creature, let's try removing the original sphere using the **Edit Face Sets** tool:

1. Find the **Edit Face Sets** tool near the bottom of the Toolbar and then click to activate it.

2. Look in the **Tool Settings** area of the header of the 3D Viewport and change **Mode** to **Delete Geometry**.

3. Click on the original gray-colored sphere to remove all of the polygons that belong to the original **Quad Sphere** shape.

Excellent – with that, we've created a little creature that we can use for sculpting.

How it works...

The **Lasso Trim** tool is somewhat similar to the **Boolean** modifier, which we learned about in the *Inserting meshes and cutting holes with Booleans* section of this chapter. The main difference is that we can draw custom shapes with the **Lasso Trim** tool.

This tool can also be used to cut away unwanted geometry when **Mode** is set to **Difference** (be aware that this can take extra time for your computer to process and that it may run slowly).

For this tool to be viable in sculpting, we will need to use the Voxel Remesher to add an even distribution of polygons across the surface of these shapes and merge all of the separate sections.

There's more...

Since we're using the 3D Cursor for depth, we can adjust how deep each of our new lasso shapes extends by moving the 3D Cursor. Try switching to **Object Mode** and use the **Cursor** tool to move the 3D Cursor (don't forget to enable the **3D Cursor** Viewport overlay so that you can see where you're moving the 3D Cursor to).

Making sure our base mesh is ready for sculpting

We've seen a lot of excellent ways to create base meshes in this chapter. Each of these techniques comes with upsides and downsides that we should be aware of. We'll conclude this chapter by going over several important things you need to know before finalizing a base mesh.

Several issues we must solve before our creations will serve as a suitable base mesh are as follows:

- Multiple objects should be joined together

- Transforms should be applied

- Non-contiguous pieces should usually be merged into a contiguous mesh

- Modifiers should be applied

- Non-mesh objects must be converted into a mesh

We'll look through some of our examples in this chapter and finish preparing them to be used as base meshes in Sculpt Mode.

Getting ready

For this section, we will be using the results from the previous sections. Some of the steps in this section don't apply to a few of the workflows discussed in this chapter, but you can follow along with any of your base mesh creations.

If you have not created any of your own base meshes, you can download and follow along with this section using with any of our examples from this chapter here: `https://github.com/PacktPublishing/Sculpting-the-Blender-Way/tree/main/Chapter04`.

How to do it...

It can be helpful to leave some areas separate to create hard transitions between shapes. For instance, eyeballs, hair, and clothing are more easily sculpted when they're kept as separate objects. However, the main body of our character will be the easiest to sculpt when we have merged all of its pieces. Our example from the *Creating and transforming primitive objects* section of this chapter does not meet this criterion.

To fix this, let's merge all of the primitive objects:

1. Select all of the mesh objects that need to be merged. This can be done by holding down the *Shift* key and clicking on each object, by pressing the *A* hotkey to select all objects, or by using the Outliner.

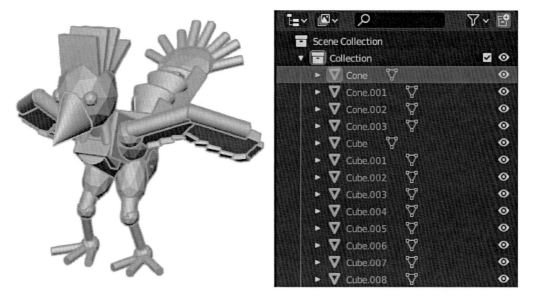

Figure 4.45 – The model is made up of many separate objects, as seen in the 3D Viewport and the Outliner

2. Make sure that only mesh objects are selected (lights and cameras should not be selected).

    One of the selected mesh pieces will be highlighted with a brighter orange color than the other objects. This object is known as the **active object**. If you do not have an active object, hold *Shift* and click on one of the selected mesh pieces to activate it. We're going to merge all of the other objects in this active object.

3. Find the **Object** menu in the top-left corner of the header of the 3D Viewport.

4. Choose **Join** to merge all of the selected objects in the active object.

Excellent – if you check the Outliner, you should only have one object left; the geometry of the other objects has been merged into the remaining object.

Our next concern is with the transforms of our remaining object. Sometimes, the **Location**, **Rotation**, and **Scale** transforms will have non-uniform values, as we can see in the Sidebar.

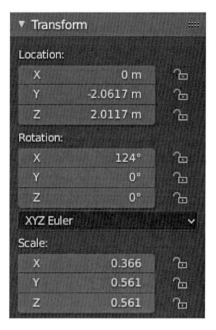

Figure 4.46 – Non-uniform transforms, as seen in the Item tab in the Sidebar

There are several things we need to consider for the best results. If we want our object to be compatible with symmetrical sculpting tools, then **X Location** should be 0 m, and ideally, **Rotation** should be 0, 0, 0 on **X**, **Y**, and **Z**.

Perhaps more important is the fact that **Scale** should always be 1, 1, 1 on **X**, **Y**, and **Z** so that our sculpting brushes behave correctly. If we try to enter **Sculpt Mode** on an object with **non-uniform scales**, the following warning will appear on the status bar at the bottom of the screen:

⚠ Object has non-uniform scale, sculpting may be unpredictable

Figure 4.47 – Object has non-uniform scale, sculpting may be unpredictable

To fix all of these issues with our transforms, we need to **apply** the transforms of our object. Applying these transforms will fix the values in our transforms while leaving our object's shape intact. Let's do this now.

5.   Open the **Object** menu in the top-left corner of the header of the 3D Viewport.

6.   Choose **Apply | All Transforms**.

Excellent – now, there's one more issue to deal with for this character. The pieces have been joined together, but the geometry of the primitive shapes is still separate. Separate parts within a single object are what are known as **non-contiguous** parts. Sometimes, non-contiguous parts can be helpful when sculpting anatomy; individual muscles can be kept non-contiguous in the early stages of a sculpt to create sharp transitions between each piece. However, these parts eventually need to be merged so that the sculpting brushes can treat the surfaces as one contiguous piece.

We learned about an excellent solution to this issue in the *Practicing the basics of the Voxel Remesher* section of *Chapter 2, Overview of Blender's Sculpting Workflows*. The Voxel Remesher can merge non-contiguous parts into one contiguous piece. If we turn on **X-ray** mode and look at this example, the difference is easy to see:

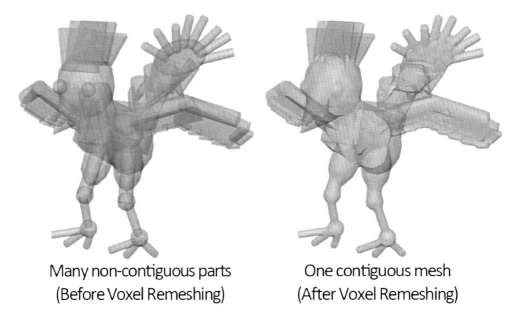

Many non-contiguous parts
(Before Voxel Remeshing)

One contiguous mesh
(After Voxel Remeshing)

Figure 4.48 – Non-contiguous versus contiguous visualized with X-ray shading

Notice how all of the intersecting geometry disappears after running the Voxel Remesher. This will make this object much easier to use as a base mesh.

Some of the techniques we have discussed in this chapter involved the use of modifiers. Because modifiers are dynamic, they can't be used in **Sculpt Mode** (with a few exceptions). To convert a modifier from its dynamic state into a state that is compatible with sculpting, we must apply the modifier:

1. Switch to **Object Mode** and select the object that has modifiers on it.

2. Navigate to the modifiers tab in the Properties editor.

3. Click on the downward arrow next to the icons at the top of the modifier settings and choose **Apply**.

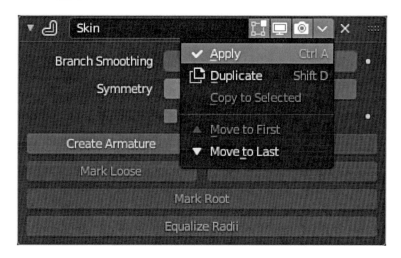

Figure 4.49 – The Apply option in the modifier settings

If you have multiple modifiers on a single object, apply them from top to bottom for the best results. You can also apply all the modifiers at the same time from the **Object** menu in the top-left corner of the header of the 3D Viewport by choosing **Apply | Visual Geometry To Mesh**.

As for objects that are created out of Metaballs or other non-mesh objects, we must convert these objects into a mesh.

4. To convert, switch to **Object Mode** and select the non-mesh object (such as a Metaball).

5. Find the **Object** menu in the top-left corner of the header of the 3D Viewport.

6. Choose **Convert To | Mesh**.

And there you have it – the final steps for converting our objects into base meshes that are ready for sculpting!

How it works...

These little bits of cleanup are necessary for our sculpting tools to behave correctly. It's a little annoying that we have to halt the creative process to take care of these issues, but it will make our lives much easier down the road. It will also improve the quality of our sculptures if we take care of these things at this early stage.

Now that you have some base meshes to play with, you can practice using the brushes and workflows that we learned about in *Chapter 3, Sculpting a Simple Character Head with Basic Brushes*, but this time, you won't have to start from a **Quad Sphere** object – you can create whatever base mesh you want!

There's more...

There is some debate as to what counts as a proper base mesh. Some artists argue that the polygons in the object must be arranged into perfect grid patterns before the object can be used as a base mesh. This process is beyond the scope of this chapter, but we will address this in *Chapter 5, Learning the Power of Subdivision and the Multiresolution Workflow*.

See also

If you would like to see our example files from this chapter, you can download them here: `https://github.com/PacktPublishing/Sculpting-the-Blender-Way/tree/main/Chapter04`.

5
Learning the Power of Subdivision and the Multiresolution Workflow

So far, in this book, we have learned how to create the larger forms of a model. However, we haven't had a chance to make any highly detailed sculptures yet. In this chapter, we'll learn about the appropriate workflow for creating highly detailed sculptures.

Before we can create detailed sculptures, we require a high-quality base mesh. We learned about all sorts of interesting techniques regarding how to create a base mesh in *Chapter 4, How to Make a Base Mesh for a 3D Sculpture*. Additionally, we learned how to use the Voxel Remesher to create a base mesh with our sculpting tools.

However, many of these base mesh creation techniques lack one major thing: a good topology for high-resolution sculpting. We will begin this chapter by learning about topology – in particular, what makes a topology good or bad for sculpting? Also, we'll learn how to use Blender's automatic **QuadriFlow Remesher** tool to generate a topology that can be used for the next part of the sculpting process.

Following this, we will learn about **Subdivision Surfaces**. Subdivision is a staple of 3D modeling software. It allows you to quickly create additional polygons for our models and, therefore, makes the model look smoother with a higher resolution.

Once we have a good understanding of how subdivision works, we can move on to the most important topic for highly detailed sculptures: **Multiresolution**. This is very closely related to subdivision, and it's a keystone element in any high-quality sculpture.

The main topics in this chapter are as follows:

- An overview of topology
- Generating an all-quad mesh with QuadriFlow
- Exploring subdivision surfaces
- Understanding when you're ready for multiresolution
- Using the Multiresolution modifier
- Recapturing details from the previous mesh
- Changing resolution for appropriate details

Technical requirements

For general requirements, please refer back to the *Technical requirements* section that was laid out in *Chapter 1, Exploring Blender's User Interface for Sculpting*.

You can download the files to follow along with this book at the GitHub link here: `https://github.com/PacktPublishing/Sculpting-the-Blender-Way`.

An overview of topology

In *Chapter 2, Overview of Blender's Sculpting Workflows*, we learned a little bit about topology. In the *Creating dynamic topology with Dyntopo* section of that chapter, we learned that **Topology** is a term we use to describe how all of the components (such as vertices, edges, and faces) of a mesh are interconnected. The topology of a model is not the same thing as the shape of the model. The positions of vertices, edges, and faces can move around and deform without changing the topology as long as none of the connecting edges are removed, rearranged, or added. For example, in the following diagram, we can observe two mesh objects with identical topology but different shapes:

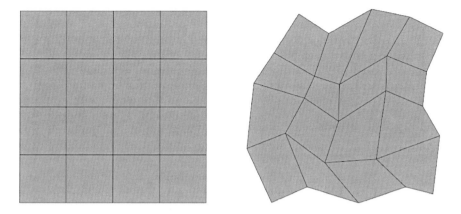

Figure 5.1 – Two objects with the same topology but different shapes

In this example, the object on the left-hand side is made out of 16 quadrilaterals (quads). The topology of these quads forms a simple grid pattern. The object on the right-hand side has the same number of vertices (25), edges (40), and faces (16), and the connections between these components are identical. The only difference is that the components have been moved around so that the shape of the object is different.

The opposite is possible as well; we can have the same shape but a different topology, as illustrated in the following diagram:

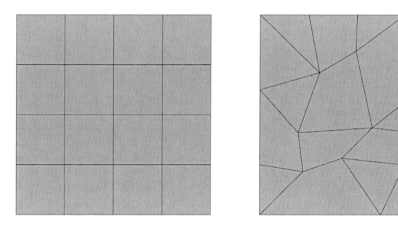

Figure 5.2 – Two objects with the same shape but a different topology

In the preceding example, each of the objects forms a square with the same dimensions. We can describe them as having the same shape. However, the object on the right-hand side has a completely different arrangement of geometry, along with a different number of vertices (21), edges (37), and faces (17). This second object has a different topology than the first object.

In the *Discovering the limitations of the basic sculpting mode* section of *Chapter 2, Overview of Blender's Sculpting Workflows*, we learned that there is a close relationship between the topology of an object and the shape of an object. The shape can be deformed, but only within a small limit. If you push the shape past this limit, the polygons will become stretched out and the topology will no longer support the shape properly. This can lead to bad (or even completely unusable) results in our sculptures.

We briefly looked at how to combat this limitation by using the dynamic topology feature. It produces a topology that looks something like this:

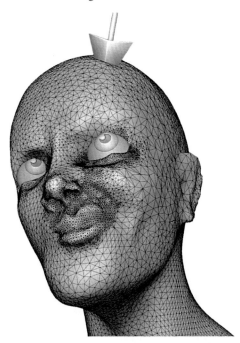

Figure 5.3 – The topology generated by the dynamic topology (Dyntopo) feature

This topology is certainly better than a bunch of stretched-out polygons, as the shapes of the sculpture are being supported by lots of little triangles. However, this type of topology has many issues. For instance, there are no clear patterns to follow, and many areas are jagged and can't be easily smoothed. This surface is prone to shading errors, and it will be nearly impossible to get crisp lines around the eyelids, upper lip, or anywhere else that requires better topology.

Because of these issues, we've avoided using the Dyntopo feature throughout this book. Instead, we've been using the Voxel Remesher to alter the topology of our sculptures and quickly generate new polygons to support the shapes we want to sculpt. The topology from this workflow appears similar to the following:

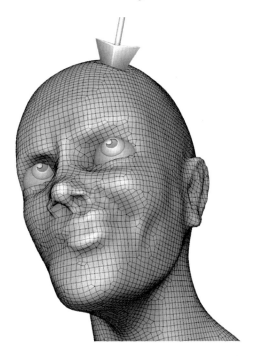

Figure 5.4 – The topology generated by the Voxel Remesher

This cleans up many of the issues that we had with our previous example, but it still has problems. The Voxel Remesher works based on a 3D grid – the generated topology always follows the grid. This is excellent for getting quick results, but it doesn't make the best topology for highly detailed sculptures.

In the *Creating a base mesh with box modeling* section of *Chapter 4, How to Make a Base Mesh for a 3D Sculpture*, we briefly touched on the idea of Edge Loops. **Edge Loops** are a crucial part of topology. Edge Loops are naturally formed in between the quads in a grid pattern. In a good topology, the edges are guided through the surface of the model giving it good **edge flow**. In the preceding example, we have a grid pattern, but we do not have a good edge flow. The edges follow the voxel grid pattern instead of flowing through the facial features of the character.

When we're ready to add details to a model, we need to rearrange the topology so that it follows the contours and details of the sculpture instead of blindly following the voxel grid patterns. A better result for high detail sculpting should look similar to the following example:

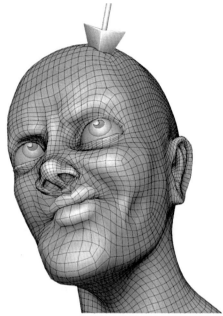

Figure 5.5 – The topology that is ready for the detail stage of the sculpting process

In the preceding example, notice how the polygons follow the contours of the lips, jaw, eyelids, brow, and other features. While this example might not be perfect (there's no such thing as perfect), it is much cleaner than either of the previous examples, and it will work well for us when we get into sculpting the highly detailed parts because the topology is reinforcing the contours and shapes of the model.

One downside to this type of topology is that it requires us to nail down the shape of the sculpture first. If we wanted to add new larger features to this character, such as a pair of horns, this topology wouldn't allow for those additions. That's why we use the Voxel Remesher and our other base mesh creation methods for the early stages of the sculpting process. When we're ready to sculpt the high-resolution details, we need to upgrade the model to this better type of topology and stop using the Voxel Remesher.

For the best results, we need to learn about the topology arrangements that will create the most efficient sculptures and how we can achieve these results. There is a lot to learn about topology. However, we're just going to focus on several of the simple ideas because this is a book about sculpting, and we want to get you back to sculpting instead of spending too much time reading about technical subjects.

In this section, we'll explore the topology of a character model and highlight some of the key features that we need to look for in a good topology.

Getting ready

Download the example `highResCharacterTopology.blend` character file from `https://github.com/PacktPublishing/Sculpting-the-Blender-Way/blob/main/Chapter05/highResCharacterTopology.blend`.

Launch Blender and open the `highResCharacterTopology.blend` file. Once you've opened the file, we're ready to explore the topology of this sculpture.

How to do it...

The character in this `.blend` file is named Lilly. Lilly is made up of many individual pieces. Each of these pieces have been given an appropriate topology to represent their shapes. Turn on the **Wireframe** display in the **Viewport Overlays** pop-over menu so that we can view her topology. With this display turned on, grid patterns will be laid on top of the character, as shown in the following screenshot:

Figure 5.6 – The high-resolution character Lilly with the wireframe overlay turned on

Take a look at the polygons on Lilly's sweatshirt – they work together to form a very clean grid pattern that follows the sleeves, torso, hood, pull strings, and other areas appropriately. Instead of thinking about the Edge Loops of this mesh, it can be helpful to look at the Face Loops. **Face Loops** are almost the same thing as Edge Loops, but they are made of faces instead of edges – who would have guessed?

Face Loops are always formed when quads are adjacent to each other. Triangles and n-gons do not contribute to Face Loops. If we place enough quads together, we will end up with very clean grid patterns that are made up of Face Loops. To visualize the Face Loops, let's hop into **Edit Mode** to explore Lilly's sweatshirt:

1. Select Lilly's sweatshirt.
2. Press the *Tab* key to enter **Edit Mode**.
3. Hover your mouse over one of the quads around the midsection of the sweatshirt.
4. Hold down the *Alt* key and click to select a face loop:

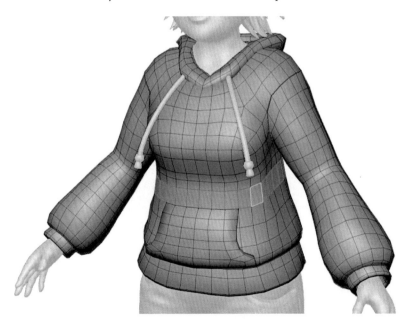

Figure 5.7 – A face loop around the midsection of the sweatshirt, highlighted in orange

All 3D software comes with shortcuts with which we select entire Face Loops like this. These loops are crucial for creating high-quality models. For now, we're just exploring the existing topology in this model. Notice how the face loop flows all the way around the character's midsection to form a complete loop. There are many loops exactly like this one that work together to form the entirety of the midsection. Try holding the *Alt* key and clicking on more faces of the model. Notice how the quads wrap around the sleeves, the hood, and the other areas to support the shape of the sweatshirt. This is a good topology.

Up next, let's explore the character's face:

1. Press the *Tab* key to exit **Edit Mode**.
2. Select Lilly's head.
3. Press the *Tab* key again to enter **Edit Mode** for the head mesh.
4. Zoom in on Lilly's head.
5. Hold down the *Alt* key and click to select a face loop near her mouth:

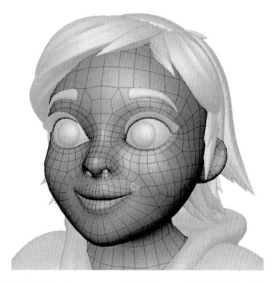

Figure 5.8 – A face loop around Lilly's mouth, highlighted in orange

Notice how the quads form a circle around Lilly's mouth area. There are several Face Loops just like this one surrounding her mouth. These concentric circles will help to reinforce the details of her lips during the high-resolution sculpting process. We can view a similar arrangement around Lilly's eyes:

1. Hold down the *Alt* key and click to select a face loop near her eye:

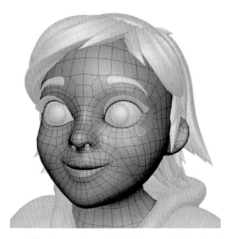

Figure 5.9 – A face loop around Lilly's eye, highlighted in orange

Once again, pay attention to how the quads form a circle around the eye. This will help us a lot when we go to sharpen the eyelids. There are other helpful loops in this character's topology as well; for instance, the jaw.

2. Orbit the 3D Viewport so that we can observe Lilly's jawline.

3. Hold down the *Alt* key and click to select the face loop that follows the jawline:

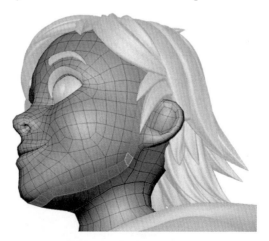

Figure 5.10 – A face loop following the contour of Lilly's jawline, highlighted in orange

This is another very common face loop to observe in good topology for a character's head. At least one face loop following the jawline will give us the structure that we need to make a pronounced jawline in the high-resolution sculpture.

Please feel free to keep exploring the topology of this character before moving on.

How it works...

Good topology is not just about grid patterns; it's about good edge flow that supports the shapes of our sculptures. The best way to visualize this edge flow is by highlighting Face Loops and Edge Loops in the topology of the model.

There's no such thing as a perfect topology. The topology just has to be arranged well enough to support the shapes we are trying to sculpt. Generally, it is a good thing to have the mesh be made entirely out of quads instead of using triangles and n-gons because only quads create Face Loops.

The Voxel Remesher does not create good Face Loops. So, next, we will learn about a better way to generate a topology that can be used for the high detail stage of the sculpting process.

Generating an all-quad mesh with QuadriFlow

So far, we've been using the Voxel Remesher to generate new polygons for our sculptures. We learned about this type of remeshing in the *Practicing the basics of the Voxel Remesher* section of *Chapter 2, Overview of Blender's Sculpting Workflows*. The advantage of the Voxel Remesher algorithm is that it generates new geometry almost instantaneously, so we can use it while we sculpt. However, the arrangement of the polygons is not ideal for a finished base mesh.

As we learned in the *An overview of topology* section of this chapter, the polygons of a base mesh should flow through the details of the model, supporting things such as the mouth, eye sockets, bridge of the nose, and more.

In this section, we will try using the **QuadriFlow remesher** to convert a model into a base mesh with good edge flow that can be used in high-resolution sculpting.

Getting ready

In this section, we need to start with a sculpture that we can remesh. You can follow the instructions in this section using a sculpture of your own. If you would rather start this section using our example, download and open the `voxelCharacterHead.blend` file at `https://github.com/PacktPublishing/Sculpting-the-Blender-Way/blob/main/Chapter05/voxelCharacterHead.blend`.

Launch Blender, and open the .blend file for your sculpture. The provided example has already been set up correctly; however, if you're using your own sculpture, switch to **Object Mode**. Open the **Viewport Overlays** pop-over menu and turn on **Wireframe**. Then, set the wireframe value to 1.000 so that we can view all the edges of the sculpture.

Once this has all been set up, we'll be ready to use QuadriFlow to remesh the sculpture.

How to do it...

Because we are in **Object Mode**, we have a variety of options available for making adjustments to the whole object, including the QuadriFlow remesh settings. With the sculpture selected, several colored tabs will appear in the **Properties** editor:

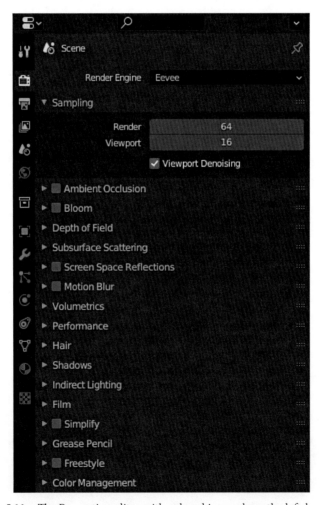

Figure 5.11 – The Properties editor with colored icons along the left-hand side

Each of these colored tabs contains settings and information about our model. To remesh this model with the QuadriFlow remesher, we need to turn our attention to the green triangle-shaped **Object Data Properties** tab:

1. Click on the green object data tab to view the settings related to the geometry of the model.

2. Scroll down to find the **Remesh** subsection of the **Object Data Properties** tab.

3. Click on the drop-down arrow to the left-hand side of **Remesh** to expand this subsection:

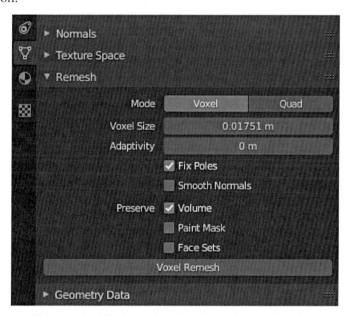

Figure 5.12 – The Remesh settings in the Properties editor

Note that the current **Mode** setting is set to **Voxel** – this should look familiar. These are the same settings that we've used to voxel remesh our sculpture. So far, in this book, we've accessed these settings via the 3D Viewport header while in **Sculpt Mode**. Now that we've switched to **Object Mode**, we can access some additional settings right here in the **Properties** editor.

To generate a base mesh with a good edge flow, we need to change the remeshing from **Mode** to **Quad**.

Important Note

The QuadriFlow remesher is a relatively recent addition to Blender. As of writing, the user interface for this feature is awkward to use, but it might be improved for future releases of Blender.

Once we've switched to **Quad** mode, we can access the QuadriFlow remesh settings by clicking on the **QuadriFlow Remesh** button. The settings pop-up menu will appear, which you can view in the following screenshot:

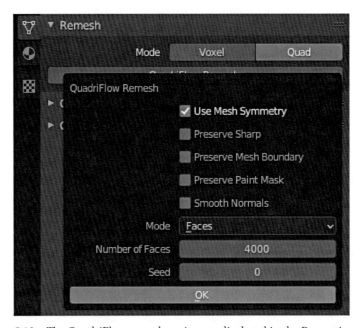

Figure 5.13 – The QuadriFlow remesh options as displayed in the Properties editor

We can adjust the target number of polygons we would like the QuadriFlow algorithm to generate. Let's try 9,000:

1. Change the **Number of Faces** setting from 4000 to 9000.

2. Click on the **OK** button.

    This could take a few seconds to process. You can observe the progress in the status bar at the very bottom of Blender's user interface. When the QuadriFlow remesher is finished, your sculpture will be updated to have a clean arrangement of quadrilateral polygons:

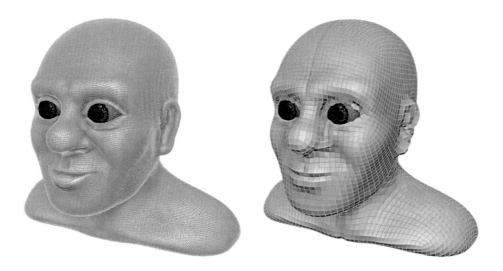

Figure 5.14 – The remeshed character before and after using the QuadriFlow remesher

Sometimes, the **Use Mesh Symmetry** option in the QuadriFlow remesh settings can leave behind holes along the symmetry line of the remeshed object. If this happens to your sculpture, you can try fixing it by performing these steps:

1. Click on the **Modifiers** tab in the **Properties** editor (it's the blue wrench-shaped tab).
2. Click on **Add Modifier**, and choose **Mirror** underneath the **Generate** column.
3. Click on the **X** toggle next to **Bisect** so that we don't introduce any unwanted geometry across the symmetry line.
4. Set the **Merge** value high enough to seal all of the holes along the symmetry line. In our example, 0.03 m works well.
5. Click on the drop-down arrow in the upper-right corner of the **Mirror** modifier and choose **Apply**.

Our example character turned out as follows:

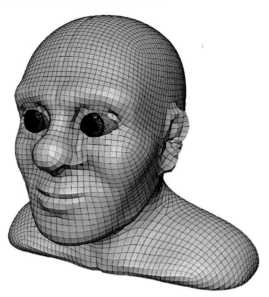

Figure 5.15 – The final topology after using the QuadriFlow remesher and fixing the holes

You might be thinking that this result looks worse than the previous version of the sculpture. However, that is to be expected for a finished base mesh. This is actually a good start. It's not supposed to have all of the details – it just needs to have a topology that supports the major shapes. By the end of this chapter, we'll have understood how to use a base mesh such as this in the multiresolution workflow to create the high-resolution details that we have been unable to create with previous methods.

How it works...

The **Quad** remesher uses the QuadriFlow algorithm to analyze the model and identify contours and major shapes. This type of remeshing will take a lot longer than voxel remeshing. However, when it's finished, the topology should follow the contours of the sculpture.

We can use QuadriFlow to convert almost any model into a base mesh that is ready for the next stages of the sculpting workflow. Many of the base meshes that we learned to create in *Chapter 4, How to Make a Base Mesh for a 3D Sculpture*, will need to be remeshed in this way. The QuadriFlow remesher works best if the input geometry has been completely merged before running the remeshing algorithm. If your input geometry is made from non-contiguous parts, you might need to run the Voxel Remesher once with a small voxel size in order to merge all of the pieces together before using QuadriFlow to generate a good edge flow for the base mesh.

There's more...

Some of the details of the original sculpture might have been lost during this remeshing process. If we keep a copy of the original sculpture around, we can reproject the details from the old sculpture onto the newly remeshed sculpture so that we get the details back. We will learn how to do this in the *Recapturing details from the previous mesh* section of this chapter.

See also

Blender's built-in option for quad remeshing uses the QuadriFlow algorithm. You can read more about the differences between the QuadriFlow remesher and the Voxel Remesher at `https://docs.blender.org/manual/en/latest/modeling/meshes/retopology.html`.

QuadriFlow is not the only option available for automatic quad remeshing. There are several premium options that are available as add-ons. An excellent place to shop for resources is the **Blender Market**: `https://blendermarket.com`. Here, there are several remeshing tools available for various use cases. The Blender Market is organized by the Blender community, so new tools are available all the time.

One of the highest quality automatic remeshing tools is the **Exoside Quad Remesher**, which is available at `https://exoside.com/quadremesher/`. This tool is not a particularly affordable option for hobbyists. However, if you require the best results possible from a one-click solution, the results of this tool are excellent.

Exploring subdivision surfaces

The **Catmull–Clark Subdivision Surface** algorithm was invented by some of the very talented engineers at Pixar. It has been a very important innovation in the 3D industry, as it provides you with a way in which to make models look smoother. This is achieved by taking input geometry and dividing all of the polygons into smaller polygons. Then, the spacing between the vertices of these new polygons is averaged to create a smooth result.

This algorithm works especially well with quadrilaterals. Each quad can be divided vertically and horizontally at the same time, which turns a single quad into a small grid of four quads. This algorithm can be repeated for multiple levels of subdivision. A second iteration on a quad will result in 16 small quads in a very clean grid pattern, as you can view in the following diagram:

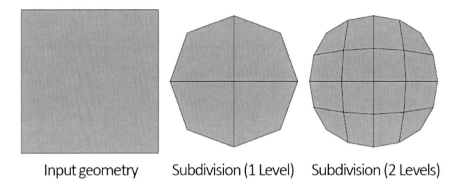

Input geometry   Subdivision (1 Level)   Subdivision (2 Levels)

Figure 5.16 – A quad with various levels of subdivision

Generally, two levels of the subdivision are enough for good results. This can be somewhat expensive for our computers to calculate because of the exponential nature of this algorithm. When working with subdivision surfaces, we tend to work with input geometry that has relatively few polygons and good edge flow.

In this section, we will take a look at what subdivision can do for our models. Later in this chapter, we will learn how subdivision is relevant to the sculpting workflow.

Getting ready

Download the example `subdivisionExamples.blend` file from `https://github.com/PacktPublishing/Sculpting-the-Blender-Way/blob/main/Chapter05/subdivisionExamples.blend`.

Launch Blender, and open the `subdivisionExamples.blend` file. Once you've opened the file, we're ready to try subdividing some models.

How to do it...

The example file has six example models, as you can see in the following diagram:

Figure 5.17 – Six example objects, from left to right: Cube, Suzanne, Hand, Bottle, Sharpener, and Cylinder

Some of these objects will work better with subdivision than others. Let's work our way from left to right and add subdivisions. We'll start with the cube:

1. Click on the **Cube** object to select it.

2. Open the **View** menu in the upper-left corner of the 3D Viewport and choose **Frame Selected**. This will zoom in and center the cube so that we can see what we will be doing in the next steps.

> **Tip**
>
> It is useful to use the **Frame Selected** option each time we work on a different object or when we work on a different piece of the same object. If you have a numpad on your keyboard, you can use the period hotkey (.) on the numpad to frame the selection. Alternatively, you can press the tilde key (~) to open the **View** pie menu and choose **View Selected** in the lower-right corner of the pie menu.

3. If the viewport ends up zoomed in too far, use the scroll wheel to zoom out until you can view the whole cube.

    Now we're ready to add subdivision to the model. In Blender, subdivision is available as a modifier. We learned a little bit about modifiers in *Chapter 4*, *How to Make a Base Mesh for a 3D Sculpture*. We will use the **Properties** editor to add a **Subdivision Surface** modifier to the cube.

4. Click on the blue wrench tab in the **Properties** editor to switch to the **Modifiers** tab.

5. Click on **Add Modifier** and choose **Subdivision Surface** from the **Generate** column in the list of modifiers.

6. Increase the **Levels Viewport** value from 1 to 2.

Excellent! The cube has gone from 6 quads to 24 quads, to 96 quads. The extra vertices of the cube have their positions averaged to create a smooth surface, as you can see in the following diagram:

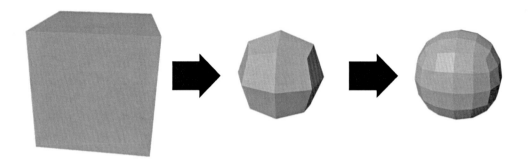

Figure 5.18 – A cube with no subdivision, one level of subdivision, and two levels of subdivision

---

Important Note

The **Subdivision Surface** modifier adds polygons to the model at an exponential rate. Two levels of subdivision are enough for most models – anything higher will usually take a long time to process. You will most likely never need to go higher than six, as subdivision levels past this point will almost always cause your computer to run out of memory and crash Blender.

The cube looks a lot smoother now because of the subdivision algorithm. The rigid corners have smoothed out and the end result is a Quad Sphere. The way in which these objects become smoother is completely dependent on the topology of the input geometry. Models with good edge flow will be better at retaining their original shapes when subdivision is applied. Let's repeat this process for each object in the scene and watch what happens to their shapes.

Tip

There is a hotkey for quickly applying a Subdivision Surface modifier to the selected object. While in **Object Mode**, press *Ctrl + 2* to add a **Subdivision Surface** modifier with two levels of subdivision.

When subdivision is applied to Suzanne (the monkey), she goes from being very blocky to looking very smooth. Her original shape has been a lot better retained than the shape of the cube. We can view a before and after comparison in the following diagram:

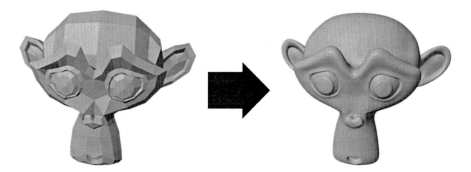

Figure 5.19 – Suzanne with no subdivision (on the left-hand side) and two levels of subdivision (on the right-hand side)

This is an excellent use case for subdivision; look at her ears, brow, and nose. Each of these shapes has had its structure defined by the topology of the input geometry – we can clearly see the polygons supporting these areas. Subdivision has emphasized each of these features by adding polygons and smoothing.

However, Suzanne is still looking a little bit faceted. A bit like a diamond, each face is catching the light, and she doesn't look very smooth yet. Instead of adding more levels of subdivision, we can request the edges of the model to blur together by applying a different type of shading to this geometry. Right now, Suzanne is using **Flat Shading**. Let's change this to **Smooth Shading**:

1. Make sure Suzanne is still selected.
2. Open the **Object** menu in the upper-left corner of the 3D Viewport and choose **Shade Smooth**:

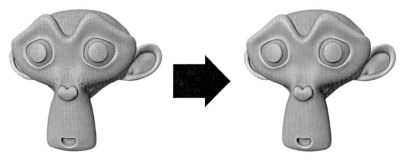

Figure 5.20 – Suzanne with flat shading (on the left-hand side) and smooth shading (on the right-hand side)

There, she's looking very smooth now. Smooth shading makes the edges between the polygons appear smoother without adding any additional geometry. This feature is not part of the subdivision surfaces algorithm, but it does work very well when used alongside subdivision.

Now, let's take a look at the hand model. Select the hand, frame it in the viewport so that we can get a good look at it, then give it two levels of subdivision. The result can be viewed in the following diagram:

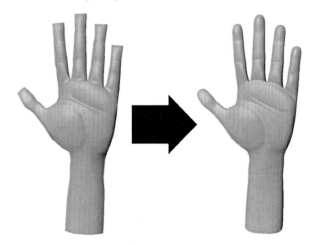

Figure 5.21 – The hand model with no subdivision and two levels of subdivision

The blocky fingertips have been completely rounded out by subdivision. Additionally, all other areas of the hand have been given extra smoothness. We can visualize this better by turning on the wireframe overlay:

3. Open the **Viewport Overlays** pop-over menu and activate the **Wireframe** overlay.

4. Observe the settings for the **Subdivision Surface** modifier in the **Properties** editor, and toggle off the **Optimal Display** setting:

Figure 5.22 – The wireframe of the subdivided hand with and without the Optimal Display setting enabled

Notice that the original topology of the hand model has a direct influence over the resulting topology of the subdivided hand. All of the original Edge Loops and Face Loops are still there; subdivision simply added divisions between these loops. It is important for our models to have good topology when we use the subdivision algorithm.

Turn off the wireframe overlay before moving on. Following this, we can look at the other examples. Select the bottle, frame it in the viewport so that we can get a good look at its spout, then give it two levels of subdivision. The result can be viewed in the following diagram:

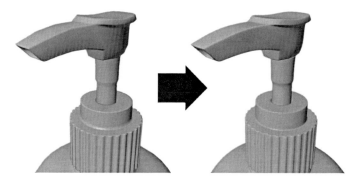

Figure 5.23 – The bottle model with no subdivision and two levels of subdivision

Here, the effect is subtle. The original model already looked pretty smooth, in part because it had smooth shading applied to it. However, in this scenario, adding subdivision is still helpful for the extremely high-level detail. This model goes from looking good to very refined and polished. We can no longer make out any jagged edges along the spout; even the smooth shaded edges look crisper.

We need to understand that subdivision is only as good as the input geometry. If the geometry doesn't have a topology that works well with subdivision, then we're going to get bad results. Let's see what happens to the sharpener model when we try to add subdivision. Select the sharpener, frame it in the viewport, then give it two levels of subdivision. The result can be viewed in the following diagram:

Figure 5.24 – The pencil sharpener model with no subdivision and two levels of subdivision

Oh, no! This model did not hold up well under subdivision. This is because the topology of this model was not created with subdivision in mind. Let's take a look at the problems within this model:

1. Turn on the wireframe overlay again so that we can view the topology of the sharpener.

2. Remove the **Subdivision Surface** modifier by clicking on the **X** toggle in the upper-right corner of the modifier settings in the **Properties** editor.

Good, now we can view the topology of the sharpener:

Figure 5.25 – The pencil sharpener's topology

It has lots of triangles and a lack of grid patterns across its surface. The left-hand side of the top area is made out of many triangles that have no discernible pattern. Similarly, the front area surrounding the circular hole is made up of many triangles, so there is no grid pattern here either. Subdivision does not work well with this type of topology. This type of model might be useful for other applications such as video games where subdivision isn't necessary. However, for our purposes, we won't be able to use a topology such as this.

Lastly, let's take a look at another problematic example: the cylinder. Select the cylinder object, frame it in the viewport, then give it two levels of subdivision. The result can be seen in the following diagram:

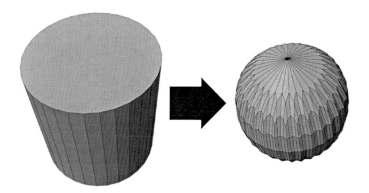

Figure 5.26 – The cylinder with no subdivision and two levels of subdivision

In the preceding example, the top of the cylinder is made from an n-gon. This n-gon becomes subdivided into one of the most infamously problematic types of topology: a **high valence pole**. There are so many edges connected to this single vertex that we end up with a strange star-shaped pattern with a wavy surface. No amount of smoothing will reduce this problem. Bad topology has ruined this model.

There's a lot more to learn about topology and how it interacts with subdivision. However, this is a book about sculpting, not topology, so it's time for us to move on.

How it works...

The subdivision algorithm is particularly good at making objects look smooth. The underlying structure of the model's topology is still there; it's just been divided and made smoother.

You might already have some guesses as to how subdivision can be useful for us in our sculpting workflow. We understand that in order to sculpt highly detailed models, we require lots of polygons. However, for the surfaces of our models to look really clean and of high quality, we need to have good topology.

Subdivision is the first part of the solution for making high-quality sculptures; the second part is multiresolution, which we will learn about shortly.

See also

There are some excellent examples of topology that are well suited for subdivision. They are available at `https://graphics.pixar.com/opensubdiv/docs/mod_notes.html`.

Understanding when you're ready for multiresolution

We took a brief look at the multiresolution workflow in the *Exploring the most powerful sculpting mode – multiresolution* section of *Chapter 2, Overview of Blender's Sculpting Workflows*. We learned that multiresolution is the best way to create highly detailed sculptures. Of course, there is a problem with multiresolution; it requires us to commit to a particular shape and create a topology that supports this shape.

The earliest stages of the sculpting workflow are all about deciding what that shape is going to be. However, it can be difficult to know when you've gone far enough and whether you're ready to start the multiresolution stage. If you switch to multiresolution too early, you might end up being unable to add large additional details to the model. However, if you switch to multiresolution too late, then some of the details that you've already sculpted could be lost in the transition.

In this section, we'll take a look at some examples that will give you a good idea regarding when you're ready to make the switch to multiresolution.

Getting ready

Download the example `voxelVSQuad.blend` character file at `https://github.com/PacktPublishing/Sculpting-the-Blender-Way/blob/main/Chapter05/voxelVSQuad.blend`.

Launch Blender and open the `voxelVSQuad.blend` file. Once you've opened the file, we'll be ready to start.

How to do it...

In this file, you'll find three vampire character heads. Let's take a look at the one on the left-hand side:

1. Click on the **head_voxelRemeshed** object on the left-hand side to select it.

2. Open the **View** menu in the upper-left corner of the 3D Viewport and choose **Frame Selected**.

   Take a look at the model for a moment. Once you're used to the way it looks, take a look at it again with the wireframe turned on.

3. Open the **Viewport Overlays** pop-over menu and activate the **Wireframe** overlay.

   Excluding the teeth and the eyes, this vampire character has been created using the Voxel Remesher. This should be obvious to you by now given the grid pattern that can be observed in the following diagram:

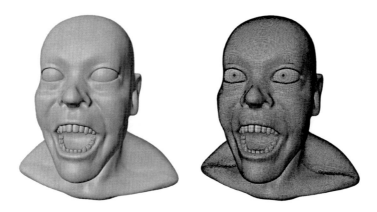

Figure 5.27 – The vampire character with the Voxel Remesher topology

This character has just the right level of detail for us to begin the multiresolution phase. But how do we know that? We're starting to bump up against the limits of what the Voxel Remesher can do. The polygon density is very high on this model and it's starting to create issues. The eyelids have been sharpened with the Pinch brush, which creates a very crisp edge. However, because of the way the Voxel Remesher works, these crisp edges will be erased if we run the Voxel Remesher again. Crisp details won't be properly preserved in the sculpting process unless we begin using multiresolution.

Additionally, there are other problems present in this model. In some areas, the topology is creating a very lumpy surface. Observe the perimeter of the upper lip; additionally, take a look at the ridge between the nostril and the corner of the mouth. These diagonal areas are fighting against the current topology, so it is not possible to create a smooth surface here until we begin multiresolution.

Some details are always lost when we convert from our old topology into our multiresolution-ready topology. For this reason, we want to avoid putting in too much detail prior to multiresolution. Don't bother trying to sculpt wrinkles, skin pores, small scars, or other little details yet. Even the sharpened eyelids are a little bit too detailed at this stage.

Before we move on to the multiresolution phase, we need to determine whether all of the major forms are in place. Do we need to add anything while we're still in the Voxel Remesher stage: horns? Elf ears? A third eye? A body? These things must all be added before entering multiresolution.

This vampire character isn't going to have a complete body, and all of the shapes we want to capture are here. All of the other details, such as the teeth and eyeballs, can be done as separate objects. So, everything is properly in place, and we can generate a better topology for the model. We already learned how to do this in the *Generating an all-quad mesh with QuadriFlow* section of this chapter.

The result from this process can be viewed on the middle vampire head in the example file. Select the middle head and frame the selection. Take a look at it with and without the wireframe overlay:

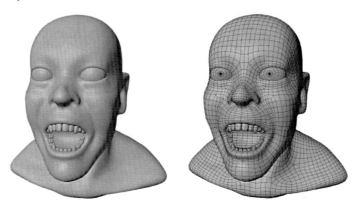

Figure 5.28 – The vampire character with multiresolution-ready topology

The difference in shape between these two versions of the model is subtle; that's a good thing! This means that most of the details were captured in the new topology. The benefit to this new topology is that it flows with the details of the sculpture. We won't get the jagged lines around the corner of the mouth or the lip anymore.

One thing worth mentioning is that we can still deform the character after this stage; facial expressions and general contortions are completely acceptable. Take a look at the third head example on the far right, as shown in the following screenshot:

Figure 5.29 – The vampire character after being smeared around relentlessly

This is the same vampire base mesh that we looked at a moment ago. The topology is exactly the same, but the shape has been smeared around like some kind of strange modern art piece. Distortions like this are acceptable even after we begin multiresolution; however, new limbs and details can't be added. In fact, the three blobs coming off the back of the vampire's head aren't part of the original topology; they had to be added as separate objects. At this stage, we can't cut holes, tear off pieces, or add new, larger forms to the sculpture.

We need to make good decisions about which shapes to capture in our topology before we begin multiresolution; surface details can be added back in later, and some distortion of the shape is acceptable.

How it works...

The shift from using the Voxel Remesher to using multiresolution can take a little bit of practice to get used to. It's a careful balance of sculpting enough detail to inform our final shapes, but not sculpting too much detail that it will then be lost in the transfer.

There's more...

If you sculpted too many details prior to multiresolution, we can recapture the details using a method laid out in the *Recapturing details from the previous mesh* section of this chapter.

Using the Multiresolution modifier

Here it is – the moment we've been hyping up for the entire book – the **Multiresolution modifier**! This is perhaps the single most important part of the high-resolution sculpting workflow.

Through the use of this modifier, we will be able to get all the benefits of a low-resolution base mesh with good topology, but we also get the benefits of a high-resolution mesh that has enough polygons to support highly detailed sculptures.

Oddly enough, we've already learned about the key ingredients of how to make multiresolution work: good topology and subdivision surfaces. The Multiresolution modifier uses the exact same algorithm as the Subdivision Surface modifier. The key differences are that multiresolution allows us to sculpt on top of each level of subdivision, allowing for higher and higher levels of detail as we increase the resolution. This is the primary way in which 3D sculptures are created in professional work.

In this section, we will try using the Multiresolution modifier on a base mesh and, finally, see the workflow come together.

Getting ready

Download the example `multiresolutionVampireHead.blend` character file at `https://github.com/PacktPublishing/Sculpting-the-Blender-Way/blob/main/Chapter05/multiresolutionVampireHead.blend`.

Launch Blender and open the `multiresolutionVampireHead.blend` file. Once you've opened the file, we'll be ready to use the Multiresolution modifier.

How to do it...

We'll start by adding the Multiresolution modifier to the base mesh:

1. Click on the **Vampire** head object to select it.

2. Click on the blue wrench tab, in the **Properties** editor, to switch to the **Modifiers** tab.

3. Click on **Add Modifier** and choose **Multiresolution** from the **Generate** column in the list of modifiers:

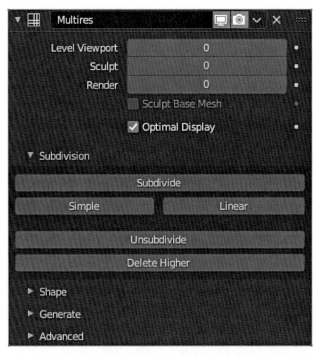

Figure 5.30 – The Multiresolution modifier settings as observed in the Properties editor

Just like the Subdivision Surface modifier, the Multiresolution modifier allows us to adjust the number of subdivision levels. This can be controlled separately between **Object Mode**, **Sculpt Mode**, and the final render by adjusting the **Level Viewport**, **Sculpt**, and **Render** settings, respectively. Currently, all three of these settings are set to 0. Unlike the Subdivision Surface modifier, we can't simply type a different number in these fields. Instead, we have to explicitly create each new subdivision level by clicking on the **Subdivide** button.

4. Click on the **Subdivide** button to create a new level of subdivision.

    Notice the current subdivision level for the **Viewport**, **Sculpt**, and **Render** settings were all incremented by 1. This uses the same algorithm for subdivision that we learned about in the *Exploring subdivision surfaces* section of this chapter. The difference here is that once we create a subdivision level, we can sculpt details onto the new level. Also, we learned that subdivision works well when we use at least two levels, so let's add another level to our Multiresolution modifier.

5. Click on the **Subdivide** button a second time to create a second level of subdivision.

    That will be enough to get us started. The vampire's head is looking much smoother now. We should try sculpting our new details at this subdivision level before subdividing further.

6. Switch to **Sculpt Mode**.

7. Choose the **Pinch** brush from the Toolbar.

8. Use the **Pinch** brush to tighten up areas such as the eyelids, eyebags, lips, philtrum, cheekbones, and more.

Using the Pinch brush is an excellent way to make a model look extra crisp. The last time we attempted to use this brush, it didn't work very well because there weren't enough polygons to pinch together. However, with the extra polygons added by the Multiresolution modifier, the Pinch brush excels. With just a little bit of creasing over the details, we can make a huge difference to the sculpture. You can have a look at our example in the following diagram:

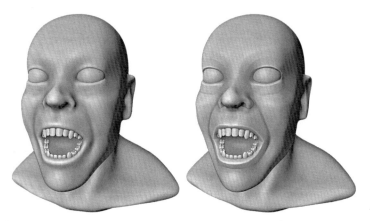

Figure 5.31 – The multiresolution sculpture before and after pinching the facial details

Of course, not every model needs to be sharpened this much, but the extra resolution will open the door to create the highest quality of art without slowing down our computers' performance to an unusable state.

Once we have entered multiresolution, we can't use the Voxel Remesher or Dyntopo. However, we should still try to work on the lowest resolution details first before increasing the resolution. For the sake of this example, let's skip ahead to a higher resolution and try making some extremely high-resolution details:

9. Click on the **Subdivide** button until the **Sculpt** level reaches 4.

10. Choose the **Draw Sharp** brush from the Toolbar.

11. Set the **Strength** value of the brush to 1.000.

12. Draw some kind of detail or pattern on the vampire's skin:

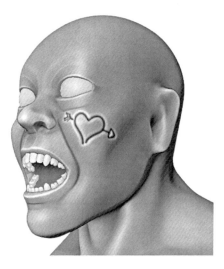

Figure 5.32 – A lovely vampire

How lovely! Drawing a pattern similar to this on a low-resolution mesh would not have been possible. One of the cooler aspects of this feature is that the details we sculpt at the higher levels of subdivision will be propagated back to the lower levels of subdivision. Try lowering the sculpting level to observe what happens to the pattern when there aren't enough polygons to support it. When you're done playing around with the sculpt level, set it back to 4 so that we can try one more brush before we end this section.

> Tip
> There are hotkeys that you can use to quickly toggle the Multiresolution modifier's sculpting subdivision level. While in **Sculpt Mode**, hold *Ctrl* and press the number key that corresponds to the number of subdivisions you want. For instance, *Ctrl + 2* will set the subdivision to level 2.

The details that we sculpt onto each subdivision level are known as **displacements**. Displacements are an efficient way for our computers to handle high-resolution sculpting, but they also allow us to do some pretty unique things. For instance, we can erase parts of the displacement to return the sculpture to its original subdivided shape:

1. Choose the **Multiresolution Displacement Eraser** brush from the Toolbar.
2. Draw over any areas that you want to erase, such as the pattern we drew with the **Draw Sharp** brush earlier.

Isn't that neat? And this is just the tip of the iceberg. We can do far more interesting things with multiresolution. In the remaining recipes of this chapter, we will explore some of the other features of multiresolution.

How it works...

Multiresolution uses a combination of subdivision and displacement to achieve extremely high-resolution details that would otherwise be impossible to create without crashing our computers. Through the use of the Multiresolution modifier, we can create details such as wrinkles in our character's skin, seams and stitching in their clothing, and more tiny details that require millions of polygons.

Important Note

Multiresolution is not interchangeable with the Voxel Remesher or Dyntopo. If you attempt to change the topology of the sculpture after beginning the multiresolution workflow, you will cause errors in the displacement and ruin the model.

Recapturing details from the previous mesh

Sometimes, we lose details during the transfer between the Voxel Remesher stage and the multiresolution stage of the sculpting process. As you practice sculpting further, you'll become a better judge of which details will transfer and which ones will be lost.

Ideally, we would always make perfect decisions about when to make the switch and no details would be lost at all. However, sometimes, it would be nice if we could recapture the lost details without having to redo any of our sculpting work. As it turns out, this is actually possible using a **Shrinkwrap** modifier and a special feature of the Multiresolution modifier called **Reshape**.

In this section, we'll try using this workflow to recapture specific details.

Getting ready

Download the example `recaptureDetails.blend` character file from `https://github.com/PacktPublishing/Sculpting-the-Blender-Way/blob/main/Chapter05/recaptureDetails.blend`.

Launch Blender and open the `recaptureDetails.blend` file. This file contains two versions of a tortoise sculpture: one that was created with the Voxel Remesher and one that has a clean topology that is compatible with the multiresolution workflow. The original voxel version contains lots of detail in the shell, toes, and head. Sadly, many of these details were lost in the new version when the new topology was created, as you can observe in the following diagram:

Figure 5.33 – A tortoise sculpture with bad topology but lots of details (on the left-hand side) and a tortoise with good topology but missing details (on the right-hand side)

That's a lot of detail to lose. It would be a shame to have to sculpt all of those details over again. So, instead, let's attempt to recapture the details into the displacement of the Multiresolution modifier.

This process is going to get a little tough for our computers to handle, so you should expect your computer to slow down a little bit during some of the steps. Essentially, we're going to require three copies of the tortoise sculpture: the original highly detailed sculpture, the one with a good topology that will be receiving the details, and a copy of this model that can be shrinkwrapped to the surface of the detailed sculpture. Additionally, we need to perform this process once for each of the objects that make up the sculpture. In this case, that means repeating the process once for the shell and once for the body.

How to do it...

Currently, we can only view the highly detailed version of the tortoise in the scene. This is because the other tortoise is part of a different **collection** that is currently inactive. Let's fix this by deactivating the detailed sculpture and activating the one with good topology:

1. Find the **Tortoise_Voxel** collection in the Outliner and click on the checkbox to the right-hand side of the collection to deactivate it.

2. Click on the checkbox to the right-hand side of the **Tortoise** collection to activate the tortoise sculpture that has a good topology:

Figure 5.34 – The two tortoise collections in the Outliner with their checkboxes circled

Now that the tortoise base mesh is visible, let's add a Multiresolution modifier to the shell.

3. Click on the **Shell** object to select it.

4. Click on the blue wrench tab, in the **Properties** editor, to switch to the **Modifiers** tab.

5. Click on **Add Modifier** and choose **Multiresolution** from the **Generate** column in the list of modifiers.

6. Click on the **Subdivide** button twice to increase the subdivision level to 2.

    Now, here's where things get tricky and a little bit confusing. We're going to duplicate the shell and shrinkwrap the duplicate onto the highly detailed tortoiseshell.

7. Open the **Object** menu in the upper-left corner of the 3D Viewport and choose
    Duplicate Objects. This will duplicate the shell and begin moving the duplicate.

8. Press the *Esc* key or right-click to cancel the movement of the duplicate shell,
    leaving it in its original position.

9. Either double-click on the name of the duplicate shell in the Outliner or press the *F2*
    hotkey to rename it to `Shell_Shrinkwrapped`:

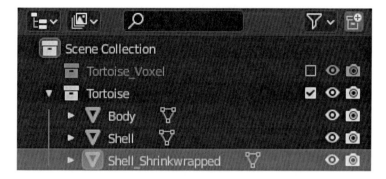

Figure 5.35 – The duplicate shell object as displayed in the Outliner

Perfect. Now we have the duplicate shell with a good topology that we can
shrinkwrap to the surface of the highly detailed shell.

10. Hide the original **Shell** object by clicking on the eyeball icon to the right-hand side
    of its name in the Outliner.

11. Select the **Shell_Shrinkwrapped** object.

12. Click on **Add Modifier** and choose **Shrinkwrap** from the **Deform** column in the
    list of modifiers.

    Now we just need to adjust the Shrinkwrap modifier settings.

13. Change **Wrap Method** to **Project**.

14. Activate both the **Negative** and **Positive** projection direction checkboxes.

15. Click on the drop-down list labeled **Target** and choose **Shell_Voxel**.

The final **Shrinkwrap** settings can be seen in the following screenshot:

Figure 5.36 – The Shrinkwrap modifier settings

We're almost there. Now we have the shell with all of the details projected onto it. This last step is a little bit awkward – we need to be able to reshape the original **Shell** object to match the shrinkwrapped shell. However, to do this, we need to be able to view both shells at once. Let's apply the modifiers to the **Shell_Shrinkwrapped** object, then we can move it to the side and unhide the original **Shell** object.

16. Click on the drop-down arrow in the upper-right corner of the **Multires** modifier and choose **Apply**.

17. Click on the drop-down arrow in the upper-right corner of the **Shrinkwrap** modifier and choose **Apply**.

18. Use the **Move** tool from the Toolbar to move the **Shell_Shrinkwrapped** object off to the side.

19. Unhide the original **Shell** object by clicking on the eyeball icon next to its name in the Outliner.

Now we should be able to view both shells at the same time. The **Shell_Shrinkwrapped** object will be off to one side, and the **Shell** object will be visible on top of the tortoise's body. This arrangement can be seen in the following diagram:

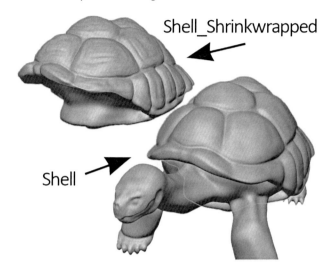

Figure 5.37 – The Shell_Shrinkwrapped object next to the Shell object

Perfect. With these two versions of the shell side by side, we can request the original **Shell** object's Multiresolution modifier to reshape itself to match the **Shell_Shrinkwrapped** object.

20. First, select the **Shell_Shrinkwrapped** object.

21. Hold *Shift* and click on the **Shell** object to add it to the selection.

22. Expand the **Shape** subsection in the Multiresolution modifier settings.

23. Click on the **Reshape** button.

And we're done! The shape of the shrinkwrapped shell has been transferred to the displacement of the shell's Multiresolution modifier. If you're happy with the result, we can delete both the **Shell_Shrinkwrapped** object and the **Shell_Voxel** object, as they are no longer needed.

Repeat these steps for the body of the tortoise and we'll be done.

How it works...

This takes a lot of steps, but the end result is worth it so that we don't have to resculpt any of our details. All of the details have been successfully recaptured and stored in the displacement of the Multiresolution modifier. From here, we can continue sculpting, adding more levels of subdivision, and sculpting even more details into the sculpture.

It is likely that some of the unwanted jagged edges will be captured from the original voxel version of the sculpture into the new multiresolution sculpture. If this happens, you can use the smoothing brush to clean up those areas.

This is by no means a necessary part of the process. You might even prefer to sculpt these details into the multiresolution version of the sculpture by hand instead of trying to salvage the details from the pre-multiresolution version of the model.

Either way, this model is now ready for sculpting extremely high details such as scales, skin wrinkles, sharp edges around the nostrils and mouth, and more.

There's more...

The latest version of Blender added a simplified way of applying the shrinkwrapped details to the Multiresolution modifier's displacement. The new way does not require you to create a duplicate of the object, nor does it require you to use the **Reshape** button. Simply, add the Shrinkwrap modifier directly to the multiresolution object and set the appropriate shrinkwrap settings that we learned about earlier. Then, click on the drop-down arrow in the upper-right corner of the **Shrinkwrap** modifier and choose **Apply**. That's all there is to it.

Changing resolution for the appropriate details

One of the hidden benefits of sculpting with the Multiresolution modifier is that we can sculpt on any level of subdivision whenever we want to. In the Voxel Remesher workflow, we have to be very strict about working from areas of low detail up to areas of high detail. However, with multiresolution, we can simply change the sculpting subdivision level and we're ready to work on a different resolution.

This doesn't come up terribly often, but it's great for fixing larger aspects of our models such as proportions, even if we've already sculpted high-resolution details. Additionally, we can take advantage of this feature to pose the character with the **Pose** brush.

In this section, we will try toggling between the subdivision levels to work on appropriate details and wrap up the chapter by creating a sculpture that poses.

Getting ready

Download the example `tortoiseMultiresolution.blend` character file at `https://github.com/PacktPublishing/Sculpting-the-Blender-Way/blob/main/Chapter05/tortoiseMultiresolution.blend`.

Launch Blender and open the `tortoiseMultiresolution.blend` file. Once you've opened the file, we can try sculpting at multiple resolutions.

How to do it...

In this file, the sculpture is a tortoise with lots of high-resolution details such as wrinkly skin and scales:

Figure 5.38 – The high-resolution tortoise sculpture

The level of detail present in this sculpture is possible because of the Multiresolution modifier. If we want to change the proportions and positions of the large forms of this character, we will have a difficult time doing so because there are nearly four million triangles at the current resolution. Let's attempt to move the front leg using the **Grab** brush:

1. Activate the **Grab** brush from the Toolbar.

2. Increase the radius of the brush so that it covers the majority of the tortoise's front leg:

Figure 5.39 – The Grab brush with a large size covering the front leg of the tortoise

3. Press your pen to the tablet and drag to stretch the tortoise's front leg outward:

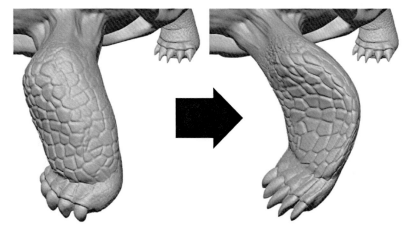

Figure 5.40 – The tortoise's leg before and after being stretched to the side via the Grab brush

Well, that didn't work very well, did it? The Grab brush has a hard time operating at this resolution because there are too many polygons. The leg didn't move uniformly, and the Grab brush put a kink in the leg's shape. Maybe we can try smoothing it out with the **Smooth** brush.

4. Hold the *Shift* key to access the **Smooth** brush.

5. Draw over the leg's surface to attempt to smooth out the kink in the leg:

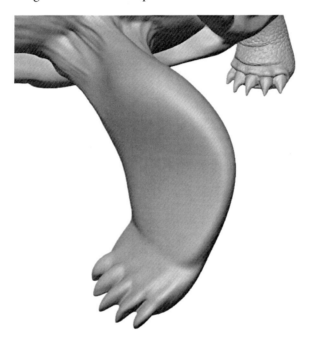

Figure 5.41 – A failed attempt to fix the kink in the leg

Unfortunately, this did not work very well at all. Because of the high resolution, the smoothing brush is only able to smooth out the surface details. The scales on the leg have been erased, but we are unable to smooth out the kink in the leg's shape.

This is a job for a lower resolution! Let's restart and try again.

6. Open the **File** menu and choose **Revert** to reset this file back to its previous state.

7. Take a look at the settings for the **Multires** modifier in the **Properties** editor and set the **Sculpt** value to 0.

Most of the details have disappeared from the sculpture, but now we can sculpt on the tortoise as if the high-resolution details don't exist. Feel free to use your sculpting brushes to change the proportions of the tortoise. Try **Grab**, **Smooth**, **Inflate**, or any other brushes you like (it doesn't have to look good; we're just experimenting right now). In our example, we've morphed the tortoise's legs into some sort of sea turtle. Once you're happy with the new shape, change the **Sculpt** value in the **Multires** modifier back up to 3. You can view our example as follows:

Figure 5.42 – Sea turtle legs with scales intact

Isn't that fascinating? Because we did all of the sculpting on the lower resolution version, we were able to utilize our sculpting tools more freely to distort the large shapes. Then, when we toggled back up to the high-resolution version, all of the details such as the scales stayed intact. Do you feel the power of the multiresolution workflow now?

Let's try a more practical example with the same workflow. We can pose the tortoise's limbs while using the lowest resolution. Blender includes an excellent brush designed specifically for this purpose – the **Pose** brush:

1. If you don't want to keep the changes you've made so far, open the **File** menu and choose **Revert** to reset this file back to its previous state.

2. Set the **Multires** modifier's **Sculpt** value to 0.

3. Activate the **Pose** brush from the Toolbar.

4. Turn off the *X axis* symmetry setting by clicking on the **X** toggle next to the butterfly icon in the header of the 3D Viewport.

5. Hover the brush over the tortoise's head.

6. Do you notice the small white line extending outward from the brush? This is a unique feature of the Pose brush. It indicates where we can pivot the sculpture from.

7. Increase the brush radius until the white line reaches the base of the tortoise's neck:

Figure 5.43 – The Pose brush reaching from the head down to the base of the neck

8. Press and drag with your pen to pose the tortoise's neck.

    To curve the neck, we can make a small adjustment with the current brush radius. Then, we can reduce the brush radius to make a small adjustment again. Keep repeating this until you've curved the neck into a pose that you're happy with.

9. When you've got the tortoise posed the way you like, set the **Multires** modifier's **Sculpt** value back up to 3:

Figure 5.44 – The tortoise in its final pose with zero subdivision levels (on the left-hand side) and three subdivision levels (on the right-hand side)

Posed characters look a lot more natural than stiff characters do, but we often save our poses for one of the final steps in the process. This would not have been easy without the multiresolution workflow.

How it works...

The Multiresolution modifier stores all of the high-resolution details in displacements that are relative to the base mesh's topology. If we reduce the resolution, any changes we make to the lower resolutions will be propagated back up to the higher resolutions.

There's more...

Because the displacements are based on the topology of the lower resolutions, we can also slide the topology around using the **Slide Relax** brush. It's easier to see what you're doing if you turn on the wireframe overlay. However, this tool will allow you to slide the topology from one area to another. In the case of this turtle, we could toggle down to the lowest resolution, slide relax the topology from the lower leg up to the upper leg, then toggle back up to the high resolution to find that the high-resolution scales have moved to the upper leg.

There are numerous other great features related to multiresolution. However, this chapter should have given you the boost you need to be able to effectively create high-resolution sculptures.

6
Using Advanced Features and Customizing the Sculpting Brushes

One key factor in creating high-quality sculptures is practice with, and mastery of, the sculpting brushes. The latest version of Blender comes with many excellent brushes that each have a place in the sculpting process. We had a chance to try many of the basic brushes in *Chapter 3*, *Sculpting a Simple Character Head with Basic Brushes*, but we can also customize our brushes to make them behave exactly the way we like. In this chapter, we'll learn about advanced brush features that will give us full control over the behavior of our brushes.

We'll start by learning about some simple adjustments that we can make to our brushes, such as custom falloff and custom stroke settings. Once we understand these features, we'll expand our knowledge with one of the most important and impactful ways to customize our brushes: **Alphas**.

Alphas are a way to add texture to our brush and create extremely fine details on the surface of our sculptures, including skin pores. We'll learn how to use automatic masks and face sets to limit our brush strokes to specific areas of the sculpture. And we'll learn how to use an assortment of advanced brushes that offer interesting new ways to refine our sculptures.

The main topics in this chapter are as follows:

- Using custom falloff
- Exploring custom stroke options
- Setting up custom alpha textures
- Using face sets as automatic masks
- Cleaving off flat sections with the Line Project tool
- Creating advanced masks with Sculpt Expand
- Posing fingers with the Pose brush

Technical requirements

For general requirements, refer back to the *Technical requirements* section in *Chapter 1, Exploring Blender's User Interface for Sculpting*.

You can download the files to follow along with this book at the GitHub link here: `https://github.com/PacktPublishing/Sculpting-the-Blender-Way`.

Several sections in this chapter will be dealing with sculptures that have an extremely high polycount (between 3 and 12 million triangles). It is important to have a lot of memory (at least 1.5 GB) and CPU processing power available so that the sculpting tools can work smoothly. It is highly recommended that you close other applications on your computer to free up resources for Blender. Web browsers such as Google Chrome are infamous for utilizing a large amount of your computer's available memory; try to close as many tabs as possible to free up memory for sculpting in Blender.

Using custom falloff

By default, the brushes have a smooth **falloff** on the sculpture. For example, if we draw with the Draw brush, the surface of the sculpture will be raised upward wherever our brush touches the surface. The pattern of this raised area has a rounded edge, strongest in the center and rounded out toward the edges with a smooth falloff curve. This smooth falloff works well in most situations, but if we learn how to customize the falloff pattern, we can make the brushes behave in more interesting ways. For instance, we can make the brush stronger at the edges, or we can intensify it even more toward the center, or we can remove the falloff so that the strength is constant across the brush's area of influence.

Getting ready

Launch Blender, and then start a new project using the sculpting preset. The Quad Sphere model that comes with the sculpting preset doesn't have enough polygons to easily demonstrate our brush falloff settings, so we should add a Multiresolution modifier. We learned all about the Multiresolution modifier in *Chapter 5, Learning the Power of Subdivision and the Multiresolution Workflow*. As we've learned, we can add a Multiresolution modifier in the blue wrench tab in the Properties editor. Use the **Add Modifier** menu, and choose **Multiresolution**. Once the modifier has been added, click **Subdivide** twice to bring the **Sculpt** level to 2.

Tip

Because adding multiresolution to our sculptures is such a common practice, there is a hotkey for quickly applying multiresolution to the selected object. While in **Sculpt Mode**, press *Ctrl + 2* to add a **Multiresolution** modifier with two levels of subdivision.

Once our Quad Sphere has two levels of subdivision, we'll be ready to experiment with different types of brush falloff.

How to do it...

Many of the brush settings are available to us in the **Tool Settings** section of the header of the 3D Viewport. However, we have access to more options if we use the **Tool** section of the Sidebar instead. Let's try adjusting the settings for the Draw brush now:

1. Choose the **Draw** brush from the Toolbar.
2. Open the Sidebar by clicking the little < indicator along the right side of the 3D Viewport or by pressing the *N* hotkey while your mouse is in the 3D Viewport.

3. Click the vertical tab along the right edge of the Sidebar labeled **Tool** to view the tool settings.

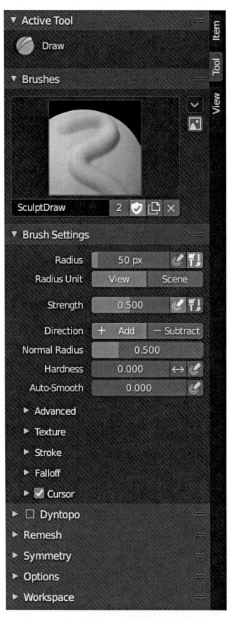

Figure 6.1 – The tool settings for the Draw brush as seen in the Tool tab in the Sidebar

> **Tip**
> Alternatively, we can view these settings in the **Active Tool and Workspace Settings** tab at the top of the Properties editor. The settings are identical in both of these menus.

Before we look at the **Falloff** settings, let's adjust the **Strength** setting of the brush and see what happens to the brush.

4. Hover your cursor over the 3D Viewport and press the *Shift + F* hotkey to begin adjusting the brush's strength.

5. Slide your cursor to increase the strength to 1.000, but don't click to confirm the new strength setting yet.

6. Take a look at the curve shape that is visible in the brush strength gizmo, which we have highlighted red in the following diagram:

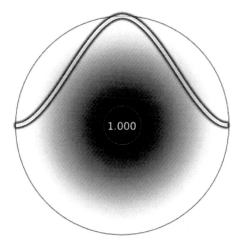

Figure 6.2 – The brush falloff curve (highlighted in red for better visibility in this image)

This curve represents the brush falloff. It currently has an eased curve in the middle and toward the edges, creating a very smooth falloff for the brush. Another way to visualize this is to look at the gradient coming from the center of the brush gizmo out toward the edges of the gizmo. The rate of falloff of this gradient matches the falloff curve.

7. When you're done observing this falloff curve, left-click or tap your pen to your tablet to confirm a strength setting of 1.000.

Now let's try out this brush so we can see how the default falloff setting behaves.

8.   Draw a small line on the surface of the Quad Sphere model.

Figure 6.3 – A line drawn with the Smooth falloff setting

This should feel very familiar because this is the default falloff setting that we've been using throughout this book. Now let's see what happens if we change to a sharper falloff.

9.   Expand the **Falloff** subsection in the tool settings in the Sidebar.

10.   Click on the drop-down list labeled **Smooth** and then choose **Sharper** from the list.

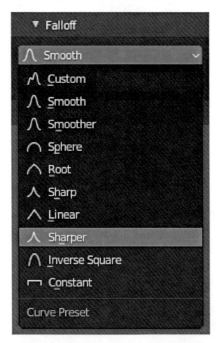

Figure 6.4 – The Sharper option as it appears in the brush Falloff drop-down list

Draw another line below the original line so we can compare the two falloff settings.

Figure 6.5 – A line drawn with the Sharper falloff setting

11. You can see how big of a difference falloff makes. Try drawing a few more lines with the **Sphere**, **Linear**, and **Constant** falloff settings.

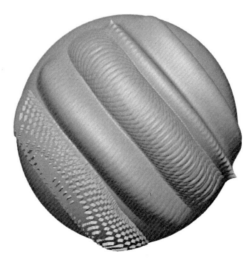

Figure 6.6 – Three more lines drawn with the Sphere, Linear, and Constant falloff settings

These shapes all have very different results. You'll notice, however, that several of these brushes have a jagged edge. Several things are causing this issue; in the next section, we'll learn how to correct this by adjusting the spacing of the brush's stroke, but for now, we can try creating a custom falloff to help with the issue.

12. Click on the falloff drop-down list, and then choose **Custom**. A custom **Curve Widget** will appear in the tool settings, as you can see in the following screenshot:

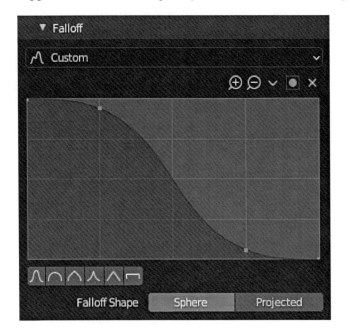

Figure 6.7 – The custom curve widget

This curve creates a symmetrical falloff for the brush; the left side represents the center of the brush with the **Control Points** curve placed at the top of the graph for full intensity. The right side represents the farthest reaches of the brush with little to no intensity.

13. Click and drag the control points to edit the **Custom** curve.

14. To increase the intensity of the brush toward the center but keep a smooth falloff at the edge, place the control points of the curve using the following screenshot as a reference:

Figure 6.8 – The custom curve widget for a high-intensity brush

With this curve, the brush will maintain full influence across approximately half of the brush area, but there is enough of a smooth falloff toward the outer edge to avoid having a jagged edge. Give it a try.

Experiment with this widget to create interesting patterns. You can create additional control points by clicking in the blank areas of the curve widget. You can even create a ripple effect by using the following screenshot as a reference:

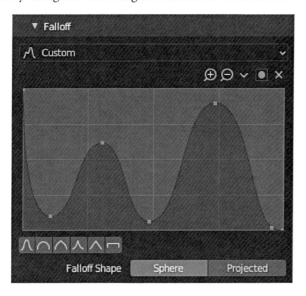

Figure 6.9 – The custom curve widget for a ripple effect

With just a few taps of the pen onto the sculpture's surface, this falloff pattern produces the result in the following image:

Figure 6.10 – The ripple effect produced by the custom curve

Custom falloff patterns like these aren't necessarily the most practical way to sculpt, but they can certainly produce interesting results like this. The default **Smooth** falloff is still the go-to setting for most brushes, but sometimes the other falloff presets come in handy as well.

How it works...

The brush falloff is an excellent way to customize our brushes. For the cleanest results, it's best to have a smooth falloff along the edge so we don't end up with a jagged transition at the edge of our brushstrokes.

The main difference between the regular Draw brush and the Draw Sharp brush is the falloff setting. There are other differences as well, but even subtle adjustments to falloff are enough to make a substantial difference in the behavior of the brush.

There's more...

Adjustments to the falloff settings go nicely with adjustments to the stroke settings. In the next section, we'll see how to use the stroke settings for a unique brush experience.

See also

- For more information on brush falloff, including some very intuitive visualizations, check out the official Blender manual page here: `https://docs.blender.org/manual/en/latest/sculpt_paint/brush/falloff.html`.

- You can read more about using the custom curve widget here: `https://docs.blender.org/manual/en/latest/interface/controls/templates/curve.html#ui-curve-widget`.

Exploring custom stroke options

All brushes must use some type of method for applying their effect to the sculpture surface. This method of application is known as the **Stroke**. Most of the default brushes in Blender use the same basic type of stroke, called **Space**. Technically, there is no way for the computer to smoothly create brush strokes; we can only create the illusion of smooth brush strokes.

When we use the **Space** option for our **Stroke Method** setting, the shape of the brush will be repeatedly stamped onto the sculpture while we draw across its surface. How often this stamping occurs is determined by the **Spacing** setting of the brush stroke. In Blender, the amount of spacing is measured as a percentage of the brush radius. If we use a high spacing value such as 500%, then the stamps will be repeated infrequently. If we use a very low spacing, such as 10%, then the stamps will be repeated very frequently.

In the following diagram, we can see several lines drawn from left to right using different spacing values:

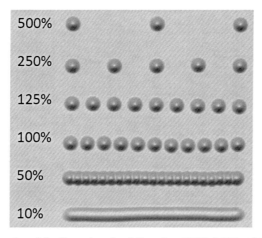

Figure 6.11 – The results of the Draw brush while using 500%, 250%, 125%, 100%, 50%, and 10% spacing

As we lower the spacing percentage, the stamps will be repeated more frequently. If we set this setting low enough, the result will look like a smooth continuous brushstroke instead of a series of stamps.

In this section, we will learn how to adjust the spacing setting for our brushes, and we will explore several other stroke methods that apply the brush shape to the model in completely different ways.

Getting ready

We can continue where we left off in the *Using custom falloff* section of this chapter. If there's no empty space left on the surface of your Quad Sphere, you can get a fresh start by deleting the **Multiresolution** modifier, adding a new **Multiresolution** modifier, and then subdividing it twice. You can use any brush falloff settings to follow along in this section, but we're going to use the custom ripple falloff that we created in the previous section for our example because it will make the examples in this section easier to see.

If you would rather start with a fresh file, use the **Sculpting** preset, select the **Draw** brush, and open the **Tool** tab in the Sidebar so that we can continue editing the settings for the **Draw** brush.

How to do it...

Currently, **Stroke Method** for the **Draw** brush is set to **Space**. We'll start by adjusting the **Spacing** setting for this stroke method and get a feel for how this changes the behavior of the brush:

1. Set the **Strength** setting of the brush to about 0.500 so that our brush strokes aren't too intense.

2. Expand the **Stroke** subsection in the tool settings in the Sidebar.

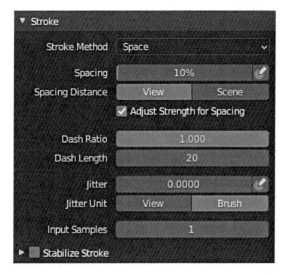

Figure 6.12 – The Stroke settings for the brush as they appear in the Sidebar

Here, we can see the Draw brush's default **Spacing** setting of **10%**. Let's see how it performs.

3.   Use the Draw brush with its default stroke settings to draw a small swoop, as seen in the following example:

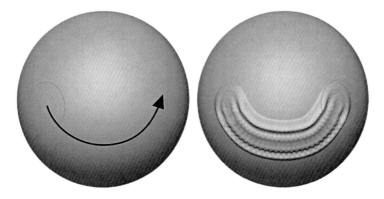

Figure 6.13 – The Draw brush with 10% spacing; this swoop looks like a mouth

The way this brush feels should be familiar because 10% is the default setting. However, in our example, we've used a custom ripple-shaped falloff for the brush that we learned about earlier in this chapter. This custom falloff highlights a small issue with this brush stroke: The spacing is too far apart and it's creating little jagged gaps between the stamped brush shape. To smooth this out, we can reduce the spacing of our brush and try again.

4. Set the **Spacing** setting of the brush all the way down to 1% so that there is as little spacing as possible.

5. Use the Draw brush with this new stroke setting to draw a small swoop above the previous swoop, as seen in the following example:

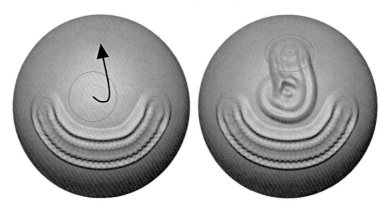

Figure 6.14 – The Draw brush with 1% spacing; this swoop looks like a nose

Notice how much smoother this brush stroke is? Sometimes, reducing the spacing like this is necessary to help us produce smooth results when using custom falloff patterns. What about less spacing though? We've got a pretty cool brush shape. If we set the spacing wide enough, we can stamp the shape in several places without smearing its edges together.

6. Set the **Spacing** setting of the brush to 200% so that there is a large amount of spacing between each stamp of the brush.

7. Use the Draw brush with this new stroke setting to draw a line from one side to the other, as seen in the following example:

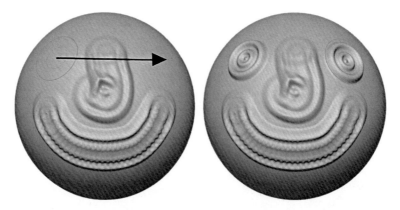

Figure 6.15 – The Draw brush with 200% spacing; these stamps of the brush look like eyes

How fun; we've made a little face! Because we used such a large brush spacing option, both eyes on this face were stamped onto the sculpture with a single continuous brushstroke. This is neat, but it isn't the most practical way to produce a single stamp of the brush. Let's try using the **Drag Dot** stroke method for a more intuitive approach.

8. Use the **Stroke Method** drop-down list to change from **Space** to **Drag Dot**.

9. Begin a brush stroke anywhere on the sculpture, and then drag the brush across the surface of the model to move the brush stamp to a new location.

    You can see that our example in the following image starts with the brush in the bottom left area and then drags upward to the top middle area:

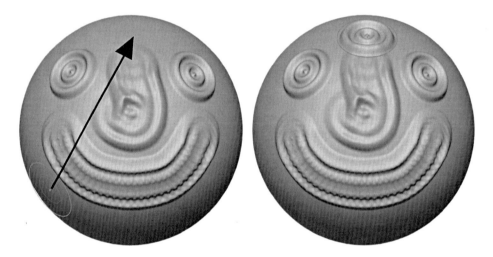

Figure 6.16 – The Draw brush with the Drag Dot stroke method

This method is excellent for placing specific details on the surface while giving us the flexibility to drag the brush stamp around in real time. When we release the pen from the surface of the tablet, only a single brush stamp is left behind on the surface of the sculpture.

There is a very similar stroke method that allows us to place the brush in a single location and then adjust the size of the stamp by dragging outward. Let's try this now.

10. Use the **Stroke Method** drop-down list to change from **Drag Dot** to **Anchored**.

11. Hover your pen over the spot you would like the brush stamp to be anchored to.

12. Press your pen down onto the tablet and then drag outward to resize the stamp in real time.

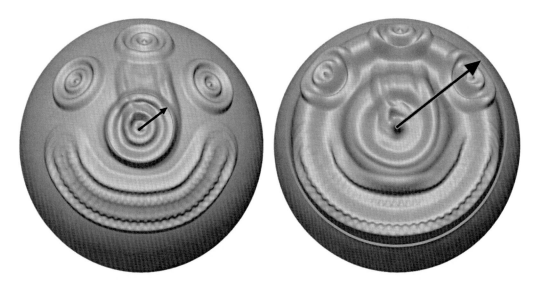

Figure 6.17 – The Draw brush with the Anchored stroke method

Isn't that neat? The Draw brush's ripple pattern is stretched across the surface of the sculpture based on how far we drag the pen. It kind of ruined the happy face we made, but that's okay; it wasn't a very good happy face anyway.

We'll explore two more stroke settings in this section. First of all, let's try a setting that can make it easier to create smooth strokes.

13. Orbit the 3D Viewport around to the back side of the sculpture so that we have a blank area to sculpt on.

14. Change **Stroke Method** back to **Space**.

15. Change the **Spacing** setting of the brush back to its default – 10%.

16. Set the **Radius** setting of the brush to a small value, such as 30 px.

17. Check the box in the Sidebar labeled **Stabilize Stroke**.

18. Press down with your pen to begin drawing on the sculpture. Instead of stamping the brush on the surface right away, a red line will appear. Keep dragging your pen to extend the red line. When the line reaches a maximum length, the brush will begin stamping onto the surface of the sculpture.

19. Continue dragging the red line around. Try drawing a curved shape, as in the following image:

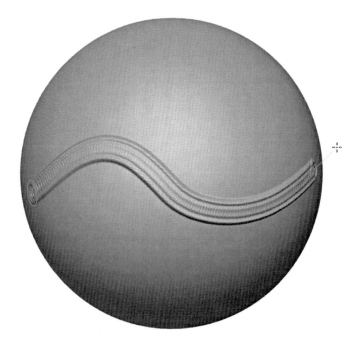

Figure 6.18 – A brush stroke stabilized by the red line

This behavior may feel odd to you. However, this is a common feature in artistic software. This feature is often called **Lazy Mouse** in other software. It works by delaying the brush stamp so that any jitter in your hand is reduced while you drag your pen across the tablet surface. This feature can help with creating intricate line details, especially if you struggle to keep your hands steady.

Sometimes, we want exactly the opposite effect. The final stroke feature we'll look at in this section will allow us to introduce a jitter effect to the brush stroke.

20. Turn **Stabilize Stroke** off.

21. Increase the **Jitter** setting to 1.0000.

22. Use the Draw brush with this new jitter setting to draw across the surface of the sculpture.

The brush's individual stamps will be scattered around randomly near the brush stroke, as you can see in the following example:

Figure 6.19 – A brush stroke scattered around the surface by the jitter feature

Great! If we need to add random details to the sculpture, this is an excellent way to do it! There are many more ways to customize the brush stroke, but these settings should give you enough to play around with for now.

The default stroke settings may be the most versatile, but every once in a while, these custom stroke settings can be very helpful. Many artists prefer to use the stabilize stroke option for detailed line work.

There's more...

These custom stroke settings are very useful when we start using brush alphas. In the next section of this chapter, we'll learn how to use alphas to give our brushes texture and use our brush stroke settings to their full potential.

See also

For more information on brush stroke settings, check out the official Blender manual page here: `https://docs.blender.org/manual/en/latest/sculpt_paint/brush/stroke.html`.

The **Curve** option is particularly interesting and worth trying out!

Setting up custom alpha textures

The default shape of each brush is a circle. This circle can be customized with the falloff settings that we learned about in the *Using custom falloff* section of this chapter. However, we can create much more intricate shapes for our brushes through the use of **Alphas**. Alphas are textures that influence the shape of the brush. They are useful for creating highly detailed patterns such as cracks, scales, and skin pores.

Because alphas are used to produce high-frequency details, they are most effective in the late stages of the sculpting workflow when we have many subdivisions to work with. We learned how to add subdivisions to our sculptures in the *Using the Multiresolution modifier* section of *Chapter 5*, *Learning the Power of Subdivision and the Multiresolution Workflow*.

Blender does not come with any alpha textures by default, but we've got you covered! This book comes with three alpha textures for you to use. In this section, we'll try setting up custom brushes with alphas for adding skin detail.

Getting ready

Go to the example files page for this chapter here: `https://github.com/PacktPublishing/Sculpting-the-Blender-Way/tree/main/Chapter06`.

Download the `oldMonk.blend` example file, as well as the `Alpha_SkinCrack01.png`, `Alpha_SkinCrack02.png`, and `Alpha_SkinPores.png` files.

> **Note**
> You may have to click on each of these files individually before the download button will appear.

Once you have all of the files downloaded, launch Blender and open the `oldMonk.blend` file. Once the file is open, we'll be ready to create and use our custom alpha brushes.

How to do it...

We can set up a custom alpha texture for the Draw brush using the Sidebar:

1. Open the Sidebar by clicking the little < indicator along the right side of the 3D Viewport or by pressing the *N* hotkey while your mouse is in the 3D Viewport.

2. Click the **Vertical** tab along the right edge of the Sidebar labeled **Tool** to view the tool settings.

As we can see in the following screenshot, the **Draw** brush is currently the active tool, so the settings in the Sidebar correspond to the **Draw** brush:

Figure 6.20 – The Active Tool settings for the Draw brush as they appear in the Sidebar

Instead of modifying the Draw brush directly, we should make a variant of the Draw brush so that we don't mess up the original Draw brush. As we can see in the preceding screenshot, the default Draw brush is actually called **SculptDraw**. Let's leave this brush intact and make a variant to which we can add an alpha texture.

3.   Click on the **Add Brush** button. (This button is represented by a pictogram with two little pages on it; it is directly to the left of the **X** button.)

Figure 6.21 – The Add Brush button

4. A new brush variant will be created with the name **SculptDraw.001**. Click on the name of the brush and rename it `SkinPores`.

5. Scroll down and expand the **Texture** subsection of the tool settings in the Sidebar.

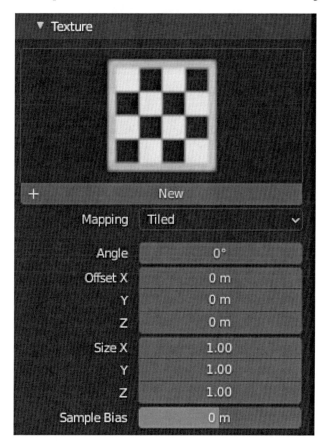

Figure 6.22 – The Texture settings for the brush as they appear in the Sidebar

6. Click on the **New** button to create a new texture slot. A new texture slot will be created with the name **Texture**.

7. Click on the name of the texture slot and rename it `SkinPores`.

8. Now we need to assign the alpha texture to this texture slot. Click on the **Show texture in texture tab.** button. (This button is represented by a pictogram with two little toggles on it; it is directly to the right of the **X** button.)

Figure 6.23 – The Show texture in texture tab. button

This will take us to a tab in the Properties editor where we can load in our alpha texture for the brush, which you can see in the following screenshot:

Figure 6.24 – The Texture tab in the Properties editor

9. Click on the **Open** button.

10. Use the pop-up file browser to select the `Alpha_SkinPores.png` file.

11. Click the **Open Image** button to load the texture file into the `SkinPores` texture slot.

12. Go back to the **Texture** settings in the Sidebar and change **Sample Bias** to `-1` m.

Excellent! Now our custom Draw brush has an alpha texture in the shape of skin pores.

The monk sculpture in this example file already has a lot of medium-sized details. It has 4 levels of subdivision, bringing it to a total of 1,643,648 quads. However, we can add more!

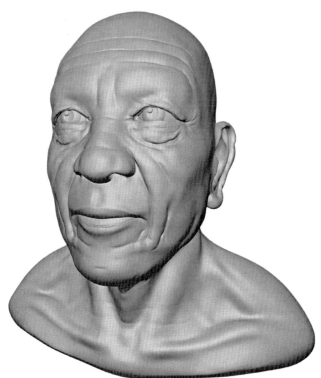

Figure 6.25 – The old monk sculpture

The monk's skin doesn't really look like skin right now due to a lack of high-frequency surface detail. The cheeks and the tip of the nose would look good with some skin pores. Let's use our new alpha brush to add these details. The details we're about to add with our custom alpha brush will have the highest quality if we add a fifth level of subdivision to the Multiresolution modifier.

> **Note**
>
> If your computer is not very powerful, it may be too slow to handle adding another level of subdivision to the sculpture. If your computer can't handle five subdivision levels, you may follow along with four instead. However, the details we make with the alpha brush will be slightly blurry due to the lower poly count.

13. Click on the blue wrench tab in the Properties editor to look at the settings for the **Multires** modifier.

14. Click on the **Subdivide** button in the **Multires** modifier to increase the sculpting subdivisions to **5**. This may take a minute or two for your computer to process.

    High-frequency details such as these will look better if they aren't perfectly symmetrical.

15. Click on the **X** button next to the butterfly icon in the header of the 3D Viewport to disable the *x* axis symmetry.

16. Lower the **Strength** setting of the brush to around 0.150.

17. Press the *F* hotkey to begin changing the **Radius** setting of the brush.

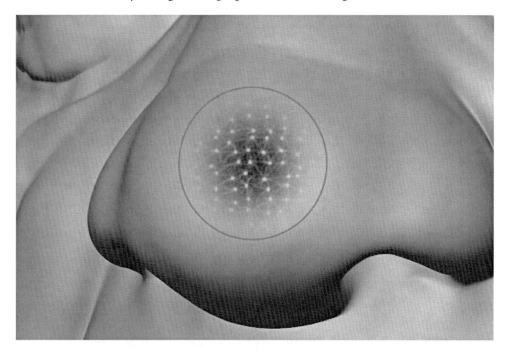

Figure 6.26 – The alpha texture as seen in the radius gizmo of the custom Draw brush

Now that our brush has an alpha texture applied to its shape, we can see the texture affecting the preview of the brush while we adjust the radius. Pick a radius that makes the little white dots match the size of real skin pores; 90px works well in our example, but your settings may vary depending on the resolution of your monitor and how zoomed in you are to the sculpture's surface.

18. Try drawing lightly on the surface of the nose to add skin pores.

19. Orbit around the nose to get a good angle on each area before each brush stroke.

20. Try adding more skin pores to the cheeks.

Our example turned out like this:

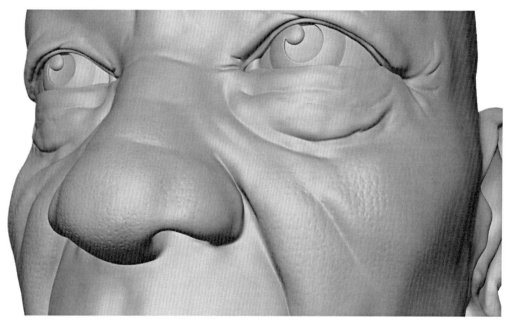

Figure 6.27 – The skin pores added to the tip of the nose and the cheeks

It's okay for these details to be subtle; we don't want to overdo it and ruin the look of the sculpture. This alpha worked really well because the texture is perfectly tiled. However, not all alphas are designed to be tiled. We can add cracks to this monk's skin using an alpha with the anchored stroke setting that we learned about in the *Exploring custom stroke options* section of this chapter:

21. Repeat *steps 3 – 12* of this section to create another custom Draw brush and texture slot called SkinCrack01. This time, load the Alpha_SkinCrack01.png file.

This alpha looks a little different from the previous one; it doesn't tile. It is meant to be stamped, so we should change two more settings for the brush.

22. Go back to the **Texture** settings in the Sidebar and change **Mapping** from **Tiled** to **View Plane**.

23. Go to the **Stroke** settings and change **Stroke Method** to **Anchored**.

    Excellent, now we can add details to the creases in this character's skin.

24. Find an area that would look good with some extra cracks, such as the wrinkles in the eye bags.

25. Position your pen over the spot you would like the anchor the crack to.

26. Press down and drag until the skin crack alpha is the size and rotation you like.

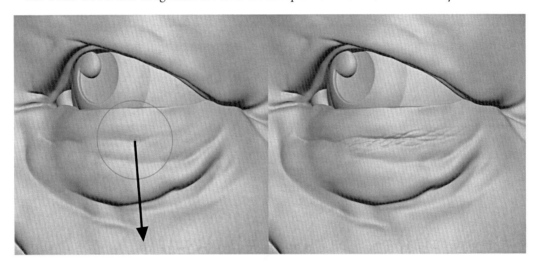

Figure 6.28 – Skin cracks added to the crease in the eye bag

It's as easy as that! You can try adding cracks like this to all of the creased areas of the skin. If you leave the *x* axis symmetry feature off, make sure you apply the cracks to both sides. A little asymmetry can make the character feel more real, but we should try to have a consistent level of detail on both sides.

Here's how our example turned out after adding skin cracks:

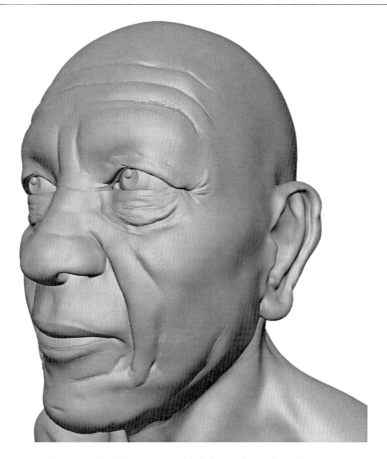

Figure 6.29 – Skin cracks added throughout the sculpture

It's subtle, but these details really add up. The crevices in the monk's skin feel more organic and detailed now that we've added some cracks to them. Lastly, let's try adding some bumpy skin texture to the surface of the monk's skin so he no longer looks so unnaturally smooth. This will be easiest to do by using an alpha with jitter and a random angle.

27. Repeat *steps 3 – 12* one more time to create another custom Draw brush and texture slot called SkinCrack02. This time, load the Alpha_SkinCrack02.png file.

28. Make sure **Stroke Method** is set to **Space**.

29. Set **Spacing** to 20%.

30. Set **Jitter** to 0.25.

31. Change **Mapping** to **View Plane**.

32. Go back to the **Texture** settings in the Sidebar and check the box for **Random** under **Angle**.

33. A new setting for **Random Angle** will appear below the **Random** checkbox. Set this setting to 90 degrees.

Perfect! Now we have a brush that can scatter rough skin details around the smooth surface by randomly rotating and stamping a simple alpha texture all over the surface of the sculpture. A little goes a long way. Be sure to use a light pen pressure and draw over any areas that need skin detail. The pattern is subtle, but with a couple of short brush strokes, you should have a result like this:

Figure 6.30 – Subtle skin detail from the jittering random angle alpha

Using this brush on the smooth areas of the monk's skin, our example turned out like this:

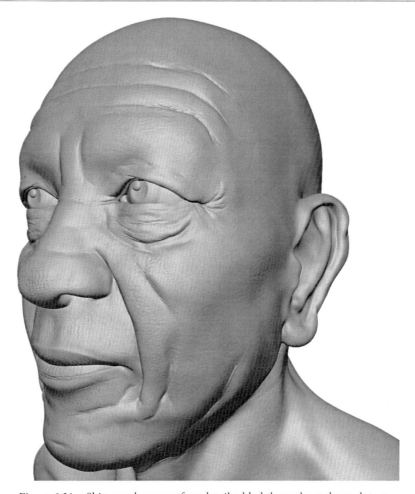

Figure 6.31 – Skin roughness surface detail added throughout the sculpture

And there you have it! This monk's skin looks a lot more realistic now that it has pores, cracks, and roughness across the surface. Little details like this would have been almost impossible to add by hand, but with custom alpha brushes, this kind of detail is easy!

How it works...

Custom brush presets can be created for any brush. In this section, we made three custom brushes grouped under the default Draw brush. We can click on the brush image in the tool settings to switch between brush presets (see *Figure 6.20*).

Alphas are an excellent way of adding fine detail to a model. Alphas are very popular with many libraries of sculpting alphas available online. When combined with custom stroke options, the types of brushes we can make are almost endless.

There's more...

We chose an old man character to demonstrate this feature because wrinkly rough details are very fitting for an old man's skin. However, the intensity of these skin details can be deceiving. We often render human skin with a feature known as **Subsurface Scattering**, which closely mimics the way light penetrates the surface and smooths out the surface details. Even young people have surface details like this in their skin. These details just become less prominent when light reacts with young healthy skin.

See also

For more information on the brush texture settings, check out the official Blender manual page here: `https://docs.blender.org/manual/en/latest/sculpt_paint/brush/texture.html`.

The **Stencil** option is especially interesting!

Using face sets as automatic masks

Some areas of our sculptures can be difficult to work with if the polygons get too close together. For example, lips are usually sculpted so close together that it becomes impossible to make adjustments to the upper lip without accidentally affecting the lower lip at the same time. We could try making a mask over one of the lips, but then we could only work on one lip at a time, and we would have to invert the mask every time we want to work on the other lip. There's a better way to automatically mask areas like this: **Face Sets**.

We got a sneak peek of face sets in the *Using the Lasso Trim tool to add and remove geometry* section of *Chapter 4, How to Make a Base Mesh for a 3D Sculpture*. Face sets are a lot like masks; they give us a way to section off parts of the sculpture. Unlike masks, face sets don't limit the influence of our brushes unless we explicitly tell them to. This is great because we can keep our face sets around for a long time and only use them when we need them. Whenever we don't need them, they can be hidden.

In this section, we'll see how face sets can be used to automatically mask areas of the sculpture, and we'll see how to create our own face sets.

Getting ready

We're going to use the `oldMonk.blend` example file again since it already comes with several face sets. We can either pick up where we left off in the previous section of this chapter, or you can download the file here: `https://github.com/PacktPublishing/Sculpting-the-Blender-Way/blob/main/Chapter06/oldMonk.blend`.

Open the `oldMonk.blend` file and we'll be ready to try using face sets.

How to do it...

Face sets are only visible when the face sets viewport overlay is active. Currently, this feature is disabled so we need to turn it on in the **Viewport Overlays** menu:

1. Make sure you're still in **Sculpt Mode** (face sets aren't available in the other modes).
2. Open the **Viewport Overlays** pop-over menu from the top-right corner of the 3D Viewport.
3. Check the box labeled **Face Sets** at the bottom of the **Sculpt** section.
4. Several areas of the sculpture will now have colors overlaid on their surface, as you can see in the following image:

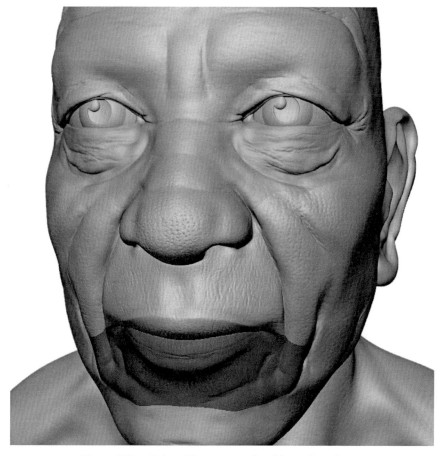

Figure 6.32 – Colored face sets on the old monk sculpture

There are three face sets on this sculpture: The green area around the underside of the eyes is a face set; the red-colored lower lip is a face set; and the gray area that makes up the rest of the sculpture is a face set. Now that we can see the face sets, we need to enable a feature for our brush that will respect the boundaries of these face sets.

5. Choose the **Grab** brush from the Toolbar or press the *G* hotkey to activate it.

6. Open the Sidebar by clicking the little < indicator along the right side of the 3D Viewport or by pressing the *N* hotkey while your mouse is in the 3D Viewport.

7. Click the vertical tab along the right edge of the Sidebar labeled **Tool** to view the tool settings.

8. Expand the **Advanced** subsection in the tool settings in the Sidebar.

9. Check the box labeled **Face Sets** in the **Auto-Masking** section.

Figure 6.33 – The Advanced settings for the brush as they appear in the Sidebar

That's all there is to it. Now, let's try pulling the lips apart with the Grab brush.

10. Drag the lower lip downward.

11. Drag the upper lip upward.

You can see our example in the following image:

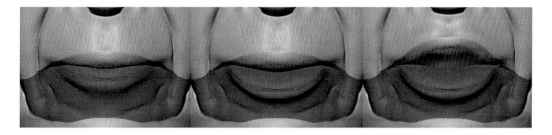

Figure 6.34 – Using face sets to adjust the lips

Using face sets has made this task easy. Did you notice how the upper lip did not move while you were adjusting the lower lip and vice versa? That's all thanks to the face sets! This sculpture came with the face sets already made. Now let's try making our own.

12. Scroll down on the Toolbar and locate and activate the **Draw Face Sets** tool.

13. Draw on the monk's nose to begin a new face set.

14. Orbit the view to make sure you've included all of the polygons that should be part of the new face set.

15. To add polygons to the new face set, hover your mouse over the colored area of the new face set (colored blue in our example), hold down the *Ctrl* key, and continue drawing over the new polygons that should be added to the face set.

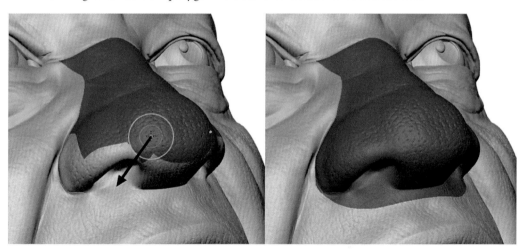

Figure 6.35 – Adding polygons to the blue nose face set

Excellent! That's how we can create face sets. There are other useful aspects of face sets as well. For instance, we can temporarily hide parts of the sculpture outside of a particular face set.

16. Hover your mouse over the colored area of the new nose face set.

17. Press the *H* hotkey to hide all polygons that don't belong to this face set.

    Pretty cool right? We can unhide the polygons by pressing the *H* hotkey again.

Face sets have other uses as well, but this should be enough to get you started with this feature.

How it works...

Face sets are based on the lowest resolution of the sculpture. Higher subdivision levels are ignored when creating face sets. We can still use them in our multiresolution workflow, but they might not match the high-resolution shape perfectly.

If you prefer to see the sculpture without the colored face sets, you can leave **Viewport Overlays** off. The **Auto-Masking** feature will still work even if the overlays are turned off.

There's more...

There are several other **Auto-Masking** options available in the brush settings. The **Topology** setting is particularly useful, although it tends to be slower than the face sets option.

See also

For more information on face sets, check out the official Blender manual page here:
`https://docs.blender.org/manual/en/latest/sculpt_paint/`
`sculpting/editing/face_sets.html`.

Cleaving off flat sections with the Line Project tool

Sculpting is usually used to create organic models such as humans, creatures, faces, hands, and other shapes that have smooth surfaces. However, it can still be useful in creating hard surfaces with our sculpting tools. One particular example is the bottom edge of the bust of a character. In classic bust sculptures, the bottom edge is usually a perfectly sharp cleaved-off section that would be difficult to achieve with our sculpting brushes.

In this section, we'll use a sculpting tool called the **Line Project** tool to try cleaving off a flat section of a sculpture.

Getting ready

We're going to use the oldMonk.blend example file again. We can either pick up where we left off in the previous section of this chapter, or you can download the file here: https://github.com/PacktPublishing/Sculpting-the-Blender-Way/ blob/main/Chapter06/oldMonk.blend.

Open the oldMonk.blend file and we'll be ready to try the Line Project tool.

How to do it...

Looking at the monk character from the front and a profile view, we can see that there is a bit of a lumpy surface below the shoulders.

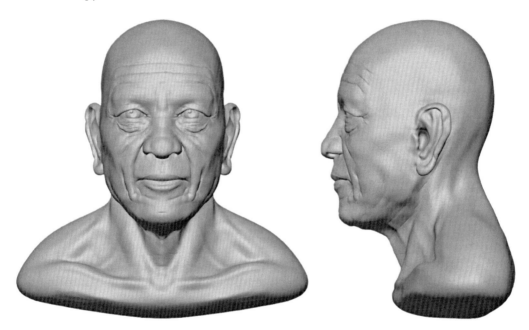

Figure 6.36 – The old monk character as seen from the front and in profile view

This looks pretty good, but we won't settle for pretty good. We can make it perfect! The best way to flatten out the bottom of this sculpture is to use the Line Project tool while our view is aligned to the side of the character:

1. Click on the positive red *X* axis in **Navigation Gizmo** in the top-right corner of the 3D Viewport to snap the view to the right side of the character.

2. Scroll down to find the **Line Project** tool on the Toolbar and click to activate it.

3. Use this tool to draw a line from the bottom left (in front of the character near the clavicle) to the top right (behind the character), as seen in the following example:

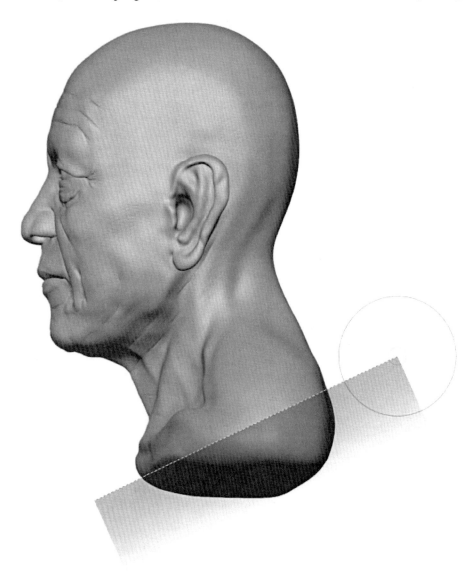

Figure 6.37 – A line drawn with the Line Project tool

4. Release the pen from the tablet surface to cleave off this section of mesh.

Excellent, that's all there is to it! Have a look at the sculpture from other angles; it should now have a perfectly flat surface underneath.

How it works...

The polygons below the line are projected onto the line so as to flatten out the surface. These polygons aren't actually removed from the model; they are just flattened out. If you need to remove geometry, it is better to do it before the multiresolution stage of the sculpting workflow.

Creating advanced masks with Sculpt Expand

Sometimes, it's important to limit the surface area that can be affected by our brushes. One way to achieve this is through the use of **Masks**. We learned a little bit about this in the *Using masks to add the ears and neck* section of *Chapter 3, Sculpting a Simple Character Head with Basic Brushes*.

The latest version of Blender includes some very powerful new ways of creating masks. In particular, we're going to look at the **Sculpt Expand** operator to create a repeating gradient pattern.

Getting ready

Nature is full of interesting patterns that can be difficult to sculpt by hand. A wonderful example of this is the underside of a gecko's foot, which can be seen in this incredible photograph by Matt Reinbold:

Figure 6.38 – The lamellae of a gecko's foot (photo by Matt Reinbold)

There are so many intricate details here! We're going to take a stylized approach to recreating this detail on the gecko foot sculpture provided. Download the example geckoFoot.blend file here: https://github.com/PacktPublishing/ Sculpting-the-Blender-Way/blob/main/Chapter06/geckoFoot.blend.

Launch Blender and open the geckoFoot.blend file. Once the file is open, we'll be ready to try using the Sculpt Expand feature.

How to do it...

The gecko foot sculpture might look detailed from the top, but orbit your view to the underside and you'll see that it's missing all of the amazing details that a gecko's foot is famous for.

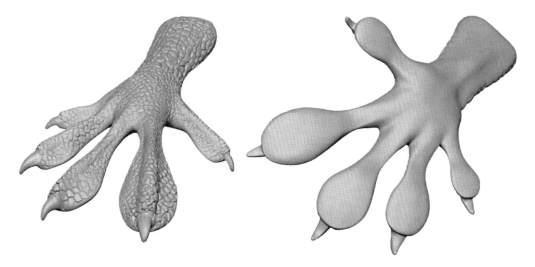

Figure 6.39 – The top side and the bottom side of the gecko foot sculpture provided

Let's try making those interesting ridges with the help of the Sculpt Expand operator! Unlike most of the tools we've used so far, Sculpt Expand is an **operator**. It is not found on the Toolbar, and it is meant to be used with hotkeys:

1. While looking at the underside of the gecko's foot, hover your pen over the tip of one of the claws. This will serve as the center point from which we will expand a mask.

2. Press the *Shift + A* hotkey to begin the **Expand Mask** operation.

> **Important Note**
> Once the operation begins, additional hotkeys for the operator will appear across the status bar at the very bottom of Blender's user interface.

3. Without bringing your pen into contact with the tablet, drag the pen slightly toward the center of the gecko's foot to begin creating a new mask.

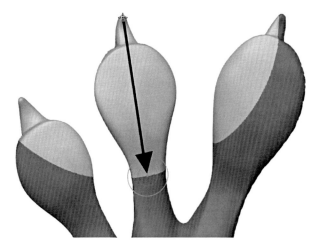

Figure 6.40 – Using the Expand Mask operator to create a mask centered around the claw tip

4. Without bringing your pen into contact with the tablet, press the *W* hotkey to increase the loop count. Keep pressing *W* or hold it down until we get enough stripes for our gecko foot pattern (see *Figure 6.41*).

5. Once we have enough stripes, press the *G* hotkey to convert each of the stripes into gradients.

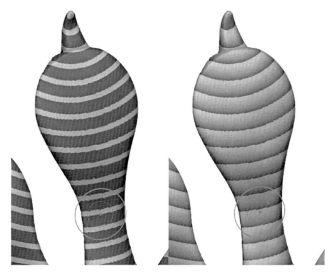

Figure 6.41 – Stripes created by increasing the loop count (left) and stripes converted to gradients (right)

6. Move your pen so that the gradients are evenly distributed, with the lightest side near the claw and the darkest side near the center of the hand.

7. Once you're satisfied with the shape of this new mask, press your pen down to the tablet to confirm the shape of the mask.

    Excellent! This type of mask would have been almost impossible to make by hand. Now we can use our Draw brush to lift up the unmasked area and create the pattern on the foot:

8. With the **Draw** brush active, expand the **Advanced** subsection in the tool settings in the Sidebar.

9. Check the box labeled **Front Faces Only** so that the **Draw** brush only affects the side of the foot that we're looking at (in this case, the underside).

10. Lightly draw over the toe to raise up the unmasked area. (You may choose to disable **Viewport Overlays** so that the mask doesn't block your view during this step.)

11. Press the *Alt + M* hotkey to clear the mask when you're finished.

12. Hold *Shift* to use the **Smooth** brush and smooth out any jagged areas.

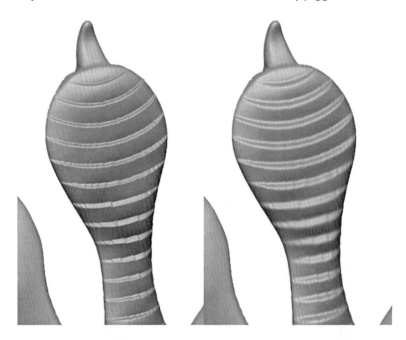

Figure 6.42 – The finished gecko toe pattern (left) with a little extra smoothing (right)

Amazing! Repeat these steps for the other four toes. When you're done, your sculpture should look something like this:

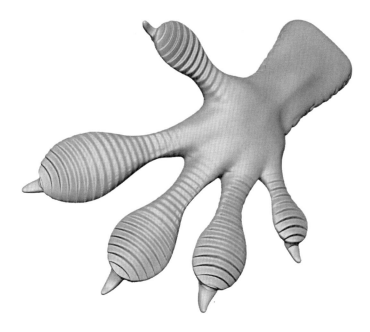

Figure 6.43 – The finished gecko toes

This is just one of the many ways that the **Sculpt Expand** feature can save us time. Imagine doing that by hand. Sculpting these details would wear out your hands so much that your fingers would look exactly like this gecko's fingers – yikes!

How it works...

Sculpt Expand works when creating masks and face sets. The *Shift + A* hotkey creates masks, while the *Shift + W* hotkey creates face sets. There are many options and hotkeys for this operator, so don't forget to check the status bar at the bottom of the screen to find new feature combinations.

There's more...

Sculpt Expand is a fantastic feature that has so much potential. There isn't enough room in this book to show off its many other capabilities, but making quick masks like this is a gateway into some really interesting stuff!

See also

- For more information on the Sculpt Expand feature, check out the developer page here: `https://developer.blender.org/D10455`.

- For a deep dive into what's possible with the Sculpt Expand feature, check out the video from the official Blender YouTube channel, *Introducing: SCULPT EXPAND | Blender Development Preview*, here: `https://www.youtube.com/watch?v=XT7h6lmE5bc`.

- The *Lamellae on a gecko's foot.* Photo made available by Matt Reinbold under the Creative Commons CC BY-SA 2.0 license. The original photo is available here: `https://www.flickr.com/photos/furryscalyman/3830578747/`.

Posing fingers with the Pose brush

We got to try the **Pose brush** earlier in this book during the *Changing resolution for appropriate details* section of *Chapter 5, Learning the Power of Subdivision and the Multiresolution Workflow.*

In this section, we'll take another look at the Pose brush and enable a feature for posing a sculpture that has joints (such as elbows or knuckles).

Getting ready

For this example, we need a sculpture that includes several joints such as knuckles. To follow along, you may either use the `geckoFoot.blend` file, or the `multiResolutionHand.blend` file from *Chapter 2, Overview of Blender's Sculpting Workflows.*

Download and open one of these files and Blender, and we'll be ready to try out the Pose brush for posing fingers.

> **Note**
>
> If your computer is not very powerful, you may need to keep the **Sculpt** subdivision level in the **Multires** modifier at a low setting to be able to follow along with this section.

How to do it...

We didn't get a very good look at the Pose brush earlier in this book because we hadn't learned much about face sets at that time. The Pose brush can be set up to respect the boundaries of the face sets and use them as points of articulation. The example file that you'll be using in this section already includes face sets at appropriate locations. All we have to do is turn on **Viewport Overlay** to see them:

1. Open the **Viewport Overlays** pop-over menu from the top-right corner of the 3D Viewport.

2. Check the box labeled **Face Sets** at the bottom of the **Sculpt** section. The colored face sets will appear on the sculpture.

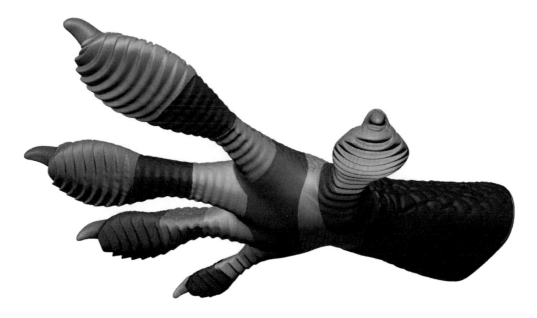

Figure 6.44 – Colored face sets on the gecko foot sculpture

3. Activate the **Pose** brush from the Toolbar.

4. Open the Sidebar and have a look at **Brush Settings**.

5. Change the **Rotation Origins** setting from **Topology** to **Face Sets**.

6. Set **Pose IK Segments** to equal the number of finger segments you would like to adjust; 3 is usually what we want.

7. Hover your pen over the tip of the appendage you want to pose. A gizmo will appear running through the length of the appendage.

Figure 6.45 – The Pose brush gizmo running through the length of the appendage

If the gizmo doesn't flow through the appendage correctly, use the *F* hotkey to adjust the radius of the Pose brush. Try to align the radius with the boundary of the face set that should serve as the first joint.

8. Press down with your pen and drag to pose the joints of the appendage.

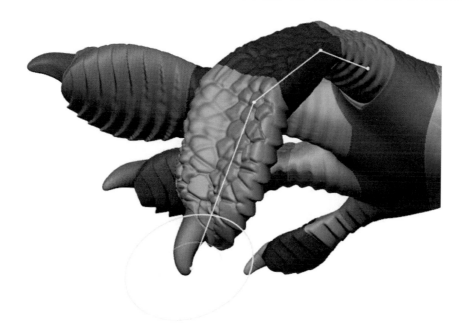

Figure 6.46 – The appendage posed with the Pose brush and face sets

And there you have it! A more advanced way of using the Pose brush. Many of the advanced sculpting features can be combined together like this in order to give you full control over the sculpting experience in Blender.

How it works...

The Pose brush works off of a principle known as **Inverse Kinematics**, which allows us to work our way backward through a chain of joints to pose an appendage.

The Pose brush is fantastic for sculptors that want to present their characters in natural poses. Keep in mind that you can only move the sculpture by relatively small amounts before the joints start to bend unnaturally. We can mitigate this by increasing the **Smooth Iterations** setting in **Brush Settings**, or by reducing the subdivision levels in the **Multiresolution** modifier before we use the Pose brush.

There's more...

The Pose brush has other options available in **Brush Settings**. Try setting the **Deformation** type to **Squash & Stretch** to change the length of an appendage.

7
Making Eyeballs

Characters are really fun to sculpt, but they look strange without eyes! As humans, we relate to living things through their eyes. This makes us hyper-aware of any problems with the eyes. As sculptors, we need to give the eyes extra attention because messed-up eyes can make our sculptures look uncanny or lifeless.

There are many ways to do eyes depending on the goal of the project. If our goal is simply to finish a sculpture as quickly as possible, we can sculpt the eyes as if they are made out of clay. We provided a set of high-quality sculpted eyes along with our example files in *Chapter 3, Sculpting a Simple Character Head with Basic Brushes*, but we'll see how to make our own in this chapter. If our goal is to make realistically rendered eyes, then we'll need to add color and materials to the eyes, so they reflect light correctly. We'll take a look at how to add some color to the eyes, so they are a little more interesting to look at. We'll explore some fun alternatives such as making insect eyes. We'll learn a more realistic way to make eyes that can be used in a high-quality render. We'll also learn a couple of ways to make cartoon-style eyes.

When we're done making the eyeballs, we'll learn how to use Constraints to aim the eyes at a target, which can make the eyes look livelier.

The main topics in this chapter are as follows:

- Creating standard clay eyeballs
- Adding color to the eyeballs
- Adding depth and realism to the eyeballs

- Creating insect eyeballs with extrusion tools

- Creating a cartoon eyeball using a Lattice

- Creating a stylized anime eye

- Aiming the eyeballs with Constraints

Technical requirements

For general requirements, refer back to the *Technical requirements* laid out in *Chapter 1, Exploring Blender's User Interface for Sculpting.*

You can download the files to follow along with this book at the GitHub link here: `https://github.com/PacktPublishing/Sculpting-the-Blender-Way`.

Creating standard clay eyeballs

While we sculpt in 3D, we tend to think of our polygons as clay instead of geometry. We learned about the **MatCap** shading option in the *Customizing solid shading mode with the pop-over menu* section of *Chapter 1, Exploring Blender's User Interface for Sculpting,* which gives the sculpture a clay-like appearance. MatCaps also give us better performance in the 3D Viewport so our computers can commit more resources to the sculpting brushes instead of shading.

Eyes look better when they have some kind of shininess to their surface. It would be nice to be able to assign a shiny MatCap to the eyes while using a matte clay MatCap for the rest of the sculpture. Unfortunately, at the time of this book's publication, Blender does not support assigning multiple MatCaps to different objects. We must share a single MatCap between all objects in the scene, so we need a different solution.

This problem predates digital sculpting, so we can learn a little from history here. Many of the most famous sculptures, including *Michelangelo's David*, had this same issue because the eyes were made out of the same slab of marble as the rest of the sculpture. The solution was to carve out the pupil of the eye while leaving a tiny bit of material behind to catch the light and give the illusion of a shiny surface. You can see this in practice in the following figure:

Figure 7.1 – The eyes of Michelangelo's David

It's a subtle but convincing effect, and it still comes in handy today when we use MatCaps in our 3D software. In this section, we'll take a look at an easy way to replicate this effect for our sculptures.

Getting ready

For this section, we will need a head sculpture that we can add eyes to. Download the provided angularHead_Start.blend file here: https://github.com/PacktPublishing/Sculpting-the-Blender-Way/blob/main/Chapter07/angularHead_Start.blend.

Launch Blender, and open the .blend file. This scene comes with the sculpture that you can see in the following figure:

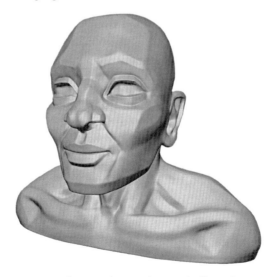

Figure 7.2 – The Angular Head example file with no eyes

Ah! Someone do something – this man has no eyes! Don't worry, we can help him; we have the technology. With this file open and ready to go, we can give this man the gift of sight.

How to do it

First off, we need to create a sphere with a special type of topology. We've mostly been using a sphere known as a Quad Sphere, but in this case, we want to use what's known as a UV Sphere:

1. Find the **Add** menu in the top-left corner of the header of the 3D Viewport.

2. Open the **Add** menu and choose **Mesh | UV Sphere**.

   Perfect, this type of sphere has a topology that works well for creating eyes, however, the poles of this sphere are currently at the top and bottom. We would like them to face front to back. We can fix this with a 90-degree rotation.

3. Open the Sidebar by clicking the little < indicator along the right side of the 3D Viewport or by pressing the *N* hotkey while your mouse is in the 3D Viewport.

4. Find the **Rotation:** option under the **Transform** section in the **Item** tab of the Sidebar.

5. Click in the first rotation field labeled **X** and type 90, then press *Enter* to apply the rotation.

   Perfect, now the UV Sphere is pointed forward so that one of its poles can serve as the iris and pupil of our eyeball. Now let's make some edits to the geometry to make it look more like an eye. To do this, we'll need to switch to **Edit Mode** and extrude some of the polygons. We learned about extruding in the *Creating a base mesh with box modeling* section of *Chapter 4, How to Make a Base Mesh for a 3D Sculpture*. Let's use some of those techniques again to form the iris and pupil.

6. Change the Interaction Mode from **Object Mode** to **Edit Mode** using the drop-down menu in the top-left corner of the header of the 3D Viewport.

7. Make sure you're using **Vertex Select** mode by clicking the corresponding icon in the header of the 3D Viewport, or by pressing the *1* hotkey.

8. Select the vertex at the very front of the sphere where all of the edges converge into a pole.

9. Open the **Select** menu in the top-left corner of the header of the 3D Viewport and choose **Select More/Less | More**. This will grow the selection to include all of the neighboring vertices.

10. Grow the selection two more times either by using the same menu option or by pressing the **Repeat Last** operator hotkey: *Shift + R.*

Your selection should look like our example in the following figure:

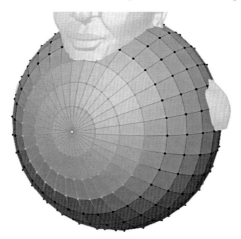

Figure 7.3 – The selected vertices in front of the UV Sphere

Now we need to extrude the selection to form the ridge around the iris.

11. Find and activate the **Extrude Region** tool from the Toolbar.

12. Click and drag inward on the yellow + of the **Extrude Region** gizmo to extrude the geometry inward, as seen in the following figure:

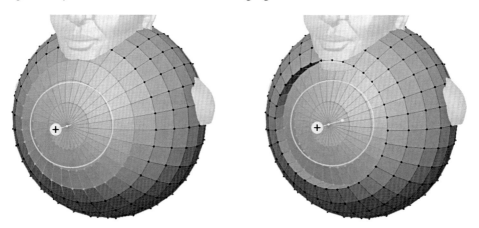

Figure 7.4 – The front of the UV Sphere extruded inward

13. Find and activate the **Scale** tool from the Toolbar.

14. Click and drag outward on the green *Y* axis of the scale gizmo to adjust the size along the *Y* axis. Keep dragging outward until the selected polygons invert and form an indent on the surface of the sphere.

15. Click anywhere within the white circle of the scale gizmo and drag slightly inward to slightly decrease the size of the selected polygons, creating a thin rim around the iris as seen in the following figure:

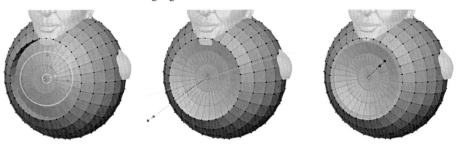

Figure 7.5 – The inverted dent of the iris formed by scaling along the Y axis then scaling inward

Perfect, this indent will serve as the iris. To form the pupil, we'll extrude the center part inward.

16. Open the **Select** menu in the top-left corner of the header of the 3D Viewport and choose **Select More/Less | Less**. This will shrink the selection.

17. Shrink the selection one more time either by using the same menu option or by pressing the **Repeat Last** operator hotkey: *Shift + R*.

18. Activate the **Extrude Region** tool from the Toolbar again.

19. Click and drag inward on the yellow + of the extrude region gizmo to extrude the geometry inward very slightly to form a thin rim around the pupil.

    Extrude a second time a little further back to give the pupil some depth as seen in the following figure:

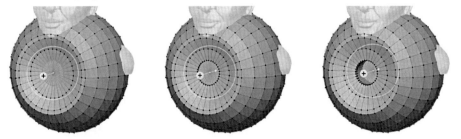

Figure 7.6 – The pupil formed with two extrusions into the sphere

We're done with our **Edit Mode** tools now.

Next, we need to place the eyeballs in the eye sockets of the sculpture.

20. Change the Interaction Mode back to **Object Mode** using the drop-down menu in the top-left corner of the header of the 3D Viewport, or by pressing the *Tab* hotkey.

21. Use the **Move** and **Scale** tools to place the eyeball in the left eye socket.

> Tip
> Instead of using the tools, you may use the Sidebar to type in exact transform values to place the eyeball. We've used the following values in our example:
> **Location:** 0.220422, -0.65479, 1.12139, and all the three values for **Scale:** 0.118379.

We can add the glint in the eye using **Sculpt Mode**.

22. Change the Interaction Mode to **Sculpt Mode** using the drop-down menu in the top-left corner of the header of the 3D Viewport.

23. While in **Sculpt Mode**, use the *Ctrl + 2* hotkey to quickly add a Multiresolution modifier with two levels of subdivision to the eye.

24. Use the **Draw** brush to sculpt a small bump on the rim of the iris as seen in the following figure:

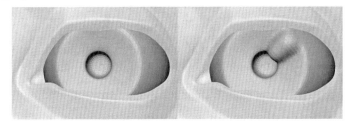

Figure 7.7 – The glint of the eye sculpted into the iris

It might not look like much, but this small detail can add a little liveliness to the eye. Now let's finish it off.

25. Change the Interaction Mode back to **Object Mode**.

26. Change the **Multires** modifier's **Level Viewport** setting to 2 so that we can see the glint of the eye in **Object Mode**.

27. Open the **Object** menu in the top-left corner of the header of the 3D Viewport and choose **Shade Smooth**. This will make the polygons of the eye appear smooth.

28. Open the **Object** menu again, and choose **Duplicate Linked**. This will make a duplicate of the eye that shares geometry with the original eye.

29. Press the *Esc* key to cancel moving the duplicate eyeball, which will place it back in its original location.

30. Find the **Location:** option under the **Transform** section in the **Item** tab of the Sidebar.

31. Click in the first location field labeled **X** to begin editing the value. Add a - before the original number to make it negative, then press *Enter* to apply. (In our example, the original value was 0.220422 and after editing it the new value is -0.220422.) This will move the duplicate eyeball into the right eye socket.

Wonderful! Our finished eyes turned out like this:

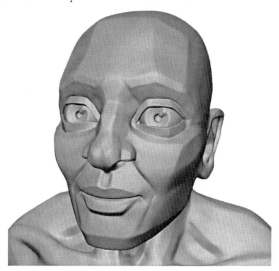

Figure 7.8 – The finished clay eyes

Now he's ready to go out and see the world!

How it works

There are many variations of this technique. Some have a larger iris that protrudes outward instead of inward. Some have no noticeable pupil indentation. Some have the sculpted glint overlap with the pupil much further than our example. All of these examples work by tricking the viewer into seeing depth in the eye with a small sheen over the pupil. Without this subtle glint in the eye, eyes tend to look lifeless and distracting.

Feel free to develop your own style. It's highly recommended that you create this type of eye early on in the creation of your sculpture so that you can shape the eyelids correctly around the eyeballs. This example character is designed in a very stylized manner, so these clay eyes complement that look. However, many art styles don't lend themselves to this type of eye, so it's common to swap out these clay eyes for something with more color and realism once we get to the late stages of the sculpture.

See also

The *David by Michelangelo* photo was made available by Jörg Bittner Unna as part of the Wikimedia Commons under the Creative Commons CC BY 3.0 license. The original photo is available here: `https://commons.wikimedia.org/wiki/File:%27David%27_by_Michelangelo_Fir_JBU013.jpg`.

Adding color to the eyeballs

Up to this point, we have not concerned ourselves with the color of our sculptures, but a small splash of color does wonders for our characters' eyeballs. Every vertex in a 3D model can store color information known as Vertex Colors. Vertex Colors can be painted with a special Interaction Mode called **Vertex Paint** mode. In this section, we'll learn how to apply color to eyeballs using **Vertex Paint** mode.

Getting ready

For this section, we will need a head sculpture with eyes that can be painted. Download the provided `coloredEyes_Start.blend` file here: `https://github.com/PacktPublishing/Sculpting-the-Blender-Way/blob/main/Chapter07/coloredEyes_Start.blend`.

Launch Blender, and open the `.blend` file. This scene comes with the sculpture that you can see in the following figure:

Figure 7.9 – The Colored Eyes example file prior to painting the eye color

She looks nice, but a little scary. Her eyes were created through a very similar process to the eyes in the *Creating standard clay eyeballs* section of this chapter. However, there is no carved detail in the front of the eye to represent the iris, pupil, and glint in the eye. Because of this, her eyes don't really look alive. Now let's try painting her eyeballs to give them some color.

How to do it

The object data for this character's eyes is linked together, so we only have to paint one and the other will automatically be updated to match. Pick either the left eye or the right eye and we can begin:

1. Select one of the eyes.

2. Open the **View** menu in the top-left corner of the header of the 3D Viewport, and choose **Frame Selected**.

3. Use the **View** menu again to choose **Viewpoint | Front**.

4. Change the Interaction Mode from **Object Mode** to **Vertex Paint** using the drop-down menu in the top-left corner of the header of the 3D Viewport.

5. In the Sidebar, expand the **Color Palette** subsection under the **Brush Settings** section of the **Tool** tab as seen in the following figure:

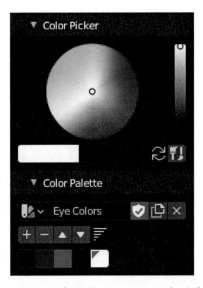

Figure 7.10 – Color Palette as seen in the Sidebar

Color palettes are an excellent way to prepare colors before we paint. This example file comes with a color palette called **Eye Colors**, which contains all the colors we'll need to paint this character's eyes. There are five color swatches in this palette. We will be using them in order from left to right.

6. Click on the first little colored square on the far left of the color palette (it's a very dark blue).

7. Set the brush **Radius** to approximately the size of the iris of the eye.

8. Use your pen to draw a large circle at the center of the eyeball. The soft edges of this circle will become the outer perimeter of the iris known as the limbal ring:

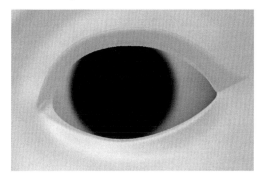

Figure 7.11 – The limbal ring painted on the eyeball

9. Click on the second little colored square in the color palette (it's a dark blue).

10. Use your pen to draw over the top of the same spot covering the dark blue circle, leaving a thin dark edge around the perimeter. This inner color will form the iris while the dark outer part from the previously painted circle will be left behind to form the limbal ring:

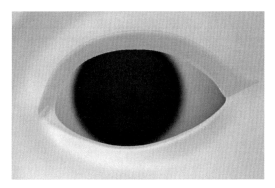

Figure 7.12 – The iris painted over the top of the limbal ring

11. Click on the third little colored square in the color palette (it's a light blue).

12. Find the **Strength** setting in the header of the 3D Viewport and click the **Strength Pressure** icon to activate pen pressure sensitivity.

13. Reduce the brush **Radius** to about one-third of the size of the iris.

14. Draw lightly with your pen under the bottom half of the iris to create a highlight in the eye and brighten up the iris:

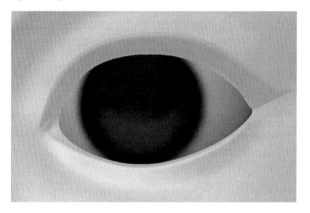

Figure 7.13 – The iris highlight painted

15. Click on the fourth little colored square in the color palette (it's black).

16. Use your pen to draw a large circle at the center of the eyeball. This will become the pupil:

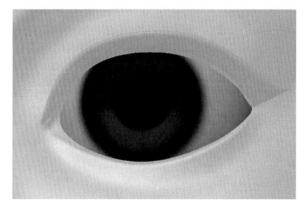

Figure 7.14 – The pupil painted

17. Click on the fifth and final little colored square in the color palette (it's white).

18. Reduce the brush **Radius** to about half the size of the pupil.

19. Use your pen to draw a large circle slightly up and to the side of the pupil. This will become the glint in the eye that gives it some fake glossiness and makes it feel alive:

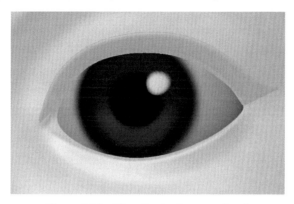

Figure 7.15 – The glint in the eye painted

This is looking pretty nice, however, when we change our Interaction Mode back to **Object Mode** the color in the eyes disappears. This is because the viewport shading is not currently utilizing Vertex Colors. Let's fix this so we can see our character's eyes properly.

20. Change the Interaction Mode back to **Object Mode**.

21. Open the **Viewport Shading** pop-over menu from the top-right corner of the 3D Viewport.

22. Under the **Color** section, click on the button labeled **Vertex**.

Perfect, now we can see the color in our character's eyes:

Figure 7.16 – The Colored Eyes example file after painting the eye color

Beautiful! Vertex Paint is just one way that we can add color to our sculptures, and for a character like this, it's an excellent way to bring the eyes to life!

How it works

In 2D painting software, we can add color to each pixel on the canvas. If we have a high number of pixels, we can create high-resolution paintings. Vertex painting is a very similar concept, but instead of painting pixels, we paint the individual vertices of the 3D model. The eyes in this example file had subdivision applied to them so that they each had thousands of vertices to work with.

Another interesting aspect of vertex painting is that the arrangement of the polygons can dictate the pattern that can be painted into the vertices. In this example, the eyes were made out of UV Spheres that have concentric rings in the arrangement of the polygons. Because of this, it is very easy to paint circles into the front of the eyes since those circles follow the pattern of the polygons.

See also

As of this book's publication, Blender's Vertex Paint mode is somewhat limited: It doesn't work correctly with the Multiresolution modifier, and Vertex Colors don't display correctly while in Sculpt Mode. There is a current development task for Sculpt Vertex Colors, which is available in experimental versions of Blender. You can follow the development progress of this feature here: `https://developer.blender.org/D5975`.

Adding depth and realism to the eyeballs

The eyes that we made in the previous sections of this chapter have been simplified to work around the limitations of the 3D Viewport and **MatCap** settings. But it is possible to create much more realistic eyes instead.

To accurately represent the depth of a real eye, we need to model two parts of the eye: an inner part that has an iris and a pupil carved into the surface, as well as an outer part of the eye that represents the cornea.

This outer part poses a problem: it requires transparency and refraction in order to correctly display the inner part through its surface. However, our current 3D Viewport settings can't handle transparency and refraction, so we need to learn a little bit about materials and rendering.

We took a very brief look at rendering in the *Exploring the viewport shading modes* section of *Chapter 1, Exploring Blender's User Interface for Sculpting*. For our purposes in this chapter, the **Material Preview** shading mode will be sufficient to visualize the refraction of the cornea. We'll learn more about rendering throughout *Chapter 10, Rendering Sculptures for Your Portfolio*.

Getting ready

For this section, we've provided a model of the inner eye and the outer eye so we can focus on creating the materials and setting up the render settings. Download the provided realisticEye_Start.blend file here: https://github.com/PacktPublishing/Sculpting-the-Blender-Way/blob/main/Chapter07/realisticEye_Start.blend.

Launch Blender, and open the .blend file. This scene comes with the two parts of the eye, which you can see in the following figure:

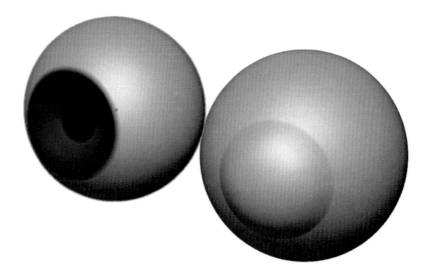

Figure 7.17 – The inner and outer eye pieces

The inner eye part on the left was created with a very similar process as the eyes we created in the *Creating standard clay eyeballs* section of this chapter, but without the fake sculpted glint in the eye. It also has Vertex Colors painted into the iris and pupil, which we learned how to do in the *Adding color to the eyeballs* section of this chapter, except there is no white glint painted into the Vertex Colors. This inward indentation of the iris closely mimics how real eyes are structured.

The outer eye on the right was made from a simple UV Sphere, and the bulge in the front represents the cornea of the eye. The cornea was created with the Quad Sphere topology, which gives a smoother appearance across the cornea. In real eyes, the cornea refracts light and has a glossy appearance. This piece of the eye is very slightly larger than the inner piece so it can fully surround it.

Both of these pieces have Subdivision Surface modifiers attached to them, so they look extra smooth. Now let's learn how to add materials to these eye parts to create a realistic eye.

How to do it

The first step is to change the viewport shading setting to **Material Preview** using the four sphere icons in the top-right corner of the 3D Viewport.

Click on the third of the four sphere icons to set the shading mode to **Material Preview**.

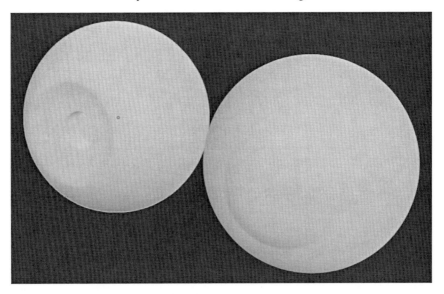

Figure 7.18 – The eye pieces in Material Preview mode

So far so good, but what happened to the color? Up to this point, we've been using the **Solid** viewport shading option, which is great for preview purposes, but now that we're in **Material Preview** mode, we need to create materials that tell the viewport how to render each object, and right now these objects are using a default material that shows up white.

Let's make a new material for the eye pieces:

1. Click on the red sphere tab in the Properties editor to switch to the **Material Properties** tab.

2. Click the **New** button to create a new material for the **Eye_Inner** object.

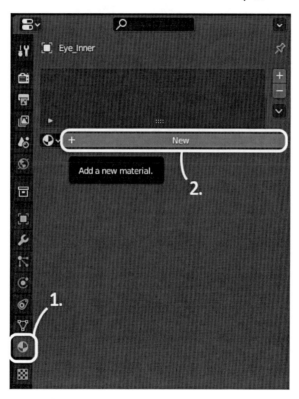

Figure 7.19 – The new material button as seen in the Properties editor

3. Click on the word **Material** and rename it to InnerEye.

Materials can be shaded in different ways. The default surface shading for new materials is called Principled BSDF, however, we need a simple type of shading called Diffuse BSDF.

4. To change the **Surface** type, click on **Principled BSDF** and choose **Diffuse BSDF**.

Figure 7.20 – Changing the Surface type to Diffuse BSDF

Now we can hook up the Vertex Colors to the color slot of the diffuse shader.

5. Click on the yellow dot to the left of the **Color** slot and choose **Vertex Color** from the **Input** column.

Figure 7.21 – Setting the Vertex Color as the input for the color slot

Excellent, we've got our color back. Now let's set up the glossy refraction material for the outer eye.

6. Select the **Eye_Outer** object.

7. Click the **New** button to create a new material for the **Eye_Outer** object.

8. Click on the word **Material** and rename it to `OuterEye`.

    For this material, we can use shading called Glass BSDF, which can be used for glossiness, refraction, and transparency.

9. To change the **Surface** type, click on **Principled BSDF** and choose **Glass BSDF**.

10. Change **Roughness** to `0.2`.

11. Change **IOR** to 1.38.

    Refraction is a special characteristic of the material, so we need to enable it under
    the **Settings** section of **Material Properties**.

12. Find the **Settings** section in the Properties editor and check the box labeled **Screen
    Space Refraction**.

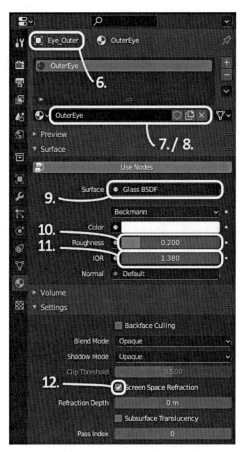

Figure 7.22 – Steps for creating the OuterEye material

Perfect, our materials are ready, and now we have enabled refraction in the render
settings.

13. Click on the gray camera-back icon in the Properties editor to switch to the **Render
    Properties** tab.

14. Find the **Screen Space Reflections** section in the Properties editor. Check the box
    and click the drop-down arrow to the left of the word **Screen Space Reflections** to
    expand the subsection.

15. Check the box labeled **Refraction** within the **Screen Space Reflections** subsection.

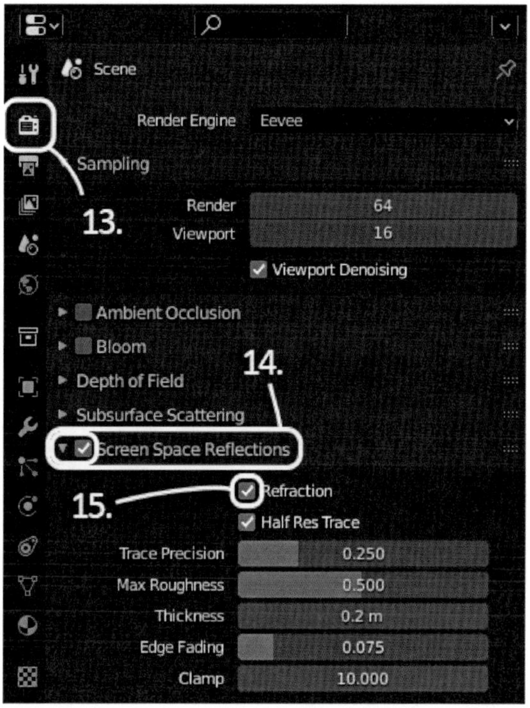

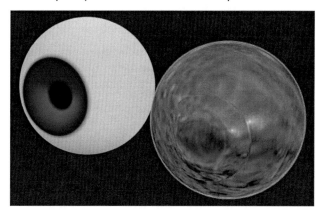

Figure 7.23 – Steps for enabling Screen Space Reflections / Refraction

Excellent, our two Eye objects should look like they do in the following figure:

Figure 7.24 – The eye pieces with their new materials

The last thing to do is to place the **Eye_Outer** object on top of the **Eye_Inner** object.

16. Find the **Location:** option under the **Transform** section in the **Item** tab of the Sidebar.

17. Click in the first location field labeled **X** and type 0, then press *Enter* to reset the position of the **Eye_Outer** object.

Lastly, we can combine these two objects together so they can be moved around as a single object.

18. Hold the *Shift* key and click on the **Eye_Inner** object to add it to the selection.

19. Open the **Object** menu in the top-left corner of the 3D Viewport and choose **Join**.

We should now see a single object in the Outliner. Let's rename it appropriately.

20. Either double-click the name of the object in the Outliner or press the *F2* hotkey to rename it to Eye.

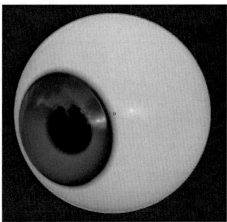

Figure 7.25 – The finished realistic eye

Now that's a pretty looking eyeball! You can copy and paste this eye into your other sculpture scenes to use it for your characters. Just remember to enable **Material Preview** mode as well as **Screen Space Reflections / Refraction** for each scene you want to use this eye in.

How it works

This is a much more realistic eye than we've made previously. However, it only works well in the **Material Preview** and **Rendered** viewport shading modes. This is because refraction is an advanced rendering effect, and without refraction, this style of eye doesn't look very good. Since we usually sculpt in **Solid** viewport shading with **MatCaps** enabled, it is typical to use one of the other types of eyes during the earlier stages of sculpting.

We can replace the eyes in our sculpture with this more realistic eye when we get to the end of the sculpting process. That way, we can render a final image with the highest quality eyes for our portfolios.

See also

The **IOR** setting for the outer eye material stands for **Index of Refraction**. This value defines the amount that light bends when interacting with the surface of the material. We used a value of 1.38 for our cornea because that is a realistic IOR value for the human cornea. For a list of IOR values for other refractive materials, you can use this handy list: https://pixelandpoly.com/ior.html.

Creating insect eyeballs with extrusion tools

Not all eyes look like human eyeballs. There are times when we can be more experimental with eye designs. Insects have very different eyes than mammals. In this section, we'll try using some technical steps to create a hexagon pattern for insect eyes.

Getting ready

For this section, we will need a head sculpture that will look good with some crazy insect eyes. Download the provided insectHead_Start.blend file here: https://github.com/PacktPublishing/Sculpting-the-Blender-Way/blob/main/Chapter07/insectHead_Start.blend.

Launch Blender, and open the .blend file. This scene comes with the sculpture that you can see in the following figure:

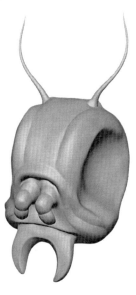

Figure 7.26 – Insect head with no eyes

Let's give this bug some eyes!

How to do it

These steps are going to get pretty technical, but a healthy dose of technical detail can really take our creations to the next level. We'll start by creating an Ico Sphere, which has a special type of topology that lends itself well to creating a hexagon pattern:

1. Hide the **Insect Head** object by clicking on the eyeball icon in the Outliner next to its name.

2. Find the **Add** menu in the top-left corner of the header of the 3D Viewport.

3. Open the menu and choose **Mesh | Ico Sphere**.

   A panel labeled **Add Ico Sphere** will appear in the bottom-left corner of the 3D Viewport. This is known as the **Adjust Last Operation** panel. Click on the **Adjust Last Operation** panel to expand the options for creating the Ico Sphere.

4. Increase **Subdivisions** to 4.

5. Either double-click the name of the Ico Sphere in the Outliner or press the *F2* hotkey to rename it to Insect Eye.

   Now that the Ico Sphere has been created, we can use a Subdivision Surface modifier to add even more polygons. Due to the arrangement of the polygons in the Ico Sphere, the subdivision algorithm will result in a pattern that we can extract hexagons from.

6. Click on the blue wrench tab in the Properties editor to switch to the **Modifiers** tab.

7. Click **Add Modifier** and choose **Subdivision Surface** from the **Generate** column in the list of modifiers.

8. Increase the **Levels Viewport** option from 1 to 2.

9. Click on the downward arrow next to the icons at the top of the modifier settings and choose **Apply**.

10. Change the Interaction Mode from **Object Mode** to **Edit Mode** using the drop-down menu in the top-left corner of the header of the 3D Viewport.

   The hexagon pattern we're looking for is buried amidst all of these extra vertices. Luckily, with just a few simple steps, we can remove the unwanted vertices, leaving behind a hexagon pattern (with a few pentagons interspersed). In order to do this, we need to find one vertex with six connecting edges as well as one vertex with five connecting edges. You can see an example of these vertices in the following figure. There will be one of these vertices in the center of each hexagon and pentagon:

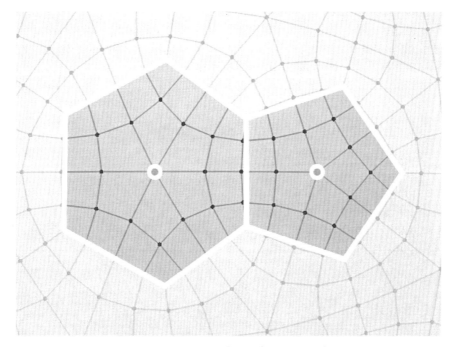

Figure 7.27 – Vertices with 5 and 6 connected edges

We need to select one of each of these vertices.

11. Select one of the vertices that has six connecting edges.

12. Hold the *Shift* key to add to the selection and select one of the vertices that have five connecting edges.

    You should now have two vertices selected, one at the center of a hexagon and one at the center of a pentagon – refer to *Figure 7.27*. Now we can use several of Blender's menu options to select all of the unwanted vertices and remove them.

13. Open the **Select** menu in the top-left corner of the header of the 3D Viewport and choose **Select Similar | Amount of Connecting Edges**.

14. Open the **Select** menu again and choose **Select More/Less | More**.

15. Open the **Mesh** menu and choose **Delete | Vertices**.

16. Open the **Select** menu one more time and choose **All**.

17. Open the **Vertex** menu and choose **New Edge/Face from Vertices**.

18. Open the **Mesh** menu again and choose **Clean Up | Limited Dissolve**.

Awesome, now we've removed all of the unnecessary vertices, leaving behind the hexagon pattern we were looking for, as you can see in the following figure:

Figure 7.28 – The sphere with a hexagon pattern

Now we can turn these hexagons into raised-up pieces to represent the bumpiness of the insect's eyes. We'll start by extruding each of these polygons individually with the Extrude Individual tool.

19. Switch to **Face Select** mode by clicking the corresponding icon in the header of the 3D Viewport, or by pressing the *3* hotkey.

20. Find the **Extrude Region** tool on the Toolbar. This tool has a small arrow indicator in the bottom-right corner to let us know that there are similar tools stacked underneath it.

21. Click and hold on the **Extrude Region** tool to open a list of similar tools and choose the **Extrude Individual** tool from the list.

22. Click and drag upward on the yellow extrude gizmo. Keep dragging until you arrive at an offset of about `0.03` m (this offset amount can be seen in the top-left corner of the 3D Viewport while dragging the extrude gizmo).

So far so good. Now let's shrink each of these polygons down slightly toward their individual centers. This can be achieved by changing our Transform Pivot Point then using the **Scale** tool.

23. Find the **Transform Pivot Point** drop-down menu in the center of the header of the 3D Viewport and choose **Individual Origins**.

Figure 7.29 – The Transform Pivot Point menu as seen in the center of the header of the 3D Viewport

24. Find and activate the **Scale** tool from the Toolbar.

25. Use the tool to scale the polygons down slightly to about 0.9 (this scale amount can be seen in the top-left corner of the 3D Viewport while dragging the scale gizmo).

26. Change the Interaction Mode back to **Object Mode**.

We've made good progress. Now let's add a modifier to bevel the hard edges and make this eye look more natural with rounded edges.

27. Navigate to the **Modifiers** tab in the Properties editor and click **Add Modifier**.

28. Choose **Bevel** from the **Generate** column in the list of modifiers.

29. Set **Amount** to 0.015 m.

30. Increase **Segments** from 1 to 2.

Perfect, now it just needs smooth shading.

31. Open the **Object** menu in the top-left corner of the 3D Viewport and choose **Shade Smooth**.

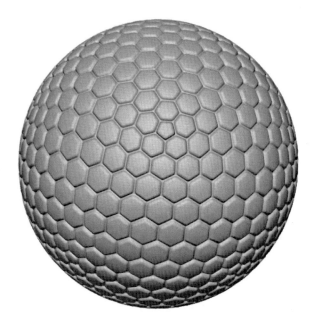

Figure 7.30 – The finished insect eye

This eye is looking pretty good. Let's place it into the eye socket in the head, then mirror it over to the other side so the insect can have two eyes.

32. Unhide the **Insect Head** object by clicking on the eyeball icon in the Outliner next to its name.

33. Use the **Move** tool from the Toolbar to place the **Insect Eye** object in the left eye socket of the **Insect Head** object.

34. Navigate to the **Modifiers** tab in the Properties editor and click **Add Modifier**.

35. Choose **Mirror** from the **Generate** column in the list of modifiers.

36. Click on the empty field in the **Mirror** modifier labeled **Mirror Object** to bring up a list of objects in the scene and choose the **Insect Head** object.

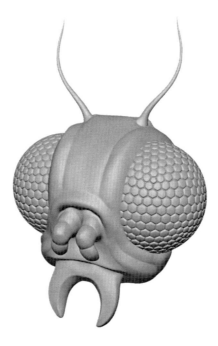

Figure 7.31 – The finished insect head

Excellent, now the insect's head is complete!

How it works

Blender comes with many tools that reduce the number of things we have to do by hand. Instead of selecting each of the problematic vertices by hand, we can identify similarity and use Blender's **Select Similar** tools to do the repetitive work for us.

The modifiers have also been very helpful for making small dynamic adjustments to the model. Remember modifiers are fully dynamic, so if you decide you want to use different settings for the Bevel modifier, you can change those settings at any time.

There's more

There are many more modeling tools like this that can be used to supplement our sculptures. It's a little less hands-on than using our sculpting brushes, but this step-by-step approach can often lead to more precise results with less manual work.

Try variations of this workflow. What would happen if you used different bevel amounts in the Bevel modifier? What would happen if you added a Subdivision Surface modifier? We encourage you to explore!

Creating a cartoon eyeball using a Lattice

We've already seen some pretty interesting ways to create an eye, but how about an eye that isn't spherical? It's common in cartoons to create elongated oval-shaped eyes.

We could sculpt a sphere into an elongated shape using the Grab brush, however, this will not allow us to rotate the eye when we want to have it look around. We need some way to deform the eye shape while maintaining the ability to rotate the eyeball. In Blender, we can achieve this through a Lattice. A Lattice is a special type of object that we can use to create a deformation cage around other objects. In this section, we'll use a Lattice to deform a spherical eyeball into an elongated oval-shaped eyeball.

Getting ready

We can use any spherical eye as a starting point. For our example, we're going to start off with the realistic eye we created in the *Adding depth and realism to the eyeballs* section of this chapter. If you have not completed that section, you can begin this section with the `realisticEye_End.blend` file, which can be downloaded here: `https://github.com/PacktPublishing/Sculpting-the-Blender-Way/blob/main/Chapter07/realisticEye_End.blend`.

Launch Blender, and open the `.blend` file. Once you've got the file open, we'll be ready to try using a Lattice object to elongate the shape of the eyeball.

How to do it

First, we need to create a Lattice object and adjust its size to fit the eyeball:

1. Open the **Add** menu in the top-left corner of the header of the 3D Viewport and choose **Lattice**.

2. Use the **Move** and **Scale** tools to adjust the position and size of the Lattice as needed to surround the eyeball as seen in the following figure:

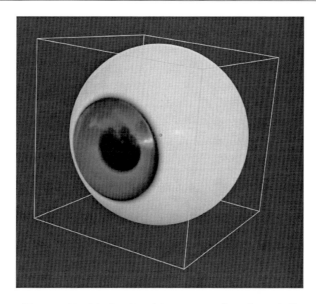

Figure 7.32 – The Lattice object surrounding the eyeball

3. Click on the **Eye** object to select it first, then hold the *Shift* key and click on the **Lattice object** to add it to the selection. The objects must be selected in this order for the next step to work properly.

4. Open the **Object** menu in the top-left corner of the header of the 3D Viewport and choose **Parent | Lattice Deform**.

5. Now the **Eye** object is attached to the **Lattice** via a **Lattice** modifier. If we edit the Lattice, the shape of the eye will deform.

6. Click on the **Lattice object** to select it.

7. Change the Interaction Mode from **Object Mode** to **Edit Mode** using the drop-down menu in the top-left corner of the header of the 3D Viewport.

8. Select the four vertices on top of the Lattice.

9. Use the **Move** tool to pull these vertices upward.

10. Use the **Scale** tool to shrink the spacing between these four vertices.

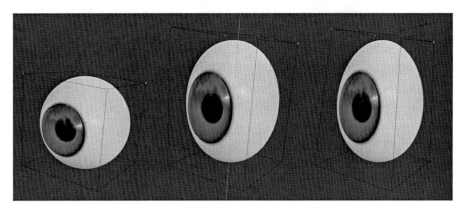

Figure 7.33 – Moving and scaling the vertices of the Lattice deforms the eyeball

11. Change the Interaction Mode back to **Object Mode** when you're finished shaping the eye.

12. Hide the **Lattice object** by clicking on the eyeball icon next to its name in the Outliner.

And that's all there is to it! Try selecting the **Eye** object and using the **Rotate** tool to aim the eye in different directions. Notice how the iris and pupil of the eye are able to rotate in new orientations while the deformed shape remains constant. That's the power of the Lattice!

How it works

The Lattice deformation works by attaching a Lattice modifier to the eyeball. As long as the modifier is attached to the eyeball, the deformation will be dynamically applied to the eyeball. We used the **Parent | Lattice Deform** option as a shortcut for creating the Lattice modifier. This option also made the Eye object a child of the Lattice object in the Outliner. This means that whenever we move the Lattice object, the Eye object will move along with it.

See also

The Lattice has many settings that make it useful for more complicated deformations. For instance, we can add more resolution to the U, V, and W dimensions of the Lattice, which will give us more vertices for customizing the shape of the deformation. You can read more about the Lattice object type here: https://docs.blender.org/manual/en/latest/animation/lattice.html.

Creating a stylized anime eye

Not all types of eyes can be created with spheres. Sometimes we want to make something that looks more like 2D art. Anime eyes are a perfect example of this. They tend to be a very flat type of shape instead of spherical.

One approach for creating this look is to model flat geometry to represent the surface of the eye, then create additional pieces to represent the iris, pupil, and glint. In this section, we'll use this approach and make use of several modifiers to complete the effect.

Getting ready

For this section, we have prepared a character sculpture created in an anime art style. Download the `animeEyes_Start.blend` file here: `https://github.com/PacktPublishing/Sculpting-the-Blender-Way/blob/main/Chapter07/animeEyes_Start.blend`.

Launch Blender, and open the `.blend` file. This scene comes with the sculpture that you can see in the following figure:

Figure 7.34 – The anime head sculpture

This character's eyes are not like the spherical eyes we've seen previously in this chapter. They have been modeled as flat planes with a subtle curvature and placed into the eye sockets. This file also comes with an extra option enabled under the **Viewport Shading** menu called **Outline**. This shading feature creates a thin outline around the perimeter of each object. This will help with the visual style of the eyes we're going to make for this character.

Now we need to make some circles for the iris, pupil, and glint in the eye, then place them on top of the flat eye planes.

How to do it

Now let's create a circle for the iris:

1. Open the **Add** menu in the top-left corner of the header of the 3D Viewport and choose **Mesh | Circle**.

2. A panel labeled **Add Circle** will appear in the bottom-left corner of the 3D Viewport. Click on this panel to expand the options for creating the circle.

3. Change **Fill Type** from **Nothing** to **N-Gon**.

4. Rename the **Circle** object to Iris.

5. Set the **Rotation: X** field in the Sidebar to 90 to rotate the circle upright.

    Good, now we need to create the pupil within the iris.

6. Change the Interaction Mode to **Edit Mode**.

7. Activate the **Inset Faces** tool from the Toolbar, and use the yellow gizmo to inset the faces, creating a perimeter of polygons as you can see in the following figure:

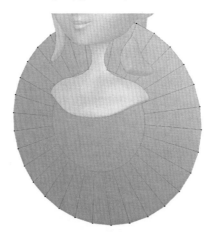

Figure 7.35 – The perimeter created from the Inset Faces tool

> **Tip**
>
> If you can't inset the faces far enough using the gizmo, then you can adjust the
> **Thickness** setting in the **Adjust Last Operation** panel in the bottom-left corner
> of the 3D Viewport. A **Thickness** value of 0.5 m works well in this case.

Now that we have the perimeter of polygons set up, we can assign materials to the
inner and outer parts to give the iris and the pupil separate colors.

8. Click on the red sphere tab in the Properties editor to switch to the **Material
   Properties** tab.

9. Click the **New** button to create a new material.

10. Click on the word **Material** and rename it to Iris.

11. Scroll down to find the **Viewport Display** section in the Properties editor and click
    the drop-down arrow to expand the subsection.

12. Click on the white color swatch labeled **Color** and use the color picker to choose
    a color for the iris. A light blue color will work nicely here.

    So far so good. Now we need a second material for the pupil.

13. Scroll back to the top of the Properties editor and click the + button in the top-right
    corner to add a second material slot to the object.

14. Click the **Assign** button to assign the selected vertices to the second material slot.

15. Click the **New** button to create a new material for the second material slot.

16. Click on the word **Material** and rename it to Pupil.

17. Scroll back down to the **Viewport Display** section and use the color picker to
    change the **Color** to black.

18. Change the Interaction Mode back to **Object Mode**.

Now our iris and pupil have some color, as can be seen in the following figure:

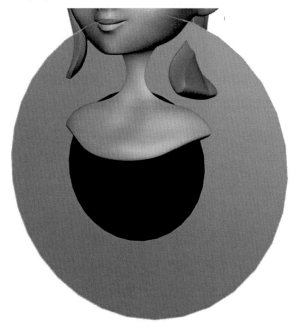

Figure 7.36 – The iris and pupil with their materials assigned

Looking good. Now we need to position the eye over the top of the eye plane in the eye socket. We can use Blender's snapping tools to help us with this process:

1. Find the **Snapping** settings next to the magnet icon in the center of the header of the 3D Viewport and click to open the pop-over menu.

2. Change the **Snap To** setting to **Face**.

3. Change the **Snap With** setting to **Center**.

4. Check the box labeled **Align Rotation to Target**.

Figure 7.37 – The snap settings

5. Use the **Move** tool to move the iris on top of the EyePlane object and hold the *Ctrl* key to activate snapping while moving.

6. Use the **Scale** tool to shrink the iris down to a reasonable size. If you would like a more stylized look for the eye, you can scale the width to be lesser than the height.

    The placement of the eye for our example can be seen in the following figure:

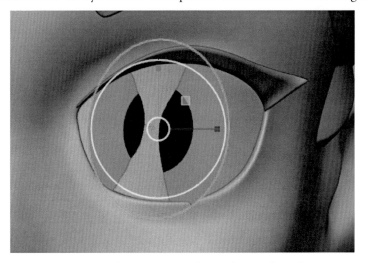

Figure 7.38 – The iris positioned over the EyePlane object

Now that the iris is in the right place, we need to shrinkwrap it to the surface of the EyePlane object so that it conforms to the subtle curvature properly:

1. Click on the blue wrench icon in the Properties editor to switch to the **Modifiers** tab.

2. Click **Add Modifier** and choose **Shrinkwrap** from the **Deform** column in the list of modifiers.

3. Change **Snap Mode** to **Above Surface**.

4. Click on the empty field in the Shrinkwrap modifier labeled **Target** to bring up a list of objects in the scene and choose the EyePlane object.

5. Set **Offset** to 0.003 m to make the iris float slightly above the surface of the EyePlane object.

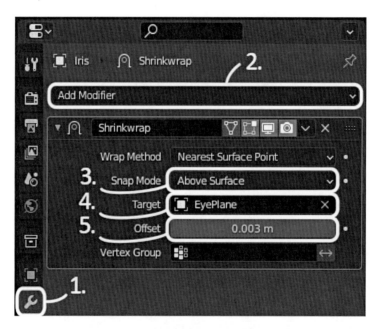

Figure 7.39 – The Shrinkwrap modifier settings

Perfect, now we can mirror the eye over to the other side:

6. Click **Add Modifier** and choose **Mirror** from the **Generate** column in the list of modifiers.

7. Click on the empty field in the Mirror modifier labeled **Mirror Object** to bring up a list of objects in the scene and choose the EyePlane object.

    Let's get rid of the flat shading so the iris looks smoother.

8. Open the **Object** menu in the top-left corner of the header of the 3D Viewport and choose **Shade Smooth**.

    We're almost done, but we should add a glint to the eye to finish off the effect. We can do this with the same process that we used to make the iris, but to save time we can duplicate the iris and remove the colored materials.

9. Make sure the **Iris** object is still selected.

10. Open the **Object** menu in the top-left corner of the header of the 3D Viewport and choose **Duplicate Objects**. This will immediately begin moving the duplicate object.

11. Hold the *Ctrl* key to activate snapping while moving and place the duplicate iris slightly up and to the right of the original. *Left-click* to place the object.

12. Use the **Scale** tool to shrink the object down to an appropriate size.

13. Rename the duplicate **Iris** object to Glint.

14. Click on the red sphere tab in the Properties editor to switch to the **Material Properties** tab.

15. Click the - button in the top-right corner twice to remove both materials from the **Glint** object.

    The glint in the eye needs to float a little higher than the iris so it doesn't interfere with the surface. Let's fix this now.

16. Click on the blue wrench tab in the Properties editor to switch to the **Modifiers** tab.

17. Increase the **Offset** of the Shrinkwrap modifier to 0.006 m.

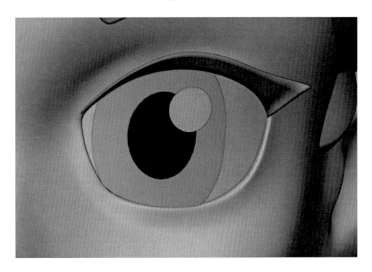

Figure 7.40 – The glint in the eye

Lastly, the glint in each eye shouldn't be mirrored because that's not how light catches the eye. Both glints should be placed in the upper-right corner of the eye so that the eyes look like they are reflecting light that is coming from the same direction. We'll need to duplicate the glint and place it on the other side by hand.

18. Click the **X** button in the top-right corner of the Mirror modifier to remove it.

19. Open the **Object** menu in the top-left corner of the header of the 3D Viewport and choose **Duplicate Objects**. This will immediately begin moving the duplicate object.

20. Hold the *Ctrl* key to activate snapping while moving and place the duplicate glint slightly up and to the right of the opposite eye. Left-click to place the object.

And we're done! You can see how our example turned out in the following figure:

Figure 7.41 – The anime head sculpture with finished eyes

You can customize this look further by duplicating the glint again, or by changing the size of the iris.

How it works

The Shrinkwrap modifier projects each vertex onto the surface of the target object. By adjusting the offset value, we can ensure that the vertices never fall below the surface of the target.

There's more

There are many other ways to create anime eyes. One other popular approach is to use **UV Unwrapping** and texture painting. This would allow us to map an image of an anime eye to the surface of an eye on a sculpture. Using this method would allow you to paint the eyes in your favorite 2D painting software and bring the result into Blender. However, texture painting is a skill that falls outside of the scope of this book, so we'll leave that topic for you to explore on your own.

Aiming the eyeballs with Constraints

We explored all sorts of interesting ways to create eyeballs in this chapter. However, all of our eyes are aimed straight forward. This can be a little jarring when presenting the finished character in a portfolio. We could rotate the eyes into a more natural position, but it's difficult to make the eyes aim at the same spot and look natural when we rotate them by hand.

This is where we can make use of Constraints. Constraints are similar to modifiers, but they are generally used to calculate some type of transformation data. In this case, we can use a constraint to aim the eyeballs at a target.

Once the constraint is added, all we have to do is position a target object and the eyes will automatically aim themselves correctly.

Getting ready

We can use any of the spherical eyes that we've created during this chapter (this excludes the anime style of eyes since they are not spheres). For our example, we're going to use the results from the *Adding color to the eyeballs* section of this chapter. If you have not completed that section, you can begin this section with the `coloredEyes_End.blend` file, which can be downloaded here: `https://github.com/PacktPublishing/Sculpting-the-Blender-Way/blob/main/Chapter07/coloredEyes_End.blend`.

Launch Blender and open the `.blend` file. Once you've got the file open, we'll be ready to add Constraints to the eyes.

How to do it

First, we need to create an empty object that will act as the target for the eyes:

1. Open the **Add** menu in the top-left corner of the header of the 3D Viewport and choose **Empty | Plane Axes**.

2. Rename the **Empty** object to EyeTarget.

3. Use the **Move** tool and place the **EyeTarget** object in front of the eyes as seen in the following figure:

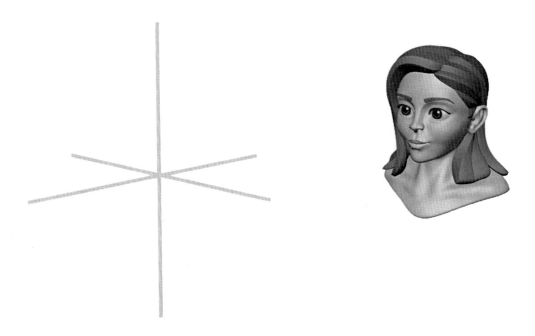

Figure 7.42 – The EyeTarget empty object floating in front of the sculpture

Don't place the **EyeTarget** object too close to the character, otherwise, the eyes will go cross-eyed when we add the Constraints. Speaking of which, let's add the Constraints now:

1. Select the left eyeball object.

2. Click on the blue timing belt icon in the Properties editor to switch to the **Constraints** tab.

3. Click **Add Object Constraint** and choose **Damped Track** from the **Tracking** column in the list of Constraints.

4. Click on the empty field in the Damped Track constraint labeled **Target** to bring up a list of objects in the scene and choose the **EyeTarget** object.

5. Set **Track Axis** to the correct axis for the eye. This will vary depending on how the eye was modeled, but in our example the *Z* axis is correct.

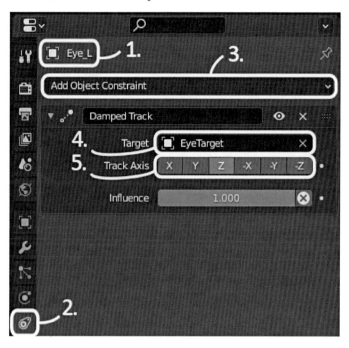

Figure 7.43 – The Damped Track constraint settings

6. Select the right eyeball object and repeat these steps.

> **Important Note**
>
> Some of the example files for this chapter came with **Copy Transforms** and **Copy Location** Constraints already attached to the right eyeball. These Constraints were attached to make symmetrical placement of the eyes easier. However, these Constraints are not intended to be an alternative to the **Damped Track** Constraint for aiming the eye. You should still add the **Damped Track** Constraint to each eye in order to get the most natural behavior.

Perfect, now all we have to do is move the **EyeTarget** object around and the eyes will follow, as you can see in the following figure:

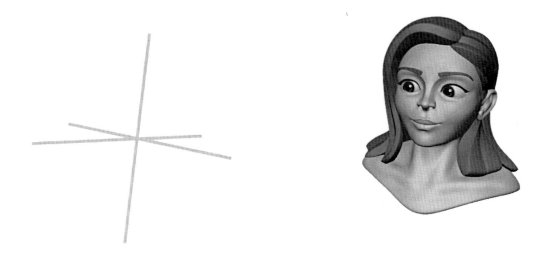

Figure 7.44 – Eyes aimed at the EyeTarget object

Little shortcuts like this cut down on the amount of manual work we have to do. We can focus on making the pose look natural instead of worrying about selecting each eye and rotating it appropriately.

How it works

The **Damped Track** constraint uses one of the object's own axes to create an aim vector toward the target object's location. We can specify the tracking axis to match the way we modeled the eye. Most of the eyes in this chapter were created from a UV Sphere object, then rotated 90 degrees, which means the Z axis points forward.

This technique can be used for most eyes and adds an excellent finished touch to any character sculpture.

8
Making Accessories and Clothing

We can't have our characters running around naked! Creating clothing and accessories for our characters is a great way to make them look more interesting. There are many ways to create accessories for our sculptures; some rely on the use of sculpting brushes, while others are best achieved with traditional modeling techniques.

In this chapter, we will explore a mixture of techniques to create several types of accessories, including a hat, earrings, and several methods for making shirts and cloth.

The main topics in this chapter are as follows:

- Making earrings
- Using Mask Extract to make a shirt
- Using the Cloth brush to add wrinkles to the shirt
- Using the Cloth Filter to create a collar for the shirt
- Preparing a shirt mesh for a cloth simulation
- Simulating cloth to wrap a shirt around a character
- Sculpting a hat with Radial Symmetry

Technical requirements

For general requirements, refer back to the *Technical requirements* section laid out in *Chapter 1, Exploring Blender's User Interface for Sculpting*.

You can download the files to follow along with this book at the GitHub link here: `https://github.com/PacktPublishing/Sculpting-the-Blender-Way`.

Important Note

This chapter includes a *Sculpting in Action* video to help demonstrate the cloth tools. You can view this video here: `https://bit.ly/3dxbBD2`. The video has demonstrations for each of the sections that are related to sculpting and simulating cloth. There is also a bonus section at the end which shows several techniques to finish sculpting asymmetrical details into the hat from the final section of this chapter.

Making earrings

Earrings are a fun accessory; there are all sorts of styles: long hoops, small rings, diamond-encrusted dangling designs, and so on. There are so many to choose from. For this section, we'll try a simple stud design with four prongs holding a diamond in the center.

Getting ready

For this section, we have provided a sculpture of a woman with vertex colors and materials already applied. With this provided scene, we can create our accessories and see them in their best quality using the Material Preview viewport shading mode. Download the womanAccessories_Start.blend file from `https://github.com/PacktPublishing/Sculpting-the-Blender-Way/blob/main/Chapter08/womanAccessories_Start.blend`.

Launch Blender and open the .blend file. This scene comes with the sculpture that you can see in the following screenshot:

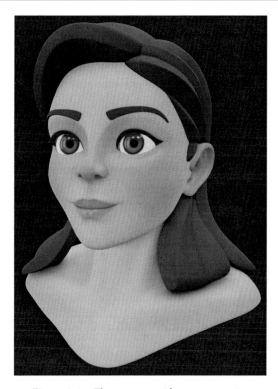

Figure 8.1 – The woman with no accessories

Let's give her some earrings to bring out the color in her eyes. A blue diamond set in gold would look really nice.

Faceted diamonds are mathematical shapes, so it would be better to generate them mathematically rather than try to sculpt them by hand. Blender comes with an add-on that will allow us to generate interesting mathematical shapes, including diamonds; we just need to enable it in Blender's **Preferences** window.

In Blender's Topbar, open the **Edit** menu and choose **Preferences**. Once the Blender **Preferences** window appears, click on the **Add-ons** tab. Use the search bar in the top-right corner to search for Extra Objects and check the box next to **Add Mesh: Extra Objects** to enable the add-on:

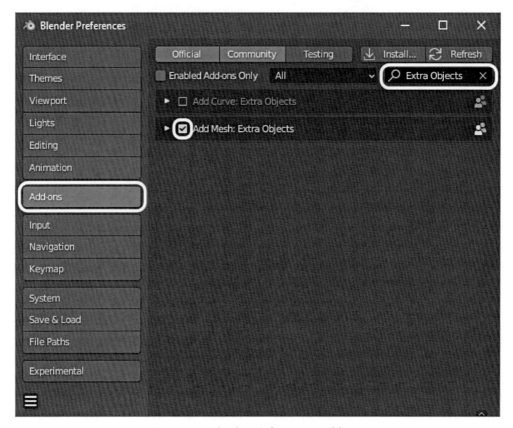

Figure 8.2 – Blender Preferences – Add-ons

Now that this add-on is enabled, additional options will appear under the **Add** menu in the 3D Viewport. Close the **Blender Preferences** window; the settings will be automatically saved. Now, we can create our diamond studded earrings.

How to do it...

First, we should hide the **Woman Head** collection so that it's not in the way while we make the earring:

1. Hide the **Woman Head** collection by clicking on the eyeball icon next to its name in the Outliner, as seen in the following screenshot:

Figure 8.3 – The eyeball icon next to the Woman Head collection

Now that that's out of the way, we can create the diamond for the earring. This will be very easy to do because of the **Add Mesh: Extra Objects** add-on that we enabled.

2. Open the **Add** menu in the top-left corner of the header of the 3D Viewport and choose **Mesh | Diamonds | Brilliant Diamond**.

3. Rename the object to `Earring_Diamond`.

Excellent – you're really good at making diamonds! We're very proud of you. Now, let's give it a glass BSDF material to make it look like a diamond.

> **Tip**
> The following instructions are very similar to the steps we took to make the `OuterEye` material in the *Adding depth and realism to the eyeballs* section of *Chapter 7, Making Eyeballs*. For detailed reference images to go along with these steps, refer back to *Figure 7.22*.

We'll adjust the settings of the material so that the surface has an appropriate color, roughness, and index of refraction that will make it look like a diamond.

4. Click on the red sphere icon in the Properties editor to switch to the **Material Properties** tab.

5. Click the **New** button to create a new material and rename the new material `Diamond`.

6. Change the **Surface** type to **Glass BSDF**.

7. Click on the **Color** swatch and use the color picker to choose a color for the diamond. This can be any color you like, but a nice color to match this character's eyes is a saturated blue with the following hue, saturation, and value settings: **H:** 0.635 **S:** 1.000 **V:** 1.000.

8. Change the **Roughness** setting to 0.125 and the **IOR** setting to 2.418:

Figure 8.4 – The diamond with a blue glass BSDF surface material

Now that we have the diamond, we need to set it in a small four-pronged gold stud.

9. Open the **Add** menu in the top-left corner of the header of the 3D Viewport and choose **Mesh | Grid**.

10. A panel labeled **Add Grid** will appear in the bottom-left corner of the 3D Viewport. Click on this panel to expand the options for creating the grid.

11. Change the **X Subdivisions** and **Y Subdivisions** settings to 3:

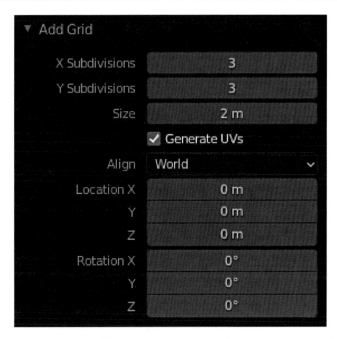

Figure 8.5 – The Add Grid settings with 3 subdivisions on X and Y

12. Rename the **Grid** object to Earring_Prongs.

13. Use the **Move** tool to move the **Earring_Prongs** object so that it sits just below the bottom point of the diamond, as seen in the following screenshot:

Figure 8.6 – The grid object moved below the diamond object

Now, we need to edit this object to turn it into the prongs of the earring. You may find these next steps easier to follow if you change **Viewport Shading** to **Solid** mode. We will do this in our example so that the reference images are easier to see in this book. You may choose to remain in **Material Preview** mode if you prefer.

Now, let's create the prongs:

1. Change the Interaction Mode to **Edit Mode**.

2. Switch to **Face Select** mode by clicking the corresponding icon in the header of the 3D Viewport, or by pressing the *3* hotkey.

3. Select the four faces in the corners of the grid, as seen in the following screenshot:

Figure 8.7 – The four corner faces of the grid selected in Edit Mode

4. Open the **Mesh** menu in the top-left corner of the 3D Viewport and choose **Delete | Faces**.

5. Switch to **Edge Select** mode by clicking the corresponding icon in the header of the 3D Viewport, or by pressing the *2* hotkey.

6.   Select the four edges around the outside of the mesh, highlighted in the following screenshot:

Figure 8.8 – The four outside edges of the mesh that should be selected

7.   Use the **Move** tool to move the edges up until they sit slightly below the perimeter of the diamond, with the diagonal angle parallel to the diamond's diagonal edge, as seen in the following screenshot:

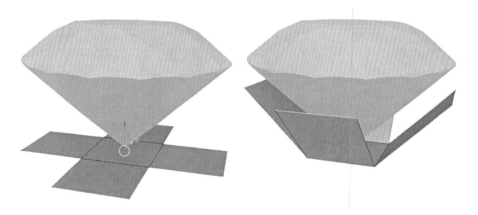

Figure 8.9 – The four outside edges raised up with the Move tool

8. Use the **Extrude Region** tool to create extra geometry near the perimeter of the diamond (about 0.55 units upward). Extrude a second time to create more geometry that extends over the top of the diamond (about 0.3 units upward). See the following screenshot for reference:

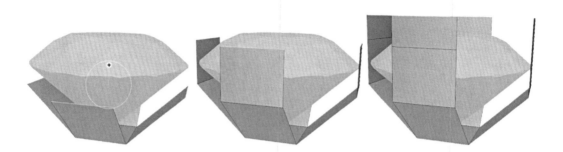

Figure 8.10 – The two extrusions made with the Extrude Region tool

9. Use the **Scale** tool to shrink the four edges inward to create the prongs that hold the diamond in place:

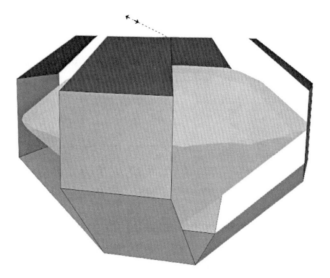

Figure 8.11 – The top of the prongs scaled inward with the Scale tool

Excellent – we're finished with **Edit Mode** now, so change the Interaction Mode back to **Object Mode**. If you switched the **Viewport Shading** mode to **Solid** as we did in our example, you can switch back to **Material Preview** mode for the rest of this section.

To finish this shape and make it look more like the prongs are holding the diamond in place, we can add some modifiers to give the prongs some thickness and a bevel.

10. Click on the blue wrench icon in the Properties editor to switch to the **Modifiers** tab.

11. Click **Add Modifier** and choose **Solidify** from the **Generate** column in the list of modifiers.

12. Set the **Thickness** setting to -0.3 m and the **Offset** setting to -0.50000.

13. Click **Add Modifier** again and choose **Bevel** from the **Generate** column in the list of modifiers.

14. Set the **Amount** setting to 0.1 m.

15. Increase the **Segments** setting from 1 to 4:

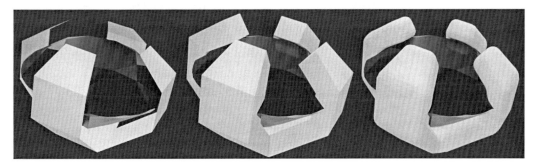

Figure 8.12 – The prongs with no modifiers (left), with a Solidify modifier (middle), and with both a Solidify and Bevel modifier (right)

We need to give the prongs some smooth shading so that we don't see any jagged edges.

16. Open the **Object** menu in the top-left corner of the 3D Viewport and choose **Shade Smooth**.

Now, let's give it a gold material to complete the effect.

17. Click on the red sphere icon in the Properties editor to switch to the **Material Properties** tab.

18. Click the **New** button to create a new material and rename the new material to Gold.

For the color of the material, we can use a hexadecimal number (also known as a hex code) to define a specific color. We've picked out the D4AF37 hex code because it works well for gold.

19. Click on the **Base Color** swatch to edit the color, and then click on the **Hex** tab and type in D4AF37.

20. Change the material's **Metallic** setting to 1.000 and the **Roughness** setting to 0.175:

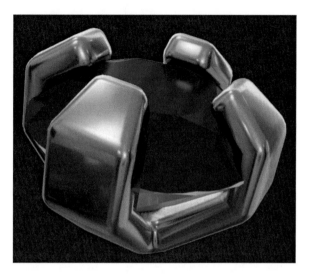

Figure 8.13 – The gold material applied to the earring prongs

Perfect – now we need to nest the **Earring_Diamond** object inside of the **Earring_Prongs** object in the Outliner.

Find the **Earring_Diamond** object in the Outliner; click and drag it on top of the **Earring_Prongs** object in the Outliner. Before letting go of the mouse button, hold down the *Shift* key and then release the mouse button:

Figure 8.14 – The Earring_Diamond object being dragged on top of the Earring_Prongs object in the Outliner (hold Shift before releasing)

Nesting one object inside of another in this way is known as parenting. When one object is parented to another, the child object will follow along wherever the parent object is transformed to. What we've achieved here is making the diamond a child of the prongs, so we can place the prongs onto the character's ears and the diamond will follow. Speaking of which, let's place the earring on the ears now:

1. Unhide the **Woman Head** collection by clicking on the eyeball icon next to its name in the Outliner.

2. Select the **Earring_Prongs** object and use the **Scale** tool to shrink it down to an appropriate size.

3. Use the **Move** and **Rotate** tools to place the **Earring_Prongs** object onto the character's left earlobe.

> **Tip**
>
> We learned about some helpful snapping settings in the *Creating a stylized anime eye* section of *Chapter 7, Making Eyeballs*. To see how to enable these settings, refer back to *Figure 7.37*.

Excellent – the last thing we need to do is mirror the two earring objects over to the other ear.

4. Click on the blue wrench icon in the Properties editor to switch to the **Modifiers** tab.

5. Click **Add Modifier** and choose **Mirror** from the **Generate** column in the list of modifiers.

6. Click on the empty field in the **Mirror** modifier labeled **Mirror Object** to bring up a list of objects in the scene, and choose the **WomanHead** object.

7. Select the **Earring_Diamond** object and repeat the previous two steps to add another **Mirror** modifier to mirror around the **WomanHead** object.

You can see how our example turned out in the following screenshot:

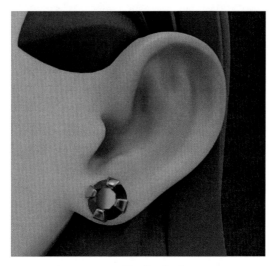

Figure 8.15 – The finished earring

Excellent – these earrings will go very nicely with the blue eyes of this character.

How it works...

The **Add Mesh: Extra Objects** add-on gives us access to many procedural shapes that can save us time when creating new objects. It might feel a little bit like cheating to use this add-on, but you're never going to be able to do a better job creating a diamond by hand than this add-on can do in a single click. You can always adjust the parameters to customize the diamond so that it will have exactly the right amount of facets for your needs.

The **Solidify** modifier takes polygons that have no thickness and extrudes them outward as evenly as possible in order to turn flat objects into solid shapes. Adjusting the offset setting will determine whether the thickness extrudes inward, outward, or somewhere in the middle.

The **Bevel** modifier adds additional edge loops around hard corners and rounds out the shape to give a more appealing, less jagged appearance to the model.

Using both of these modifiers together allows us to create complex shapes without having to model very much by hand in **Edit Mode**.

There's more...

There are many other ways we can make earrings; you could try making a basic ring shape with the Torus primitive mesh object from the **Add** menu. You could try making intricate wire patterns with the **Skin** modifier that we learned about in the *Using the Skin modifier to turn wireframe structures into thick skins* section of *Chapter 4, How to Make a Base Mesh for a 3D Sculpture.*

Aside from diamonds, the **Add Mesh: Extra Objects** add-on will let us create other helpful shapes such as **Round Cube**, which includes an operator preset to generate a Quad Sphere like the one that comes with the sculpting preset. There are also **Gears** and many other interesting extra objects. Explore and have fun!

See also

We chose our gold color from a list of hex codes online. For an excellent list of gold-color hex codes, check out the following link: `https://www.rapidtables.com/web/color/Gold_Color.html`. The color we used to create the gold in this section is labeled **Metallic gold**.

Using Mask Extract to make a shirt

There are several ways to create clothing for our sculptures. One of the easiest ways to begin the clothing creation process is through a mask extraction. This will allow us to create a mask with the mask tools and then duplicate the masked area into a separate object. The benefit of this is that we can create the clothing as a separate object that is easier to work with. The shape of the duplicate object will already fit the form of the original sculpture, giving us an excellent starting point.

Getting ready

For this section, we can pick up where we left off in the *Making earrings* section of this chapter. If you have not completed that section, you can begin this section with a fresh copy of the `womanAccessories_Start.blend` file, which you can download here: `https://github.com/PacktPublishing/Sculpting-the-Blender-Way/blob/main/Chapter08/womanAccessories_Start.blend`.

Launch Blender and open the `.blend` file. You will be able to follow along with this section whether or not you made the earrings.

How to do it...

Mask extractions are an awesome feature, but unfortunately, as of this book's publication, Blender does not support extracting masks from multiresolution sculptures. As a workaround for this limitation, we will start by duplicating the **WomanHead** object, reducing its subdivision level, and then applying the Multiresolution modifier:

1. Change **Viewport Shading** to **Solid** mode.

2. Select the **WomanHead** object.

3. Open the **Object** menu in the top-left corner of the header of the 3D Viewport and choose **Duplicate Objects**. This will make a duplicate called **WomanHead.001**, which will immediately begin moving around with your mouse movements.

4. Press the *Esc* key to cancel moving the duplicate object, which will place it back in its original location.

5. Rename the **WomanHead.001** object to `TemporaryHead`.

6. While the **TemporaryHead** object is selected, open the **View** menu in the top-left corner of the header of the 3D Viewport and choose **Local View | Toggle Local View**. This will hide all objects other than the **TemporaryHead** object.

7. Click on the blue wrench icon in the Properties editor to switch to the **Modifiers** tab.

8. Decrease the **Level Viewport** subdivision level from 3 to 2.

9. Click on the downward arrow near the top-right corner of the **Multires** modifier and choose **Apply**.

    Perfect – we will use this duplicate head object to paint and extract our mask.

10. Change the Interaction Mode to **Sculpt Mode**.

11. Activate the **Mask** brush on the Toolbar.

12. Set the brush **Radius** setting to something large enough to easily paint over the shoulders of the character, around `150 px`.

13. Set the brush **Strength** setting to `1.000`.

    Use your graphics tablet to draw over the shoulders and around the neck of the character to create a mask in the shape of the shirt. Follow our example from the following screenshot:

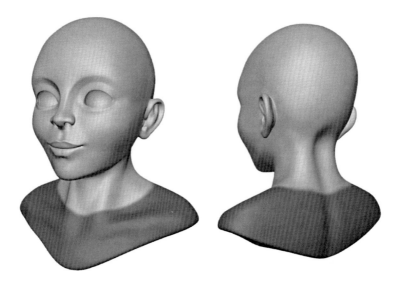

Figure 8.16 – The masked area that we will extract the shirt from

Be sure to get the underside as well. Once you have the mask painted onto the character, we can extract it.

14. Open the **Mask** menu in the top-left corner of the 3D Viewport and choose the **Mask Extract** option.

15. Uncheck the **Extract as Solid** option; then click the **OK** button.

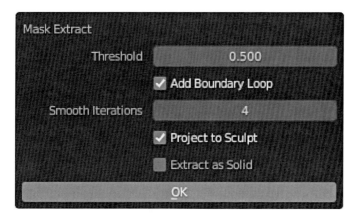

Figure 8.17 – The Mask Extract options

This will create a new object called **Mesh** from the masked area. Blender will automatically change the Interaction Mode to **Object Mode** and select the new object. Let's keep going.

16. Open the **View** menu in the top-left corner of the header of the 3D Viewport and choose **Local View | Toggle Local View**, which will make all of the other objects visible again.

17. Rename the new **Mesh** object to Shirt.

18. Now that we've finished the extraction, we no longer need the **TemporaryHead** object; delete it by right-clicking on it in the Outliner and choosing **Delete**.

To help the shirt stand out, we should give it a material.

19. Change **Viewport Shading** to **Material Preview** mode.

20. Select the **Shirt** object.

21. Click on the red sphere icon in the Properties editor to switch to the **Material Properties** tab.

22. Click the **New** button to create a new material and rename it to Shirt.

23. Click on the **Surface** type drop-down list and choose **Velvet BSDF**.

24. Click on the **Color** swatch and use the color picker to choose a color for the shirt. For our example, we went with a light reddish pink with the E73F56 hex code.

This color looks good, but the shirt is mostly underneath the surface of the character's shoulders, as you can see in the following screenshot:

Figure 8.18 – The shirt underneath the surface of the character's shoulders

Let's fix this using the **Inflate Mesh Filter** tool.

25. Change the Interaction Mode to **Sculpt Mode**.

26. Activate the **Mesh Filter** tool on the Toolbar.

27. Find **Tool Settings** at the top of the 3D Viewport and use the drop-down list to change **Filter Type** to **Inflate**.

28. Hover your pen over your graphics tablet near the middle of the 3D Viewport. Press the tip of your pen onto your graphics tablet to begin using the Mesh Filter. Keep your pen pressed to the tablet and drag it to the right to begin inflating the shirt. Keep inflating until all parts of the shirt are above the shoulders, as seen in the following screenshot:

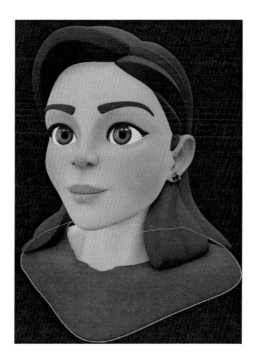

Figure 8.19 – The shirt inflated until it is above the surface of the character's shoulders

And there you have it – an extracted shirt! Nice work – extracting a mask like this is the first step to making high-quality clothing. We'll try to improve the quality of this shirt in the subsequent sections of this chapter.

How it works...

Mask extractions are an excellent way to create the basic shapes of clothing that match the shape of the character. The extracted mask is treated the same as any other object in Blender. Once we have an extraction for a piece of clothing, we can sculpt details into it to create a detailed final result.

See also

As we mentioned at the start of this section, Blender does not currently support extracting masks from multiresolution sculptures, which is why we had to start this section by duplicating the head. In future versions of Blender, these steps may not be necessary. Eventually, we will be able to extract masks directly from the multiresolution object.

There is a current development task for fixing this issue; you can follow the development progress of this feature here: `https://developer.blender.org/T79949`.

Using the Cloth brush to add wrinkles to the shirt

3D software packages such as Blender often come with the ability to perform cloth simulations; this means that the computer can move the polygons around and make them interact like cloth – bunching up, folding, wrinkling, draping over surfaces, and so on.

We'll learn more about cloth simulations by the end of this chapter. One of the disappointing things about cloth simulations though is that they are performed by the computer, and the only way to adjust the outcome of the simulation is to adjust the input parameters and run the simulation over again. This means that it's not a very hands-on way to work.

Blender recently introduced a revolutionary new feature to the sculpting toolset – the Cloth brush. The Cloth brush is a special type of brush that is able to run a cloth simulations in real-time while we sculpt. This will allow us to drag the surface of a sculpture around, which will act like cloth while we sculpt, giving us the best of both worlds – a hands-on sculpting experience alongside a computer simulation.

This is an advanced brush; therefore, it is difficult to master. It includes many deformation modes that allow us to simulate cloth in many ways, including Drag, Pinch Point, and Expand. Each of these allows us to control the cloth simulation in different ways. However, the complexity of this brush doesn't end there. Using the Cloth brush involves heavily on adjusting tool settings in the Sidebar. We recommend reading through *Chapter 6, Using Advanced Features and Customizing the Sculpting Brushes*, before attempting to use the Cloth brush.

In this section, we will try using the Cloth brush to add wrinkles to a simple shirt mesh.

Getting ready

For this section, we will pick up where we left off in the *Using Mask Extract to make a shirt* section of this chapter. If you have not completed that section, you can begin this section with a fresh copy of the clothBrush_Start.blend file here: https://github. com/PacktPublishing/Sculpting-the-Blender-Way/blob/main/ Chapter08/clothBrush_Start.blend.

Launch Blender and open the .blend file. Once you've got the file open, we'll be ready to try out the Cloth brush.

How to do it...

First, let's prepare our workspace for using the Cloth brush:

1. Change **Viewport Shading** to **Solid** mode.

2. With the **Shirt** object selected, change the Interaction Mode to **Sculpt Mode**.

3. Find and activate the **Cloth** brush on the Toolbar (you may need to scroll down).

4. Make sure the Sidebar is open and the **Tool** tab is active.

> Tip
>
> If needed, hover your mouse over the left-side edge of the Sidebar until your mouse cursor changes to the resizing cursor; then click and drag to the left to expand the Sidebar so that all of the text is properly visible.

5. Within the **Tool** tab of the Sidebar, we can see lots of important settings for the Cloth brush. Let's set these settings to allow for subtle dragging and wrinkling of the shirt:

    Set the **Radius** setting to around 75 px.

    Set the **Simulation Area** setting to **Dynamic**.

    Set the **Deformation** setting to **Drag**.

    Set the **Force Falloff** setting to **Plane**.

    Set the **Cloth Mass** setting to 1.000.

Set the **Cloth Damping** setting to 0.800:

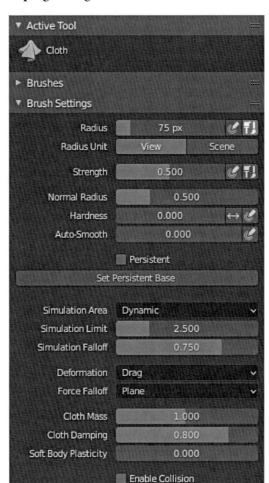

Figure 8.20 – The Cloth brush settings as seen in the Sidebar

The Cloth brush works best with symmetry turned off.

6. Find the symmetry settings in the top-right corner of the 3D Viewport header and click the **X** toggle to deactivate **X-Axis Symmetry**.

    It will be easier to work if the hair isn't blocking our view.

7. Hide the **Hair** collection by clicking on the eyeball icon next to its name in the Outliner.

    Perfect – now that we have all the right settings, let's try making some wrinkles in the shirt with the Cloth brush.

8. Draw from the center of the chest toward the character's left shoulder:

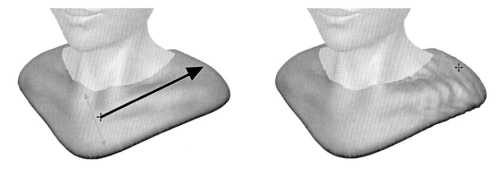

Figure 8.21 – Wrinkles added to the character's left shoulder

9. Draw from the center of the chest again, but this time, drag toward the character's right shoulder:

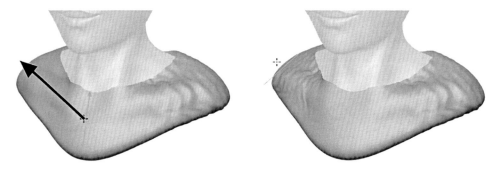

Figure 8.22 – Wrinkles added to the character's right shoulder

Great! The **Drag** deformation style for the Cloth brush mostly leaves the shirt in its original shape, but it drags wrinkles across the surface.

> Tip
> If your results did not turn out like this, try undoing the brushstroke by pressing the *Ctrl + Z* hotkey, and then try the brushstroke again. If you continue to have strange or unpredictable results, try reducing the brush **Radius** setting and the brush **Strength** setting. We've tried to guide you with settings that will work well for this example, but due to the Cloth brush using a simulation, your results may vary.

In our example, the center of the chest ended up without any wrinkles, so let's try a different deformation style to pinch the cloth together in the center area of the shirt.

10. Set **Deformation** to **Pinch Point** and **Force Falloff** to **Radial**. Use the brush to draw left to right and right to left across the chest area:

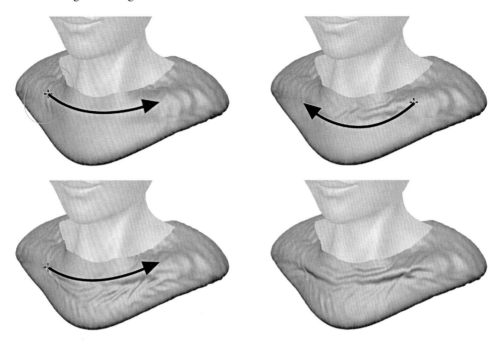

Figure 8.23 – Cloth pinched together across the chest

The front of the shirt is looking pretty good now, but the back could use some work. Just for fun, let's try one more deformation type for the back.

11. Set **Deformation** to **Expand**. Use the brush to draw across all of the flat areas of the back of the shirt:

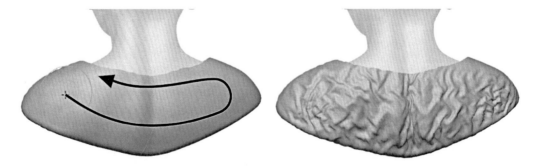

Figure 8.24 – Cloth expanded on the back of the shirt

Now that we're done sculpting, we can unhide the **Hair** collection.

One small issue remains – this shirt is looking a little jagged and rough. This is typical of cloth simulations, as the polygons bunch together. An easy way to make it look smoother is to add a Subdivision Surface modifier.

12. Click on the blue wrench icon in the Properties editor to switch to the **Modifiers** tab.

13. Click **Add Modifier** and choose **Subdivision Surface** from the **Generate** column in the list of modifiers.

The default number of subdivision levels displayed in the viewport (**Levels Viewport**) is 1. This is plenty for this use case, so we can leave it at this setting. However, Blender will use a different setting when we render the final image of this sculpture. Currently, this alternative setting is set to 2, which is unnecessary. We should set the **Render** level to 1 as well so that the shirt will look the same in the final render as it does in the viewport:

Figure 8.25 – The results from the Cloth brush

Awesome – these extra wrinkles really make the shirt look like it's made from cloth. If the effect is too strong, you can always try smoothing some of the wrinkles with the Smooth brush or use the Smooth Mesh Filter to reduce the intensity of the wrinkles all at once.

How it works...

We adjusted quite a few settings in the Sidebar to get the Cloth brush to behave correctly. The Simulation area is an optimization option. Simulations are slow for our computers to run, so by default, the Cloth brush only simulates the Local area near your brush. We changed this to **Dynamic** so that the Simulation area will update dynamically across the surface as we drag. This gives us fast performance while using the Cloth brush, without the limitations of a Local area simulation.

Deformation modes are perhaps the most important setting for the Cloth brush; they fundamentally change the nature of the cloth simulation. We tried the following three types of deformation modes:

- **Drag** behaves like sliding a tablecloth across a table with your hands.
- **Pinch Point** is almost like dragging the nozzle of a vacuum cleaner on a shirt.
- **Expand** is similar to bunching up a piece of fabric.

There are other types to explore as well. We also tried using two different settings for **Force Falloff**. The **Plane** setting helps the simulation affect long linear areas, similar to pulling up the tubes of a pair of socks. The **Radial** setting limits the cloth simulations to small circular areas. This setting has a major effect on the behavior of the **Deformation** setting.

Cloth Damping works alongside **Cloth Mass** to slow down the cloth as it moves. If these settings are too low, the Cloth brush will become very touchy; every small adjustment will tend to make the polygons go crazy and give us unusable results.

As you can see, there are many settings to adjust for this brush. We encourage you to explore these settings and discover new ways to use the Cloth brush.

There's more...

The Cloth brush is best used in small strokes to create wrinkles and cloth patterns. It is not meant as a complete replacement for doing things by hand, nor is it a complete replacement for full cloth simulation tools. Its usefulness lies somewhere in between. You'll notice that we did not use the Cloth brush to create the general shape of the shirt; instead, we used the Cloth brush to add cloth-like wrinkles to the already existing shirt geometry.

If we need to simulate cloth draping over a surface, that is a task better suited to a full-featured cloth simulation, which we will have learned about by the end of this chapter.

See also

- The Cloth brush was added as a major new feature in Blender 2.83. This brush comes with an expansive feature set, and we've really only scraped the surface of what it can do in this section. You can watch the official Cloth brush demonstration video here: `https://www.youtube.com/watch?v=t3W1cl3BYwc`.

- Many improvements have been made to the Cloth brush since its introduction; you can read up on some of the major improvements that came with Blender 2.91 on the official Blender blog here: `https://code.blender.org/2020/10/cloth-sculpting-improvements-in-blender-2-91/`.

- There's much more to read in the documentation as well: `https://docs.blender.org/manual/en/latest/sculpt_paint/sculpting/tools/cloth.html`.

Using the Cloth Filter to create a collar for the shirt

What an exciting time to be alive – a real-time cloth simulation for our sculptures is such an amazing tool at our disposal. In the previous section of this chapter, we tried out the Cloth brush, which allowed us to simulate cloth directly under our brushstrokes. In this section, we will take things a step further and use several advanced features together in order to make a pleated collar for our character's shirt.

Getting ready

For this section, we will pick up where we left off in the *Using the Cloth brush to add wrinkles to the shirt* section of this chapter. If you have not completed that section, you can begin this section with a fresh copy of the `clothFilter_Start.blend` file here: `https://github.com/PacktPublishing/Sculpting-the-Blender-Way/blob/main/Chapter08/clothFilter_Start.blend`.

Launch Blender and open the `.blend` file. Once you've got the file open, we'll be ready to create a collar for the shirt with the Cloth Filter.

How to do it...

We're going to be using both face sets and masks in this section, so first, let's make sure the appropriate viewport overlays are enabled:

1. Open the **Viewport Overlays** pop-over menu from the top-right corner of the 3D Viewport and check the box labeled **Face Sets** at the bottom of the **Sculpt** section.

2. Make sure the **Mask** overlay is enabled as well.

    Masks will not be properly displayed in **Sculpt Mode** while we have a Subdivision Surface modifier enabled on an object, so we need to temporarily disable this modifier.

3. Click on the blue wrench icon in the Properties editor to switch to the **Modifiers** tab.

4. Find the little computer monitor icon at the top of the **Subdivision** modifier labeled **Display modifier in viewport** (hover over the icon to see this label). Click this icon to disable the modifier.

    Lastly, let's hide the hair again so that we can see what we're doing:

5. Hide the **Hair** collection by clicking on the eyeball icon next to its name in the Outliner.

    Perfect – from here, we need to create the geometry for the collar by extruding the neck hole of the shirt:

6. With the **Shirt** object selected, change the Interaction Mode to **Edit Mode**.

7. Switch to **Edge Select** mode by clicking the corresponding icon in the header of the 3D Viewport, or by pressing the *2* hotkey.

8. Hold down the *Alt* key and click to select the edge loop around the perimeter of the neck hole in the shirt, as seen in the following screenshot:

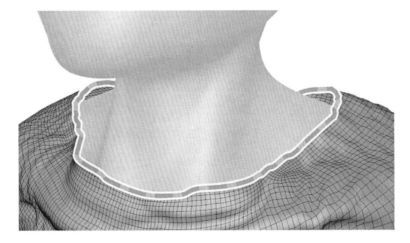

Figure 8.26 – The edge loop around the neck hole

9. Use the **Extrude Region** tool to create extra geometry around the neck; pull it upward high enough for the desired thickness of the shirt collar. You can see our example in the following screenshot:

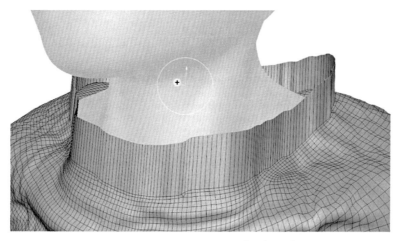

Figure 8.27 – Extra geometry for the collar

10. Use the **Scale** and **Move** tools as needed to fit the collar to the neck. Check your work from several angles to make sure the collar stays above the surface of the neck.

    Now we're going to create two face sets to define the collar of the shirt.

11. Switch to **Face Select** mode by clicking the corresponding icon in the header of the 3D Viewport, or by pressing the *3* hotkey.

12. Hold down the *Alt* key and click to select the newly created face loop around the perimeter of the neck hole in the shirt, as seen in the following screenshot:

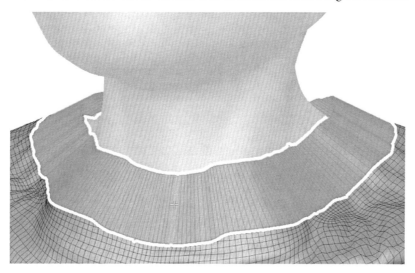

Figure 8.28 – The face loop around the neck hole

13. Change the Interaction Mode to **Sculpt Mode**.

14. Open the **Face Sets** menu in the top-left corner of the 3D Viewport and choose the **Face Set** from **Edit Mode** selection option.

    This will create a new face set based on the polygons that we had selected in **Edit Mode**. Now, let's go back into **Edit Mode** to make a small change to the selection and create a second face set.

15. Change the Interaction Mode back to **Edit Mode**.

16. Open the **Select** menu in the top-left corner of the 3D Viewport and choose the **Checker Deselect** option.

    A panel labeled **Checker Deselect** will appear in the bottom-left corner of the 3D Viewport. Click on this panel to expand the options.

17. Change the **Deselected** option to 2 and change the **Selected** option to 4:

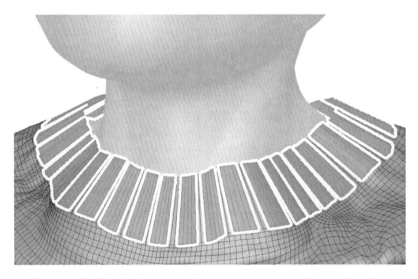

Figure 8.29 – The face loop around the neck after using Checker Deselect

18. Change the Interaction Mode to **Sculpt Mode** again.

19. Open the **Face Sets** menu again and choose **Face Set** from **Edit Mode** selection.

    Perfect – now we should have two face sets around the collar, one thin and one thick. Our example looks like this:

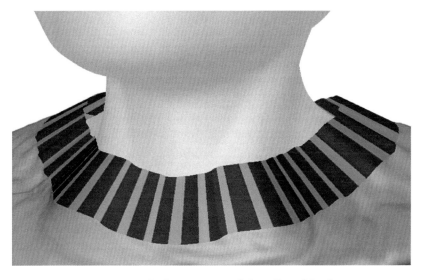

Figure 8.30 – The face sets around the collar of the shirt

We're finished with the preparatory work; now, we can do the fun part. We'll create a mask from one of these face sets using the Sculpt Expand feature. Then, we'll puff up the collar with the Cloth Filter:

1. Hover your brush over the thicker of the two face sets around the collar (the purple one in our example).

2. Press the *Shift + A* hotkey to begin the **Expand Mask** operation.

3. Hold the *Ctrl* hotkey to snap the **Expand Mask** operation to the boundary of the face set.

4. Click or tap with your pen to confirm the new mask and complete the **Expand Mask** operation.

   Now that we have our mask, we can inflate the collar with the Cloth Filter.

5. Find and activate the **Cloth Filter** tool on the Toolbar (you may need to scroll down).

6. Find **Tool Settings** at the top of the 3D Viewport and use the drop-down list to change **Filter Type** to **Inflate**.

   This next part will be difficult to see because the viewport is currently cluttered with face sets and masks, so it will be helpful to temporarily disable all of our viewport overlays.

7. Click on the **Viewport Overlays** icon in the top-right corner of the 3D Viewport to disable all overlays.

The masks and face sets are still there, and they will behave as if they were visible. But now we don't have to deal with the visual clutter while we use the Cloth Filter.

8. Hover your brush anywhere in the 3D Viewport; touch down with the pen and drag to the right to begin using the Cloth Filter to inflate the collar.

9. Lift your pen from the tablet when you're satisfied with the amount of inflation for the collar. Our example looks like this:

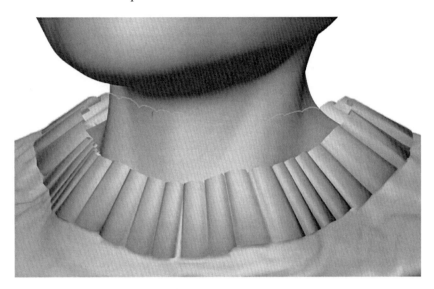

Figure 8.31 – The collar inflated with the Cloth Filter

Excellent – we're finished with **Sculpt Mode**. Now, we can put a few finishing touches on the shirt, and we'll be done:

1. Click on the **Viewport Overlays** icon to re-enable all overlays.

2. Change the Interaction Mode to **Object Mode**.

3. Go to the **Modifiers** tab in the Properties editor and click the little computer monitor icon at the top of the **Subdivision** modifier to re-enable the Subdivision Surface modifier.

4. Click **Add Modifier** and choose **Solidify** from the **Generate** column in the list of modifiers.

5. Unhide the **Hair** collection by clicking on the eyeball icon next to its name in the Outliner:

Figure 8.32 – The finished shirt

Fantastic – creating face sets and masks are great ways to control the Mesh Filter and the Cloth Filter. In this case, it allowed us to create a really comfy-looking collar for this character's shirt!

How it works...

The Cloth Filter is very similar to the Mesh Filter that we learned about in the *Smoothing the lumpy and jagged surfaces of the sculpture* section of *Chapter 3, Sculpting a Simple Character Head with Basic Brushes*. The major difference is that the Cloth Filter simulates cloth just like the Cloth brush does, which gives us a way to create wrinkles and other cloth-like behavior across the entire mesh.

The Cloth Filter also respects the masked area, so by creating a mask, we were able to limit the areas of the mesh that were inflated.

Preparing a shirt mesh for a cloth simulation

Throughout this chapter, we've explored several features for creating a shirt; we used mask extractions, the Cloth brush, and the Cloth Filter. But there is another way to create clothing for our characters that can produce more natural cloth-like results. We can use a cloth simulation to wrap clothing around our sculptures.

A cloth simulation is a technique that predates the Cloth brush and the Cloth Filter. Fundamentally, it's a similar idea – the computer uses a set of parameters to apply physics to a mesh so that it behaves like cloth. There are several benefits to simulating cloth: we can specify edges that will be sewn together, we can make the simulation collide with the surface of the sculpture, and we can run the simulation across the entire mesh at once.

In this section, we will learn how to prepare a mesh so that it is compatible with a cloth simulation.

Getting ready

For this section, we have provided the torso of a mannequin with a guide for a shirt shape that we can use to build a shirt. Download the mannequinShirt_Start.blend file here: https://github.com/PacktPublishing/Sculpting-the-Blender-Way/blob/main/Chapter08/mannequinShirt_Start.blend.

Launch Blender and open the .blend file. Once the file is open, we can begin creating the shirt for the mannequin.

How to do it...

We'll start by creating the mesh for the shirt:

1. Open the **Add** menu in the top-left corner of the header of the 3D Viewport and choose **Mesh | Plane**.

2. A panel labeled **Add Plane** will appear in the bottom-left corner of the 3D Viewport. Click on this panel to expand the options for creating the plane:

    Set **Location X** to 1 m.

    Set **Location Y** to -0.9 m.

    Set **Location Z** to 7 m.

    Set **Rotation X** to 90.

3. Rename the **Plane** object to Shirt.

    Now, we need to set up a material for the shirt so that it is visually distinct from the mannequin.

4. Click on the red sphere icon in the Properties editor to switch to the **Material Properties** tab.

5. Click the **New** button to create a new material and rename it Shirt.

6. Scroll down to find the **Viewport Display** section in the Properties editor and click the drop-down arrow to expand the subsection.

7. Click on the white color swatch labeled **Color** and use the color picker to choose a color for the shirt. We'll use the 6AADE7 hex code, but feel free to choose any color that makes the shirt stand out on the mannequin:

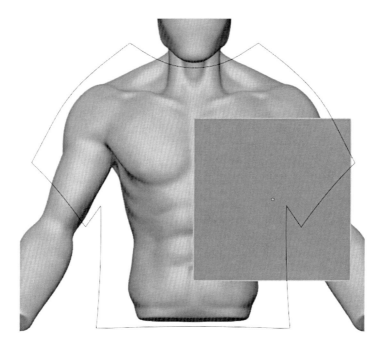

Figure 8.33 – The Shirt object with the new material applied

Now, we can get back to working on the shape of the shirt:

8. Open the **Object** menu in the top-left corner of the header of the 3D Viewport and choose **Apply | All Transforms**.

9. Click on the blue wrench icon in the Properties editor to switch to the **Modifiers** tab.

10. Click **Add Modifier** and choose **Mirror** from the **Generate** column in the list of modifiers.

11. Within the **Mirror** modifier, check the box labeled **Clipping**.

Applying the transforms of the shirt has moved the center of the object back to the center of the grid; enabling the **Clipping** setting of the **Mirror** modifier will keep the middle vertices glued to the centerline. Now, we only have to model one half of the shirt and the other half will automatically be mirrored for us.

Now, let's begin making the shirt using the **ShirtShapeGuide** outline as a reference.

12. With the **Shirt** object selected, change the Interaction Mode to **Edit Mode**.

13. Use the **Move** tool to drag the plane down and to the left so that it fits into the bottom area of the reference shirt shape, as seen in the following screenshot:

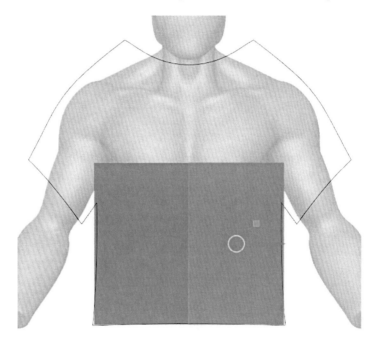

Figure 8.34 – The plane fitted into the bottom of the ShirtShapeGuide object

14. Switch to **Edge Select** mode by clicking the corresponding icon in the header of the 3D Viewport, or by pressing the *2* hotkey; then select the top edge.

15. Use the blue arrow of the **Move** tool to lower the top edge to meet the corner of the armpit of the shirt, as seen in the following screenshot:

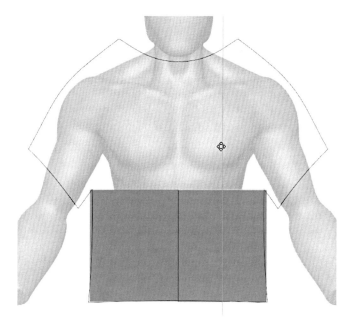

Figure 8.35 – The top edge lowered into the armpit

16. Activate the **Extrude Region** tool, and then click and drag along the white circle of the gizmo to extend the top of the shirt to meet the base of the collar of the shirt:

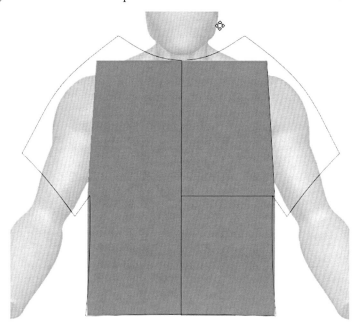

Figure 8.36 – The top edge extruded upward to the collar

17. Select the upper-right-side edge.

18. Use the **Extrude Region** tool to extrude extra geometry to form the sleeve.

19. Switch to **Vertex Select** mode by clicking the corresponding icon in the header of the 3D Viewport, or by pressing the *1* hotkey.

20. Select the vertex of the sleeve nearest the shoulder and use the **Move** tool to place it in the shoulder area of the **ShirtShapeGuide** outline.

21. One at a time, select and move the two vertices of the sleeve into the corners of the sleeve in the **ShirtShapeGuide** outline.

    When you're finished with these steps, your result should look like this:

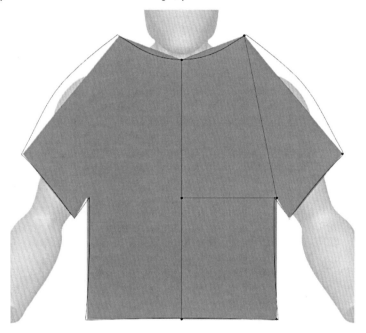

Figure 8.37 – The vertices of the shirt placed correctly

Excellent – we have our basic shirt shape. However, parts of the shirt aren't as curved as the reference guide. We need to add a few more edge loops to support the curvature of the collar and the shoulder.

22. Activate the **Loop Cut** tool from the Toolbar.

23. Hover your mouse over the bottom middle area of the shirt; a yellow vertical line will appear from the bottom up through the collar. Click to cut an edge loop into the mesh.

24. Hover your mouse over the top-right edge of the sleeve; a yellow vertical line will appear to cut through the sleeve. Click to cut an edge loop into the mesh.

25. Use the **Move** tool to adjust the positions of the new vertex in the middle of the collar and the new vertex at the top of the sleeve. Align these two vertices with the **ShirtShapeGuide** outline.

    After cutting the new edge loops and moving the vertices, your results should look like this:

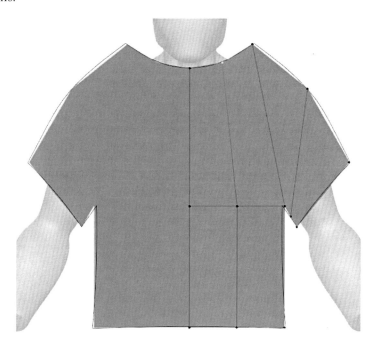

Figure 8.38 – The shirt after cutting new edge loops and correctly placing the new vertices

So far, so good. However, the cloth simulation will work best if the polygons are evenly sized. Right now, the quads are much taller than they are wide. To fix this, we can insert more horizontal edge loops.

26. Activate the **Loop Cut** tool again, find **Tool Settings** at the top of the 3D Viewport, and set the **Number of Cuts** setting to 2.

27. Hover your mouse over the lower-right edge of the sleeve; a yellow horizontal line will appear to cut across the sleeve into the torso. Click once to cut two edge loops into the mesh.

28. Hover your mouse over the bottom-right-side edge of the waist; a yellow horizontal line will appear to cut across the waist to the other side. Click once to cut two edge loops into the mesh:

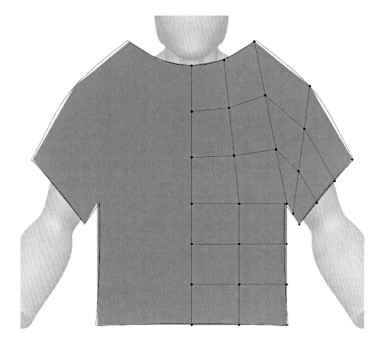

Figure 8.39 – The extra edge loops cut through the shirt, dividing it into even quads

Cloth simulations require hundreds or sometimes thousands of polygons. Now that the polygons are evenly cut, we can subdivide the mesh to create more polygons.

29. Open the **Select** menu in the top-left corner of the 3D Viewport and choose **All**.

30. Open the **Edge** menu in the top-left corner of the 3D Viewport and choose **Subdivide**.

31. A panel labeled **Subdivide** will appear in the bottom-left corner of the 3D Viewport. Click on this panel to expand it if it is not already expanded.

32. Set **Number of Cuts** to 6.

We have all of our geometry for the front of the shirt; now, we need to create the back.

33. Orbit the 3D Viewport so you can see the side and some of the back of the mannequin sculpture.

34. Activate the **Extrude Region** tool, and then click and drag along the yellow + button of the gizmo to extrude the shirt backward through to the backside of the mannequin (about -2.25 units backward).

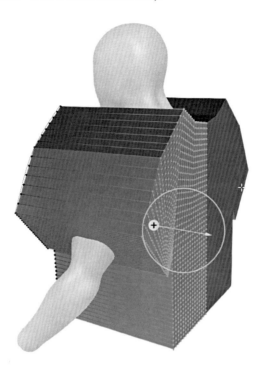

Figure 8.40 – The shirt extruded backward

You may notice some darkened shading on the shirt. This is because extruding backward like this resulted in the polygons being inside out. To fix this, we can recalculate the normal facing direction of the polygons.

35. Open the **Select** menu in the top-left corner of the 3D Viewport and choose **All**.

36. Open the **Mesh** menu in the top-left corner of the 3D Viewport and choose **Normals | Recalculate Outside**.

   We're almost done; in this next sequence of steps, we're going to remove unwanted polygons around the neck hole, sleeve hole, and waist hole:

37. Switch to **Face Select** mode by clicking the corresponding icon in the header of the 3D Viewport, or by pressing the 3 hotkey.

38. Orbit the 3D Viewport as needed so that you can see the bottom of the shirt.

39. Click and drag to box-select the polygons on the very bottom of the shirt:

Figure 8.41 – The polygons that need to be deleted

40. Open the **Mesh** menu in the top-left corner of the 3D Viewport and choose **Delete | Faces**.

41. Repeat these steps to remove the polygons that are covering the sleeve holes and the neck hole.

    One last thing – the cloth simulation will allow us to use loose edges as if they were pieces of string to sew the cloth together. To do this, we can remove the polygons around the perimeter of the shirt, leaving behind sewing edges.

42. Click on the positive red X axis in the navigation gizmo in the top-right corner of the 3D Viewport to snap the view to the right side of the mannequin.

43. Turn on the **X-ray** feature in the top-right corner on the 3D Viewport header. This will allow us to see through the polygons of the shirt, and it will allow our selection tools to select hidden geometry.

44. Click and drag to box-select the polygons in the middle of the shirt that bridge the front to the back; be careful not to select the front and back polygons.

45. Open the **Mesh** menu in the top-left corner of the 3D Viewport and choose **Delete |
    Only Faces**.

> **Important Note**
>
> Make sure you choose the **Only Faces** option, not the **Faces** option. The
> difference here is that choosing **Only Faces** will leave behind the connecting
> edges that the cloth simulation can use to sew the front and the back of the
> shirt together.

46. Turn the **X-ray** feature back off.

47. Change the Interaction Mode to **Object Mode**.

48. Select and delete the **ShirtShapeGuide** object.

Save your work; we're done preparing the shirt for the cloth simulation:

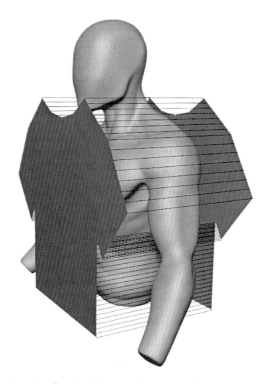

Figure 8.42 – The finished shirt mesh prepared for a cloth simulation

It doesn't look like much yet, but this shirt has all of the polygons we need for a high-quality
cloth simulation, and the connecting edges will be used to sew the shirt together. We'll
learn how to use the cloth simulation tools in the next section of this chapter.

How it works...

The tools we used in this section are all traditional modeling tools. We got some practice with tools such as these already in *Chapter 4, How to Make a Base Mesh for a 3D Sculpture*. It is useful to practice these modeling tools because we can use them to be very deliberate in the creation of our 3D assets.

Modeling for a cloth simulation is a little different than regular modeling. It's a good idea to start from a plane primitive object because planes have no thickness, and cloth simulations are designed to work with meshes that have no thickness. The thickness can be added via a Solidify modifier after we run the cloth simulation.

One of the excellent things about cloth simulations is that they closely emulate how real-life clothing is made. Flat patterns are created and then sewn together. If you want inspiration for your own clothing designs, have a look at real clothing patterns; if they work in real life, there's a good chance they will work in Blender's cloth simulation.

Simulating cloth to wrap a shirt around a character

Now that we have a mesh that is compatible with cloth simulation, we can use it to run a cloth simulation and wrap the cloth around the sculpture.

Cloth simulations have many settings to adjust to customize the style of the simulation; we're going to use a preset to make our cloth behave like cotton. We also need to enable collision on the object that the cloth will wrap around; otherwise, the cloth will phase right through the surface of the object.

Once we're finished in this section, we'll have a shirt that wraps around the character in a very realistic fashion.

Getting ready

For this section, we can pick up where we left off in the *Preparing a shirt mesh for a cloth simulation* section of this chapter. If you have not completed that section, you can begin this section with a fresh copy of the `clothSimulation_Start.blend` file here: `https://github.com/PacktPublishing/Sculpting-the-Blender-Way/blob/main/Chapter08/clothSimulation_Start.blend`.

Launch Blender and open the `.blend` file. Once the file is open, we can set up the cloth simulation.

How to do it...

We'll start by enabling a collision on the mannequin object:

1. Select the mannequin object and navigate to the **Physics** tab (represented by the blue orbiting moon icon) in the Properties editor.

2. Click the button labeled **Collision** to enable physics collisions on the mannequin:

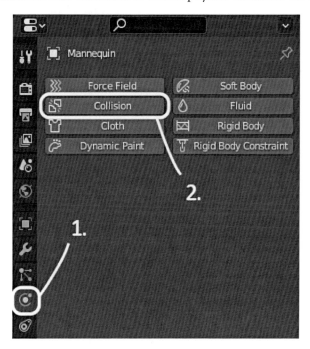

Figure 8.43 – The Physics tab in the Properties editor

Now, we need to add cloth physics to the shirt.

3. Select the **Shirt** object.

4. Click the button labeled **Cloth** in the **Physics** tab of the Properties editor.

    Great – now a cloth simulation has been added to the shirt. Before we run the simulation, we need to adjust a few settings to make it behave like a shirt. Luckily, Blender has a few presets for us to use. We'll use the cotton preset for our example, but feel free to experiment:

5. Click on the **Cloth Presets** icon at the top right of the **Cloth** settings, highlighted in the following screenshot:

Figure 8.44 – The list of cloth presets

6. Click on **Cotton** from the list of cloth presets.

    Next, we'll adjust a couple of settings to make sure that the simulation is high quality and the edges get sewn together.

7. Increase the **Quality Steps** setting to 10.

8. Scroll down and expand the **Shape** subsection of the cloth settings.

9. Check the box labeled **Sewing** in the **Shape** subsection.

10. Set the **Shrinking Factor** setting to -0.05.

Excellent – the high setting we've used for **Quality Steps** will make sure the cloth doesn't crumple through the surface of the mannequin. The **Sewing** feature will use the edges that connect the front and the back of the shirt to sew the two halves together, and the negative **Shrinking Factor** will puff up the shirt slightly so that it drapes over the body nicely and creates some loose wrinkles.

Now that the settings are set, we're ready to run the simulation!

> **Important Note**
> Cloth simulations are very intense operations for our computers to run. It's a good idea to save your work before trying to run the simulation in case your computer runs out of memory and Blender crashes.

Now that the settings are set, we're ready to run the simulation!

Simulations run over time. Because of this, we need to use the Timeline editor to run the simulation. The Timeline can be found at the bottom of Blender's user interface, as seen in the following screenshot:

Figure 8.45 – The Timeline editor

The Timeline has a blue indicator to show us what our current animation frame is. Right now, the current frame of animation is 0. As the simulation runs, this indicator will move forward to show the current frame. The playback controls are in the center of the header of the Timeline; this is where we'll find the buttons to control the simulation:

1. Click the **Play Animation** button or press the *Spacebar* hotkey to begin the simulation.

2. Watch the simulation play; the results should look good around frame 15 or so.

    Because we are simulating several thousand polygons with a high number of quality steps, the simulation is expected to run slowly. Depending on the speed of your computer, it could take a whole minute or more to process 15 frames of the simulation.

3. When you're happy with the shape of the cloth, click the **Pause Animation** button or press the *Esc* hotkey to stop the simulation:

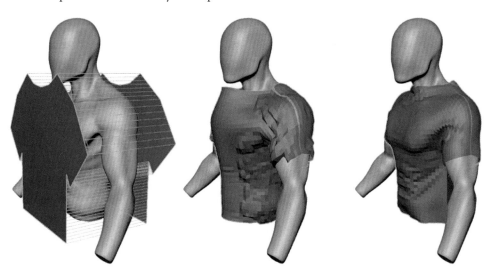

Figure 8.46 – The shirt before, during, and after running the simulation

When the simulation is finished, we can make a few adjustments to make the cloth look smoother and give it thickness.

4.   Open the **Object** menu in the top-left corner of the 3D Viewport and choose **Shade Smooth**.

5.   Click on the blue wrench icon in the Properties editor to switch to the **Modifiers** tab.

6.   Click **Add Modifier** and choose **Subdivision Surface** from the **Generate** column in the list of modifiers.

7.   Set the **Render** subdivision level to 1 to match the **Viewport** subdivision levels.

8.   Click **Add Modifier** again and choose **Solidify** from the **Generate** column in the list of modifiers:

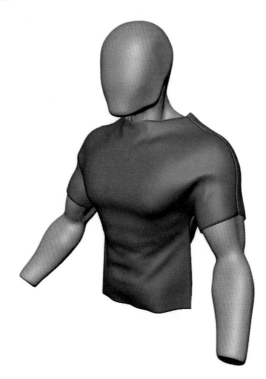

Figure 8.47 – The finished shirt after adding the Subdivision Surface and Solidify modifiers

Fantastic – the shirt is finished! If you're happy with the shape of the shirt from the simulation, we need to take an extra step to ensure that Blender keeps the cloth in this shape (otherwise, the shape may reset the next time we open this file).

9.   Click on the downward arrow next to the icons at the top of the **Mirror** modifier settings; then choose **Apply**.

10. Click on the downward arrow next to the icons at the top of the **Cloth** simulation settings; then choose **Apply**.

    Once these two modifiers are applied, the shape will be locked in. If you would like to completely close up the sewing edges, here's one last trick (this will only work if you've applied the modifiers in the previous two steps).

11. With the **Shirt** object selected, change the Interaction Mode to **Edit Mode**.

12. Switch to **Edge Select** mode by clicking the corresponding icon in the header of the 3D Viewport, or by pressing the *2* hotkey.

13. Open the **Select** menu in the top-left corner of the 3D Viewport and choose **Select All by Trait | Loose Geometry**.

14. Open the **Mesh** menu in the top-left corner of the 3D Viewport and choose **Delete | Collapse Edges & Faces**.

15. Change the **Interaction Mode** back to **Object Mode**.

Now, that's a fine-looking shirt!

How it works...

The cloth simulation is the classic way to create convincing clothing for characters in 3D; it has been used to create clothing long before the Cloth brush and the Cloth Filter were added to Blender. As the cloth simulation runs, each vertex of the cloth moves with a set of parameters that we provided when we chose a cloth preset. Depending on the parameters, the vertices might be stiff or stretchy. Each vertex checks for collision with objects that have collision enabled; if they bump into an object, they will move accordingly so that they don't penetrate the surface of the other object.

The loose edges in the mesh can be treated as sewing guides; as the simulation runs, the edges shrink and sew the pieces of cloth together. This is an excellent way to make clothing because it very closely emulates the way clothes are made in real life.

There's more...

We learned about the Cloth brush and the Cloth Filter earlier in this chapter. You can use these tools to add more wrinkles to the shirt that we created in this section. Check the tool settings for the **Enable Collision** and **Use Collisions** options for the Cloth brush and the Cloth Filter respectively. Temporarily disabling the **Multires** modifier on the mannequin object will improve performance when using collision with the sculpting tools.

See also

Blender's cloth simulation has many parameters to explore. You can read up on what each of the cloth settings does in Blender's documentation here: `https://docs.blender.org/manual/en/latest/physics/cloth/settings/index.html`.

Sculpting a hat with Radial Symmetry

Our mannequin could use a nice hat to go with his fancy new shirt. Some clothing items are more easily made with our sculpting tools, so we'll take a break from the cloth simulation in this section. There are many types of hats that we could make, but we'll go with a simple beanie for this section.

Beanies have a special type of symmetrical shape – they aren't just symmetrical from left to right; they have a repeating pattern that surrounds the entire hat. We have a symmetry setting for our sculpting tools called Radial Symmetry that can help us create this effect without having to repeat our brush strokes around the surface of the hat manually.

Getting ready

For this section, we can pick up where we left off in the *Simulating cloth to wrap a shirt around a character* section of this chapter. If you have not completed that section, you can begin this section with a fresh copy of the `clothSimulation_End.blend` file here: `https://github.com/PacktPublishing/Sculpting-the-Blender-Way/blob/main/Chapter08/clothSimulation_End.blend`.

Launch Blender and open the `.blend file`. With a clear view of the mannequin object, we're ready to sculpt a hat.

How to do it...

We'll start by creating a base mesh for the hat:

1. Open the **Add** menu in the top-left corner of the header of the 3D Viewport and choose **Mesh | UV Sphere**.

2. A panel labeled **Add UV Sphere** will appear in the bottom-left corner of the 3D Viewport. Click on this panel to expand the options for creating the sphere:

   Set **Location X** to 0 m.

   Set **Location Y** to 0 m.

   Set **Location Z** to 9.5 m.

3. Rename the **Sphere** object Hat.

Now, we need to set up a material for the hat so that it is visually distinct from the mannequin.

4. Click on the red sphere icon in the Properties editor to switch to the **Material Properties** tab.

5. Click the **New** button to create a new material and rename it Hat.

6. Scroll down to find the **Viewport Display** section in the Properties editor and click the drop-down arrow to expand the subsection.

7. Click on the white color swatch labeled **Color** and use the color picker to choose a color for the shirt. We'll use the D677E7 hex code, but feel free to choose any color that makes the hat stand out from the mannequin:

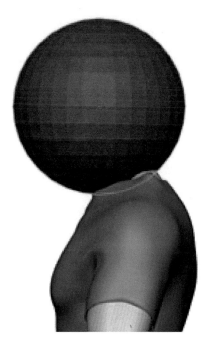

Figure 8.48 – The hat object with its new material

Now, we can finish making the base mesh for the hat.

8. With the **Hat** object selected, change the Interaction Mode to **Edit Mode**.

9. Click on the positive red *X* axis in the navigation gizmo in the top-right corner of the 3D Viewport to snap the view to the right side of the hat.

10. Turn on the **X-ray** feature in the top-right corner of the 3D Viewport header.

11. Switch to **Face Select** mode by clicking the corresponding icon in the header of the 3D Viewport, or by pressing the *3* hotkey.

12. Click and drag to box-select the bottom half of the sphere:

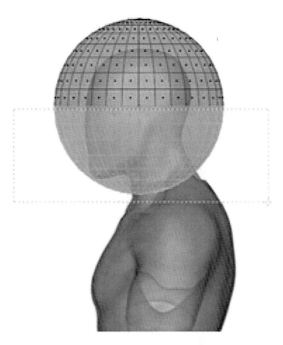

Figure 8.49 – The bottom half of the sphere that should be deleted

13. Open the **Mesh** menu in the top-left corner of the 3D Viewport and choose **Delete | Faces**.

   This will leave behind a hole in the bottom of the sphere that we need to fill with polygons. Luckily, Blender has a way to automatically fill holes like this with a grid pattern.

14. Switch to **Edge Select** mode by clicking the corresponding icon in the header of the 3D Viewport, or by pressing the *2* hotkey.

15. Open the **Select** menu in the top-left corner of the 3D Viewport and choose **Select All by Trait | Non Manifold**.

   This will select the edges that make up the perimeter of the hole that was left behind when we deleted the bottom faces. Now, let's adjust our viewport so we can see it from the bottom.

16. Turn the **X-ray** feature back off.

17. Click on the negative blue -*Z* axis in the navigation gizmo in the top-right corner of the 3D Viewport to snap the view to the bottom of the hat.

18. Open the **View** menu in the top-left corner of the header of the 3D Viewport and choose **Local View | Toggle Local View**. This will hide all objects other than the **Hat** object.

19. Open the **Face** menu in the top-left corner of the 3D Viewport and choose **Grid Fill**.

20. A panel labeled **Grid Fill** will appear in the bottom-left corner of the 3D Viewport. Click on this panel to expand it if it is not already expanded.

21. Adjust the **Offset** setting until the newly created grid of polygons are aligned straight from top to bottom and left to right, as seen in the following screenshot:

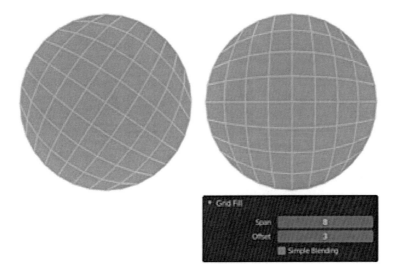

Figure 8.50 – The new grid of polygons filling in the bottom of the sphere before adjusting the Offset (left) and after adjusting the Offset (right)

> **Important Note**
> The **Offset** setting is relative to the original orientation of the grid. In our example, an **Offset** setting of 3 aligned the grid correctly. However, you may need a different setting, depending on the original orientation of the grid.

Now that we've filled in the hole in the bottom, let's make the rim for the beanie.

22. Orbit the 3D Viewport so that you can see the side of the **Hat** object.

23. Switch to **Face Select** mode by clicking the corresponding icon in the header of the 3D Viewport, or by pressing the *3* hotkey.

24. Hold down the *Alt* key and click on one of the faces along the bottom of the hat to select the face loop around the bottom.

25. Find the **Extrude Region** tool on the Toolbar. This tool has a small arrow indicator in the bottom-right corner to let us know that there are similar tools stacked underneath it.

26. Click and hold the **Extrude Region** tool to open a list of similar tools, and choose the **Extrude Along Normals** tool from the list.

27. Click and drag on the yellow gizmo to extrude a rim around the base of the hat (about 0.1 units outward):

Figure 8.51 – The bottom face loop of the hat extruded

28. Change the Interaction Mode to **Object Mode**.

29. Open the **View** menu in the top-left corner of the header of the 3D Viewport and choose **Local View | Toggle Local View**.

30. Find the **Rotation:** option under the **Transform** section in the **Item** tab of the Sidebar.

31. Click in the first rotation field labeled **X** and type -15; then press *Enter* to apply the rotation. This will tilt the hat backward so that it aligns better to the head.

32. Open the **Object** menu in the top-left corner of the 3D Viewport and choose **Shade Smooth**:

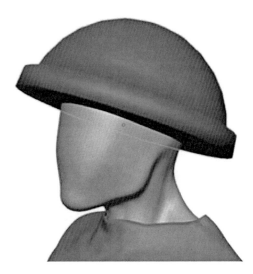

Figure 8.52 – The finished hat base mesh

Excellent – the base mesh is finished. Now, let's try sculpting it into a proper beanie with multiresolution and Radial Symmetry.

33. Click on the blue wrench icon in the Properties editor to switch to the **Modifiers** tab.

34. Click **Add Modifier** and choose **Multiresolution** from the **Generate** column in the list of modifiers.

35. Click the **Subdivide** button four times to create 4 levels of subdivision.

36. Change the Interaction Mode to **Sculpt Mode**.

37. Switch to the **Tool** tab in the Sidebar and expand the **Symmetry** subsection.

    Instead of using the mirror symmetry that we're used to, we're going to use Radial Symmetry to make our brushstrokes encircle the hat.

38. Click in the **Radial Z** field and type 3 2 to use 32 points of symmetry around the hat.

39. Find and activate the **Elastic Deform** brush on the Toolbar.

> Tip
>
> The Elastic Deform brush is very similar to the **Grab** brush, but it has a slightly different behavior with its falloff. The surrounding geometry will be pulled along with the main geometry, which leads to more realistic deformations when sculpting objects that should behave like cloth.

40. Set the brush **Radius** setting to something large enough to cover the lower half of the hat, around 170 px.

41. Hover your brush over the far-right side of the rim of the hat; then press down and drag inward to reshape the hat to better fit the form of the head, as seen in the following screenshot:

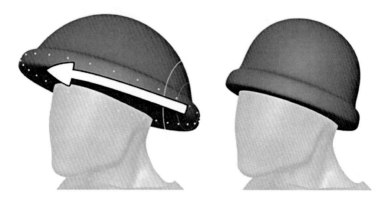

Figure 8.53 – The hat reshaped to fit the head with the Elastic Deform brush and Radial Symmetry

Now, let's draw some vertical lines into the hat to form the classic beanie fabric pattern.

42. Activate the **Draw Sharp** brush on the Toolbar.

43. Set the brush **Radius** setting to something very small for drawing lines, around 8 px.

44. Set the brush **Strength** setting to 1.000.

45. Use your graphics tablet to draw lines into the hat from bottom to top and top to bottom.

Remember to orbit around the sculpture between brushstrokes so that you can sculpt across the top and bottom of the hat. Follow our example in the following screenshot:

Figure 8.54 – The hat with woven lines carved in with the Draw Sharp brush

Tip

As you orbit the 3D Viewport around the sculpture, you may notice the hat becomes blurry; this is because Blender is using an optimization feature called Fast Navigate, which toggles to a lower subdivision level while orbiting. This optimization may be necessary for complex sculptures, but in this case, it's just a visual distraction. You can turn off this feature in **Options** in the top-right corner of the 3D Viewport header.

Finally, let's intensify the boundary between the rim of the hat and the upper part of the hat.

46. Use your graphics tablet to draw a short line around the rim of the hat. Radial Symmetry will do most of the work here:

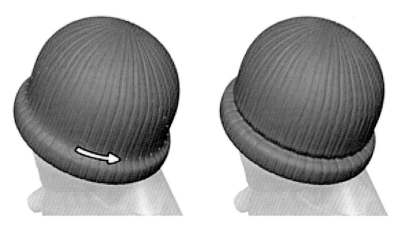

Figure 8.55 – A sharp line added to the rim of the hat with the Draw Sharp brush

Fantastic! Radial Symmetry has made it really easy to make the symmetrical details of this hat. We can always take this design further by disabling Radial Symmetry and sculpting some asymmetrical details, such as tapering on the sides of the head, cloth folds, and other adjustments to the shape. To disable Radial Symmetry, type 1 in the **Radial Z** field of the Sidebar:

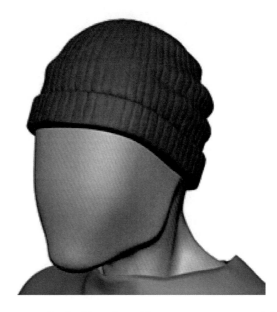

Figure 8.56 – The finished hat after adding some asymmetrical detail

Be sure to check out the bonus section of the *Sculpting in Action* video for this chapter to see our example of how to add asymmetrical details to this hat sculpture.

How it works...

Radial Symmetry effectively duplicates our brushstrokes across the surface of the model around the model's origin point. Because we created the hat base mesh out of a UV Sphere primitive object, its origin point is where the sphere's center used to be. We also rotated the object by -15 degrees on the X axis while in **Object Mode**, which also tilted the Z axis of the model by -15 degrees, so the Radial Symmetry follows this tilt as well.

It is most effective to create symmetrical details in a model first because it reduces the amount of work that we have to do by hand. However, most objects look best with a little asymmetrical detail, which we can add after disabling our symmetry settings.

There's more...

We can use several brushes to improve the quality of this hat once we're finished with the Radial Symmetry stage. This is a great example of where we can take advantage of sculpting at lower resolutions on the Multiresolution modifier, which we learned about in the *Changing resolution for appropriate details* section of *Chapter 5, Learning the Power of Subdivision and the Multiresolution Workflow*. In the case of this beanie sculpture, the high-resolution details had to be added first so that the **Radial Symmetry** feature would work properly. However, we can still sculpt low-resolution details such as wrinkles or changes to the general shape of the hat by switching to lower levels of subdivision. When we sculpt on the lower resolutions, the woven line patterns at the higher resolutions will be preserved.

See also

This chapter's *Sculpting in Action* video includes two demonstrations for this section of the chapter – one for the main instructions and one that's included as a bonus, which demonstrates how to take this hat sculpture to the next level using several techniques we've learned throughout this book to sculpt asymmetrical cloth details: `https://bit.ly/3dxbBD2`.

9
Creating Teeth, Eyebrows, and Hair

Most character sculptures require secondary features before they look complete. In this chapter, we will explore creating teeth, eyebrows, and hair for our sculpted characters. We'll start by making teeth and inserting them into a character's mouth. Next, will take a look at creating eyebrows. It's easy to forget to make eyebrows for our characters, but they are an important part of the face! Finally, we will try several methods for creating hair for our sculptures.

Hair (including eyebrows and facial hair) can be created in several ways, depending on the desired art style of your sculpture. The most common methods for creating hair are as follows:

- **Mesh Hair**: This is a very manual way to create hair using classic box modeling techniques and modifiers. This method is useful for creating hair with strong stylized shapes. It is common to use this style of hair when we need to use a small number of polygons. For example, video games designed for low-end mobile devices typically can't handle characters with tens of thousands of polygons, so mesh hair is a great way to optimize performance.

- **Particle Hair**: This is the best choice for realistic hair, where individual strands of hair are created to look the way hair does in real life. The first half of the process for creating this type of hair is very technical: particle settings for the hair can be adjusted to produce the desired number of hairs, length, curliness, and frizziness. The second half of the process is more artistic: the hair strands are shaped with grooming tools (similar to combing hair in real life). This style of hair is typically used for characters in animated films.

- **Hair Cards**: This style of hair is very similar to hair particles, but instead of individual strands, hair is grouped together into flat polygon cards that protrude from the character's head. Each of these polygons has a picture of hair attached to it with transparency around the edges. When enough of these simplified hair cards are placed together, they look like realistic hair. This is typically used for hair in video games instead of hair particles because having tens of thousands of individual hair particles is too much for most video game engines to handle, even on high-end computers and game consoles.

- **Sculpted Hair**: This is a great way to block out organic hair shapes with brushes. This method for creating hair is no different than creating any other part of the sculpture. It does have some drawbacks, though: it's hard to control the way hair flows across the head, and it is difficult to produce clean lines and shapes. Hair made with this method tends to look more like clay than hair, which may or may not fit your art style.

- **Hair Curves**: This is a great way to create stylized flowing hair with absolute control. Curves are made from a small number of simplified control points. These control points are smoothly connected together mathematically to produce very clean lines and shapes. This gives us a high level of control over the shape of the hair while the computer does most of the hard work.

Creating realistic hair with particles and hair cards is a very complex subject. Unfortunately, both of these methods require a lot of additional knowledge about 3D modeling, texturing, and materials, which we don't have time to go into detail about in this book. However, we will take a brief look at creating particle hair for realistic eyebrows and leave hair cards for you to research on your own.

This chapter will primarily focus on methods for creating stylized hair since it can be created with sculpting tools.

The main topics in this chapter are as follows:

- Creating tusks and teeth for an orc
- Creating stylized mesh eyebrows with modifiers
- Creating realistic eyebrows with hair particles

- Extracting hair from the scalp
- Visualizing the silhouette of sculpted hair
- Roughing out the shape of sculpted hair
- Adding surface details to sculpted hair
- Creating long flowing hair with curves

Technical requirements

For general requirements, refer to the *Technical requirements* section laid out in *Chapter 1, Exploring Blender's User Interface for Sculpting*.

You can download the files to follow along with this book at the GitHub link here: `https://github.com/PacktPublishing/Sculpting-the-Blender-Way`.

> **Important Note**
>
> This chapter includes a Sculpting in Action video to help demonstrate the hair sculpting process. You can view this video here: `https://bit.ly/3Gsd6hY`.
>
> The video has two demonstrations for the sculpted hair section of this chapter, including a bonus section at the end which shows how to take the hair sculpture to the next level by adding small details.

Creating tusks and teeth for an orc

Everyone needs a healthy smile, even orcs. Some pieces of our sculptures are most easily created as separate objects, and teeth are an excellent example of this. Keeping teeth separate ensures that we will have a sharp transition between the mouth and the teeth. This is because polygons of separate objects can never blend together through the use of the Voxel Remesher or any other means.

In this section, we will sculpt two types of teeth and place them in the provided character's mouth.

Getting ready

For this section, we have provided an orc head that needs some teeth. Download the `orcTeeth_Start.blend` file from `https://github.com/PacktPublishing/Sculpting-the-Blender-Way/blob/main/Chapter09/orcTeeth_Start.blend`.

Launch Blender and open the `.blend` file. This scene comes with the sculpture that you can see in the following image:

Figure 9.1 – An orc who needs to learn how to smile

Once the file is open, we can begin creating teeth for the orc.

How to do it...

We'll start by creating a pair of tusk-like canine teeth that we can place in the lower corners of the mouth:

1. Open the **Add** menu in the top-left corner of the header of the 3D Viewport and choose **Mesh | UV Sphere**. Rename the sphere object to Tusk.

2. Open the **View** menu in the top-left corner of the header of the 3D Viewport and choose **Local View | Toggle Local View**. This will hide all objects other than the **Tusk** object.

3. Change the Interaction Mode to **Sculpt Mode**.

4. Activate the **Snake Hook** brush on the Toolbar.

5. Use a large brush radius and drag upward on the top of the sphere to elongate the shape into a tusk-like shape, as seen in the following image:

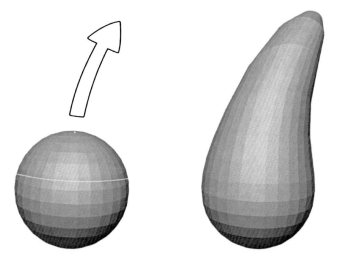

Figure 9.2 – The tusk shape made by elongating the sphere with the Snake Hook brush

6. Change the Interaction Mode back to **Object Mode**.

7. Open the **View** menu and choose **Local View | Toggle Local View** to make the other objects visible again.

8. Use the **Move**, **Rotate**, and **Scale** tools to place the **Tusk** object onto the distended gap in the orc's lower lip, as seen in the following image:

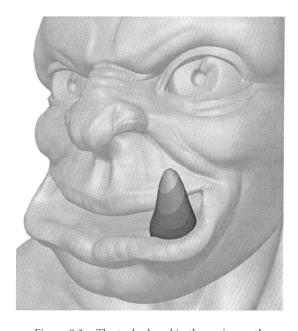

Figure 9.3 – The tusk placed in the orc's mouth

9. Click on the blue wrench icon in the Properties editor to switch to the **Modifiers** tab.

10. Click **Add Modifier** and choose **Mirror** from the **Generate** column in the list of modifiers.

11. Click on the empty field in the Mirror modifier labeled **Mirror Object** to bring up a list of objects in the scene and choose the **Orc** object.

Now that we've got the tusks placed in the mouth, let's add some details.

1. Change the Interaction Mode to **Sculpt Mode**.

2. Click **Add Modifier** from the **Modifiers** tab and choose **Multiresolution** from the **Generate** column in the list of modifiers.

3. Click the **Subdivide** button twice to create two levels of subdivision.

> **Important Note**
>
> The **Multiresolution** modifier conflicts with most other modifiers while in **Sculpt Mode**. The mirrored half of the tusk will disappear as soon as we add subdivision levels. Don't worry, this is just a limitation of **Sculpt Mode**, the mirrored tusk will come back when we return to **Object Mode**.

For this next part, we can use any of the brushes to make the tusks look interesting. For our example, we'll use the **Scrape** brush to make the tusks look rough with hard edges:

1. Activate the **Scrape** brush from the Toolbar.

2. Set the brush **Radius** to a medium size, around 100 px.

3. Set the brush **Strength** to 1.000.

Use your graphics tablet to sculpt hard edges into the tusk. This works best if you follow the shape of the tusk from top-to-bottom, or bottom-to-top like you're whittling a stick. Avoid side-to-side motion.

Don't forget to orbit around the tusk as you slowly chisel away at the edges of the tusk. If you need to, you can use **Local View** to focus on the tusk and get a better view while you sculpt. Try to refine the tip of the tusk to look sharp. When you're finished shaping the tusk, change the Interaction Mode back to **Object Mode**.

If needed, make more adjustments with the **Move, Rotate,** and **Scale** tools until you're happy with the placement of the tusks. You can see how ours turned out in the following image:

Figure 9.4 – The sculpted tusks

That's quite the mouthful! This orc still needs a bunch of small teeth, though. Sometimes when sculpting we end up with repeating patterns and symmetry. In this case, we've got symmetrical tusks because of the Mirror modifier. This is a really excellent way to work because we only have to sculpt one tusk and the other will remain perfectly synchronized with all of the newly sculpted details.

However, this only works for symmetrical placement of objects, and everyone knows that orcs have asymmetrical randomly crooked teeth! We can't use the Mirror modifier to make asymmetrical teeth, but we can still keep all of the teeth synchronized by making **linked duplicates**. Let's make one more tooth and use it to place linked copies around the mouth.

First, we'll make a regular duplicate of the tusks as a starting point:

1. Select the **Tusk** object.

2. Open the **Object** menu in the top-left corner of the header of the 3D Viewport and choose **Duplicate Objects**. This will make a duplicate called **Tusk.001**; this duplicate will immediately begin moving around with your mouse movements.

3. Move the duplicate tusk object toward the center of the mouth, then left-click or press the *Enter* key to place the object.

    This is a regular duplicate. It will not be linked nor kept in sync with the original **Tusk** object.

4. Rename the **Tusk.001** object to Tooth.

5. Find the **Mirror** modifier in the **Modifiers** tab and click the **X** button in the top-right corner of the Mirror modifier to remove it.

6. Use the **Scale** tool to shrink the tooth so that several teeth can fit in the mouth.

7. Use the **Move** and **Rotate** tools to place the **Tooth** object inside the mouth.

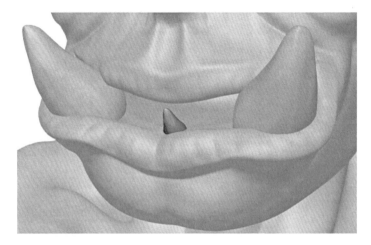

Figure 9.5 – The tooth scaled to fit and placed in the mouth

Now that we have the first tooth, we can begin making linked duplicates for the other teeth.

8. Open the **Object** menu in the top-left corner of the header of the 3D Viewport, and choose **Duplicate Linked**.

> **Important Note**
> Make sure you choose the **Duplicate Linked** option, not the **Duplicate Objects** option, otherwise the duplicate teeth will not be properly linked and synchronized.

9. Use the **Move**, **Rotate**, and **Scale** tools as needed to place the linked duplicate of the tooth in an appropriate place inside of the mouth.

10. Repeat *steps 8* and *9* until you've made a mouth full of linked duplicate teeth:

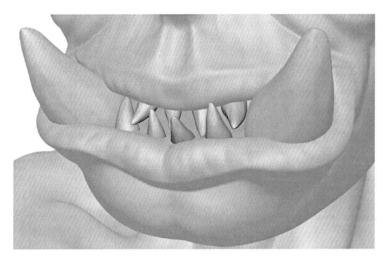

Figure 9.6 – The mouth full of teeth

Excellent! Now that we have all of the teeth, we can try making adjustments to them. The amazing thing about linked duplicates is that any change we make to one of these objects will be applied to all of the other objects.

Let's try using the Scrape brush to file down the sharp tip of one of the teeth:

1. Select any of the teeth (excluding the tusks) and change the Interaction Mode to **Sculpt Mode**.

2. Use the **Scrape** brush to scrape away the fine tip of the tooth and make the tooth flat.

3. Change the Interaction Mode back to **Object Mode**.

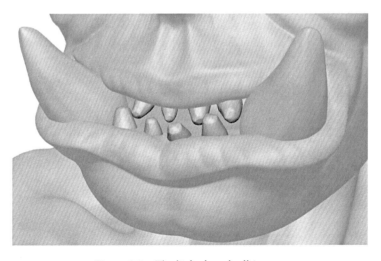

Figure 9.7 – The linked teeth all in sync

And that's all there is to it. All of the changes we made to the tooth are applied to all of the other linked teeth. The orc's smile is complete:

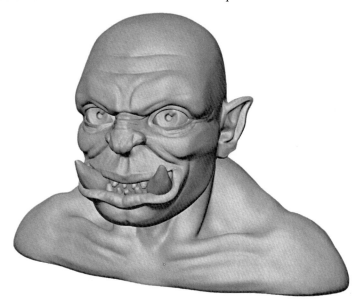

Figure 9.8 – The orc with a happy smile

Linked duplicates like this come in handy all the time. Crooked orc teeth are just one application.

How it works...

Keeping the teeth as separate objects gives us a lot of freedom. We don't have to worry about the teeth being included in the base mesh of the head. We can use the Voxel Remesher on the teeth while not affecting the head. We can add a separate Multiresolution modifier to the teeth so that we can add polygons only where they are needed.

Making linked duplicates is also very beneficial because the teeth are sharing object data. Any change we make to one of the linked teeth will be propagated to all of the other teeth regardless of location, rotation, or scale.

There's more...

Using multiple objects like this is very efficient for Blender's performance since only the object currently active in **Sculpt Mode** has to be manipulated by the sculpting tools. One of the default Viewport Overlays in **Sculpt Mode** is called **Fade Inactive Geometry**, this overlay makes all of the inactive objects slightly transparent so that we can easily tell which object is active.

There is a quick way to switch between active sculpting objects without leaving **Sculpt Mode**: hover your pen over the object you would like to switch to, then press the **Transfer Mode** hotkey, which is *D* in Blender version 2.93.

Important Note

In Blender version 3.0, this hotkey was changed to *Alt + Q*. This is because the Transfer Mode operator was upgraded to work with other Interaction Modes, but the original hotkey wasn't available in the other Interaction Modes.

Creating stylized mesh eyebrows with modifiers

This method for creating eyebrows will start with making a basic eyebrow shape using tools in **Edit Mode**, then we'll snap the vertices of the eyebrow to the character's face. Once we have the basic eyebrow in place, we can finish giving the eyebrow thickness by adding several modifiers.

This type of eyebrow will work well for art styles that rely on strong exaggerated shapes.

Getting ready

For this section, we can pick up where we left off in the *Creating tusks and teeth for an orc* section of this chapter. If you have not completed that section, you can begin this section with the stylizedEyebrows_Start.blend file, which can be downloaded here: https://github.com/PacktPublishing/Sculpting-the-Blender-Way/ blob/main/Chapter09/stylizedEyebrows_Start.blend.

Launch Blender and open the .blend file. Once the file is open, we can begin creating the eyebrows for the orc.

How to do it...

We'll start by creating the basic shape of the eyebrow with a plane:

1. Open the **Add** menu in the top-left corner of the header of the 3D Viewport and choose **Mesh | Plane**.

2. A panel labeled **Add Plane** will appear in the bottom-left corner of the 3D Viewport. Click on this panel to expand the options for creating the plane.

    Set the **Size** to 0.1 m.

Set **Location X** to 0.25 m.

Set **Location Y** to -1 m.

Set **Location Z** to 1.2 m.

Set **Rotation X** to 90.

3.   Rename the **Plane** object to Eyebrows.

4.   Click on the negative green -*Y* axis in the **Navigation Gizmo** in the top-right corner of the 3D Viewport to snap the view to the front view of the orc's face.

5.   With the **Eyebrows** object selected, change the Interaction Mode to **Edit Mode**.

6.   Click and drag outward on the red *X* axis of the scale gizmo to adjust the size along the *X* axis. Keep dragging outward until the plane is as wide as you want the eyebrow to be; in our example, a scale of 3.25 works well.

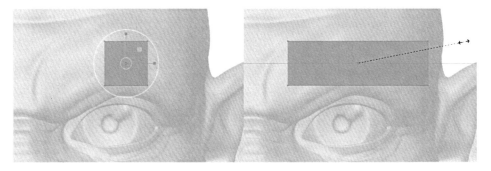

Figure 9.9 – The plane scaled along the X axis to make it wider

7.   Activate the **Loop Cut** tool from the Toolbar, find the **Tool Settings** at the top of the 3D Viewport, and set the **Number of Cuts** to 4.

8.   Hover your mouse over either the top or bottom edge of the plane. A yellow vertical line will appear to cut through the plane. Click once to cut four edge loops into the mesh.

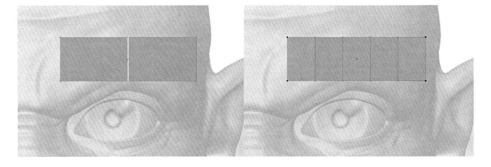

Figure 9.10 – Extra edge loops cut into the plane

Excellent! That should give us enough geometry to work with. Now we can enable our vertex snap settings and shape the eyebrow to fit the brow of the head:

1. Find the **Snapping** settings next to the magnet icon in the center of the header of the 3D Viewport and click to open the pop-over menu.

2. Change the **Snap To** setting to **Face**.

3. Check the box labeled **Project Individual Elements**.

4. Activate the **Rotate** and **Scale** options under the **Affect** section.

Figure 9.11 – The snap settings

Now that the snap settings are set correctly, click on the magnet icon in the header of the 3D Viewport to activate snapping.

5. Use the **Move**, **Rotate**, and **Scale** tools to transform the vertices to make the eyebrow shape as seen in the following image:

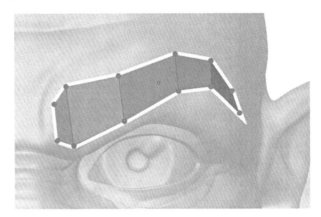

Figure 9.12 – The vertices transformed to make the eyebrow shape (the polygons in this image have been highlighted for better visibility in this book)

Important Note

The polygons of the eyebrow will become difficult to see after snapping them to the character's face. This is because parts of the polygons are now underneath the surface of the character's face. The example eyebrow in the previous image has been altered to better show the placement of the vertices. However, the polygons will not be as visible on your screen as they are in this image.

Orbit the 3D Viewport around the character to make sure the eyebrow shape looks good from all angles; it should slightly wrap around the side of the brow. Adjust the vertices as needed, and when you're finished change the Interaction Mode back to **Object Mode**.

Once we're back in Object Mode, we can enable smooth shading and add modifiers to finish the eyebrows:

1. Open the **Object** menu in the top-left corner of the 3D Viewport and choose **Shade Smooth**.

2. Click on the blue wrench icon in the Properties editor to switch to the **Modifiers** tab.

3. Click **Add Modifier** and choose **Mirror** from the **Generate** column in the list of modifiers.

4. Click on the empty field in the Mirror modifier labeled **Mirror Object** to bring up a list of objects in the scene and choose the **Orc** object.

5. Click **Add Modifier** again and choose **Solidify** from the **Generate** column in the list of modifiers.

6. Set the **Thickness** to 0.4 m and the **Offset** to 0.0000.

7. Click **Add Modifier** again and choose **Bevel** from the **Generate** column in the list of modifiers.

8. If the Bevel modifier introduces a kink into the surface of the eyebrows. Try increasing the **Angle** of the bevel threshold, for the best results don't exceed 85 (a setting of 80 works well in our example).

9. Click **Add Modifier** one last time and choose **Subdivision Surface** from the **Generate** column in the list of modifiers.

10. Set the **Levels Viewport** to 2.

When you're done, you should have four modifiers in the stack, as shown in the following image:

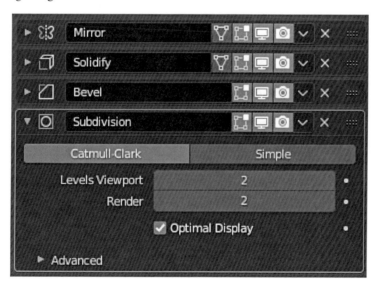

Figure 9.13 – The finished modifier stack

That's a whole bunch of modifiers! They all work together to turn the simple eyebrow shape into a thick pair of blocky mesh eyebrows. Perfect for this stylized orc!

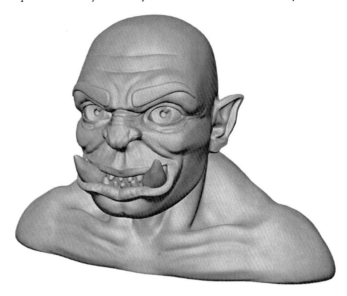

Figure 9.14 – The orc with a beautiful pair of eyebrows

As one last step to clean up the eyebrows' transforms, open the **Object** menu and choose **Apply | All Transforms**. This will center the transform origin of the eyebrows, which keeps things clean for any future edits we may want to make to the eyebrows.

The great thing about making the eyebrows this way is that it's very easy to make adjustments to the shape. Simply go back into **Edit Mode** and move the vertices around. The modifier stack will be reevaluated and any changes you make will be applied to the eyebrows automatically.

How it works...

The snap settings we used made it very easy to project the individual vertices of the eyebrow onto the orc head sculpture. This way, we can work quickly and precisely.

We took full advantage of the modifier stack to create this eyebrow. The modifier stack is evaluated from top to bottom. The Mirror modifier saves us from having to make the eyebrow on both sides of the head. The Solidify modifier gives the flat eyebrows some thickness by extruding outward. The Bevel modifier creates sharp edges with extra edge loops around the perimeter of the eyebrow. Finally, the Subdivision Surface modifier adds polygons to the eyebrows and makes them look smooth. The Bevel modifier helps the eyebrow retain its shape when the Subdivision Surface modifier smooths the surface of the eyebrow.

Using these modifiers helped a lot with creating these stylized mesh eyebrows for the orc. Mesh hair for the head can be created through a similar process, along with **Edit Mode** tools such as extrude.

There's more...

This character's art style is very blocky, so this blocky style of mesh eyebrow suits him well.

However, we can add details to the eyebrows with our sculpting tools if we so choose. Before we can sculpt the eyebrows, we need to apply all four of the modifiers from top to bottom. A fast way to apply all modifiers is to convert the object to a mesh by choosing **Object | Convert | Mesh**. This will work even though the object is already a mesh.

Once the modifiers are applied, the eyebrows will behave the same as any other mesh. We can use **Sculpt Mode** to add details however we see fit.

Creating realistic eyebrows with hair particles

The most realistic way to create hair for our sculptures is by using a **particle system**. Particles are useful in 3D software for creating hundreds of small objects in a distributed pattern. Particles can be useful for simulating specs of dust floating in the air, sparks flying off of a piece of machinery, or thousands of hair strands.

A deep dive into particles is beyond the scope of this book, so we will focus on a small introduction to how to use hair particles to create realistic eyebrows for a character.

Getting ready

For this section, we have provided an old monk character who is currently completely bald. Download the `realisticEyebrows_Start.blend` file from `https://github.com/PacktPublishing/Sculpting-the-Blender-Way/blob/main/Chapter09/realisticEyebrows_Start.blend`.

Launch Blender, and open the `.blend` file. This scene comes with the old monk character that you can see in the following image:

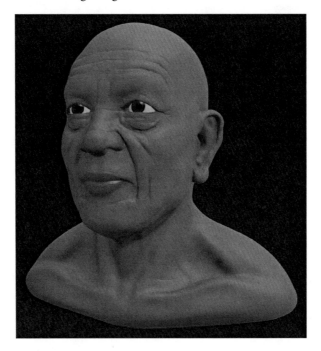

Figure 9.15 – Bald old monk with realistic materials

We usually don't want to create particle hair for our sculptures until we've finished all of the other stages of sculpting. This character model has been finished, and realistic materials have been created for the character so that his skin looks like real skin instead of clay. We have also created a hair material ahead of time so that the eyebrows can have a proper hair color.

Once you've opened this file, we can begin creating realistic eyebrows for this old monk character.

How to do it...

We'll start by creating a **vertex group** to control the density of the eyebrow hair particles. Vertex groups are similar to masks, but they can be used for many purposes outside of **Sculpt Mode**:

1. Navigate to the **Object Data** tab (represented by the green triangle icon) in the Properties editor.
2. Click the + button next to the **Vertex Groups** subsection to create a new vertex group.

3.   Rename the vertex group `Eyebrows_Density`.

Figure 9.16 – The Vertex Groups subsection in the Object Data tab of the Properties editor

Now we can use an Interaction Mode called **Weight Paint** to paint the area for the eyebrows and add influence to the vertex group.

4.   Change the **Viewport Shading** to **Solid** mode for better visibility and performance.

5.   Open the Interaction Mode drop-down list in the top-left corner of the header of the 3D Viewport and choose **Weight Paint**.

From here, we can use the pen of our graphics tablet to paint the influence of the **Eyebrows_Density** vertex group. The influence of the vertex group is indicated by the colors we see on screen: dark blue represents 0% influence, while bright red means 100%. Green, yellow, and other colors represent partial influences.

6. Use the **Draw** tool to paint the area where eyebrow hairs should appear, as shown in the following image:

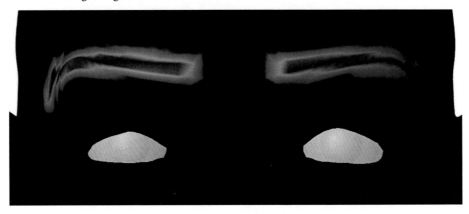

Figure 9.17 – The eyebrows painted in Weight Paint mode

7. Change the Interaction Mode back to **Object Mode**.

    Now we can add the particle system to the **OldMonk** object to create the hair for the eyebrows.

8. Navigate to the **Particles** tab (represented by the blue dots and lines icon) in the Properties editor.

9. Click the + button to create a new particle system along with particle settings for the particle system.

10. Rename the new **ParticleSystem** to Eyebrows and rename the **ParticleSettings** to EyebrowSettings.

11. Click the **Hair** button to change the particle type to hair.

    Now the old monk will be covered in hair, as seen in the following image:

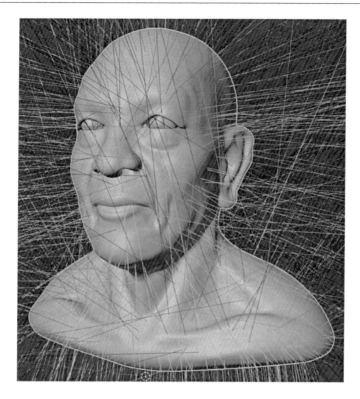

Figure 9.18 – The old monk with out-of-control eyebrow hair

Let's tame these crazy eyebrows by using our **Eyebrows_Density** vertex group to control the density of these hairs.

12. Scroll down to the **Vertex Groups** subsection of the particle system and click the arrow to expand it.

13. Click on the empty field labeled **Density** to bring up a list of vertex groups and choose the **Eyebrows_Density** vertex group.

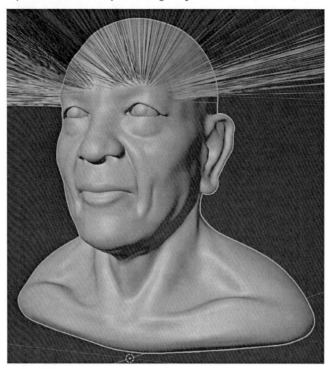

Figure 9.19 - Eyebrows controlled with the Density vertex group

That's a good start, but the hairs are still way too long. Let's fix that now.

14. Scroll up to the **Emission** subsection and set the **Hair Length** to 0.003 m.

    Now that the hairs are a reasonable length, we can groom them. This process is somewhat similar to sculpting; we can use the **Comb** tool to shape the hair particles artistically.

15. Open the **Interaction Mode** drop-down list in the top-left corner of the header of the 3D Viewport and choose **Particle Edit** (this mode is only available on objects that have a particle system attached).

16. Use the **Comb** tool to drag over the hairs and comb them into an appropriate shape, as shown in the following image:

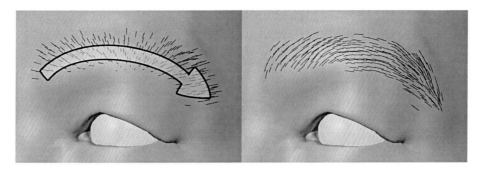

Figure 9.20 - The eyebrow groomed with the Comb tool

The hairs will behave very similarly to real-life hair while we comb them. It may take several brush strokes to get a desirable shape. Don't forget to orbit the 3D Viewport while combing so that the eyebrows cling to the contours of the brow appropriately. Try to taper the outer edges of the eyebrow so that it gets thinner at the end. Once we have the general shape, we can clean up any extra hairs with the **Cut** tool.

17. Activate the **Cut** tool from the Toolbar and drag over the top and bottom of the outer edge of the eyebrow to trim the hairs. Try to taper the shape of the eyebrow, as shown in the following image:

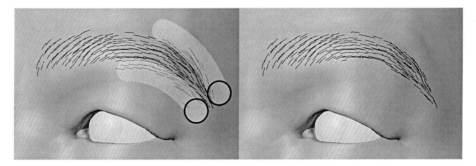

Figure 9.21 - The eyebrow trimmed with the Cut tool

The hair particles we've created so far are the primary hairs of the particle system, sometimes referred to as **parent hairs**. We typically keep the number of parent hairs relatively low so that they are easy to control with our grooming tools. When we want to make the hair look more dense, we can enable **child hairs**. Child hairs cannot be edited with our grooming tools; instead, these hairs are created by the particle system to clump together around the parent hairs. This allows us to make very dense hair without having to comb thousands of hairs by hand. We can also choose to display a small number of child hairs in the viewport, while rendering a much higher amount in the final render so that our viewport performance doesn't slow down, but our final render will look amazing!

In our case, this old monk's eyebrows are going to be very thin, so we will only need a small number of child hairs for both the viewport and the render:

1. Expand the **Children** subsection of the Particle Properties..

2. Click the **Simple** button.

    Set the **Display Amount** to 5 (we're keeping this number low for better performance in the viewport).

    Set the **Render Amount** to 5 (try a higher number if you want more eyebrow hairs in the final render).

    Set the **Radius** to 0.002 m.

    This will populate the surrounding two-millimeter area around each parent hair with five child hairs.

    We're almost finished. Now we need to fix the thickness of the hair and give the hair the correct material so it looks correct in the rendered image and Material Preview shading mode.

3. Expand the **Hair Shape** subsection.

4. Set the **Diameter Root** to 0.02 m.

5. Expand the **Render** subsection.

6. Click on the empty field labeled **Material** to bring up a list of available materials and choose the **OldMonk_Hair** material.

7. Change the **Viewport Shading** to **Material Preview** mode.

Excellent, the eyebrows are done. Our example turned out like this:

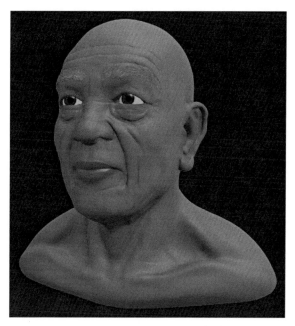

Figure 9.22 - Eyebrows on fleek

Groomed hair like this is the best way to create realistic hair. We can control the hair in a very natural way with our grooming tools, but we also get to have fine control over the style of the hair through the particle settings.

How it works...

Particle hair is a complex subject that could fill a book all by itself, so we can't explain all of the details here. All you need to know for now is that hairs are created by the particle system wherever the density vertex group has influence. Once the hairs are created, our grooming tools can take over to give us artistic control and comb the hair the way we would comb hair in real life.

There's more...

We've really only scratched the surface of what's available in Particle Edit mode. Additional strands of hair can be added. Individual hairs can be lengthened or shortened as needed. We can puff up the hairs to lift them off of the surface, somewhat similar to using a hairdryer.

There are also many details that we can add in the particle settings. We can add clumping to the hair so that the child hairs clump together with the parent hairs. We can add roughness to the hair to make it look frizzy. We can add curliness or braided details, all by adjusting the settings in the particle system.

We encourage you to play around with these settings. Don't limit yourself to a single particle system; you can create additional particle systems for facial hair, the scalp, and more!

See also

Hair particles are excellent for realistic hair, but they usually can't be used for video games. A common solution for this is to replace the hair particles with hair cards.

Particles can be converted to curves to be used as the basis for hair cards. To convert the particles, first, click the **Convert** button for the hair particle system in the **Modifiers** tab of the Properties editor, then choose **Object | Convert | Curve**. Once the particles are converted to curves, the curves can be extruded into hair cards with the **Extrude** setting under the **Geometry** subsection of the green **Object Data** tab in the Properties editor. Once the hair cards are created, a hair texture can be applied to create the final look of the hair.

This process is straightforward in theory, but it requires a lot of practice with tools that are beyond the scope of this book, so we will leave you to research hair cards on your own. To learn more about the hair card creation workflow, we recommend this two-part video tutorial by *Emmanuel. W (Luwizart)*:

* *Generate hair cards with blender particle system – Part 1*: https://www.youtube.com/watch?v=sCkvKlJXZg4

* *Generate hair cards with blender particle system – Part 2*: https://www.youtube.com/watch?v=ZTU8k9uZF2Y

Extracting hair from the scalp

Most methods for creating stylized hair begin with creating hair for the scalp. The easiest way to achieve this is using a mask extraction. A mask extraction will allow us to paint a mask onto the character's scalp, then duplicate the masked area into a separate object to form the basic shape of the character's hair. We used mask extractions once before in the *Using mask extract to make a shirt* section of *Chapter 8, Making Accessories and Clothing*. This section will be very similar, but instead of making a shirt, we will be making hair for the scalp of our character. Once we have the basic hair shape, we can continue to work on the hair with our sculpting tools.

Getting ready

For this section, we can use any bald character sculpture as a starting point. You can use your own creation, or you can choose from several characters we've provided with the previous chapters of this book:

- The child from `childHead.blend`

- The character we sculpted from `simpleCharacterHead_Bonus.blend`

- The vampire from `multiresolutionVampireHead.blend`

- The old monk from `oldMonk.blend`

- The angular head from `angularHead_End.blend`

- The orc from `stylizedEyebrows_End.blend`

These would all be excellent candidates for making hair, but why stop at realism? Maybe the turtle from `recaptureDetails.blend` would like some hair too!

For our example, we'll use the child from `childHead.blend`, which can be downloaded here: `https://github.com/PacktPublishing/Sculpting-the-Blender-Way/blob/main/Chapter01/childHead.blend`.

Launch Blender and open the `.blend` file containing the character you would like to make hair for. Once you've got the character file open, we recommend switching the **Viewport Shading** to **Solid** mode. Make sure **Mask** is enabled under the **Sculpt** subsection of the **Viewport Overlays** (this option is only available in **Sculpt Mode**).

How to do it...

Mask extractions are a great way to get started with stylized hair. Unfortunately, as of this book's publication, Blender does not support extracting masks from multiresolution sculptures. If you are working with a character sculpture that has a Multiresolution modifier, we need to use a workaround for this limitation by disabling the modifier:

1. Select the character's head object and change the Interaction Mode to **Sculpt Mode**.

2. Click on the blue wrench icon in the Properties editor to switch to the **Modifiers** tab.

3. Click on the monitor icon at the top of the **Multires** modifier to temporarily disable the modifier.

Sometimes this will dramatically change the shape of the sculpture. In our example, you can see that the neck of the child loses all detail and turns into a thin cylinder that is not representative of the high-resolution version:

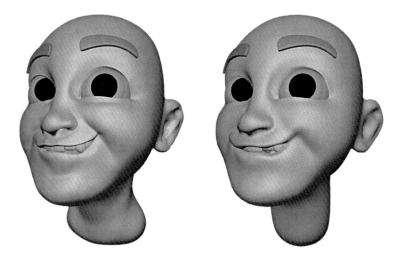

Figure 9.23 – Multiresolution enabled (left) and disabled (right)

This is happening because the details of the neck were sculpted while the Multiresolution modifier was enabled, which means none of the changes to the shape were applied to the base mesh. Luckily, Blender provides a way to transfer these changes to the base mesh to correct the shape:

4. Expand the **Shape** subsection in the Multiresolution modifier settings.

5. Click the **Apply Base** button.

The base mesh shape will now match the high-resolution sculpture as closely as possible. This may not be necessary if the base mesh is already a close match to the high-resolution sculpture, but it is helpful in our example.

With the Multiresolution modifier disabled, we can paint the mask for the extraction.

1. Activate the **Mask** brush on the Toolbar.

2. Set the brush **Radius** to something large enough to easily paint large areas of the scalp.

3. Set the brush **Strength** to 1.000.

4. Activate the *X* axis symmetry from the top-right corner of the 3D Viewport header.

5. Use your graphics tablet to draw over the scalp, behind the ears, across the back of the neck, the hairline, and the entire back of the head. Follow our example in the following image:

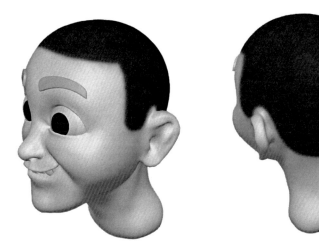

Figure 9.24 – The masked scalp area

Orbit the 3D Viewport while you paint the mask, be sure to fill in the entire area for the hair. Once you have the mask painted onto the character, we can extract it.

6. Open the **Mask** menu in the top-left corner of the 3D Viewport and choose the **Mask Extract** option.

7. Setting for the **Mask Extract** operation will appear. Leave the settings at their defaults and click the **OK** button.

    This will create a new object called **Mesh** that matches the shape of the mask. Blender will automatically change the Interaction Mode to **Object Mode** and select the new object.

8. Rename the new **Mesh** object to Hair_Scalp.

    The **Extract As Solid** option from the **Mask Extract** operation has added a **Solidify** modifier to this new object in order to give it thickness. The modifier has been labeled **geometry_extract_solidify**. Let's adjust the offset and thickness now.

9. With the **Hair_Scalp** object selected, navigate to the **Modifiers** tab in the Properties editor.

    Set the **Offset** of the Solidify modifier to 0.0000.

    Set the **Thickness** to 0.03 m.

> **Important Note**
> Depending on the size of the sculpture, and how thick you want the hair to be, you may need a different **Thickness** value.

Now that we've finished the extraction, we can turn the Multiresolution modifier for the head back on:

1. Select the character's head object, and then click on the monitor icon at the top of the **Multires** modifier to reenable the modifier.

   Excellent, now we have an extracted mesh for the scalp that we can sculpt on. To help this new mesh stand out, we should give it a material.

2. Select the **Hair_Scalp** object.

3. Click on the red sphere icon in the Properties editor to switch to the **Material Properties** tab.

4. Click the **New** button to create a new material and rename the new material to Hair.

5. Change the **Base Color** to your choice of hair color, we chose the hex code B1582C for our example (this is the color that will appear in **Material Preview** and **Rendered** viewport shading).

6. Scroll down to the **Viewport Display** section and change the **Color** to a dark gray, we chose the hex code B1B1B1 for our example (this is the color that will appear in **Solid** viewport shading).

   Excellent. We're almost done, just a couple of things to clean up before this hair can be sculpted.

7. With the **Hair_Scalp** object selected, navigate to the **Modifiers** tab of the Properties editor.

8. Click the drop-down arrow in the top-right corner of the **geometry_extract_solidify** modifier and choose **Apply**.

   The **Add Boundary Loop** option from the **Mask Extract** operation has added a face loop around the perimeter of the extracted mesh. This face loop will help to preserve the shape of the mesh when we add subdivisions with a Multiresolution modifier. Let's add multiresolution now.

9. Click **Add Modifier** and choose **Multiresolution** from the **Generate** column in the list of modifiers.

   If you started with a character that had a Multiresolution modifier, then there is a slight issue to deal with before we can move on. The multiresolution data from the original head sculpture has been copied over to the extracted hair. Even though we've added a brand-new Multiresolution modifier and the current subdivision levels are set to **0**, the displacement data from the original head is still present.

In our example, the child's **Head** object had **2** levels of subdivision, so the extracted **Hair_Scalp** object also has two levels. We could bring these subdivision levels back simply by typing 2 in the **Level Viewport**, **Sculpt**, and **Render** settings. Unfortunately, this seldom produces the desired result; the displacement can easily become erratic because the extracted mesh is missing some of the original polygons. The most reliable course of action is to remove the displacement data and start fresh.

10. With the subdivision levels set to **0**, click the **Delete Higher** button in the **Subdivision** subsection of the **Multires** modifier.

    Excellent. Now we have a completely fresh start, and we can subdivide again.

11. Click the **Subdivide** button to create **1** level of subdivision.

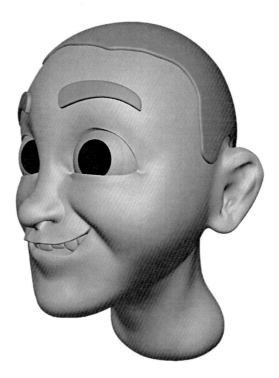

Figure 9.25 – The finished extraction for the scalp hair, ready for sculpting

Perfect, now we have our extracted scalp hair, ready for sculpting!

How it works...

The extracted scalp helps to define the volume of the hair. We can use this as a starting point for the character's hair. The hair makes a significant difference to the overall look and feel of the character, so it's important to block out the silhouette, size, and shape of the hair as early and as quickly as possible before we try to add any details to it.

There's more...

The next part of the process is to use our sculpting tools to edit the extracted scalp. Adjust the shape with Grab, Elastic Deform, and Snake Hook. Increase the volume with Inflate. Draw parting lines with Crease and Draw Sharp. Once we're happy with the shape of the hair we can add details to it to make it look like proper hair. We will learn how to do all of this in the subsequent sections of this chapter.

Visualizing the silhouette of sculpted hair

There are many situations where visualizing the silhouette of our sculptures can be helpful. Sculpting hair is an excellent example of this because hair contributes a lot to the shape of a character's silhouette. It is important to think about the silhouette when preparing to sculpt something complicated, such as hair, because it allows us to determine whether the shapes are aesthetically pleasing early in the process. Surface details, such as individual strands of hair, do not contribute to the silhouette. It is easy to become distracted by the small details while we work on the large forms of the hair sculpture, so it can be helpful to view the model without any surface detail while we block out the major forms of the hair.

In this section, we will learn how to customize Blender's viewport settings to show our sculpture's silhouette.

Getting ready

For this section, we can pick up where we left off in the *Extracting hair from the scalp* section of this chapter. If you have not completed that section, you can begin this section with the `childHead_ExtractedHair.blend` file, which can be downloaded here: `https://github.com/PacktPublishing/Sculpting-the-Blender-Way/blob/main/Chapter09/childHead_ExtractedHair.blend`.

Launch Blender and open the `.blend` file. Once the file is open, we can set up the user interface for silhouette visualization.

How to do it...

One aspect of Blender's user interface that we have not covered yet is the ability to split areas into multiple editors. For example, we can split the Outliner into two sections and turn one of these sections into a 3D Viewport. Let's do this now:

1. Move your mouse over the horizontal edge that divides the Outliner and the Properties editor.

2. Right-click on the dividing edge to bring up a list of **Area Options** and choose **Horizontal Split**.

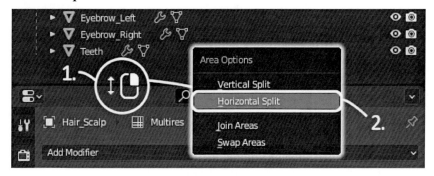

Figure 9.26 – Horizontal Split

A horizontal line will appear under your mouse. Move this line to where you would like to split the area. About halfway through the Outliner will work well for our purposes.

3. Left-click to split the area:

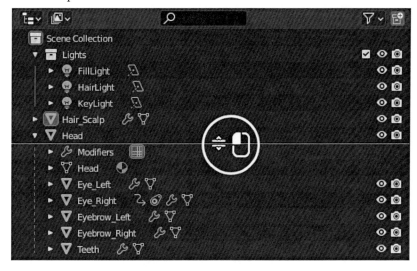

Figure 9.27 – Split the Outliner in half

Now we have two Outliner editors, an upper and a lower. Functionally, they are the same, which isn't particularly useful, so let's change the upper one into a 3D Viewport.

4. Click on the **Editor Type** icon in the top-left corner of the upper Outliner area to bring up a list of other editor types, and choose **3D Viewport** from the list:

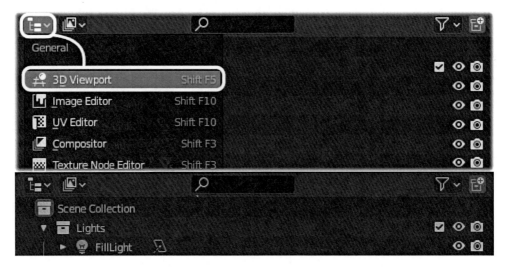

Figure 9.28 – Change the upper Outliner into a 3D Viewport

Great! Now let's customize the settings for this viewport. It's a little cramped right now, so we'll start by maximizing it to fill the entire window.

5. Right-click on the header (the header is transparent, but you can right-click in any of the places that have icons, such as the viewport shading options). A menu will appear. Choose **Header | Maximize area**. Alternatively, you can hover your mouse over the secondary 3D Viewport and press the *Ctrl + Space* hotkey to maximize the area.

6. Change the **Viewport Shading** to **Solid** mode.

7. Click on the little down arrow to the right of the viewport shading modes to open the **Viewport Shading** pop-over menu.

8. In the **Lighting** section, click the **Flat** button to remove shading from the objects.

9. In the **Color** section, click the **Single** button to use a single color to display all objects.

10. Click on the white color swatch to edit the display color. Choose black by sliding the value slider along the right side of the color picker all the way to the bottom. Alternatively, you can use the hex code 000000 to set the color to black.

11. In the **Background** section, click the **Viewport** button to use a custom color specific to this 3D Viewport.

12. Click on the gray color swatch to edit the background color. Choose white by sliding the value slider along the right side of the color picker all the way to the top. Alternatively, you can use the hex code FFFFFF to set the color to white.

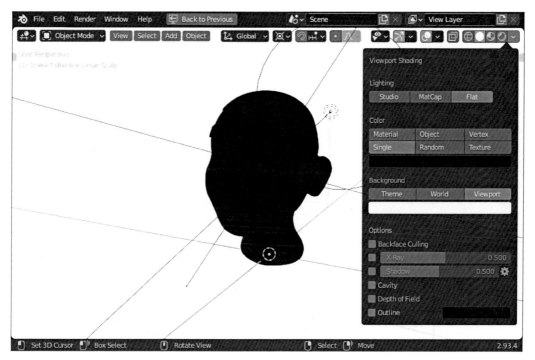

Figure 9.29 – The custom shading for the 3D Viewport

Perfect! Now we can remove some of the extra clutter from this viewport.

13. Click on the **Viewport Overlays** icon in the top-right corner of the 3D Viewport to disable all overlays.

14. Click on the **Show Gizmo** icon to the left of the **Viewport Overlays** icon to disable all viewport gizmos.

15. Press the *N* hotkey to close the Sidebar (if it's not already closed) and press the *T* hotkey to close the Toolbar (if it's not already closed).

16. Right-click on the header (the header is transparent, but you can right-click in any of the places that have icons, such as the viewport shading options). A menu will appear: choose **Header** then uncheck the box labeled **Show Header**.

17. Minimize the 3D Viewport either by clicking the **Back To Previous** button in the top-left corner of the user interface or by pressing the same *Ctrl + Space* hotkey that we used a moment ago to maximize the area.

18. Left-click and drag the space between the small 3D Viewport and the Outliner as needed to get a good view of the sculpture's silhouette.

Fantastic! Now we can see the silhouette of the sculpture in our customized 3D Viewport while we work in the main 3D Viewport.

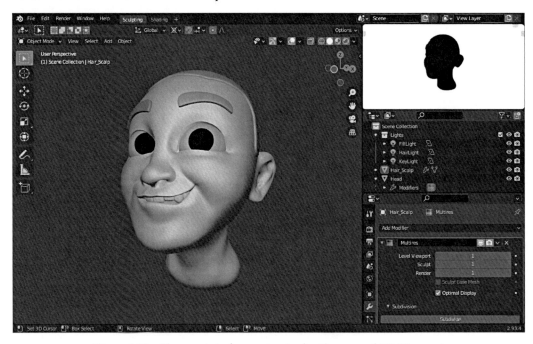

Figure 9.30 – The user interface customized with a second 3D Viewport

It would be nice to be able to keep the angle of the two 3D Viewports perfectly in sync. Unfortunately, as of this book's publication, Blender does not have an easy way to do this. However, we can make it work by adding a camera to the scene, then matching the viewports via the camera's viewpoint. Let's do this now to keep the viewing angles of the 3D Viewports in sync:

1. Open the **Add** menu in the top-left corner of the header of the main 3D Viewport and choose **Camera**.

2. Open the **View** menu in the top-left corner of the header of the main 3D Viewport and choose **Align View | Align Active Camera to View**.

3. Hover your mouse over the main 3D Viewport and scroll in to zoom. Keep zooming in until you can't see the yellow border of the camera anymore.

4. Open the Sidebar by clicking the little < indicator on the right side of the main 3D Viewport or by pressing the *N* hotkey while your mouse is in the main 3D Viewport.

5. Switch to the **View** tab of the Sidebar and find the **View Lock** subsection.

6. Check the box labeled **Camera to View**.

    From now on, zooming, panning, and orbiting will move the camera object along with the main 3D Viewport. All we need to do now is match the silhouette viewport to the camera.

7. Hover your mouse over the secondary 3D Viewport and press the tilde key, ~, to open the **View** pie menu, then choose **View Camera** in the bottom-left corner of the pie menu.

8. Keep your mouse over the secondary 3D Viewport and scroll in to zoom. Keep zooming in until you can't see the border of the camera anymore. Try to match the zoom level of the main 3D Viewport as closely as possible.

Now we're finished. The two viewports will stay in sync!

This is not a flawless solution; there are still some actions that can cause the viewports to get out of sync, but you can always realign the camera using the **View | Align View | Align Active Camera to View** option. Although, you may have to temporarily toggle off the **Lock Camera to View** option if you need to adjust the zoom level.

How it works...

Blender's user interface is highly customizable. We can have multiple copies of each editor open at once. In this case, it was helpful to use a second 3D Viewport. Each 3D Viewport can have its own shading settings. By using the flat shading mode, we are able to visualize only the silhouette of the sculpture. This will help us focus on the large details while we sculpt the hair, while eliminating the surface detail. We will still sculpt primarily in the main 3D Viewport, but remember to check what the silhouette looks like frequently. This technique is particularly helpful for sculpting hair, but you can use it any time you would like to focus on the silhouette.

Roughing out the shape of sculpted hair

Now that we have an extracted scalp mesh, we can use it to create the basic hair shape. This can be thought of as the planning phase of sculpting the hair. We will not be sculpting individual strands of hair or adding any small details yet. We must first define the volume, parting lines, and general flow of the hair. An important aspect of the planning phase is to visualize how the hair contributes to the character's silhouette, so we recommend following the instructions in the *Visualizing the silhouette of sculpted hair* section of this chapter.

In this section, we will use our sculpting tools to rough out the shape of the hair so that we can visualize the way the hair will look on the character before adding details.

Getting ready

For this section, we can pick up where we left off in the *Visualizing the silhouette of sculpted hair* section of this chapter. If you have not completed this section, you can begin this section with the `childHead_ExtractedHair_WithSilhouette.blend` file, which can be downloaded here: `https://github.com/PacktPublishing/Sculpting-the-Blender-Way/blob/main/Chapter09/childHead_ExtractedHair_WithSilhouette.blend`.

It is helpful to use reference photos when designing a character's hair. This will help us determine which areas have volume and contribute to the shape of the hair the most. We've chosen these images of a cheerful child as reference:

Figure 9.31 – Cheerful Boy in Overalls (photos by Marina Abrosimova)

You don't have to limit yourself to photos of the same person, but do try to find photos that show the hair from multiple angles so you can see where the hair originates from and what direction it flows in.

We need to think of the hair not as one whole blob, but as divided sections that each have mass, volume, and direction. If we try to think of the hair as one continuous shape across the entire head, we will get lost and be unable to produce a satisfying result.

Using the reference image, we can simplify the hair to its major shapes and identify how each shape flows across the head:

Figure 9.32 – Hair sectioned into major shapes

In the preceding image, we can see that the red section of hair in the front behaves as one solid shape, swooping down across the forehead. The blue section is similar, but it flows across the top and toward the side of the head instead of across the front. The two yellow sides each have volume and puff outward away from the head. There is also a small amount of hair visible on the back of the neck which we've highlighted purple; even this small piece contributes to the silhouette.

These sections clump together to form distinct shapes that we must try to capture in the earliest stages of sculpting the hair.

Once we've got our reference images ready, we can begin shaping the hair with our sculpting tools.

How to do it...

Before we think about the strands and the flow of the hair, we need to establish volume. In other words, we must give the appropriate amount of thickness to the hair in each area of the head. We can do this most easily with our Inflate brush, Grab brush, and Snake Hook brush. We'll start by adding volume to the front, top, and sides:

1. Select the **Hair_Scalp** object and change the Interaction Mode to **Sculpt Mode**.

2. Activate the **Inflate** brush.

3. Set the brush **Strength** to 1.000.

4. Use your graphics tablet to draw over the hair in front of the character's face, right above the eyes, as shown in the following image:

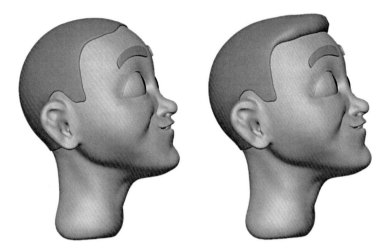

Figure 9.33 – Hair in the front before and after being inflated

This subtle adjustment has already made the shape of the hair feel more natural. Remember to check the silhouette. Notice how inflating this section has added a substantial amount of volume to the character's hair:

Figure 9.34 – The silhouette of the hair before and after being inflated

This contribution to the volume and silhouette is what we should be checking for at this stage. The top of the head, sides, and little part in the back all need a bit of volume. Keep working with the Inflate brush until you have something similar to the following image:

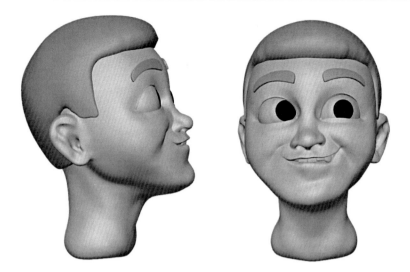

Figure 9.35 – Volume added to the top, sides, and back of the hair with the Inflate brush

So far so good. This initial pass with the Inflate brush has already made the hair feel more natural.

> **Important Note**
>
> If this is your first time sculpting hair, we recommend using a short hair style. If you're feeling more advanced and you would like to use this technique with long hair, you will need to apply the Multiresolution modifier, then use the Voxel Remesher to add polygons to support the shape of the long hair while you shape the volume and silhouette. We covered the Voxel Remesher in the *Using the Voxel Remesher in a low-to-high detail workflow* section of *Chapter 2, Overview of Blender's Sculpting Workflows*.

We've got the basic volume of the hair started, but we haven't followed our reference image very closely. Looking back at the reference, we can see that the hair is not symmetrical. Hair is almost never symmetrical. The origin of the hair strands, the flow of the hair sections across the head, and the parting line of the hair will always look best with some asymmetry involved.

We should turn off symmetry, then we can refine the shape of the hair to better match the segments we outlined in our reference:

1. Deactivate the *X* axis symmetry from the top-right corner of the 3D Viewport header.

2. Activate the **Snake Hook** brush.

Use your graphics tablet to pull a section of hair from the front, slightly down and to the side across the forehead area, as shown in the following image:

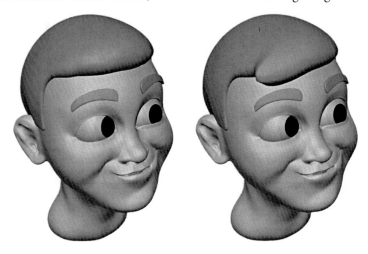

Figure 9.36 – The front swoop of the hair created with the Snake Hook brush

This hair swoop is inspired by the red section that we outlined in *Figure 9.32*. It's fine if this doesn't match the reference exactly. Focus on what looks best for the character you're sculpting. The reference is just there to help us define the main sections of the hair. Using the blue section of hair outlined in *Figure 9.32* as a reference, let's add a few more swoops with the **Snake Hook** brush across the top of the head following the same general flow:

Figure 9.37 – Additional swoops of hair added with the Snake Hook brush

As we can see from the reference, this swoopy hair originates on the character's left side, then flows over to the character's right side. The little swoops we've made with the **Snake Hook** brush do a pretty good job at highlighting the ends of these sections, but right now we have no definitive origin for this hair. We can fix this by carving in the parting line on the character's left side. A parting line is one of the most obvious places where hair originates.

Look again at the far-right image in *Figure 9.32*. Notice how the blue section of hair and the yellow section of hair originate at the same point then flow in opposite directions? This creates a very distinct shape in the character's hair at the parting line. Let's add this with the **Crease** brush:

1. Orbit the 3D Viewport so we can see the left side of the character's head (the opposite side of the swoops we created with the **Snake Hook** brush).

2. Activate the **Crease** brush.

3. Set the brush **Strength** to 1.000.

    Use your graphics tablet to carve the parting line into the hair, as shown in the following image:

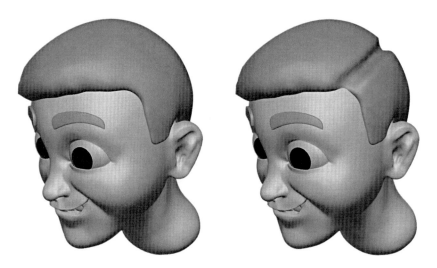

Figure 9.38 – The parting line carved into the hair with the Crease brush

This is a good start. Use the **Smooth** brush, **Inflate** brush, and **Grab** brush as needed to refine this shape.

Figure 9.39 – The parting line of the hair refined with other brushes

The parting line of the hair helps make the hair look real. It will also give a clear direction of flow when we get to the detailing phase because hair always flows outward from the parting line. Check the silhouette at this stage, you should be able to see a definitive wedge cut into the shape of the hair at the parting line. Hair flows outward from this wedge, as you can see highlighted in the following image:

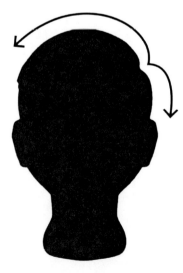

Figure 9.40 – The silhouette of the parting line of the hair

This is a really excellent start to the shape of the hair. Let's use the **Crease** brush across the top of the head to reinforce the sections we made earlier with the **Snake Hook** brush:

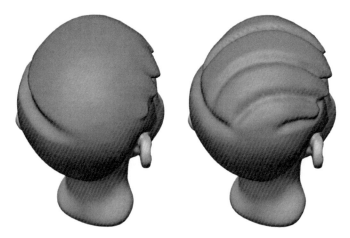

Figure 9.41 – The reinforced sections of hair flowing across the head

That should be enough for this planning phase of the hair. Check your work from every angle and make sure the silhouette looks good. The general shape of the hair won't change much past this phase. If it doesn't look good now, adding individual strands of hair and other details won't make it look a whole lot better.

Depending on the complexity of the hair shape you've sculpted, you may need to use the QuadriFlow remesher to generate new edge flow for the sculpted hair. Usually, it is easier to sculpt details into the hair if the flow of the polygons matches the flow of the hair sections that we've sculpted. In our example, the hair flows diagonally against the original topology. Another issue is that the polygons at the tips of the hair where we used the **Snake Hook** brush have become bunched up. Using QuadriFlow will fix both of these issues, as you can see in the following image:

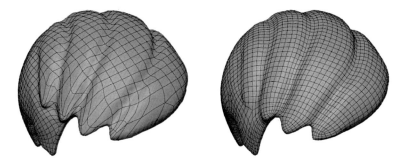

Figure 9.42 – The hair before and after using QuadriFlow to remesh it

We learned how to do this in the *Generating an all-quad mesh QuadriFlow* section of *Chapter 5, Learning the Power of Subdivision and the Multiresolution Workflow*. If you choose to do this, make sure you apply the Multiresolution modifier first. When you use QuadriFlow, disable the **Use Mesh Symmetry** option and enable the **Smooth Normals** option. Once the new all-quad mesh has been generated, add a new Multiresolution modifier.

This last bit of preparation will make sculpting details much easier.

How it works...

Roughing out the main shapes of the hair is an important first step in making the hair look aesthetically pleasing. Reference images help a lot in determining how the hair can be broken down into manageable sections.

Depending on the art style you're trying to achieve, this phase might be all you need to make convincing hair for your character since all of the major landmarks of the hair are in place already. Next, we will learn some techniques to add detail to the hair.

See also

The *Cheerful Boy in Overalls* photos were made available by Marina Abrosimova on `https://www.pexels.com/` under the free-to-use Pexels License. The original photos are available here: `https://www.pexels.com/@marina-abrosimova-3319804`.

Adding surface details to sculpted hair

It's time to add some detail to the hair. Artistically, it is not generally a good idea to sculpt every individual hair; the results usually end up looking too busy and visually distracting. It is better to sculpt details that give the impression of hair layered onto the surface. Most art looks best when broken down into a hierarchy of detail: large forms, medium forms, and small forms.

We've established the largest forms of hair by roughing out each of the sections of hair. But right now, it looks like a blob of clay because it has no medium or small detail. Our next step will be to add some medium-sized details to the hair to emphasize the flow of the hair strands within each section.

There are many ways to do this, and you can work your way down to very intricate small details if you're willing to put in the time and effort. In this section, we will learn some simple techniques that will give good results with relatively little tedious work.

Getting ready

For this section, we can pick up where we left off in the *Roughing out the shape of sculpted hair* section of this chapter. If you have not completed that section, you can begin this section with the `childHead_HairDetails_Start.blend` file, which can be downloaded here: `https://github.com/PacktPublishing/Sculpting-the-Blender-Way/blob/main/Chapter09/childHead_HairDetails_Start.blend`.

Launch Blender and open the `.blend` file. Once the file is open, we can begin detailing the hair with our sculpting tools.

How to do it...

If we try to think of the hair as one continuous shape across the entire head, we will get lost and be unable to produce a satisfying result. We need to break it down into individual pieces in a layered hierarchy of detail. We outlined the largest sections of the hair using our reference image in the *Roughing out the shape of sculpted hair* section of this chapter. Now we need to divide these sections into smaller clumps that have depth and direction.

We'll start by using the Clay brush with our drawing tablet's pressure to build up tapered swoops of hair in layers. Then we can smooth away unwanted details with the Smooth brush and refine the rest of the details using the Draw Sharp brush.

First, let's prepare a few sculpting settings:

1. Select the hair object and change the Interaction Mode to **Sculpt Mode**.

2. Click the **Subdivide** button in the **Multires** modifier to add more subdivision levels to the hair. In our example, we'll need **3** levels of subdivision at this stage.

   If your computer can handle it, disable the **Fast Navigate** option from the **Options** menu in the top-right corner of the 3D Viewport header. This will require more computer processing power, but it will allow Blender to display the sculpture at its highest subdivision level while orbiting the viewport. (If your computer begins to slow down, you may need to turn this feature back on).

3. Orbit the 3D Viewport so we can see the back of the hair.

   Now let's set up the Clay brush and sculpt the first layer of hair.

4. Activate the **Clay** brush on the Toolbar.

   Set the brush **Radius** to a large size, around `135 px`.

   Set the brush **Strength** to `0.750`.

> **Important Note**
>
> The extracted hair mesh has polygons inside of the character's head that face inward. Usually, we can ignore these polygons, but some areas where the hair becomes very thin could be problematic. Some brushes can inadvertently affect the inner polygons while we sculpt on the outer polygons. If this happens to you, you can tell the brush to only affect the outer polygons by enabling the **Front Faces Only** setting in the **Brush** menu in the **Tool Settings** of the 3D Viewport header.

We're going to use the pressure of the drawing tablet to draw tapered clumps of hair. It will be easiest to start from the bottom and work our way up since this will give us a natural layering for the hair:

1. Start with your brush at the very bottom edge of the hair. Touch down with light pressure and drag upward with increasing pressure to draw a clump, as shown in the following image:

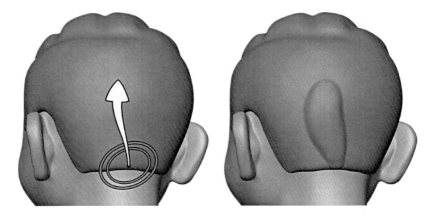

Figure 9.43 – The first clump of hair drawn with the Clay brush

It may take a little experimenting to get this right. Feel free to undo with the *Ctrl + Z* hotkey and try again as many times as you need to so you can practice using the pressure. Add some slight curvature to the brush stroke to make the hair look wavier. When you're happy with this clump of hair, we can continue making more clumps around the lowest part of the hair.

2. Keep drawing tapered clumps of hair to fill out the base of the hair, as shown in the following image:

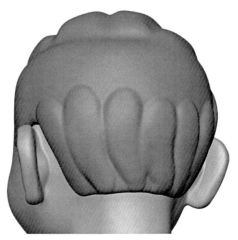

Figure 9.44 – The first layer of hair sculpted with the Clay brush

This will form the bottom layer of the hair. Before we sculpt the next layer, we should smooth out the tops of these clumps so that they don't conflict with the next layer.

3. Hold down the *Shift* key to temporarily switch to the Smooth brush.

4. Use the Smooth brush to smooth out the tops of the clumps we made with the Clay brush.

5. Release the *Shift* key to return to the Clay brush.

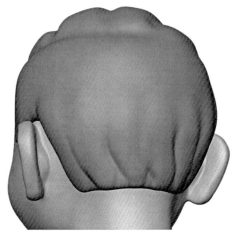

Figure 9.45 – The tops of the hair clumps smoothed with the Smooth brush

6.   So far so good. Let's repeat these steps to make a second layer, slightly above the first layer, overlapping some of the original clumps.

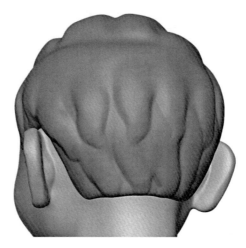

Figure 9.46 – The second layer of hair sculpted with the Clay brush and tops smoothed with the Smooth brush

7.   One more time, let's draw a third layer. For this third layer, instead of smoothing out the tops of the hair clumps, we will tuck them into the parting line of the hair. Only smooth slightly if you need to, but try to preserve the general shape of each clump as it tucks into the parting line.

8.   Make sure to add small clumps of hair above the ears. At this point, all of the space below the parting should have clumps of hair sculpted in.

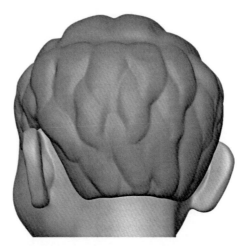

Figure 9.47 – The third layer of hair sculpted with the Clay brush; clumps tucked into the parting line

Perfect! We've got the layers of the hair established. However, they are looking pretty soft around the edges. We can use the Draw Sharp brush to sharpen the edges of these hair clumps.

1. Activate the **Draw Sharp** brush on the Toolbar.

2. Set the brush **Radius** to a large size, around 110 px. It needs to be large enough that we can use it to draw a tapered edge, not an extremely sharp line.

3. Leave the brush **Strength** at 0.500 so that we don't have a harsh transition at the edge of the brush strokes.

   Let's customize the brush with a few settings from the **Tool Settings** section of the 3D Viewport header.

4. Activate the pen pressure icon for the brush **Radius**.

5. Open the **Stroke** menu and check the box labeled **Stabilize Stroke**.

6. Change the draw **Direction** of the brush to **Add** by clicking the + button.

We can use this brush to emphasize the clumps of hair. We will trace over the soft corners of the hair clumps to create a definitive ridge to each clump.

> Tip
> The **Stabilize Stroke** feature will make it easier to make smooth brush strokes. It works by making the brush lag slightly behind where your pen is. It can take a little practice to get used to how this feature works. If you don't like this feature you can disable it, but we recommend using it to produce clean line work.

Pick a clump of hair and trace along the left side edge with a slight margin. Continue the stroke to the tip of the hair clump, as shown in the following image:

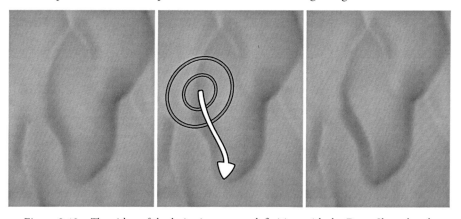

Figure 9.48 – The ridge of the hair given more definition with the Draw Sharp brush

Sharpening just one of these clumps might not feel like it changed much yet. But little details like this will add up. Use this same technique to sharpen the rest of the hair clumps. You should see a very pronounced difference once all of the clumps have been sharpened, as you can see in the following image:

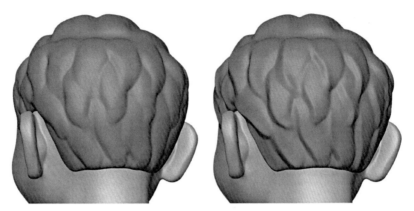

Figure 9.49 – The hair clumps before and after using the Draw Sharp brush to enhance the edges

In our example, we chose to only emphasize the left side of each clump because it makes the hair layers look like they are tucking into each other, but if you would like to emphasize both the left and the right side, go ahead.

Next, let's use the Clay brush again to add some definition to the hair in the top section of the head:

1. Orbit the 3D Viewport so we can see the top of the hair.

2. Activate the **Clay** brush on the Toolbar.

   Set the brush **Radius** to a medium size, around 50 px.

   Leave the brush **Strength** at 0.750.

3. Pick one of the hair sections on the top of the head and draw a strip of hair from the tip to the parting line, as shown in the following image:

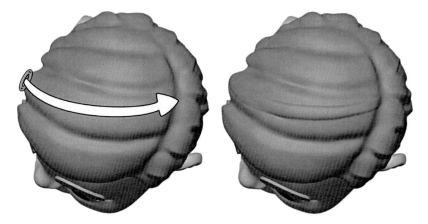

Figure 9.50 – The top of the head with one strand added with the Clay brush

That's a good start. Draw more strips like this following along the established flow of the hair. Keep repeating this for all of the sections of hair on the top of the head. When you're finished, the hair on the top of the head should look like it has strands running through each section. You can see our example in the following image:

Figure 9.51 – The top of the head with many strands of hair sculpted with the Clay brush

Excellent! Simply by following the flow of the original large forms, we've broken the top hair down into smaller strands and added some medium detail to the sculpture.

Some of the details we've added might look a little bit soft, or blurry. We can sharpen and enhance some of the details of the hair by adding another level of subdivision and using the Draw Sharp brush again:

1. Click the **Subdivide** button in the **Multires** modifier once to add another level of subdivision to the hair. In our example, this will bring the sculpting subdivision level to **4**.

2. Activate the **Draw Sharp** brush on the Toolbar.

3. Change the draw **Direction** of the brush to **Subtract** by clicking the - button in the **Tool Settings** section of the 3D Viewport header.

4. Set the brush **Radius** to a small size, around 40 px. It needs to be large enough that we can use it to draw a tapered edge, not an extremely sharp line.

5. Leave the brush **Strength** at 0.500.

6. Use the Draw Sharp brush to trace in between each clump of hair to sharpen the grooves.

This will take some time to finish, and the result will be subtle, but it will go a long way to making the edges of the hair look distinct. You can see a before and after comparison of our example in the following image:

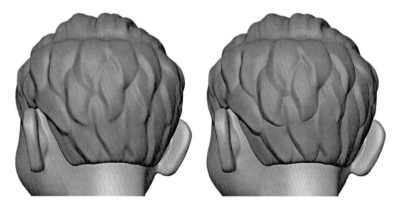

Figure 9.52 – The hair on the back of the head before and after tracing the edges with the Draw Sharp brush

We can also sharpen the lines along the parting line of the hair, and through the top sections of the hair. Again, the effect here will be subtle, but it makes it look very sharp:

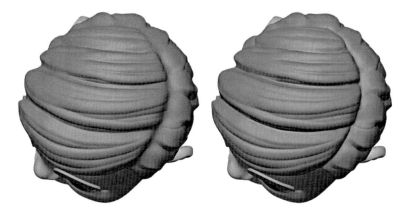

Figure 9.53 – The hair on the top of the head before and after tracing the edges with the Draw Sharp brush

And there we have it; with just a few steps and a lot of repetition we've taken this hair from a large blob of clay into something that resembles proper stylized hair. This style of hair might be enough for you, but we can always add more detail. The best way to do this is to use the Draw Sharp brush to split the medium-sized hair clumps into smaller strands of hair. You can see our example in the following image:

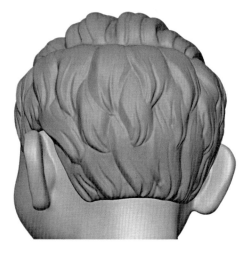

Figure 9.54 – The hair with small details and hair strands added

Be sure to check out the bonus section of the *Sculpting in Action* video for this chapter to see our example of how to add small details to the hair.

How it works...

The Clay brush is an excellent choice for quickly building up large forms, but the edges of each brushstroke can often look a little too soft and undefined. We can add definition to the edges of these forms using the Draw Sharp brush with a large radius and a carefully applied amount of pressure. The Stabilize Stroke option helps us make clean line work without the shakiness of our hands interrupting the smooth flow of the brushwork.

Building up these forms in layers can give the impression of hair without having to sculpt the individual strands. We can break down these forms further if we need to, depending on what we need for our chosen art style.

Sculpting hair like this takes a lot of practice. It may take you several attempts to achieve a result you're happy with. Keep at it and refine your own personal style.

See also

This chapter's *Sculpting in Action* video includes two demonstrations for this section of the chapter – one for the main instructions and one that's included as a bonus, which demonstrates how to take the details of this hair to the next level: `https://bit.ly/3Gsd6hY`.

As stated at the beginning of this section, trying to sculpt intricate details, such as individual hair strands, often results in unsatisfying artwork. A better way to think about making aesthetically pleasing art is to break it down into a hierarchy of detail, like we did with our large, medium, and small details of the hair. The philosophy behind the hierarchy of detail is very well explained by *Gleb Alexandrov* in his presentation at the Blender Conference 2017: *The Secret of Making High-Quality Art (in Blender and Everywhere)*, which you can watch here: `https://www.youtube.com/watch?v=qMH_J_vcoqE`.

Creating long flowing hair with curves

The final way we can create hair for our sculptures is by using curves. **Curves** are sometimes known as splines, NURBS paths, or Bézier curves. These objects are made up of a small number of control points that we place in 3D space with our transform tools. Blender connects these control points together with smooth lines, which creates mathematically perfect curvature that would otherwise be difficult to make by hand.

We can give these curves thickness with a bevel profile, which can be used to make patterns that look like hair strands. This technique is excellent for making long hair. In this section, we will take a quick look at how to create a strand of stylized hair with curves, which you can use for your characters.

Getting ready

For this section, we will keep it simple and create our hair curves in a fresh `.blend` file.

Launch Blender and choose **File | New | General** to create a new Blender project. Remove the default cube object by choosing **Object | Delete** from the menu in the top left of the 3D Viewport. Once the cube is removed, we can begin making hair curves.

How to do it...

Let's begin by creating the path for the hair. This will be somewhat like an individual hair, but after we give it thickness, it will act more like a group of long hairs working together to form a section of hair:

1. Open the **Add** menu in the top-left corner of the header of the main 3D Viewport and choose **Curve | Path**.

2. Rename the new **NurbsPath** object to `Hair_Path`.

3. With the **Hair_Path** object selected, change the Interaction Mode to **Edit Mode**.

    Although this is not a mesh object, Blender's user interface for editing this object in **Edit Mode** is very similar to editing the vertices of a mesh. We can see that this object is made from five control points.

Figure 9.55 – The control points of the path (this image has been edited for better visibility in this book)

Each control point can be selected and moved around the same way we would select and move around the vertices of a mesh.

4. Select a control point and use the **Move** tool to move it around.

5. Repeat this for each of the control points to make an interesting shape.

    You should see a curved line appear, connecting the control points together.

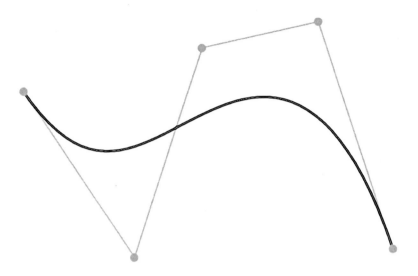

Figure 9.56 – The smooth curve can be seen connecting the control points (this image has been edited for better visibility in this book)

This smooth curve is the path that Blender is generating between the control points. This is the important shape to pay attention to while moving the control points around. Keep moving the points around until you have a shape that you're happy with.

Now let's give this path some thickness and detail. This can be done with a **Bevel Profile**:

1. Navigate to the **Object Data** tab (represented by the green curve icon) in the Properties editor.

2. Expand the **Geometry** section and the **Bevel** subsection.

3. Click the button labeled **Profile** to choose a custom bevel profile for the curve.

4. Increase the **Depth** setting to 0.5 m to give the curve thickness.

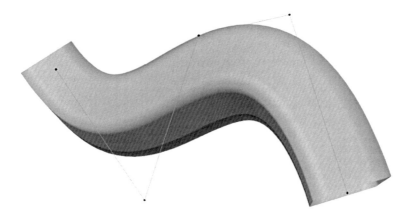

Figure 9.57 – The curve with thickness

The shape of this thickness is determined by the bevel profile widget in the Properties editor. The bevel widget is the very large square area below the **Preset** drop-down menu. The default bevel profile is a diagonal line running from the top left to the bottom right of the square, as we can see in the following image:

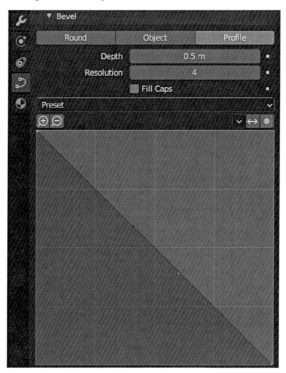

Figure 9.58 – The default bevel profile

This behaves very similarly to the Curve Widget we learned about in the *Using custom falloff* section of *Chapter 6, Using Advanced Features and Customizing the Sculpting Brushes*. By manipulating the curve in the bevel profile, we can adjust the shape of the bevel on the curve. We can add control points to the bevel profile by clicking and dragging on the diagonal line in the Properties editor. This will allow us to create interesting shapes very quickly.

5. Click on the diagonal line in the bevel profile to add a control point.

6. Drag the control point to change the shape of the bevel profile.

7. Add as many points as you like to customize the shape.

Our example of a basic stylized hair shape can be seen in the following image:

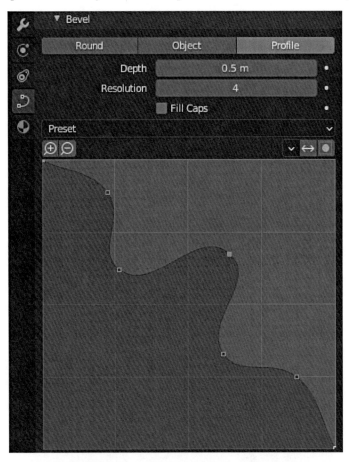

Figure 9.59 – Example bevel profile for stylized hair

Simply by changing the bevel profile, the shape of the curve is updated to match the new pattern. Our example can be seen in the following image:

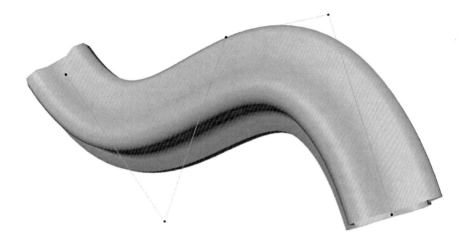

Figure 9.60 – The resulting bevel shape on the curve from the new bevel profile

So far so good. We can also adjust the radius of specific points along the curve. This is most useful for closing off the tip of the curve to make it look more like hair instead of a tube with a hole at the end:

1. Select the control point at the tip of the path.

2. Open the Sidebar by clicking the little < indicator on the right side of the main 3D Viewport or by pressing the *N* hotkey while your mouse is in the main 3D Viewport.

3. Switch to the **Item** tab of the Sidebar.

4. From here, we can change properties that belong to the selected control point.

5. Change the **Radius** to 0.000 to collapse the end of the hair strand.

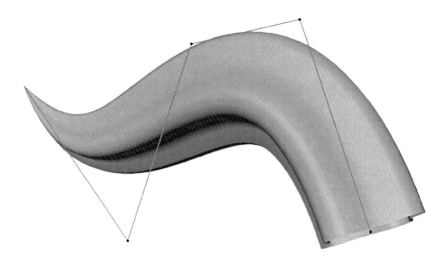

Figure 9.61 – The finished hair strand

Excellent! We now have a complete strand of stylized hair made from a curve. The greatest thing about this workflow is that we can adjust the shape of the path as often as we like, and the shape of the hair will update to match. We can extend the hair either by extruding or subdividing the control points to make the path longer.

We can also duplicate the control points to make more hairs and begin styling a character's hair with them. Select the control points you would like to duplicate, then choose **Curve | Add Duplicate** from the top-left corner of the 3D Viewport. With enough duplicates you can create hair for a character's entire head, like the example in the following image:

Figure 9.62 – An example hairdo made from curves

This is an example character we saw earlier in this book from the
`highResCharacterTopology.blend` file. Take it as inspiration and try to use this
technique to make hair for your own characters!

How it works...

Hair curves are a very popular way to create long flowing hair for our sculptures. They
offer a lot of flexibility to us as artists, while the computer does most of the hard work to
calculate the smooth curves.

Styling this type of hair takes a lot of practice. We should remember what we've learned
throughout this chapter. Try to break down the hair into main sections that we can
represent with these hair curves. Think about the origins of the hair and how to layer the
hair to give it volume.

There's more...

As an alternative to the bevel profile, we can use a second curve object to define the bevel shape of the hair path object. First, you'll need to create the second curve object. Usually, a **Curve | Circle** object is the best choice. Navigate to the green **Object Data** tab of the Properties editor and change the **Bevel** type to **Object** instead of **Profile**. From here, you can edit the Circle object in **Edit Mode** to customize the bevel shape.

You can also use a third curve object as a **Taper Object** to define the thickness of the hair strand along its length.

Another exciting tool to play with is the **Tilt** value of each control point. This will allow us to twist the hair along the path. A quick way to adjust the Tilt is to select a control point and press the *Ctrl + T* hotkey.

There's also no reason we have to limit ourselves to using curves just for hair. Curves are excellent for making ropes, chains, straps, tentacles, or any other long curvy shapes for our sculptures.

See also

If you would like to see an example of a complete head of hair made with curves, check out the example character in the `highResCharacterTopology.blend` file here: `https://github.com/PacktPublishing/Sculpting-the-Blender-Way/blob/main/Chapter05/highResCharacterTopology.blend`.

Feel free to explore this example file. Expand the **Hair** collection in the Outliner and try selecting each piece of the hair. Change the Interaction Mode to **Edit Mode** and see how the curves were used to shape the hair for this character.

10
Rendering Sculptures for Your Portfolio

We've worked hard to learn many interesting sculpting tools, tips, and techniques, and now we've got some awesome sculptures to show off in our portfolios! But before we upload any images of our artwork for the world to see, we should make sure that our sculptures can be seen in the best light – literally! We should add lights to the scene and set up materials for the sculptures so that they look amazing! Once we have our lights in place, we can **render** the artwork.

Rendering is what our computers do to calculate the appearance of 3D objects in the scene. Rendering can be done with varying quality, depending on our needs. Technically, our computers are always rendering our sculptures into the 3D Viewport. Viewport rendering is usually done with relatively low-quality settings so that our computers' processing power can be dedicated to the sculpting tools instead of the rendering process.

We learned a little bit about how Blender draws objects in the 3D Viewport in the *Exploring the viewport shading modes* section of *Chapter 1, Exploring Blender's User Interface for Sculpting*. We know that **Solid** mode with **MatCap** shading works well while we sculpt because this mode prioritizes fast sculpting performance over visual quality. However, this shading mode doesn't look the best for presenting a finished piece of art. This is where the **Rendered** shading mode comes in.

When we use the term *render*, we typically aren't referring to the solid viewport shading mode. Instead, we use the term to refer to the highest quality type of rendering that is used for producing the final image after we've created all of the 3D objects. This is the type of rendering that we will learn to do in this chapter.

The main topics in this chapter are as follows:

- Setting up Rendered mode
- Adding three-point lighting to the scene
- Lighting up the environment with an HDRI
- Creating a clay material for the sculpture
- Using a camera to render the sculpture
- Setting up a turntable for a 360-degree render
- Exporting the final render

Technical requirements

For general requirements, refer back to the *Technical requirements* section laid out in *Chapter 1, Exploring Blender's User Interface for Sculpting.*

You can download the files to follow along with this book at the GitHub link here: `https://github.com/PacktPublishing/Sculpting-the-Blender-Way`.

This chapter will rely more heavily on your graphics card than any of the previous chapters because rendering is a task typically performed by the graphics card. The Blender Foundation has made efforts to support as many graphics cards as possible. However, some rendering settings are limited by your operating system and graphics card manufacturer. **GPU rendering** on macOS is currently not supported, so you will have to use **CPU rendering** instead, which tends to be slower. GPU rendering support on macOS is in the works, with a target release in Blender 3.1; you can follow the development of this feature here: `https://developer.blender.org/T92212`.

Another small limitation is that some denoising features such as the **OptiX AI denoiser** are only available on **NVIDIA** graphics cards. For a better understanding of which rendering features your computer supports, you can read more here: `https://docs.blender.org/manual/en/latest/render/cycles/gpu_rendering.html`.

You will be able to follow along with this chapter with most computers, but some parts of the rendering process may take much longer than normal if your computer doesn't support GPU rendering and denoising.

Setting up Rendered mode

Rendering is the highest-quality way to view our sculptures, but it is also the slowest way for our computers to draw 3D objects. This trade-off is worth it as long as we choose the appropriate settings that will make our renders look good.

The first thing we need to understand is that the process of rendering is performed by a **render engine**. Blender is not a render engine; we use Blender to sculpt and model our 3D objects, but when it's time to render, we need to choose which render engine to use. This is typical of all 3D software; it's not a problem for us because there are many render engines to choose from. Blender includes two render engines out of the box, **Eevee** and **Cycles**.

- **Eevee** is a real-time *rasterizing* render engine that prioritizes fast speed over realistic lighting. A render from this type of render engine usually takes less than one second to process. This is most closely comparable to high-quality video game graphics. The results from this type of render engine can look really fantastic. However, certain shortcuts are taken to keep the render engine working fast, which means the lighting isn't as realistic as other engines. You can read more about the Eevee render engine here: https://docs.blender.org/manual/en/latest/render/eevee/introduction.html.

- **Cycles** is a *path tracing* (a type of *ray tracing*) render engine that prioritizes realistic light calculations over speed. A render from this type of render engine usually takes a few minutes or sometimes hours to process. This type of render engine is typically used in professional animated movies. If you want the absolute best quality possible and you want precise artistic control over the quality of the lighting, this is the best type of render engine to use. You can read more about the Cycles render engine here: https://docs.blender.org/manual/en/latest/render/cycles/introduction.html.

> **Important Note**
>
> At the time of writing this book, the Blender Foundation is preparing to release Blender 3.0. This upcoming version of Blender includes an updated version of Cycles (internally known as **Cycles X**). Render times are much faster in this updated version. We recommend using this new version of Blender if you choose to render your sculptures in Cycles. You can read about the Cycles X improvements here: https://code.blender.org/2021/04/cycles-x/.

Both of these render engines are fairly easy to get started with. In this section, we will learn how to tell Blender which render engine we want to use and how to set up the render settings to take advantage of our graphics card.

Getting ready

For this section, we're going to use one of our previous example files to help demonstrate the difference in visual quality between the Eevee and Cycles render engines. The skin, eye, and hair materials from the old monk example can be rendered in either engine, but the resulting image will be different in each engine. We'll use the `realisticEyebrows_End.blend` file to demonstrate these differences. You can download the file here: `https://github.com/PacktPublishing/Sculpting-the-Blender-Way/blob/main/Chapter09/realisticEyebrows_End.blend`.

Launch Blender and open the `.blend` file. Once the file is loaded, we can set up our render settings.

How to do it...

Let's start by enabling our graphics card as a Cycles render device in the user preferences:

1. Open the **Edit** menu from Blender's Topbar and choose **Preferences**.
2. Once the **Blender Preferences** window appears, click on the **System** tab.
3. Find the **Cycles Render Devices** section.

> **Important Note**
>
> These settings will be different, depending on your computer's operating system and graphics card. There are several computation backend options here: **None**, **CUDA**, **OptiX**, and **OpenCL**.
>
> The **None** option means that rendering will be performed on your computer's **Central Processing Unit (CPU)** instead of the **Graphics Processing Unit (GPU)**. This will still produce high-quality results, but rendering will take much longer.
>
> The **CUDA** option is a computation backend for rendering with NVIDIA graphics cards; it has a wide range of compatibility for many graphics cards.
>
> The **OptiX** option is a newer backend for rendering with NVIDIA graphics cards. It has less compatibility with old graphics cards, but it renders faster than CUDA.
>
> The **OpenCL** option is primarily used for AMD graphics cards. It is slower than the NVIDIA backends, but it's still faster than CPU rendering. OpenCL will no longer be supported in the upcoming Blender 3.0 release. Implementation of an alternative backend (**HIP**) is in development to support AMD graphics cards. Other implementations are in the works to support Intel graphics cards in the future.
>
> If your hardware doesn't support these backends, you will see this warning: **No compatible GPUs found for path tracing Cycles will render on the CPU.**

4. Choose the computation backend that works for your computer; we will use **Optix** in our example.

5. Enable the checkbox for your commute device (**NVIDIA GeForce GTX 1660 Ti** in our example):

Figure 10.1 – The Cycles Render Devices section of the Blender Preferences window

These settings are part of Blender's user preferences, so they will be automatically saved and retained between Blender projects. You should only have to set up these options one time. You can close the **Preferences** window when you're finished. Once these settings are enabled, Blender will be able to use your graphics card for GPU rendering in the Cycles render engine.

Now, let's try rendering the old monk character in Eevee and Cycles to see the difference between the two render engines:

1. Navigate to the **Render** tab (represented by the gray camera-back icon) in the Properties editor.

2. Make sure that **Render Engine** is set to **Eevee**:

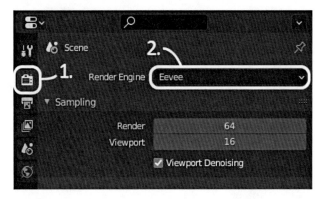

Figure 10.2 – The Render Engine option in the Render tab of the Properties editor

3. Now that we've told Blender which render engine to use, we can activate the viewport render mode. Let's see what the old monk looks like when rendered in Eevee.

4. Change the viewport shading to **Rendered** mode by clicking the fourth shading mode sphere icon in the top-right corner of the 3D Viewport:

Figure 10.3 – Rendered shading mode in the Viewport Shading options

This will tell Blender to use our choice of render engine to draw the objects in the 3D Viewport. Since we chose Eevee, the old monk will now be rendered with Eevee, as you can see in the following screenshot:

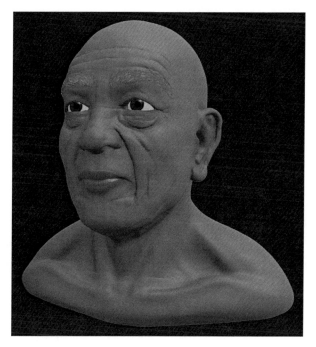

Figure 10.4 – The old monk character rendered in Eevee

If you're thinking that this looks the same as the **Material Preview** shading mode, you are correct. The **Material Preview** shading mode always uses Eevee under the hood to render the objects in the viewport without needing to switch to **Rendered** shading mode. This means that the render results will look the same between Material Preview and Eevee's Rendered shading mode unless we use custom lighting in the Rendered mode. However, custom lighting has been disabled for this example file, so the results are identical.

Let's try changing the to the Cycles render engine to see some very different results:

1. Change **Render Engine** to **Cycles** in the **Render** tab of the Properties editor.

2. Change the **Device** to **GPU Compute**. (The **GPU Compute** option will only work if you have a compatible graphics card set up in the **Cycles Render Devices** section of the preferences that we set up at the beginning of this section. If you do not have a compatible graphics card, you can leave the **Device** setting set as **CPU**.)

> **Important Note**
>
> The first time you use the OptiX rendering backend, viewport rendering might take a few minutes to start. You will see a message in the top-left corner of the 3D Viewport that says **Loading render kernels (may take a few minutes the first time)**. This can take around five minutes to process the first time. If you don't want to wait, you can use CUDA instead of OptiX.

Once rendering begins, you will notice that the image starts off looking really pixelated and noisy, but over time, the image becomes clearer as long as you don't move the camera or any of the objects in the scene. An example of the rendering progress can be seen in the following screenshot:

Figure 10.5 – The noisy render of the old monk in Cycles

> **Important Note**
>
> As this is a graphically intense process, you will likely hear your computer's fans spin up to full speed. This is expected and completely normal; it will not damage your computer.
>
> If you are using CPU rendering, your computer may slow down considerably. Basic tasks such as using an internet browser have to share resources with the rendering process, so they will likely slow down as well. It is recommended that you don't use other applications at the same time as rendering.

This slow rendering progression is a downside to using a path tracing render engine such as Cycles. The rendering has to start over each time the camera, objects, or lights are moved. However, the final result of a Cycles render is almost always of a higher quality than that of an Eevee render, as you can see in the following screenshot:

Figure 10.6 – The old monk character rendered in Cycles

Note that this render has much more accurate lighting across the surface of the character's skin. The reflections in the eyes are more realistic, the eyebrow hair has more depth, and the crevices of the skin are more appropriately dark. Other subtle details come through more clearly, such as the light penetrating the rim of the ear to give it a subtle red glow.

Both of these render engines can be tweaked to produce very pleasing results, but realistic materials and lighting are more easily achieved with Cycles. Most of the rest of the information throughout this chapter will be helpful for using both render engines; you may choose whichever engine suits your needs. We will be focusing on Cycles because it does a better job with accurate lighting, which is really important for rendering sculptures.

How it works...

Rasterizing engines such as Eevee are most common in video games. They work by converting the 3D models to pixels on our screen and running simplified shading algorithms to color each pixel. Extra features like shadows, bloom, and ambient occlusion can be added for a more complete image. However, each of these features uses shortcuts that sacrifice accuracy in order to keep the rendering happening in real time.

These days, rasterizing engines have come a long way and can produce very high-quality results. You may be completely satisfied with the renders that Eevee can produce, especially because the renders are instantaneous. However, Eevee does have some shortcomings and isn't always the best choice.

Path-tracing engines such as Cycles are considered to be the most accurate high-quality way to render. They work by casting rays of light into the scene from the camera, and then tracing the path of the light as it bounces off of each surface. The path each ray of light takes is dictated by the qualities of the materials of each surface that the light hits.

Each ray of light is calculated similarly to the way light works in real life, so the lighting looks very realistic in this type of rendering engine. However, tracing these paths of light takes a long time and a lot of processing power. Unfortunately, light that scatters around the scene often leads to image **noise**. Many materials have complex surfaces that require more than one path to be traced for each pixel in the final image. This means that we need additional **samples** to reduce image noise. This is why the image starts off really noisy and clears up over time.

We can watch as Cycles renders each path tracing sample in the top-left corner of the 3D Viewport. The more samples, the less noisy the image will be; **256** samples are used in our example file. This setting can be adjusted in the **Sampling** subsection of the **Render** tab of the Properties editor.

There's more...

Material Preview mode is closely related to **Rendered** mode. This mode ignores the **scene lights** and the environment lighting (aka the **scene world**) so that we can focus on developing the look of the materials before we render. A default set of environment lighting is used instead to evenly light the scene so that the objects can be seen. This can be controlled from the **Viewport Shading** pop-over menu by enabling the **Scene Lights** and **Scene World** settings.

It is important to know that **Rendered** mode requires us to set up our own lights and environment lighting settings. If we do not set these up, our renders will be very dark and not very appealing. This did not affect our example file because the **Scene World** setting under the **Viewport Shading** pop-over menu was disabled for this file ahead of time. Because of this, Blender used the default environment lighting from **Material Preview** mode to render instead of using the scene's custom environment lighting, which has not been set up for this file.

We will learn how to set up lights for the scene as well as environment lights in the next two sections of this chapter.

Adding three-point lighting to the scene

A major part of rendering is lighting. Without lights, our render would be completely dark, and it would be impossible to see anything. Up to this point, we've been working in **Viewport Shading** modes such as **Solid**, **MatCap**, and **Material Preview**, each of which gives us default lighting so that we don't have to worry about lights while we work on our sculptures. But now is the time to be more creative with our lighting and customize the look and feel of our finished sculpture by placing our own lights in the scene instead of using default lighting.

We can use a classic setup for lighting called **three-point lighting**. This type of lighting is an easy way to get started and produces high-quality results. A diagram of this lighting setup can be seen in the following screenshot:

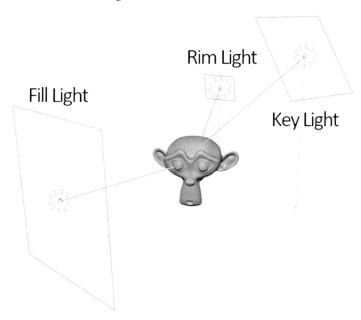

Figure 10.7 – The typical three-point lighting setup

This involves a **Key Light** that lights the subject from the front; this is the primary source of light for the subject. This light is typically placed slightly above the subject, but its position can be adjusted as needed to produce alternative moods. A secondary **Fill Light** is used to soften the image and fill in the harsh shadows of the subject that are created by the **Key Light**. This light usually needs to be placed 90 degrees off from the **Key Light** so that it can add light to the shadowy areas. Lastly, a bright **Rim Light** is used from behind to help separate the subject from the background. This light is sometimes known as a **back light** or **hair light**. Without it, the subject's silhouette tends to blend into the background and feel less pronounced.

In this section, we will learn how to add lights to the scene to create this setup.

Getting ready

For this section, we can use any finished sculpture. However, some of the example files provided with this book already have lights added and render settings adjusted. Since we will be focusing on how to set up render settings from scratch, we recommend using either your own creation or the orc from `stylizedEyebrows_End.blend`, which you can download here: `https://github.com/PacktPublishing/Sculpting-the-Blender-Way/blob/main/Chapter09/stylizedEyebrows_End.blend`.

Launch Blender and open the `.blend` file. Once the file is loaded, we can set up our lights.

How to do it...

Let's start by adding the first light in the three-point lighting setup – the key light:

1. Open the **Add** menu in the top-left corner of the header of the 3D Viewport and choose **Light | Area**.

2. Rename the new light `Key Light`.

3. Use the **Move** tool to place the light in front and slightly to the side of the sculpture:

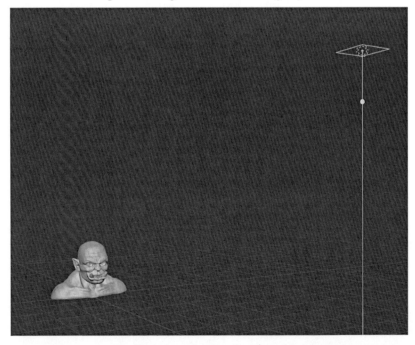

Figure 10.8 – The key light in front and to the side of the sculpture

Now that we have the light in position, let's aim it at the sculpture. We could use our **Rotate** tool, but this light comes with a gizmo that we can use to aim it at the sculpture. There is a yellow dot in front of the area light; this dot can be dragged onto any surface to aim the light at the target surface. Let's try it now.

4.   Click and drag the yellow dot gizmo onto the sculpture to aim the light:

Figure 10.9 – The key light aimed at the sculpture

We can't see the effect of this light in the viewport until we switch to the **Rendered** viewport shading mode. You can use either Eevee or Cycles for this, but we'll use Cycles in our example.

5.   Navigate to the **Render** tab (represented by the gray camera-back icon) in the Properties editor.

Change **Render Engine** to **Cycles**.

Change **Device** to **GPU Compute** if your computer supports it.

6.   Change **Viewport Shading** to **Rendered** mode:

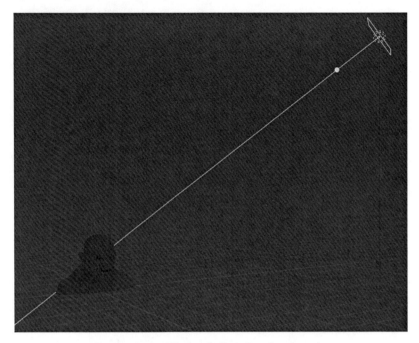

Figure 10.10 – The key light in Rendered mode

Great – now we can see the effect of the light on the surface of the sculpture. However, the light is very dark. The intensity of a light source is affected by several factors: the distance of the light to the subject, the power of the light, and the size of the light's area. In our example, the light is at a far distance, which means we need to increase the power and the size.

7.   With the area light selected, navigate to the **Object Data** tab (represented by the green lightbulb icon) in the Properties editor.

Increase the **Power** setting to 1500 W.

Increase the **Size** setting to 2 m.

Excellent – because we are mimicking studio lights, we can use really high wattage values like this to add a lot of brightness to this main source of light. The size of the light has a big impact on the sharpness of the shadows. Small lights produce hard shadows and large lights produce soft shadows:

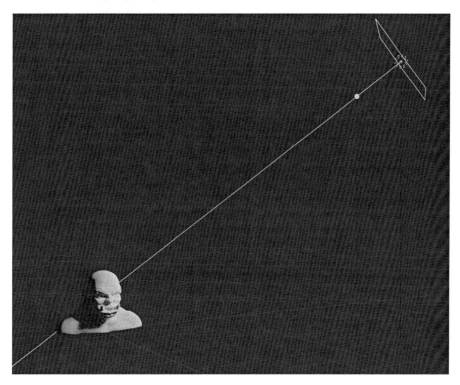

Figure 10.11 – The key light with more power and a larger size

While we're making adjustments to the key light, we can add some color to it.

8. Click on the **Color** swatch and use the color picker to choose a color for the key light. For our example, we went with a subtle greenish color with the hex code 9DFFD8.

Here's how our example looks so far with the colored key light:

Figure 10.12 – The orc rendered with the key light

This light acts as the main light for the three-point lighting setup. It will control the general mood of the lighting.

> **Tip**
>
> Feel free to try positioning this light at other angles. Moving the key light below the sculpture is a great way to make things look sinister.

The key light has left behind some dark shadowy areas. Our next step is to add a fill light to fill in these areas:

1. Open the **Add** menu in the top-left corner of the header of the 3D Viewport and choose **Light | Area**.

2. Rename the new light `Fill Light`.

3. Use the **Move** tool to place the light in front and slightly to the side of the sculpture, opposite of the key light.

4. Aim the fill light at the sculpture either with the **Rotate** tool or the aim gizmo.

   Increase the **Power** setting to `500 W`.

   Increase the **Size** setting to `5 m`.

5. Click on the **Color** swatch and use the color picker to choose a color for the fill light. For our example, we went with a complimentary purple color with the hex code `D495FF`:

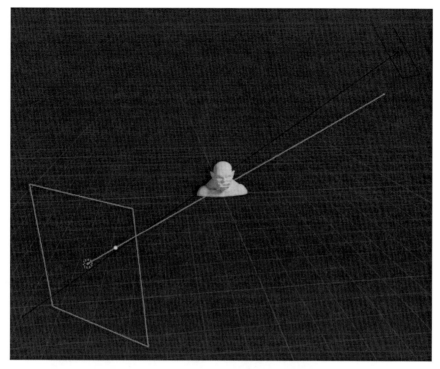

Figure 10.13 – The fill light positioned to the side of the sculpture

Here's how our example looks with the fill light added:

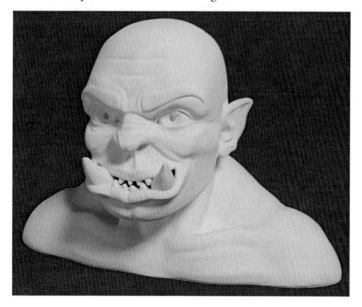

Figure 10.14 – The orc rendered with the key light and fill light

The fill light is much less bright than the key light. It's meant to be complementary; it shouldn't upstage the key light. Because of its large size, the fill light produces soft shadows, and it does an excellent job at filling in the hard shadows from the key light.

The final light we should add is the rim light:

1. Open the **Add** menu in the top-left corner of the header of the 3D Viewport and choose **Light | Area**.

2. Rename the new light `Rim Light`.

3. Use the **Move** tool to place the light behind the sculpture.

4. Aim the rim light at the sculpture either with the **Rotate** tool or the aim gizmo.

    Increase the **Power** setting to `3000 W`.

    Leave the **Size** setting set to `1 m`.

5. Click on the **Color** swatch and use the color picker to choose a color for the rim light. For our example, we went with a strong deep blue color with the hex code `3400FF`:

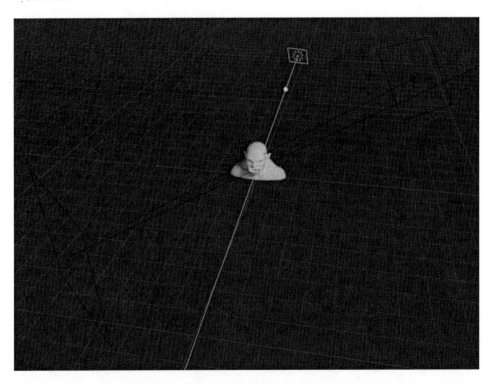

Figure 10.15 – The rim light positioned behind the sculpture

Here's how our example looks with the rim light added:

Figure 10.16 – The orc rendered with the key light, fill light, and rim light

The rim light is typically the brightest light in the scene; it casts a bright light across the back of the sculpture, creating a rim of light that helps to make the sculpture stand out from the background.

To keep our .blend file organized, let's add all of the lights to a collection:

1. Select all three lights.
2. Open the **Object** menu in the top-left corner of the header of the 3D Viewport and choose **Collection | Move to Collection**.
3. A small window labeled **Move To Collection** will appear under your mouse cursor; click the **+ New Collection** button.
4. Name the new collection Lights and click the **OK** button.

And that's all there is to the three-point lighting setup. This setup can be modified as much as you like to produce a different look for your sculpture.

How it works...

Blender's lights closely mimic real lighting, so we can use real-world techniques to produce lighting for our sculptures. Three-point lighting is one of the most tried and true types of lighting in professional media production. It's far from the only way to light a subject, but it produces high-quality results with ease.

There's more...

In this section, we used only one type of light, but Blender offers four main types of lights:

- **Point**: A point light is similar to a small light bulb; all of the light comes from a single point in 3D space and emanates outward in all directions.

- **Sun**: This is a directional light; its position in 3D space is ignored. All light from this type of light is parallel and closely simulates the light from the sun; it is useful for filling the scene with light the way the sun does in real life.

- **Spot**: This light produces a cone of light exactly like the lights used in theater. It is excellent for creating a dramatic look.

- **Area**: This type of light emits from a large surface area and closely mimics studio lights. It is excellent for adding lots of light and giving fine control over the hardness of the shadows that it produces.

When you're comfortable with the basics of setting up lights, feel free to experiment with some of these other light types to customize the look of your renders.

See also

The Blender Foundation has an official video showcasing a three-point lighting setup, available here: `https://www.youtube.com/watch?v=RDbrOpnIY7Q`.

Lighting up the environment with an HDRI

There is an additional type of lighting for our scenes that we need to consider when creating high-quality renders – **environment light**. This type of light is present in the scene without being tied to a specific light object in the Outliner. There are two main types of environment light that we can use. The first type is known as **ambient light**. This is a basic type of lighting that adds brightness to the entire scene evenly. By default, Blender has a small amount of ambient light enabled. However, this type of lighting isn't used very often in modern renders because it's not a realistic way to light a scene. The most realistic and popular way to add environment lighting is through the use of a **High Dynamic Range Image (HDRI)**.

An HDRI is a spherical 360-degree image of an environment that contains an incredibly large amount of lighting information in each pixel. These images are usually created with a special photography process that captures what an environment looks like at numerous exposure levels, and then stores all of the data in a single image that we can control with our 3D software. HDRIs are typically stored in the `.hdr` or `.exr` file formats. It's important to know that these files are not interchangeable with regular images that have been stored in the following image formats: `.png`, `.jpg`, `.tga`, `.tiff`, and other non-HDR formats.

In this section, we will learn how to load an HDRI into Blender's **world** properties, which will allow us to use the realistic lighting information from the image to cast light into the scene and onto the surface of our sculpture.

Getting ready

For this section, we can pick up where we left off in the *Adding three-point lighting to the scene* section of this chapter. If you have not completed that section, you can begin this section with the `threePointLighting_End.blend` file, which can be downloaded here: `https://github.com/PacktPublishing/Sculpting-the-Blender-Way/blob/main/Chapter10/threePointLighting_End.blend`.

We will also need an HDRI to add to the environment. We have provided one for you to use, which can be downloaded here: `https://github.com/PacktPublishing/Sculpting-the-Blender-Way/blob/main/Chapter10/phalzer_forest_01_4k.exr`.

Launch Blender and open the `.blend` file. Once the file is open, we can set up the environment lighting for the scene.

How to do it...

Environment light is part of the **World** properties tab of the Properties editor. However, controlling the HDRI is done through the **Shader** editor. This is a special type of editor that will allow us to connect *nodes* together to control the lighting and materials. This editor is not present in the current workspace, so let's start by changing over to the **Shading** workspace:

1. Click on the **Shading** tab at the top of the user interface:

Figure 10.17 – The Shading workspace tab

> **Important Note**
> The available workspaces will be different depending on how the file was created. Our example file was created from the sculpting preset, so it includes the **Sculpting** and **Shading** workspaces. If you do not see the **Shading** workspace tab, you can add it by clicking + and choosing **General | Shading**.

Clicking on this tab will rearrange the entire user interface with new editors and a layout that is suited for setting up the environment lighting. This workspace includes six editors, as you can see in the following screenshot:

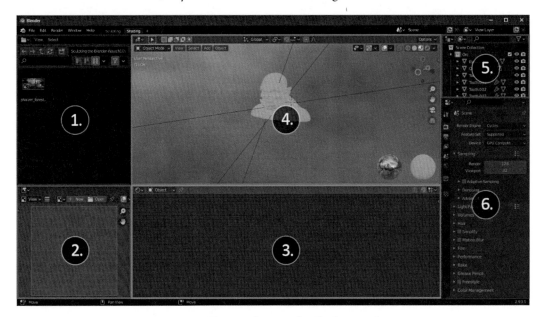

Figure 10.18 – The six editors in the Shading workspace

There are several new editors available to us in this workspace:

1. The **File Browser** will allow us to browse for texture files, such as the HDRI that we've downloaded for this project. Alternatively, you can use your operating system's file browser, but Blender includes this editor so that you never have to leave Blender's UI to browse for files.

2. The **Image** editor gives us a preview of our image and texture assets that we've loaded into Blender. We can also use this editor to paint textures, but that's beyond the scope of this book.

3. The **Shader** editor is our main focus for this section. This allows us to create a network of nodes to customize our environment lighting and materials for our sculptures.

    This workspace also includes three editors that we have used previously in our other workspaces:

4. The **3D Viewport**.

5. The **Outliner**.

6. The **Properties** editor.

Changing to this workspace has also changed the shading mode of the 3D Viewport to **Material Preview** mode. **Material Preview** mode is meant for exactly the opposite of what we're trying to achieve here; it provides us with a default set of lighting so that we can focus on creating materials without having to worry about adding lights to the scene and without having to set up the environment light. As you can see, **Material Preview** includes a colored background for the viewport, which is actually a built-in HDRI. Unfortunately, this built-in HDRI is only for preview purposes and can't be used in **Rendered** mode.

Since we're here to learn about rendering and setting up the environment light ourselves, **Material Preview** mode will not be helpful now.

Let's switch to **Rendered** mode and learn how to set up a custom HDRI:

1. Change **Viewport Shading** to **Rendered** mode.

    The Shader editor's default mode allows us to edit materials for the selected object in the scene. This can be seen in the top-left corner of the header of the Shader editor. In order to set up environment lighting, we need to change this mode to work with the **World** settings.

2. Change the shader type from **Object** to **World** using the drop-down menu in the top-left corner of the header of the Shader editor:

Figure 10.19 – The Shader Type drop-down menu

Excellent – now we can see the nodes that are responsible for the environment lighting. There are currently two nodes, a **Background** node and a **World Output** node, as you can see in the following screenshot:

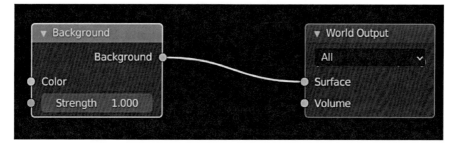

Figure 10.20 – The Background node and World Output node

The **Background** node is a shader node that tells the render engine what **Color** the environment should be as well as how much **Strength** the environment light should have. The default **Color** value is a dark gray with the hex code 404040. It may be difficult to see, but there is a color swatch to the right of the word **Color**; clicking on this color swatch will open a color picker, which can be used to pick an alternative color for the **Background** node.

The **World Output** node has a slot for **Surface** and a slot for **Volume**, which each take information from other nodes in the node network. The **Background** lighting information from the **Background** node is currently hooked up to the **Surface** slot of the **World Output** node.

The connection between these two nodes is often referred to as a **noodle**. Nodes only contribute to the render results when their noodles are hooked up.

At the moment, this scene is using the most basic type of environment lighting – ambient light. A single color is being used to add some brightness to the entire scene. It is difficult to visualize the contribution of this light because of the three area lights present in the scene. Let's disable these lights for now so that we can more easily see the environment light.

3. Hide the **Lights** collection by clicking on the eyeball icon next to its name in the Outliner.

    Now, let's try adjusting the **Color** value of the **Background** node and see what happens to the ambient light.

4. Click on the dark gray color swatch of the **Background** node to open the color picker and pick a different color. Don't forget that you can adjust the brightness slider along the right side of the color picker. For our example, we've picked an orange color with the hex code C76315:

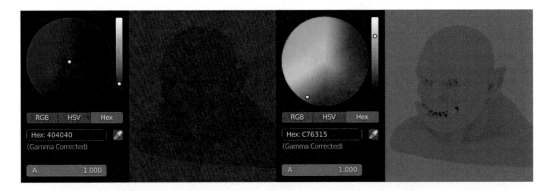

Figure 10.21 – The ambient light color changed from gray to orange

Note that the color of the background in the 3D Viewport changes. More importantly, colored light is being cast onto the sculpture from the environment. Evenly lit environments like this aren't very realistic or visually pleasing, so it's time to replace this singular ambient light color with an HDRI. We can do this by adding a node in the Shader editor.

5. Open the **Add** menu in the top-left corner of the header of the Shader editor and choose **Texture | Environment Texture**. This will make a new **Environment Texture** node; this new node will immediately begin moving around with your mouse movements.

6. Move the new node to the left of the **Background** node and left-click to place it:

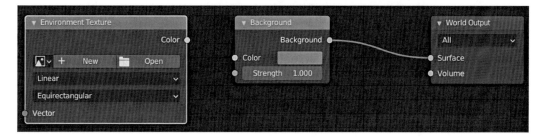

Figure 10.22 – The Environment Texture node placed to the left of the Background node

This new node is a type of texture node. It requires an image texture to work correctly. In our case, we will be loading the HDRI into this node.

7. Click the **Open** button on the **Environment Texture** node. This will open a file browser window.

8. Navigate to the directory where you downloaded the phalzer_forest_01_4k. exr file. Select it and click the **Open Image** button to load it into Blender.

    Now that the texture is loaded into the node, we need to hook up the **Environment Texture** node's **Color** output into the **Background** node's **Color** input.

9. Click and drag from the yellow dot on the right side of the **Environment Texture** node to begin creating a noodle from the **Color** output.

10. Drag the noodle to the yellow dot on the left side of the **Background** node to make a connection between the nodes:

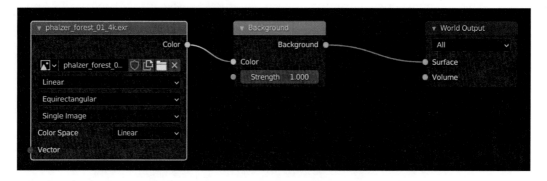

Figure 10.23 – The Environment Texture node hooked up to the Background node

Now that the connection has been made, the lighting information stored in the HDRI texture will be used to color the background and cast light onto the sculpture. Note that the color swatch on the **Background** node has been replaced by this connection because the swatch is no longer needed. Instead, the color value of each pixel in the HDRI is sampled by the **Environment Texture** node and passed into the **Color** slot of the **Background** node. This simple setup creates very pleasing results, as shown in the following screenshot:

Figure 10.24 – The orc sculpture lit with the HDRI

Note that this is not just a background image. The most important aspect of this environment texture is the realistic light that it casts into the scene. The results can be subtle, but there's no better way to make a render look realistic.

We can re-enable the **Lights** collection to bring back our area lights now.

The lights in this collection are looking a lot more subtle now because their brightness is very low relative to the brightness of the sun in the HDRI. Feel free to either increase the power of these lights or remove them altogether to suit the visual style you want for your render.

How it works...

HDRIs are very large texture files; each pixel contains values of color and light. Unlike regular images, there is a very high dynamic range that can be represented by each pixel. The vast difference in brightness between a light source and a regular surface can't be properly represented in a regular image. These brightness values are key to illuminating a 3D render.

There's more...

We can control the rotation of the HDRI if we add a **Vector | Mapping** node and an **Input | Texture Coordinate** node. Hook up the **Vector** output of the **Mapping** node into the **Vector** input of the **Environment Texture** node. Then, hook up the **Generated** output of the **Texture Coordinate** node into the **Vector** input of the **Mapping** node. This setup can be seen in the following screenshot:

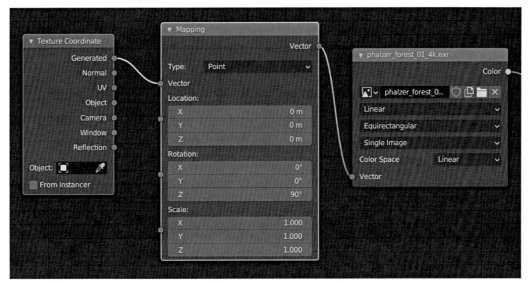

Figure 10.25 – The Texture Coordinate and Mapping nodes added to control the rotation of the HDRI

The coordinates needed for sampling the texture are being generated by the **Texture Coordinate** node. Now, you can control the rotation of the HDRI by adjusting the **Rotation Z** value of the **Mapping** node.

If we don't want to use the HDRI for the background, but we still want to use it for casting light into the scene, we can add a few nodes to replace the background with a solid color. To achieve this, we need to add a **Color | MixRGB** node and an **Input | Light Path** node.

The **Mix** node will be used to blend between two colors. Hook up the **Color** output of the **Environment Texture** node into the **Color1** slot and use the color swatch to choose a background color for the **Color2** slot; we chose solid black (hex code 000000) for our example. Then, hook up the **Color** output of the **Mix** node into the **Color** input of the **Background** node. To mix the colors properly, hook up the **Is Camera Ray** output from the **Light Path** node into the **Fac** input on the **Mix** node. The final node setup can be seen in the following screenshot:

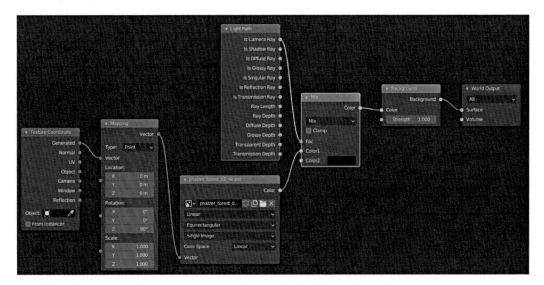

Figure 10.26 – The nodes required to use the HDRI for lighting and a solid color for the background

Nodes give us a lot of control over the way the environment is rendered. This finished node network is available in the hdriEnvironmentLighting_ End.blend file, which can be downloaded here: https://github.com/ PacktPublishing/Sculpting-the-Blender-Way/blob/main/Chapter10/ hdriEnvironmentLighting_End.blend.

See also

Creating HDRIs requires specialized camera equipment and software. You don't need to make them yourself because there are many places to download high-quality HDRIs from the internet. The HDRI used in this example was provided by **Poly Haven** (formerly **HDRI Haven**), which is one of the most widely used collections of HDRIs available online. The HDRIs from this website are free to use: `https://polyhaven.com/hdris`.

Creating a clay material for the sculpture

Up to this point, our sculptures have been displayed with a default light gray material. But it doesn't have to be like this! We can create custom materials for our sculptures to make them look like they are made out of wood, metal, dirt, or any other substance we like.

> **Important Note**
>
> While sculpting, we used MatCaps to preview what our sculptures would look like with different colors. However, MatCaps are not the same as materials, and they can't be used for rendering.

Materials for rendering can be created using the Shader editor. Most modern render engines use **Physically Based Rendering** (**PBR**), also known as **Physically Based Shading** (**PBS**). This means that we can represent an almost limitless variety of materials with different colors, roughnesses, metallic properties, emissive properties, and much more by dialing in properties of the shader nodes using a standardized set of values. These values are based on the properties of materials in real life. All of the properties we need to represent most materials have been compiled together into one large node in the Shader editor known as the **Principled BSDF**.

For this section, we will stick to a very simple approach to creating materials. We'll hook up a set of image textures from a premade **texture set**. Texture sets are a collection of image texture files that contain information about material properties, including **color**, **displacement**, **normal**, and **roughness**. These image textures can be hooked up to their respective slots in the Principled BSDF node to create the material.

Getting ready

For this section, we can pick up where we left off in the *Lighting up the environment with an HDRI* section of this chapter. If you have not completed that section, you can begin this section with the `hdriEnvironmentLighting_End.blend` file, which can be downloaded here: `https://github.com/PacktPublishing/Sculpting-the-Blender-Way/blob/main/Chapter10/hdriEnvironmentLighting_End.blend`.

We will also need a set of textures to use for our material. We have provided a clay texture set for you to use. It consists of four image textures, which can be downloaded here: `https://github.com/PacktPublishing/Sculpting-the-Blender-Way/tree/main/Chapter10/Clay004_2K-PNG`.

Make sure you have the HDRI from the previous section downloaded as well; otherwise, the environment lighting will not render correctly.

Launch Blender and open the `.blend` file.

Creating a material from a texture set is fairly straightforward; we saw how to add an image into the Shader editor in the *Lighting up the environment with an HDRI* section of this chapter. The process for adding textures for materials is very similar, but we have to add one image texture node for each texture in the texture set, which is very tedious. Blender comes with an add-on that makes many node-related tasks easier; we just need to enable it in Blender's **Preferences**:

1. In Blender's Topbar, open the **Edit** menu and choose **Preferences**. Once the **Blender Preferences** window appears, click on the **Add-ons** tab.

2. Use the search bar in the top-right corner to search for `Node Wrangler` and check the box next to **Node Wrangler** to enable the add-on.

3. Now that this add-on is enabled, several new hotkeys will be available to us in the Shader editor. Close the **Blender Preferences** window; the settings will be automatically saved.

How to do it...

Now, we can create a clay material for the sculpture:

1. If the 3D Viewport isn't already set to the **Rendered shading** mode, switch to it now.

    Our Shader editor is currently set to the **World** shader type. In order to create a material, we need to switch to the **Object** shader type.

2. Change the shader type from **Object** to **World** using the drop-down menu in the top-left corner of the header of the Shader editor.

    The **World** nodes will disappear, and now the Shader editor will display the nodes that belong to the material of the active object. However, no object is currently selected, so we won't see any nodes yet. Let's select the sculpture.

3. Click to select the **Orc** object in the 3D Viewport.

    Now that we have an active object, a button will appear in the header of the Shader editor:

Figure 10.27 – The New button in the header of the Shader editor

4. Click the button labeled **+ New** in the header of the Shader editor to create a new material for the active object.

The new material's name will be displayed where the **+ New** button used to be. Its default name is **Material**, which is a terrible name.

5. Click on the **Material** word to edit the name of the material and rename it Clay.

Now that we have a new material, two new nodes will appear inside of the Shader editor, a **Principled BSDF** node and a **Material Output** node, as you can see in the following screenshot:

Figure 10.28 – The Principled BSDF node and Material Output node

The **Principled BSDF** node is huge and contains many options, but don't let that intimidate you. We will leave most of the values at their defaults and only change the few that are needed to customize our clay material. Instead of hooking up our textures by hand, we can use one of the hotkeys that we enabled from the **Node Wrangler** add-on.

6.   Click on the **Principled BSDF** node to select it.

7.   Hover your mouse over the Shader editor and press the **Add Principled texture setup** hotkey, which is *Ctrl + Shift + T*. This will open a file browser window.

8.   Navigate to the directory where you downloaded the four images in the Clay004_2K-PNG texture set.

9.   Select all four textures: Clay004_2K_Color.png, Clay004_2K_Displacement.png, Clay004_2K_NormalGL.png, and Clay004_2K_Roughness.png.

10.   Click the **Principled Texture Setup** button to load all of the images into Blender.

It might take a moment to load. When it's finished, eight new nodes will be added to the Shader editor and automatically hooked up, as shown in the following screenshot:

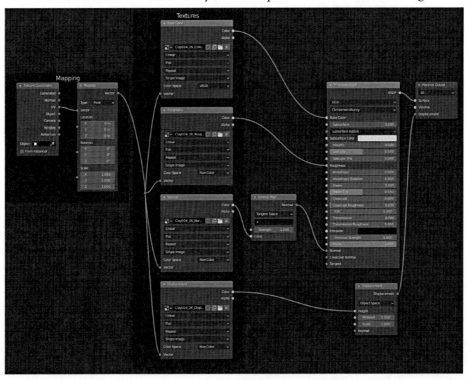

Figure 10.29 – The new nodes added by the Principled Texture Setup button

> **Tip**
>
> If your computer is running slowly while editing the shader nodes, you can pause Cycles' viewport rendering by clicking the pause button in the top-right corner of the 3D Viewport header. Just remember to click the button again to resume rendering when you're ready.

Four of these new nodes are **image texture** nodes, one for each of the textures in the texture set. The **Base Color** node is set to use the **sRGB Color Space** since the image texture contains color data. The **Roughness**, **Normal**, and **Displacement** nodes are set to use the **Non-Color Color Space** since these image textures contain non-color data about their respective properties for the material.

All four of the image texture nodes are receiving their coordinates from the **Mapping** node, which is hooked up to the **UV** space output of the **Texture Coordinate** node. Textures can be sampled from several alternative texture coordinates by using the different outputs of this node.

The final two nodes are the **Normal Map** node and the **Displacement** node. Each of these nodes converts their input textures to be compatible with their respective properties.

We almost have everything we need with this setup. However, the textures are currently being sampled with the **UV** texture coordinate. **UVs** are special coordinates that we can make for our 3D models so that textures can be precisely mapped onto the surface of the models.

Making UVs is not easy with high-resolution sculptures, so let's use an alternative texture coordinate to automatically project the textures onto the sculpture without needing to make UVs:

1. Click and drag from the top purple dot on the right side of the **Texture Coordinate** node to begin creating a noodle from the **Generated** output.

2. Drag the noodle to the top purple dot on the left side of the **Mapping** node labeled **Vector**.

    This will replace the previous connection with a new connection between the **Generated** output and the **Vector** input. Now, the textures will get their mapping coordinates from the generated coordinate space instead of the UV coordinate space.

    One last bit of cleanup to make the **Generated** texture space behave better is to use **Box** projection instead of the current **Flat** projection and add a small amount of blending.

3. Find the drop-down list on the **Base Color** node labeled **Flat**.

4.   Open the drop-down list and choose **Box**.

5.   A new field will appear below the drop-down list labeled **Blend**; set this to 0.200.

6.   Repeat these steps for the **Roughness, Normal**, and **Displacement** nodes.

Excellent – our finished node setup can be seen in the following screenshot:

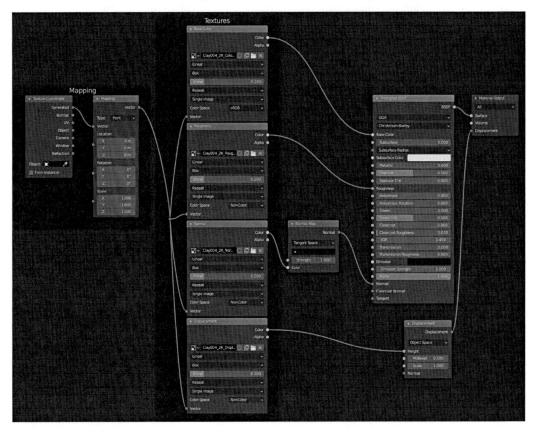

Figure 10.30 – The finished node setup for the Clay material

Almost done; now we need to assign this finished **Clay** material to the other objects in the scene.

7.   Open the **Select** menu in the top-left corner of the header of the 3D Viewport and choose **Select All by Type | Mesh**.

8.   Open the **Object** menu in the top-left corner of the header of the 3D Viewport and choose **Link/Transfer Data | Link Materials**.

This will copy the material from the active object to all of the other mesh objects in the scene.

Now our sculpture has a clay material that makes it look much more detailed than it used to, as you can see in the following screenshot:

Figure 10.31 – The orc sculpture with the finished Clay material

There are many more ways to customize the materials of our sculptures. Different texture sets can be used to make the sculpture look like it's made from all sorts of materials. We chose this clay material for our example because traditional sculpting is done with clay, and it has a charming look while being easy to set up.

How it works...

PBR is the modern standard for making materials. The great thing about this is that there are numerous libraries of materials that will all be compatible with Blender and many other 3D software packages. The **Principled BSDF** node is a standard implementation of PBR properties into a single node.

The textures in a texture set are often referred to as **maps**. Each type of map delivers some type of data to the surface of the object. The **Base Color** map is the most straightforward type of texture; it supplies the color of the surface. The **Roughness** map determines how matte or shiny the surface will be; subtle variations throughout the roughness texture make the surface catch the light in a realistic way. The **Normal** map adds bumpy surface details that make objects look really detailed. The **Displacement** map raises and lowers the polygons of a mesh to add extra small details. This is very similar to a normal map but much more pronounced. Displacement textures aren't always necessary. At the time of this book's publication, displacement textures don't work in the Eevee render engine. Some texture sets include additional maps to control other properties of the material as well.

Texture sets can be created from source images taken from a camera, or they can be generated from scratch using procedural nodes. Once the texture set has been created, it can be easily hooked up in most 3D software to produce realistic results.

Mapping the texture set onto a model can be done with UVs or by using a box projection. The box projection method is useful because it works for all shapes with no additional setup required. The downside to a box projection is that it tends to produce ugly seams in some areas. These seams can be hidden with a small amount of blending to blur the edges of the projected textures.

There's more...

Materials such as these are easy to reuse across many sculptures and projects. The upcoming Blender 3.0 release will come with the brand-new **Asset Browser** that will make it easy to create a library of materials and apply them to objects in your scenes. You can read about the Asset Browser here: `https://wiki.blender.org/wiki/Reference/Release_Notes/3.0/Asset_Browser`.

See also

You can read more about the Principled BSDF node here: `https://docs.blender.org/manual/en/latest/render/shader_nodes/shader/principled.html`.

There are several free collections of texture sets available online. Here is a short list of excellent resources:

- **Poly Haven**: `https://polyhaven.com/textures`
- **textures.com**: `https://www.textures.com/browse/pbr-materials/114558`
- **cgbookcase**: `https://www.cgbookcase.com/textures/`
- **3DTextures.me**: `https://3dtextures.me/`
- **3Dassets.one**: `https://www.3dassets.one/`
- **ambientCG**: `https://ambientcg.com/`

The **Clay004** texture set we used in this section was provided by ambientCG, licensed under CC0 1.0 Universal: `https://ambientcg.com/view?id=Clay004`.

Using a camera to render the sculpture

Modern 3D software allows us to use viewport rendering, which allows us to see nearly instantaneous results directly in our viewport while we work. However, viewport rendering is only intended for preview purposes. When we're happy with our preview render, we can move on to creating the final render. Blender needs to know which angle to create the final render from and which settings to use. Blender gets this information from the active camera.

A **camera** is a special type of object that contains several settings specific to rendering. Just like a camera in real life, we can position the camera, rotate it, frame our subject, adjust the focal length of the lens, and much more.

In this section, we will go through the basics of setting up a camera so that we can produce a final render of our sculpture.

Getting ready

For this section, we can pick up where we left off in the *Creating a clay material for the sculpture* section of this chapter. If you have not completed that section, you can begin this section with the `clayMaterial_End.blend` file, which can be downloaded here: `https://github.com/PacktPublishing/Sculpting-the-Blender-Way/blob/main/Chapter10/clayMaterial_End.blend`.

Make sure you have all of the textures from the previous section downloaded as well; otherwise, the clay material and environment lighting will not render correctly.

Launch Blender and open the `.blend` file. Once the file is loaded, we can set up our camera for rendering.

How to do it...

For this part of the process, we don't need to use the **Rendered** viewport shading mode; it will only slow us down while we set up the camera. You can stay in **Rendered** mode if you like, but for our example, we will switch to **Solid** mode.

First things first – we need to add a camera:

1. Open the **Add** menu in the top-left corner of the header of the 3D Viewport and choose **Camera**.
2. Positioning the camera can be achieved the same way as any other 3D object by using the **Move** and **Rotate** tools. However, it is easier to snap the camera to the angle of our viewport instead.

3. Open the **View** menu in the top-left corner of the header of the 3D Viewport and choose **Align View | Align Active Camera to View**.

    This will align the camera object to match the current viewing angle of the 3D Viewport, as shown in the following screenshot:

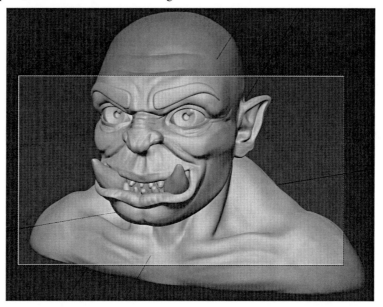

Figure 10.32 – The camera aligned with the 3D Viewport

Notice the yellow border inside of the viewport? This is the framing of the camera; the dark areas outside of this border will not appear in the final render.

We can keep the camera locked to the viewport with a setting in the Sidebar.

4. Open the Sidebar by clicking the little < indicator along the right side of the main 3D Viewport or by pressing the *N* hotkey while your mouse is in the main 3D Viewport.

5. Switch to the **View** tab of the Sidebar.

6. Find the **View Lock** subsection of the Sidebar and expand it if it isn't already expanded.

7. Check the box labeled **Lock Camera to View**.

    Now, every time we pan, zoom, or orbit the 3D Viewport, the camera object will stay synchronized to the viewing angle of the 3D Viewport. Now, let's pick a camera angle that showcases our sculpture nicely.

> **Important Note**
>
> Choosing the camera angle is typically done before finalizing the placement of the lights. We already set up the lights earlier in this chapter, but feel free to adjust the positions of the lights as needed to match your preferred camera angle.

Rendering with a camera is very similar to taking a photograph with a camera in real life. Just like in photography, part of picking a good camera angle requires adjustments to the focal length of the camera lens.

8. With the camera selected, navigate to the **Object Data** tab (represented by the green camera icon) in the Properties editor.

9. Find the **Focal Length** setting under the **Lens** subsection.

    The **focal length** of the camera determines how much perspective distortion the image will have. Low focal length values such as 12 mm will result in an exaggerated fisheye effect. Medium values like 50 mm are considered to be better for general purposes. Slightly higher values up to 115 mm are often used for character portraits. And huge values like 300 mm or higher are used for telephoto landscape photos. You can see the dramatic difference in perspective between 12 mm and 115 mm in the following screenshot:

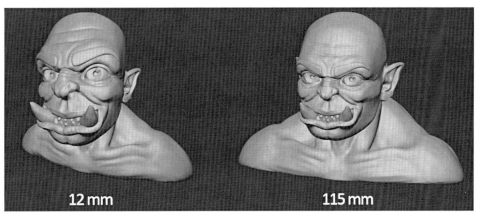

Figure 10.33 – 12 mm versus 115 mm focal length

10. Set the **Focal Length** setting to match the look you want for your render.

    There is no correct setting here; it all depends on the look you want to showcase your sculpture in. The default setting is 50 mm because it is a fairly neutral setting. But we'll use 115 mm for our example since it is closer to what's typically used for characters.

Now that the **Focal Length** is set, move the camera into position to pick an angle you want to render the sculpture from.

> **Tip**
>
> Photographers often use composition guides such as the **rule of thirds** to help frame the subject in a pleasing way. We can turn on **Composition Guides** for the camera under the **Viewport Display** subsection of the **Object Data** tab in the Properties editor.

You can see the camera angle we've chosen for our example in the following screenshot:

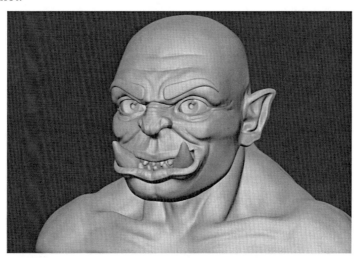

Figure 10.34 – The chosen camera angle to render the sculpture from

Once you're happy with the camera angle, it's a good idea to disable **Lock Camera to View** so that you don't accidentally move the camera again.

Now, we can render the image to see the results from the camera.

11. Open the **Render** menu from Blender's Topbar and choose **Render Image** or press the *F12* hotkey.

Regardless of the current viewport shading mode, this will render the final image using our chosen render engine – in our case, Cycles. By default, the render will appear in a new window. Our example render turned out like this:

Figure 10.35 – The rendered image of the sculpture

> **Important Note**
> Rendering in this way usually takes longer than viewport rendering since it is done with more samples and higher resolution. Expect it to take at least 5 minutes or considerably longer, depending on your computer's processing power.

Once the image finishes rendering, you can save it to your computer:

1. Open the **Image** menu from the header of the Render window and choose **Save As...**; a file browser will appear.
2. Use the file browser to choose a location, image format, and name for the rendered image, and then click the **Save As Image** button.

And there you have it – your first render is complete!

How it works...

Rendering the final image is slightly different from viewport rendering. Viewport rendering allows us to skip setting up a camera and several other settings, such as render resolution. This is great for preview purposes, but we should be sure to set up everything properly when it's time to do a final render.

We will take a look at how to give our render a final layer of polish using the other render settings in the *Exporting the final render* section of this chapter.

There's more...

Blender's cameras also support other tools from real-life photography, including depth of field. **Depth of field** allows us to focus on part of an object while the rest of the object becomes slightly blurry. This is often a desirable effect for artistic reasons. With the camera selected, the **Object Data** tab in the Properties editor will display a **Depth of Field** subsection. A **Focus** object can be chosen, and a low **F-Stop** value can be set to give the image some blurriness. Try focusing on the **Eye_L** object with an **F-Stop** value of **1.4**, and then render the final image again.

The results will be subtle if the camera is far away from the subject, but a subtle blur effect like this can make the render feel more realistic, and the blurriness can help direct the audience's attention to the important parts of the sculpture.

Setting up a turntable for a 360-degree render

When we render our sculptures, we need to make a decision about how we want to present our artwork. Sometimes, our goal is to make an artistic composition with a nice camera angle, artistic use of lighting and shadow, and other features such as depth of field. This is what we focused on in the *Using a camera to render the sculpture* section of this chapter when we rendered the example orc sculpture.

However, artistic renders like this don't showcase the sculpture from every angle, and sometimes the lighting can make it difficult to see the details of the sculpture itself. When it comes to making portfolio pieces, it can be helpful to render your sculpture in a way that shows off your sculpting skills more than your lighting and rendering skills.

For this purpose, it is common to center the sculpture in the camera view, brightly light it, and animate it rotating 360 degrees so that it can be seen from every angle. This is called a **turntable**.

In this section, we will learn how to set up a turntable so that we can render a short animation of our sculpture rotating 360 degrees.

Getting ready

For this section, we can pick up where we left off in the *Using a camera to render the sculpture* section of this chapter. If you have not completed that section, you can begin this section with the `cameraSetup_End.blend` file, which can be downloaded here: `https://github.com/PacktPublishing/Sculpting-the-Blender-Way/blob/main/Chapter10/cameraSetup_End.blend`.

Make sure you have all of the textures from the previous section downloaded as well; otherwise, the clay material and environment lighting will not render correctly.

Launch Blender and open the `.blend` file. Once the file is loaded, we can set up our turntable.

How to do it...

Part of setting up a turntable requires the use of the Timeline editor for animation. Our current workspace doesn't include a Timeline editor, so we need to add a new workspace from Blender's Topbar:

1. Find the workspaces listed at the top of Blender's user interface. In our example, there are only two workspaces available, **Sculpting** and **Shading**, but there is also a + button in the Topbar for adding other workspaces.

2. Click the + button to add a workspace and choose **General | Animation**.

    This will rearrange the user interface with a layout that is suited for animation. This workspace comprises editor types that we've seen in our other workspaces. This includes two 3D Viewports, the Outliner, Properties editor, and a Timeline, as you can see in the following screenshot:

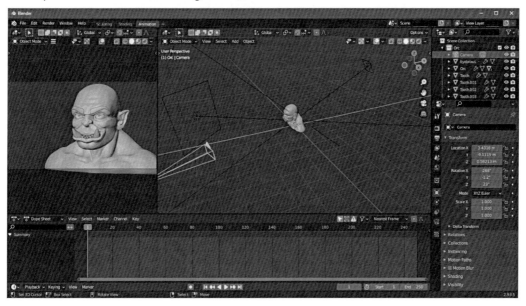

Figure 10.36 – The Animation workspace

The 3D Viewport on the left is aligned to the camera, while the 3D Viewport on the right gives us a better view of the objects in the scene.

Now that we have a timeline editor available to us, we can set up the turntable. The easiest way to do this is to place an empty object in the center of the scene and animate it spinning 360 degrees.

3. Open the **Add** menu in the top-left corner of the header of the 3D Viewport and choose **Empty | Plane Axes**.

4. Rename the **Empty** object to Turntable.

Now, we need to place a keyframe on the **Rotation Z** transform field of the **Turntable** object:

1. With the **Turntable** object selected, navigate to the **Object** tab (represented by the orange square icon) in the Properties editor.

2. Click on the small dot to the right of the **Rotation Z** transform field to place a keyframe:

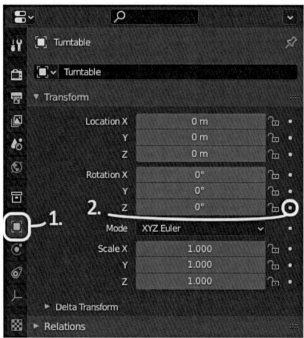

Figure 10.37 – The Rotation Z keyframe indicator

Clicking this dot will have several effects:

-   The small dot will turn into a diamond shape, indicating that there is an animation keyframe on this field for the current frame of animation.

-   The **Rotation Z** field will turn yellow, indicating that the field is controlled by animation data.

-   Orange dots will appear in the Timeline editor underneath the blue current frame indicator to show where the keyframes are on the timeline – in this case, frame **1**.

Let's have our turntable make a full revolution over the course of 5 seconds. By default, Blender plays animations at 24 frames per second, so this will require 120 frames of animation:

1. Change the **End** setting in the bottom-right corner of the Timeline editor from **250** to 120.

    Now, we need to place a second keyframe at the end of the animation. Animations that loop work best if we give them one additional frame, so our second keyframe should go on frame **121**.

2. Drag the blue current frame indicator to frame **121**.

Changing the current frame will have several effects:

- The small diamond shape next to the **Rotation Z** field will become hollow, indicating that there is an animation keyframe on this field but not on the current frame of animation.

- The **Rotation Z** field will turn green, indicating that the field is controlled by animation data but there is no keyframe on the current frame.

Now, let's rotate the **Turntable** object one full rotation and add a keyframe to frame **121**:

1. Click to edit the **Rotation Z** field, type 360, and then press *Enter*.

    The field will turn orange, indicating that the value of the field has been updated but a new keyframe has not yet been inserted.

2. Click on the small hollow diamond to the right of the **Rotation Z** transform field to insert a second keyframe.

Clicking the hollow diamond will have several effects:

- The hollow diamond will become solid, once again indicating that there is an animation keyframe on this field for the current frame of animation.

- The **Rotation Z** field will turn yellow again, indicating that the field is controlled by animation data.

- More orange dots will appear in the Timeline editor underneath the blue current frame indicator to show where the keyframes are on the timeline – in this case, frame **121**.

Excellent – we have our animation keyframes in place; the **Turntable** object will now rotate 360 degrees around its *Z* axis over the course of 120 frames. To see this in action, press the **Play Animation** button in the middle of the bottom of the Timeline or press the *spacebar*.

When you're finished viewing the animation, press the *Esc* key to cancel playing the animation and return to frame **121**.

There's one remaining issue with our animation keyframes. They have ease-in and ease-out motion curves applied to them. This means that the turntable's rotation will speed up and slow down at the beginning and end of the animation instead of rotating at a constant rate. Let's fix this now:

1. Open the **Select** menu in the top-left corner of the header of the Timeline and choose **All**.

2. Open the **Key** menu in the top-left corner of the header of the Timeline and choose **Handle Type | Vector**.

The orange dots on the Timeline will change to squares to indicate the new handle type. Play the animation again and you'll see that the **Turntable** object rotates at a constant rate and the animation loops seamlessly.

Now, we need our camera and our lights to rotate around the sculpture. This can be done by nesting the camera and the lights inside of the turntable empty as child objects. Children follow the transforms of their parent automatically, so when the turntable rotates, the camera and the lights will too:

1. Drag the blue current frame indicator to frame **1**.

2. Click to select the **Camera** object.

3. Hold the *Shift* key down and click on the following objects to add them to the selection: **Key Light**, **Fill Light**, and **Rim Light**.

4. Lastly, hold the *Shift* key and click to add the **Turntable** object to the selection.

5. Open the **Object** menu in the top-left corner of the header of the 3D Viewport and choose **Parent | Object**.

   This will make the **Camera** object and the three lights children of the **Turntable** object. Play the animation and you'll see the four objects spinning around the sculpture. We can also see what the animation looks like from the camera's perspective in the 3D Viewport on the left side of the UI.

   The current position of the camera is a little awkward for the turntable, so let's center its position and aim it straight at the sculpture.

6. Click to select the **Camera** object.

7. With the **Camera** object selected, navigate to the **Object** tab (represented by the orange square icon) in the Properties editor.

8. Let's adjust some of the transform values to center the sculpture in the camera's framing:

Change **Location X** to 0 m.

Change **Location Y** to -11 m.

Change **Location Z** to 0.825 m.

Change **Rotation X** to 90.

Change **Rotation Y** to 0.

Change **Rotation Z** to 0.

Now that the camera is positioned correctly, the turntable is ready. Play the animation to see how it looks. If you're happy with the animation, we can render it as a video. There are several options and considerations for rendering animations, so we will save that for the *Exporting the final render* section of this chapter.

How it works...

Turntables are a great way to showcase a sculpture from all angles. We typically want to aim our camera straight at the sculpture and use lighting that avoids dark shadows. Interesting camera angles and artistic shadows can look good for artistic renders, but they tend to hide the details of our sculpture that we're trying to showcase in a 360-degree render.

Choosing where to place our keyframes for looping animations can be a little confusing. For our turntable, we inserted two keyframes – one with 0 degrees of rotation and one with 360 degrees of rotation. 0 degrees and 360 degrees result in exactly the same angle. Because of this, including both of these frames would cause the animation to repeat an identical frame and stutter each time the animation loops. This is why we placed our 360-degree keyframe on **121**, even though we end the animation playback at frame **120**. Ending the animation one frame early ensures that the extra frame is not repeated, so we get a seamless loop.

Exporting the final render

There are several quality settings to consider when rendering and exporting our work; let's not trip at the finish line. Some of our render settings will be different, depending on the render engine we've chosen. We're going to stick with Cycles for this section. Let's discuss some of the settings we need for a high-quality render in Cycles.

We briefly mentioned the concept of samples and noise in the *Setting up Rendered mode* section of this chapter. Path tracing engines such as Cycles require multiple samples to create the final image. If we use a low number of samples, the image will render quickly, but the image will also have more undesirable noise. If we use a high number of samples, the image will take longer to render, but the noise will be significantly reduced.

There is no magic number for how many samples we need. Scenes with many lights and complex material properties require more samples than scenes with few lights and simple materials. Our orc example only requires a small number of samples to remove the noise, around 32–128. This is because the clay material is very simple to render. Our old monk example requires a slightly higher number of samples to remove the noise, around 256–512. This is because the old monk's skin and eyes materials have more complex properties such as subsurface scattering and refraction. If we use many lights and introduce other features such as a shallow depth of field and caustics, it will require considerably more samples to clean up all of the noise, sometimes as high as 1,024–4,096.

Reducing noise is important for a high-quality render, but there are a few other things we should set up as well, including resolution and file format.

In this section, we will make some small adjustments to Blender's output settings to make sure that our renders are exported with the highest quality. We'll also learn a little bit about the Blender community and where you can go to share your finished artwork.

Getting ready

For this section, we can use the artistic render that we set up in the *Using a camera to render the sculpture* section of this chapter, or we can use the 360 setup that we prepared in the *Setting up a turntable for a 360-degree render* section of this chapter.

If you have not completed either of these sections, you can download the `cameraSetup_End.blend` file from here: `https://github.com/PacktPublishing/Sculpting-the-Blender-Way/blob/main/Chapter10/cameraSetup_End.blend`, or you can download the `turntableSetup_End.blend` file here: `https://github.com/PacktPublishing/Sculpting-the-Blender-Way/blob/main/Chapter10/turntableSetup_End.blend`.

Make sure you have all of the textures from the previous sections downloaded as well; otherwise, the clay material and environment lighting will not render correctly.

Launch Blender and open the `.blend` file. Once the file is loaded, we can go over our export settings.

How to do it...

Some of the settings we need to adjust are split between the **Render** tab and the **Output** tab of the Properties editor. We'll start with the **Render** settings.

If you see noise in your render, try increasing the number of samples:

1. Navigate to the **Render** tab (represented by the gray camera-back icon) in the Properties editor.

2. Expand the **Sampling** subsection.

   We can independently set the number of samples used in the 3D Viewport render and the number of samples used in the final render. Increase the number of samples in the **Render** and **Viewport** fields as needed to reduce noise in the final render and viewport renders respectively. We typically want to keep the **Viewport** samples low so that we have fast previews in the viewport while we set up our lights and other settings. We can use a higher number of samples for the render since it doesn't need to be fast.

   Now, let's set up the resolution and file format for the export:

3. Navigate to the **Output** tab (represented by the gray printer icon) in the Properties editor.

4. Expand the **Dimensions** subsection.

   From here, we can set the render resolution. The default **1920 x 1080** setting is the resolution for HD video. If you're exporting to social media such as Instagram, you can change this to a square ratio such as **1080 x 1080**. Rendering with high samples takes a long time, so it is common to temporarily lower the resolution to do a pre-final render. We can do this by lowering the % slider to something small such as **25%**. Don't forget to bring this back up to **100%** when you're ready for the final render.

   Finally, we should set our file output settings.

5. Expand the **Output** subsection.

   By default, the rendered images will be saved to the /tmp\ directory on your computer. You can change this using the folder icon to browse for a new output location.

   If you're saving a single image, we recommend the following settings:

   Set **File Format** to **PNG**.

   Set **Color** to **RGB**.

   Set **Color Depth** to **8**.

6. With the render settings set, open the **Render** menu from Blender's Topbar and choose **Render Image** or press the *F12* hotkey.

    If you're saving an animation (such as the turntable), you can use the same settings to render out an image sequence, or you can use the following settings to render a video file:

    Set **File Format** to **FFmpeg Video**.

    Set **Color** to **RGB**.

7. Expand the **Encoding** subsection and set the following settings:

    Set **Container** to **Quicktime**.

    Set **Video Codec** to **H.264**.

    Set **Output Quality** to **High Quality**.

    Using the Eevee render engine to render the turntable animation will save a considerable amount of time since the animation has to render 120 individual frames.

8. With the render settings set, open the **Render** menu from Blender's Topbar and choose **Render Animation** or press the *Ctrl + F12* hotkey.

How it works...

There are many quality settings that can be set up differently between viewport renders and final renders. For example, the **Render** tab in the Properties editor has a subsection for adjusting the amount of sampling Cycles will use. You'll notice we can set different values for **Viewport** and **Render**. It is typical to use a low number of samples (around 32) in the Viewport so that the rendering happens as quickly as possible. A higher number of samples (around 128) is used for the final render because it will improve the quality of the final image and reduce noise, although it takes a lot longer to process the image. Sometimes, it is necessary to use extremely high values for the final render (around 4096). Having a separate setting for the viewport render samples is especially convenient in these extreme cases.

Some other settings are dependent on final renders as well. The Multiresolution modifier can be set to use a low subdivision level in the viewport but a high value in renders. Objects in the Outliner can be set to appear in the viewport but not in the final render, or vice versa.

Customizing these values will allow us to retain the flexibility of a fast viewport rendering while taking full control over the look of the final render.

There's more...

Increasing the number of samples is not the only way of reducing noise in Cycles renders. There are several **denoising** algorithms that we can use, including the **OptiX AI denoiser** and **Open Image Denoise**. Denoising can be enabled under the **Sampling** subsection of the **Render** tab of the Properties editor. Denoising can speed up render times. However, you should be aware that high-frequency details (such as skin pores) often get erased by denoising algorithms, as they can be mistaken for noise.

We can also adjust the **Color Management** settings at the bottom of the **Render** tab of the Properties editor. Try adjusting the **Look** option to give the render lower or higher contrast, depending on your artistic tastes.

See also

Incredible – you've made it to the end of the book! Now the only thing left is to share your sculptures with the online Blender community! Although we primarily used our orc sculpture for this chapter, you can go through this process with any of your sculptures that you've made throughout this book.

There are some great places to share your renders online. For professional portfolio work, `https://www.artstation.com/` is an excellent place to post. There is an active Reddit page for Blender here: `https://www.reddit.com/r/blender/`. You can use the #b3d hashtag on Twitter and Instagram to let people know you made your art using Blender. You can also share your 3D models to `https://sketchfab.com/` (however, you may need to reduce the polygon count of your sculptures before you can upload; try the **Decimate** modifier to quickly reduce the polycount).

There is an annual community sculpting event called **Sculpt January**. Throughout the month of January, there's a new prompt every day, providing you with a sculpting challenge. Check out the official Twitter account here: `https://twitter.com/sculptjanuary`.

Thank you so much for purchasing this book. I hope you've found it helpful. If you decide to share your work on social media, I would love to see your sculptures; tag me on Twitter `@Xury46`. It's been a pleasure helping you get started on your sculpting journey!

Index

Other Books You May Enjoy

If you enjoyed this book, you may be interested in these other books by Packt:

Blender 3D By Example - Second Edition

Oscar Baechler, Xury Greer

ISBN: 978-1-78961-256-1

- Explore core 3D modeling tools in Blender such as extrude, bevel, and loop cut
- Understand Blender's Outliner hierarchy, collections, and modifiers
- Find solutions to common problems in modeling 3D characters and designs
- Implement lighting and probes to liven up an architectural scene using EEVEE
- Produce a final rendered image complete with lighting and post-processing effects
- Learn character concept art workflows and how to use the basics of Grease Pencil
- Learn how to use Blender's built-in texture painting tools

3D Game Design with Unreal Engine 4 and Blender

Justin Plowman

ISBN: 978-1-78934-515-5

- Create a fully functioning game level of your own design using Blender and Unreal Engine 4

- Customize your level with detailed 3D assets created with Blender

- Import assets into Unreal Engine 4 to create an amazing finished product

- Build a detailed dynamic environment with goals and an ending

- Explore Blender's incredible animation tools to animate elements of your game

- Create great environments using sound effects, particle effects, and class blueprints

Packt is searching for authors like you

If you're interested in becoming an author for Packt, please visit `authors.packtpub.com` and apply today. We have worked with thousands of developers and tech professionals, just like you, to help them share their insight with the global tech community. You can make a general application, apply for a specific hot topic that we are recruiting an author for, or submit your own idea.

Share Your Thoughts

Now you've finished *Sculpting the Blender Way*, we'd love to hear your thoughts! Scan the QR code below to go straight to the Amazon review page for this book and share your feedback or leave a review on the site that you purchased it from.

https://www.amazon.in/review/create-review/error?asin=%3C1801073872%3E

Your review is important to us and the tech community and will help us make sure we're delivering excellent quality content.